Jun 2019

The Nightingale's Sonata

The Nightingale's Sonata

THE MUSICAL ODYSSEY OF
Lea Luboshutz

THOMAS WOLF

PEGASUS BOOKS
NEW YORK LONDON

THE NIGHTINGALE'S SONATA

Pegasus Books Ltd.
148 W 37th Street, 13th Floor
New York, NY 10018

First Pegasus Books cloth edition June 2019

Pages from the autograph manuscript of César Franck's Sonata in A major for violin and piano reproduced on pages 18, 78, 174, 250, and 306 with permission from The Morgan Library & Museum, New York.

Interior design by Maria Fernandez

Library of Congress Cataloging-in-Publication Data is available.

ISBN: 978-1-64313-067-5

10 9 8 7 6 5 4 3 2 1

Printed in the United States of America
Distributed by W. W. Norton & Company
www.pegasusbooks.us

For the Family

CONTENTS

DRAMATIS PERSONAE

Because there are so many characters in this story, the following alphabetical list provides a quick guide to help identify some of them. I have included both general biographical information as well as ways in which they are related to the main characters. Death dates are current through 2018. Because the main characters are referred to so often, I have used initials for them as follows:

- LL = Lea Luboshutz
- OG = Onissim Goldovsky
- RK = Rashel Khin
- BG = Boris Goldovsky
- IGW = Irina Goldovsky, later Irene Wolf

I have also followed certain rules:

1. *I have used a single spelling for Russian surnames to make it easier to track relatives even though in Russian, males and females have different endings for the same family name (e.g., Goldovsky for a man and Goldovskaya for a woman). In this list, I use the masculine ending for both (Goldovsky).*
2. *In parenthesis, I have provided nicknames or alternative names for characters who are referred to in multiple ways in the text. For example Katherine Luboshutz is also called "Gitel" and "Babushka."*
3. *In the case of married women, I have listed them alphabetically under their married surnames.*
4. *In cases where women used their maiden names as their stage or literary names and did not take their husband's name, the entry is under the maiden name (as for example Anna Luboshutz and Rashel Khin).*
5. *At the end of the alphabetical list is a listing of tsars and tsaritsas* *mentioned in the text, with birth and death dates as well as the dates of their reigns.*

---

* While some in English use the term *tsarina* or *czarina*, the correct term is *tsaritsa*.

Auer, Leopold (1845–1930) Hungarian violinist and pedagogue who taught both in Russia and later in the United States. He invited LL to study with him in St. Petersburg but the family could not afford to send her. Later, he taught with LL at the Curtis Institute of Music.

Auer, Nadine Pelikan (1855–1932) Russian-born first wife of violinist Leopold Auer (they divorced in 1901). Friend of OG and RK.

Bergonzi, Carlo (1683–1747) Italian luthier, possible maker of a violin that LL played prior to purchasing the Nightingale Stradivarius.

Bok, Mary Louise Curtis (1876–1970) Daughter of Cyrus Curtis (founder of Curtis Publishing Company). Philanthropist and founder of the Curtis Institute of Music in Philadelphia. Her first husband was Edward Bok. Her second husband was Efrem Zimbalist. Patron and friend of LL.

Chaliapin, Fyodor Ivanovich (1873–1938) Russian singer who performed and toured with both of the Luboshutz sisters and introduced LL to Sol Hurok in Paris.

Dohnanyi, Ernst von (1877–1960) Hungarian-born composer, pianist, and conductor. Conducted orchestra in one of LL's first concerts in New York and later became BG's piano teacher in Budapest.

Druian, Rafael (1922–2002) Student of LL; Russian-born American violinist and conductor who served as concertmaster for the New York Philharmonic, the Cleveland Orchestra, and other ensembles and purchased LL's Stradivarius violin after her death.

Duncan, Isadora (1877–1927) American dance pioneer; Pierre Luboshutz was her accompanist in Russia and she helped him emigrate. Friend of the Luboshutz family.

Elisabeth (HRH) (1891–1967) Queen consort of Belgium as the spouse of King Albert I, she was a fine violinist who studied with Ysaÿe and, after hearing LL, invited her to play at the palace.

Feldshtein, Solomon Mikhaelovich (dates unknown) Russian lawyer; first husband of RK and the father of her only child.

Flesch, Carl (1873–1944) Hungarian violinist and pedagogue who taught at the Curtis Institute of Music until 1928 and played first violin in the first iteration of the Curtis String Quartet. He left, in part, in protest over LL's appointment to the faculty.

Franck, César (1822–1890) French composer of the sonata for violin and piano that became an important part of the family history of LL and OG.

Goldovsky, Anna Osipovna Garkavi (date unknown–1909) Stepmother of OG (second wife of OG's father, Boris Isaakovich Goldovsky). Sister of jurist Vladimir Osipovich Garkavi, who introduced OG to the field of law.

Goldovsky, Boris Isaakovich (dates unknown) OG's father. Merchant of the Second Guild.

Goldovsky, Boris Onissimovich (1908–2001) Second child of OG and LL. Director of opera departments at Tanglewood Music Center, New England Conservatory of Music, Cleveland Institute of Music, and Curtis Institute of Music where he had been a student of Fritz Reiner; founder of New England Opera Theatre and Goldovsky Opera Theater.

Goldovsky, Dmitri Yurievich (1931–1988) Son of Yuri Goldovsky and oldest grandchild of LL and OG.

Goldovsky, Irina Onissimovna See Wolf, Irene Goldovsky.

Goldovsky, Margaret Codd (1911–2004) BG's wife, fellow student at the Curtis Institute of Music, and a professional singer during the early years of their marriage.

Goldovsky, Onissim Borisovich (1865–1922) Russian lawyer and political activist born in Vilnius. Named for his maternal grandfather. Married to RK. Later fathered three children with LL.

Goldovsky, Rosa Onissimovna (dates unknown) Mother of OG who was divorced from her husband when OG was five years old.

Goldovsky, Yuri Onissimovich (1907–1931) First child of OG and LL.

Grzhimali, Ivan Voitsekhovich See Hřímalý, Jan.

Gurkov, Solomon Izrailevich See Hurok, Sol.

Hofmann, Josef Kazimierz (1876–1957) Polish-American pianist who became director of the Curtis Institute of Music and toured with LL. The two quite possibly were lovers at the time.

Hřímalý, Jan [Grzhimali, Ivan Voitsekhovich] (1844–1915) Czech-born violinist and teacher of LL at the Moscow Conservatory where he was a professor from 1869 to 1915.

Hurok, Sol [Solomon Izrailevich Gurkov] (1888–1974) Russian-born American impresario who managed LL, Luboshutz & Nemenoff, and many other well-known classical music performers.

Joachim, Joseph (1831–1907) Hungarian violinist, conductor, composer, and teacher. A close collaborator of Johannes Brahms, he is widely regarded as one of the most significant violinists of the 19th century. Refused to teach LL.

Katzman, Sergei (dates unknown) Odessa-based rabbi, father of Katherine Katzman Luboshutz and Mischa Katzman. Grandfather of LL, Anna, and Pierre Luboshutz.

Khin,[*] **Rashel Mironovna** (1863[**]–1928) Wife of OG. Author of successful novellas, stories, and plays, as well as translations into Russian of the works of George Sand, Émile Zola, and other French authors.

Koni, Anatoli Fedorovich (1844–1927) Liberal jurist, senator, writer. Longtime intimate of RK and family friend and associate of OG's mentor Prince Aleksandr Urusov.

Koussevitzky, Serge Alexandrovich (1874–1951) Russian double bass player and impresario who in 1924 moved to the United States and became music director and conductor of the Boston Symphony Orchestra. Engaged members of the Luboshutz and Goldovsky families in his many musical endeavors.

Kreutzer, Leonid (1884–1953) Russian-born pianist who was an important teacher at the Berlin Hochschule für Musik (Conservatory). He took on BG as a student and conducted the orchestra for BG and LL's first Berlin concerto concert there. Also briefly LL's lover.

Kuzin, Svetlana "Sveta" (1962–) Great-granddaughter of Anna Luboshutz and Nikolai Shereshevsky. Primary Russia-based researcher for this book.

Luboshutz, Anna (1887–1975) LL's younger sister, an accomplished cellist who married the physician Nikolai Shereshevsky and made her home in Russia all of her life.

Luboshutz, Katherine "Gitel" Katzman [later called "Babushka"] (1865–1940) Daughter of Rabbi Sergei Katzman, wife of Saul Luboshutz, mother of LL, Anna Luboshutz, and Pierre Luboshutz. She ran a piano store in Odessa and supported her family there. Eventually joined the family in the United States.

Luboshutz, Lea (1885–1965) Odessa-born daughter of Katherine Katzman and Saul Luboshutz. Sister of Anna and Pierre. Mother of Yuri, Boris, and Irina Goldovsky.

---

[*]   Some writers use Rashel's married name when referring to her, as in "Khin-Goldovskaya." However, most refer to her simply as Khin, the name she used in literary works.

[**]   There is controversy about Rashel's birth year. The year given here is confirmed by her diary.

Concert violinist who emigrated to the United States where she joined the faculty of the Curtis Institute of Music.

Luboshutz, Pierre (1890–1971) Son of Katherine Katzman and Saul Luboshutz, brother of LL and Anna Luboshutz, a pianist and with his wife Genia Nemenoff, half of the famed piano duo team of Luboshutz & Nemenoff.

Luboshutz, Saul (date unknown–1925) Violin teacher; father of LL, Anna Luboshutz, and Pierre Luboshutz; husband of Katherine Katzman; first teacher of LL.

Mintslov, Rudolf Rudolfovich (1845–1904) OG's mentor at a law firm he joined in 1888.

Mlynarski, Emil Szymon (1870–1935) Russian-born violinist, conductor, composer, and pedagogue. A student of Leopold Auer, he was, after LL's father, her first violin teacher for three years in Odessa. Later joined the Curtis Institute of Music faculty in Philadelphia where he taught BG conducting.

Naumburg, Aaron (1859–1928) Wealthy businessman and philanthropist, active in both the visual and performing arts and interested in supporting women artists. Paid for LL's Stradivarius violin ("Le Rossignol," or "The Nightingale").

Nemenoff, Genia (1905–1989) Pianist, French-born daughter of a Russian family, the Jacobs, that had settled in Paris to establish a branch of the family fur business. Genia later married and became the performing partner of pianist Pierre Luboshutz.

Polyakov, Lazar Solomonovich (1843–1914) Russian entrepreneur and banker. His Moscow villa with the small chapel that his devout Orthodox Jewish wife, Rozalia, used regularly is now the Bolshaya Bronnaya Synagogue. Was one of LL's earliest patrons and gave her an Amati violin.

Prince, Sidney (1865–1929) Partner in Asiel & Co., a financial services firm, and for ten years a member of the New York Stock Exchange Governing Committee. Patron of LL and BG who made possible the latter's studies with Dohnanyi in Budapest.

Prokofiev, Sergei Sergeyevich (1891–1953) Russian composer, pianist, and conductor. LL premiered his first violin concerto in New York.

Rozanov, Vasily Vasilievich (1856–1919) Philosopher, friend, and major influence on the young OG. Husband of writer Polina Suslova. Later in life, their friendship ended over Rozanov's anti-Semitism.

Safonov, Vasily Ilyich (1852–1918) Russian pianist, teacher, conductor, and composer. Director of the Moscow Conservatory during the years that the Luboshutz children were students.

Schnabel, Artur (1882–1951) Austrian pianist considered one of the greatest of all Beethoven interpreters and one of the most important pedagogues of his time who became BG's teacher in Berlin.

Serkin, Rudolf (1903–1991) Czech-born pianist, cofounder of the Marlboro Music Festival in Vermont, director of Curtis Institute of Music, and teacher of Andrew Wolf.

Shereshevsky, Nikolai Adolfovich (1885–1961) Prominent physician and researcher who married Anna Luboshutz in 1913. A victim in the so-called "Doctors' Plot," Stalin's attempted effort to falsely accuse Jewish doctors of illegal activities, he was later exonerated.

Silverstein, Joseph "Joey" (1932–2015) American violinist and conductor who served as concertmaster of the Boston Symphony Orchestra from 1962 to 1984. Performed with Andrew Wolf in the latter's final concert.

Stern, Isaac (1920–2001) Russian-born American violinist with whom Andrew Wolf collaborated and toured as assisting pianist for many years.

Stradivari, Antonio (1644–1737) One of the greatest violin makers of all time. LL owned and played his golden period instrument called "Le Rossignol," or "The Nightingale."

Suslova, Polina [aka Apollinaria Prokofyevna Suslova] (1839–1918) Wife of the philosopher Vasily Rozanov and former mistress of Fyodor Dostoevsky. She sent a letter to the authorities that resulted in OG's arrest.

Urusov, Prince Aleksandr Ivanovich (1842–1900) Distinguished Russian legal figure and the man most responsible for OG's training in the law. OG's recollections of him were published after Urusov's death.

Wolf, Andrew (1943–1985) Billy Wolf and IGW's fourth child, a Curtis graduate and pianist. Married to Linda Lunt Wolf and father of Anna and Heather.

Wolf, Irene Goldovsky [called Irina until she moved to the United States in 1929] (1917–2010) Third child of OG and LL. Married Walter L. "Billy" Wolf in 1933 and had six children.

Wolf, Thomas (1945–) Billy Wolf and IGW's fifth child. A flutist and arts consultant and this book's author. Married Dennie Palmer Wolf and father of Lea and Alexis.

Wolf, Walter Loeb "Billy" (1908–2002) Part of an important Philadelphia Jewish family. Married IGW and fathered six children: Alexandra, Nicholas, Catherine, Andrew, Thomas, and Lucy.

Ysaÿe, Eugène (1858–1931) The violinist and pedagogue to whom Cesar Franck dedicated his violin and piano sonata. LL was selected to play for him at the Moscow Conservatory and he invited her to study with him in Belgium, where he coached her on the Franck sonata.

Zimbalist, Efrem (1890–1985) Violinist who first met LL when they were concertmasters of their respective conservatory orchestras in Russia. Later, both taught at the Curtis Institute of Music, where he became director in 1941. Married first to the singer Alma Gluck, he later married Mary Curtis Bok.

RUSSIAN TSARS AND TSARITSAS MENTIONED IN THE TEXT
(listed in chronological order of their reigns)

Tsar Peter I "the Great" (1672–1725). Reigned 1682–1725.

Tsaritsa Catherine II "the Great" (1729–1796). Reigned 1762–1796.

Tsar Paul I (1754–1801). Reigned 1796–1801.

Tsar Alexander I (1777–1825). Reigned 1801–1825.

Tsar Nicholas I (1796–1855). Reigned 1825–1855.

Tsar Alexander II "the Liberator" (1818–1881). Reigned 1855–1881.

Tsar Alexander III (1845–1894). Reigned 1881–1894.

Tsar Nicholas II (1868–1918). Reigned 1894–1917.

Tsaritsa Alexandra Feodorovna (1872–1918) Hessian-born empress consort by virtue of being the spouse of Nicholas II, she reigned 1896 to 1917. A granddaughter of Queen Victoria of England who, though raised a Protestant, converted and became Russian Orthodox.

For a complete list of characters with birth and death years and short descriptions, please go to www.nightingalessonata.com/list-of-characters.

INTRODUCTION

⏤∾⏤

Late in my mother's life, she gave me a gift—a silver *podstakannik* or Russian tea-glass holder with a beautiful front enameled portrait. Two small boys in pale turn-of-the-century linen suits lean toward each other, their serious dark eyes above full pink cheeks and half smiles. The image of the boys—tender, elegant, and safe—sits on the tranquil enamel surface, capturing a moment of calm not only in their lives but also in the life of Imperial Russia.

Though the image depicts two children, the significance of the object had much to do with my grandmother Lea Luboshutz. The boys in the portrait are her two sons, my uncles Yuri and Boris. Lea had commissioned the *podstakannik* while still a young violin prodigy. It was to be a gift to my grandfather Onissim, a much older lawyer and patriot who had once been her patron and was now the father of her three children—Irina (my mother) and my two uncles.

The beautiful article was a family heirloom, but while others ascribed much sentimental value to it, I did not. As a child, I saw it every night at the family dinner table when my father took his tea. Though pretty, it seemed nothing special. After my mother died, I had the object appraised, mostly to see whether it might yield clues about my family's history and especially something about my grandmother. I was astonished to learn that it was quite valuable.

The *podstakannik* had been made around 1915 by a German-born silversmith, Feodor Rückert, who worked in Moscow, often for the House of

Fabergé. That seemed to support a family legend about its provenance, one I had never really believed (my family often told tall tales about the past). It was said that my grandfather had received the gift just a few years before his death—a death that had forced Lea to completely reinvent her life and those of her family members. In family lore, Onissim's death was somehow mysteriously linked to the Russian Revolution . . . but beyond that I was not permitted to ask questions.

Having to reinvent herself and her life would have been nothing new to my grandmother. In her first twenty-five years, she had already transformed herself from a poor Yiddish-speaking Jewish girl living in the provinces of Imperial Russia into a cultural icon living a lavish lifestyle in Moscow—a place closed to most Jews. By the time she gave the gift to Onissim, she spoke both perfect Russian and fluent French, traveled internationally, and dined with royalty. She had plenty of her own money—enough to purchase not only the *podstakannik* but also many more articles of value. She had certainly made the most of her talent and her opportunities. But a couple of years after giving Onissim the gift, she was again reduced to poverty; and a few years after that, she was a political exile living in another country. Once more, she would have to start again.

The *podstakannik* was linked to a tumultuous historical period. It had traveled from Moscow to Odessa and back again during the Revolution, entrusted to Lea's mother, Gitel, for safekeeping. Then, after Onissim's death, Gitel smuggled it out of Russia along with valuable jewelry. The story family members loved to tell was of Gitel sewing the lovely object, together with whatever valuables that could be pawned, to the inside of a feather duvet, thus outwitting suspicious authorities over and over again. Miraculously, the fragile enamel arrived unharmed in the United States after a decade-long journey from Moscow to Odessa, back to Moscow, to Berlin, Paris, and finally to Philadelphia where it remained until my mother's death.

Beyond these family stories, I knew very little, except for a disquieting fact that I learned in my mother's final years. Yes, Lea had given the tea-glass holder to Onissim, who had showered her with jewels during their life together. Yes, my grandparents loved each other very much and had three children together. But no, that was not the full story. Lea, the master of reinvention, had recast this story to suit her needs after she left Russia. As I was startled to learn, Lea and Onissim had actually never been married. In fact, Onissim had another "real" wife.

When my mother gave me the gift of the tea-glass holder, she told me that I should find out more about my grandmother and the family's history and tell their stories. But after she died, much time passed and I had done nothing about it. Indeed, I was close to seventy, a grandparent myself. The people I could ask were long dead. Family papers came to me, and I put them in storage—photographs, letters, diaries, diplomas, official documents, as well as memoirs, both published and unpublished. The family was nothing if not loquacious and, in their time, many of them were famous. Yet, I hadn't looked at any of it. I told myself I was simply too busy.

Then in the summer of 2012 everything changed. After returning from playing some concerts, I began organizing old CDs to ensure that performances by musician family members would not be lost. These included recordings by various relatives of the older generation and also by my brother Andy, who had died of a brain tumor at an early age. And then, there it was: a recording of my brother's final performance of César Franck's sonata for violin and piano from January 1985—the last music he had ever played publicly. I had never listened to the recording—not once, though I had been with him at that last harrowing performance. When I first received the CD about a month after the concert, replaying the event was simply too painful. But why had almost *three decades* passed without my ever listening to it?

The Franck sonata. For a hundred years, it had been part of Lea and my family's history. The composition was linked to their greatest triumphs and most heart-wrenching tragedies. It helped them survive political turmoil, anti-Semitic persecution, revolution, emigration. It had helped Lea meet people and forge lifelong partnerships that would serve her aspirations for the family. The sonata had been associated with her happiest times, her love affairs, and economic success. It had marked moments of abject poverty. She had made it a calling card as she and the family moved from country to country. "The Franck" was, for us, what family portraits, traditions, prayers, war medals, or quilts might be for others—it was a talisman, the touchstone of who we were and could be.

The Franck is an unusual piece of music. It is unlike almost every sonata that preceded it in one important respect. Its predecessors are full of tunes and themes—different ones for each movement. But the Franck has a single, central, thematic idea. It occurs in each of the four movements. Over the course of the work, the shape of this central idea is reinvented. Sometimes it is slow, sometimes fast, sometimes bright, at other times dark; sometimes exuberant, at other times like a wisp of smoke.

As I looked at the CD, I stood unmoving. Suddenly things became clear. Reinvention was a common thread, certainly; but reinvention around a core theme: That was at the heart of the sonata, and it was at the center of Lea and the family's story. The single theme for Lea and the family for over a century had been "live a good life." It was never stated, never discussed, yet always understood. As in the four movements, this core idea took shape and expression in different ways for specific family members and at various times.

For Lea, living a good life was always thought of in terms of the family—helping herself and them escape poverty and persecution while achieving fame through music. For her father, the idea of a good life had a religious connotation—the word *good* standing for ethical values and living life for others. For her partner Onissim, a good life was one to be enjoyed by all Russians, one that could only be achieved by embracing the values of César Franck's adopted homeland in France, even if it took a revolution and considerable personal risk. For my generation, the Franck sonata meant living a life according to a set of seemingly impossible high standards of family accomplishments.

My brother Andy and I and others in our generation owed a huge debt to those who came before us. None of them had an easy life. There had been struggles, disappointments, and tragedies. But it was Lea to whom they had all looked for inspiration and strength. She had worked hard to achieve her dream. But now she and the rest of those earlier generations were gone and I realized that I needed to honor my debt. In addition to the treasure trove of material I already had, there was much more in archives in various countries. There were relatives I had never met. It was time for me to go back in time, recover Lea's and the family's stories, and in that way come to the Franck sonata once again.

The
Nightingale's Sonata

The Families of Lea Luboshutz and Onissim Goldovsky

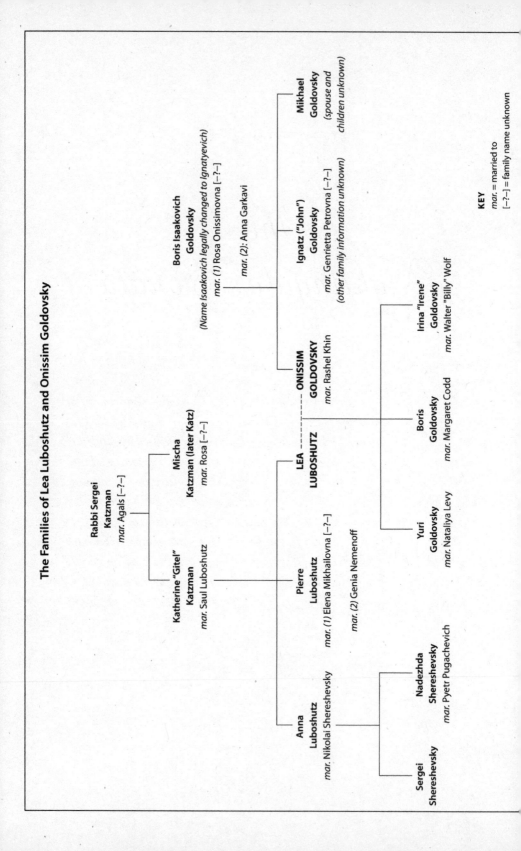

Rabbi Sergei Katzman
mar. Agals [–?–]

Mischa Katzman (later Katz)
mar. Rosa [–?–]

Katherine "Gitel" Katzman
mar. Saul Luboshutz

Pierre Luboshutz
mar. (1) Elena Mikhailovna [–?–]
mar. (2) Genia Nemenoff

Anna Luboshutz
mar. Nikolai Shereshevsky

Sergei Shereshevsky

Nadezhda Shereshevsky
mar. Pyetr Pugachevich

LEA LUBOSHUTZ

ONISSIM GOLDOVSKY
mar. Rashel Khin

Yuri Goldovsky
mar. Nataliya Levy

Boris Goldovsky
mar. Margaret Codd

Irina "Irene" Goldovsky
mar. Walter "Billy" Wolf

Boris Isaakovich Goldovsky
(Name Isaakovich legally changed to Ignatyevich)
mar. (1) Rosa Onissimovna [–?–]
mar. (2): Anna Garkavi

Ignatz ("John") Goldovsky
mar. Genrietta Petrovna [–?–]
(other family information unknown)

Mikhael Goldovsky
(spouse and children unknown)

KEY
mar. = married to
[–?–] = family name unknown

PRELUDE

(1853 to 1885)

❧

The year was 1853. The Belgian musician César Franck began writing a sonata for violin and piano. After composing some of the music, he sent the work to the legendary pianist and composer, Franz Liszt. But some time after doing so, Franck abandoned the project. A few years later, he took up the idea of a violin sonata again. This time he had a special incentive. He wanted to dedicate the work to Liszt's daughter, Cosima, who had recently married Hans von Bülow, Liszt's most talented pupil. Again, the project came to nothing. Whether it was Franck's inability to muster inspiration or his suspicion that the von Bülow's marriage was headed for disaster, he set the work aside. He was prescient. By 1865, Cosima had fallen in love with composer Richard Wagner and borne his child. By that time, Franck had become completely disillusioned and disappointed with his attempts to write a violin sonata.

That is the same year of another great disappointment that opens my family story. . . .

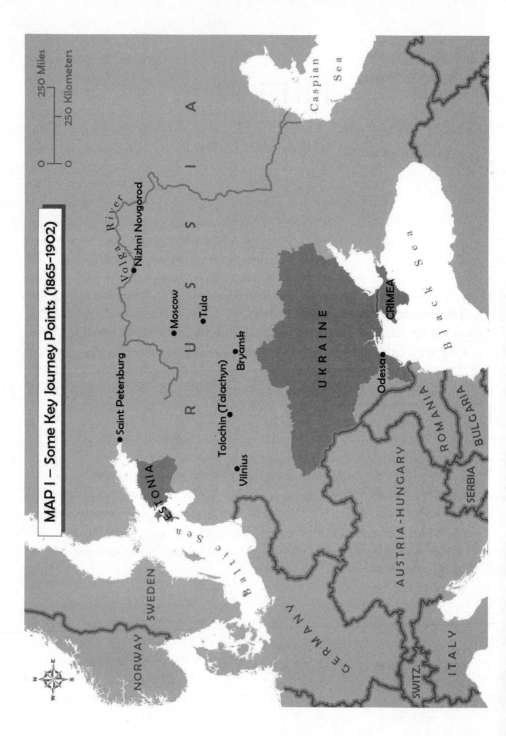

MAP I – Some Key Journey Points (1865–1902)

NORWAY

SWEDEN

ESTONIA

Baltic Sea

GERMANY

SWITZ.

ITALY

AUSTRIA-HUNGARY

SERBIA

ROMANIA

BULGARIA

R U S S I A

● Saint Petersburg

Volga River

● Nizhni Novgorod

● Moscow

● Tula

Tolochin (Talachyn) ●

Vilnius ●

Bryansk ●

UKRAINE

CRIMEA

Odessa ●

Black Sea

Caspian Sea

250 Miles

250 Kilometers

0

0

N
E
S
W

2

The Odessa Family

As my great-grandmother Katherine was to tell her family many years later, her birth in 1865 had been a great disappointment to her father, Rabbi Sergei Katzman of Odessa. Like many rabbis (and, in fact, like many Jews everywhere), he had wanted his firstborn to be a boy. A son would have brought many advantages to his poor but religious family. After all, a son could make his way in the world without any help from his father. A girl needed a husband and finding one could cost money; failing that, a daughter could end up a dependent old maid. Such were not idle considerations. But the great joke among his congregants was that the rabbi actually got what he wanted in nearly every respect. Even as a child, Katherine was a tiger—headstrong and not easy to control. In time, she also became ambitious and developed a remarkable head for business. This latter trait she seemed to have inherited from her mother, Agals, who handled the family money and, according to family legend, distributed it sparingly.

In the year 1880, when Katherine was fifteen, the rabbi learned from a *shadchan* (a marriage broker) that Saul Luboshutz would soon be asking for her hand in marriage. The news came as a surprise, but the rabbi was not displeased. He immediately retired to his small study to deliberate. On the one hand, Saul was a good Jew. The rabbi knew him from the synagogue, where Saul was a reliable and regular attender and often helped make up the *minyan* when attendance was light. Saul clearly knew his Torah—no small thing—and he did not appear to have enemies. Finding a husband for Gitel (as everyone called Katherine) might not be so easy. She had a reputation for being pigheaded. More importantly, she would not come with a dowry (by this time, there were six other children and not much money). Offers might not be numerous. All these were arguments for the match.

On the other hand, Saul was from a different generation than Gitel—the rabbi guessed Saul must be close to forty-five, thirty years older than his daughter. Gitel was maybe a little too young for marriage, though the rabbi certainly did not want to be stuck with an old maid. There was also the economic angle. Saul was a violin teacher. In Odessa, they were a dime a dozen, and Saul had not exactly captured the market of promising children from wealthy merchant families. How would they live? Well, Gitel was practical. It wouldn't be the first time a woman supported her family while her husband spent his days in prayer and study. On the whole, the rabbi thought the idea had merit and he passed on this information to the matchmaker, pending, he said, a discussion with his daughter.

Gitel herself was also mulling over the match. Near the end of her life, she confessed to her children that she had had no illusions. She knew the decision would not be primarily hers, and her father probably wanted to give Saul his blessing (about her mother Agals's opinion, she mentioned not a word). Besides, Gitel liked Saul. The fact that he was poor would be nothing new. She had grown up poor and, unlike her father, had no illusions about God's role in the equation. God, to the extent he existed, helped those who helped themselves. Gitel already had shown some aptitude for doing just that and, unbeknownst to her father and Saul, she had some money tucked away. She had ideas about how she and Saul might make a nice living by buying and selling pianos. As Saul was a musician, he could help with advice about the quality of the instruments. Soon the rabbi accepted Saul's proposal, on the condition that he wait until Gitel turned sixteen.

How could I possibly have known what my great-great-grandfather thought about the possibility of his daughter marrying Saul Luboshutz, sixty-five years before I was born? It is simple. Members of my family were storytellers, and this was one of those stories passed down from my great-grandmother to her daughter, Lea, to my mother, and eventually to my generation. As a child, I assumed it was true—as I did all of Lea's stories. Where there were gaps in the family history, I filled them in—often erroneously.

For example, Gitel's father was never named in this particular story and I assumed he was "Rabbi Katz" because his son, Gitel's brother, went by the name Mischa Katz once he moved to America. But much later I saw Gitel's death certificate and found that her father's name had actually been Sergei Katzman. So obviously, Mischa had shortened his name when he came to the United States, though I never found out why. Nor was it explained until much later that Saul's family name had not been Luboshutz. In Russia, it had been Luboshits and had been changed in the 1920s because the last syllable "shits" (with its obvious scatological meaning) was not a moniker suitable for America. These were small things but they were emblematic of a larger problem. Family members were not always reliable historians—sometimes they left things out, sometimes they dissembled, and at other times they made things up, especially when it made a particular narrative juicier or more amusing. And the inaccuracy of their narratives was not limited simply to the storytelling that came at family gatherings or in chance conversations. Many of my relatives actually wrote autobiographies, both published and unpublished. Yet these, too, I gradually learned, were not always reliable.

Saul and my great-grandmother Gitel were married in 1881. But the celebrations were clouded by political storms sweeping the Russian Empire that were starting to threaten Jews even in remote Odessa. Russia had captured Odessa from the Ottoman Empire in 1794. But Odessans, who prided themselves on the city's origins—Ancient Greek—saw themselves as sophisticated cosmopolitans. Russians were a minority throughout the 19th century, and the city was home to Germans, French, and Italians as well as Ukrainians, Greeks, and East Europeans. French, rather than Russian, was the language of daily life.

True, Odessans lived in the shadow of Russia's gray steppes to the north. But they preferred to look to the south, where steep cliffs dropped down to a vast port and its seemingly endless opportunities for building a better life. Late in her life, Saul and Gitel's daughter Lea would recall in an unpublished memoir her idyllic childhood of "horse-drawn trolleys and droshkas, a sunny and sweet climate, and long walks to the Black Sea, where we sometimes went swimming in the summer . . . It was a clear city, with straight streets, magnificent trees, and gorgeous parks."[1]

More than one thousand ships arrived in Odessa each year, delivering silk, wine, nuts, spices, and furniture and picking up Russian grain destined for Italy, France, and England. Children—if they were brave enough to hurtle down the famous two-hundred-step staircase to the waterfront—could immerse themselves in a world of polyglot traders and sailors from Europe, the Americas, Africa, and the Far East. Odessans of all nationalities, classes, and faiths mingled in a traditional evening stroll, promenading along wide boulevards, enjoying the balmy sea air, and pausing for free concerts in the city's many small parks.

One of Odessa's oldest buildings was the theater, completed in the first decade of the 19th century. In 1810, its famous opera house, designed by the French architect Jean-François Thomas de Thomon and seating more than sixteen hundred (in a city of only thirty thousand), opened. It was there that Saul would introduce each of his children to the performances of great visiting musicians, often purchasing a single standing-room ticket and holding a child on his shoulders.

At the time of Saul and Gitel's marriage, Jews accounted for one-third of the city's population. Odessa was part of the Pale of Settlement, a strip of land running from Poland and Lithuania to the Black Sea. In 1791, Catherine the Great had declared that Russian Jews had to live within the borders of the Pale, trapping them in this vast, impoverished territory on the periphery of the empire. Most of the Pale was composed of half-starving rural settlements, or shtetels, and a handful of Polish, Lithuanian, and Ukrainian cities long past their prime. By creating the Pale, Catherine not only helped solve what many Russians considered the "Jewish problem" but in the South at least it helped populate sparsely occupied territories and establish commercial control over areas that had been annexed from the Ottoman Empire.

But Odessa was a growing metropolis, offering employment as well as the chance for Jews to meld unnoticed into the city's multicultural social life. Jews flocked to the city from elsewhere in the Pale and some even prospered. At the peak of their success, Jewish entrepreneurs held about half of the city's trading and manufacturing licenses and they dominated the business of exporting Russian grain to Europe. An Odessa-based Jewish firm, Rabinowitch and Co., was the first Russian company to trade with China. Restrictions on Jewish employment in Russia were relaxed in Odessa, and Jews became doctors, pharmacists, lawyers, bankers, inn-keepers, and bakers. The imperial government permitted the first Russian-Jewish school to open in Odessa in 1826 and the first Jewish newspaper was published there in 1860.

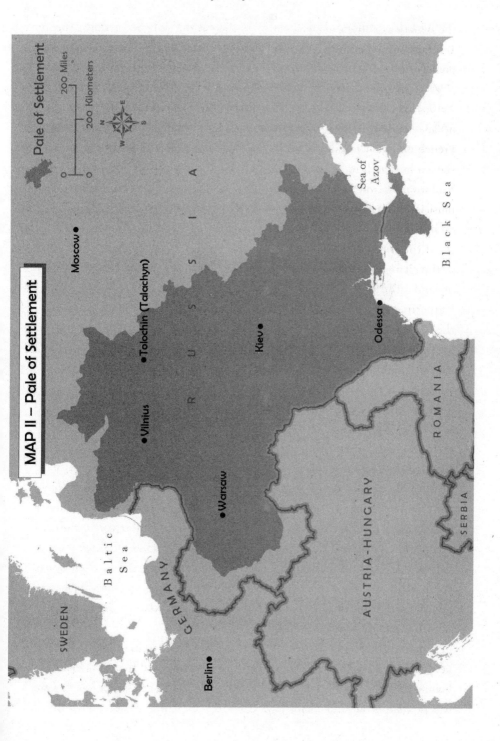

MAP II – Pale of Settlement

Pale of Settlement

200 Miles

200 Kilometers

Moscow

Tolochin (Talachyn)

R U S S I A

Kiev

Vilnius

Odessa

Warsaw

Sea of Azov

Black Sea

Baltic Sea

SWEDEN

GERMANY

Berlin

AUSTRIA-HUNGARY

ROMANIA

SERBIA

But Lea's memories and a handful of success stories belied a more complex reality for most Odessan Jews. One-third of the city's Jewish families were poor enough to need food assistance on the Holy Days and one-fifth were destitute. Poverty and overcrowding worsened as Jews were expelled from Moscow, St. Petersburg, and rural Ukraine and fled to the relative safety of Odessa. Saul and Gitel, with their tiny apartment and struggling piano business, were considered solidly middle class by the standards of Jewish Odessa.

Special Taxes on Jews in the Russian Empire
Tax on kosher slaughter
Tax on the sale of kosher meat
Tax on rental income
Tax on profits and dividends on a business
Tax on owning a printing press
Legacy duties
Fee for lighting candles on the Sabbath
Fee for wearing a yarmulke

Like all Russian Jews, the Luboshutzes were considered "aliens" (*inorodzhi*) under Russian law and they enjoyed "privileges" bestowed by the Tsar, rather than rights. These privileges were defined by a thicket of decrees, regulations, instructions, clarifications, orders, and amendments. An 1889 compilation of the rules pertaining to Jews in Russia ran to 290 pages. Jews were not allowed to own land and they were barred from the military officer corps, the civil service, academia, and the judiciary. They paid special taxes on kosher meat, yarmulkes, Sabbath candles, rental income, and business profits. Even worse, the Jews of Odessa were periodically targeted by mob violence. The term *pogrom* originated in Odessa, where Jews were attacked by Greeks in 1821 and 1859 and by Russians in 1871.

The most terrifying pogrom of the 19th century occurred in 1881—the year of Gitel's marriage to Saul. For weeks, rumors circulated that Jews had been behind the assassination of Tsar Alexander II in St. Petersburg. Well aware of the tensions around them, Jews tried to stay behind closed doors. But it was impossible to avoid work, shopping, and attending services. Eventually, armed gangs appeared, attracting growing mobs as they roamed the streets searching for Jews, including women, children, and the elderly. The mobs were ruthless and often murderous. If they couldn't find Jews to assault, they burned and ransacked Jewish homes and businesses. As usual with Russian pogroms, the police either stood by or joined the attackers, leaving Jews without any protection at all.

In an eerie foreshadowing of 20th-century Europe, Odessa in the spring of 1881 turned overnight from a center of culture, tolerance, and globalism into a bloodbath for the Jews. It was probably at this point that Gitel and Saul vowed do whatever was necessary to take the children of their union out of the Pale of Settlement.

According to family legend, Saul wanted to have children, but Gitel told him they had to wait until the "business" was established. Saul had no head for business, nor any interest in it. It was Gitel who rode the horse cart down the streets of Odessa, shouting, "Pianos for sale; does anyone have a piano for sale?" When she found an instrument she could afford, it was Gitel who arranged to have it loaded onto the cart and then unloaded at their two-room apartment, often getting her younger brother Mischa to assist. It was Gitel who arranged for repairs. Her customers were other poor Jews, so there was little room for markup. Often all she allowed was a polishing of the keys and buffing up of the exterior, the only jobs she felt she could entrust to Saul.

Gitel's greatest challenge was not in finding pianos, nor in selling them. She was a salesperson at heart. Her problem was Saul. Gitel knew that cleaning a piano and making it look good took little work and virtually no money. But as a musician, Saul knew what was inside the piano—the sound board, the strings, the action—and he knew that many of Gitel's pianos were worth little more than the price of firewood. According to my grandmother, Lea, who wrote about her parents in her memoir, the two fought constantly about Gitel's aggressive pricing, and he undermined her by warning potential customers. His unfortunate tendency to tell the truth drove Gitel to distraction, so she often insisted that he go off to the synagogue when she expected a customer.

"Go to the synagogue." It was a great family joke when I was growing up. Whenever someone told my great-uncle Pierre that he wasn't doing something right, he would laugh and say, "Go to the synagogue; I am busy." He remembered his mother's constant refrain to his father. He would say it in jest to his sister (my grandmother), even though she had not set foot in a synagogue in years.

According to Lea, Saul was scrupulously honest in other ways. He knew that they were supposed to purchase a permit to sell pianos and that a tax was due once the instruments were sold. Gitel felt that she made little enough on these transactions to bother with additional expenses and details. She told Saul to mind his business—she would get her brother Mischa to help. Saul's job teaching violin brought in just about enough to keep him in the cigarettes that he smoked constantly and to allow him to give a few kopecks to beggars, which, as a good Jew, he always felt he should do. It was Gitel who paid for everything else. If Saul wanted a family, Gitel knew that it would be her responsibility to find the support. And find it she did. Within three years, she had saved enough to tell Saul she was ready for a child. Their prayers were soon answered with a first child—Lea, my grandmother.

Boy Child in the Jerusalem of the North

While I knew a great deal about my grandmother and her family, I knew almost nothing about my grandfather Onissim Goldovsky. His photograph hung on my wall, so I was familiar with his face. As to what he was like as a person, my grandmother had described him in almost mythic terms, but there were few facts to go along with this Godlike image. Part of the problem was that so many years had elapsed since his life and death. He was a generation older than Lea—indeed, Onissim was born the same year as Lea's mother, Gitel, though she lived a much longer life and moved to America. Onissim died in Russia in 1922, a few years after the Revolution, so it was no easy task to go back to 1865 to trace his roots. And there was another problem: For all the years I was growing up, there had been a reticence in the older generation of my family to talk about him. There were clearly secrets they did not wish to share.

When I finally started digging into the historical record, I was astonished. Onissim had been famous—an important figure about whom one could construct a verifiable and impressive résumé. I did not need the kind of family stories that described Lea and her forebears—many of which I often questioned anyway. In Onissim's case, there was published material—much of it written by Onissim himself (including at least one article considered important enough to be reprinted a century after his death). I learned that he spent evenings with literary lions like Lev Tolstoy and Maxim Gorky in Russia and Émile Zola in France. There were his political speeches, letters, various diaries. If I needed extra validation, there was the fact that in the early 20th century, an American journalist, Herman Bernstein, traveled to Moscow to interview him as one of the potential leaders of the new Russia for the *New York Herald*. Wherever I pulled at a thread of information, there would be a ball of string. And the more I learned about Onissim, the better I understood why my grandmother, who was still an adolescent when her love affair with the much older man began, had worshipped him. I could understand why she wanted to link her life with his and had been willing to make serious personal compromises in order to do so.

Though Gitel and Onissim—each a first child—were both born in 1865, other details of their births were quite different. If Gitel came from a poor family in Odessa and her birth had been something of a disappointment, Onissim's birth in Vilnius, a city more than 700 miles north of Odessa, was a celebrated event.* Onissim's father, Boris Isaakovich Goldovsky, was an established man of business. He and his wife, Rosa Onissimovna

---

* Onissim's birth is recorded as January 6, 1865. However, in Russia, the Julian calendar (Old Style) was used until February 14, 1918. Dates in the Julian calendar differ somewhat from those in use today throughout the world—the so-called Gregorian calendar (or New Style). Unless otherwise indicated, all Russian dates prior to February 14, 1918, are given according to the Julian calendar (or Old Style dates). Onissim's birthday according to our current calendar would be January 18. [For those interested, simple conversion tables are provided on the Internet.]

Goldovsky, were thrilled that their firstborn was a son. In good Jewish tradition, the boy was named for a deceased grandfather, in this case Rosa's father.[2]

Though Onissim's parents could be optimistic about his prospects given their social and economic position, historical forces were producing headwinds. In 1865, Vilnius was a city nostalgic for its illustrious past and a place growing increasingly hostile to Jewish families like the Goldovskys. It had once been the capital of the Grand Duchy of Lithuania and the cultural capital of the Polish-Lithuanian Commonwealth. During the Middle Ages, the Commonwealth was considered one of the Great Powers, stretching from the Baltic to the Black Sea and rivaling Russia, the Holy Roman Empire, and the Habsburg Empire for dominance of Eastern Europe. More important for our story, it was also the most tolerant state in Europe, welcoming Polish Catholics, Orthodox Russians, Lutherans, Jews, and even a handful of Muslims. Special laws protected Jews' rights to practice their religion and maintain their customs, including the right to do business on Sundays.

Throughout the Middle Ages, Jewish communities fleeing persecution in Germany, Italy, Spain, Portugal, and Hungary settled in Vilnius. In 1648, a wave of refugees arrived from nearby Ukraine, where a Cossack uprising had killed more than 100,000 Jews. For these refugees, Vilnius was the "Jerusalem of the North" (*Yerushalaim d'Lita*)—a place where they could preserve their traditions and produce some of the most important scholarship of the era. Kabballah, Hasidism, Orthodox Judaism, Zionism, and Jewish Socialism were all born in Lithuania.

The Polish-Lithuanian Commonwealth, however, was less a melting pot than a patchwork of cultures. The Jews, like the Catholics and the Lutherans, generally kept to themselves. Visitors described Vilnius's Jewish Quarter as an exotic microcosm of the centuries-old Jewish lifestyle. Residents spoke Yiddish, followed ancient styles of dress, and observed daily, weekly, and yearly rituals. While few were wealthy, Vilnius's Jews made reasonable livings as shopkeepers, traders, innkeepers, and doctors. The vast majority of Lithuanian Jews, however, lived in the countryside, in small villages called "shtetls." By the middle of the 18th century, the Polish-Lithuanian Commonwealth was home to a quarter of the Jews in Europe, approximately 700,000 people.

Everything changed in 1795, when the Commonwealth was partitioned and the Russian Empire claimed Lithuania. Vilnius and most of the surrounding countryside were integrated into the Pale of Settlement and subjected to harsh Russification measures designed to stamp out any vestiges of Polish or Jewish nationalism. Before Onissim's birth, but within the lifetimes of his parents, Jewish self-government was abolished and Jewish schools were forced to teach their students in Russian. Traditional clothes and sidelocks were banned. Jewish boys became subject to conscription into the Russian army and a whole profession of official kidnappers emerged, charged with tracking down boys who tried to escape the draft. Vilnius was flooded with Russian soldiers and secret police who were notorious for stealing from Jewish shops and harassing Jews on the street.

By the time Onissim was born, the Jews of Vilnius, like the Jews of Odessa, were aspiring above all to escape "beyond the Pale." For all the differences between them, both Onissim's and Lea's parents understood that achievement, as well as wealth, could be the answer and both saw in their firstborn children the opportunity for a better life.

Onissim was sixteen and attending school in Moscow when the 1881 pogroms broke out across the Pale of Settlement. Vilnius was spared the worst of the violence. But repression, discrimination, and industrialization combined to impoverish Jewish communities across the Pale, and Vilnius's Jewish Quarter was gradually transformed into a ghetto of hopelessness and despair. Onissim Goldovsky had to excel if he wanted to be free of the turmoil.

A Troubled Family

❧

My grandmother Lea and my grandfather Onissim both came from intensely ambitious Jewish families. Lea's, as it turned out, was also an intensely loyal and loving one. Onissim's was not. In time, I would understand why Onissim came to crave a kind of familial warmth and harmony that his own family lacked. It was clearly something that attracted him to Lea.

Onissim's father, my great-grandfather Boris Goldovsky, was a serious man and a strict father, a wealthy Jew by Vilnius standards. He was a Merchant of the Second Guild, which was a status so far above that of Saul Luboshutz (a so-called petty bourgeois) that the Luboshutz and Katzman families could barely imagine it. Boris had considerable capital and a comfortable position for a Jew in business—equivalent to an upper-middle-class life today. He enjoyed various economic and political privileges, including the right to purchase an exemption from military service. His three children were all sons—something that must have pleased the ambitious father.

Onissim's brother Ignatz was a year younger and for some reason went by the English nickname John as transliterated into Russian. The other brother Mikhael (Mischa) was three years younger. All three sons would become professionally successful as their father had hoped, but also serious and taciturn. There was little levity in the household and an absence of family harmony appears to date from the time the boys were quite young and lost their mother, Rosa. Onissim, the oldest, was only five. Boris had remarried almost immediately and the children lived with the new couple. But Rosa had not died; Boris had had an adulterous love affair,[3] which resulted in his divorcing Rosa and marrying his paramour, Anna Osipovna Garkavi. He did not permit Rosa to see the children again for years.

Here then was a clue to Onissim's later behavior and feelings about women and family. His father had divorced his mother and banished her in order to be with someone else. In Russia at that time, men had the power to do such things. But Onissim knew it was wrong—especially the banishing part. While he too would find himself straddled between a wife and a lover (who turned out to be my grandmother, Lea), he would be unable to make a break with either of them for many years. My mother would be one of the products of that ambivalence.

Unsurprisingly, Onissim and his brothers never liked Anna. She was a poor substitute for their real mother. She did not care much for the boys and was often unkind and angry—the classic profile of a wicked stepmother. From an early age, Onissim was the protector and surrogate caregiver for his younger brothers, and here again was another clue. As Onissim grew older he would develop a philosophy of life and politics shaped around the idea of caring not only for members of one's family, but more generally for one's fellow man.

Onissim never forgave Anna for usurping his mother's place in the family, according to diary entries of Onissim's wife, Rashel Khin. On the occasion of his father and stepmother's twenty-fifth anniversary on January 19, 1896, Onissim "was almost dying when he had to make the official congratulatory 'speech' to Anna Osipovna. He HAD to pronounce words that he knew were false, to appear joyful, to kiss her . . . All this so as not to spoil his father's holiday—his father who is now an ill and miserable hypochondriac." The entry goes on: "Their mother is still alive and . . . she still cannot forget that her oldest children were taken away from her. It was a torture for her. There are no boundaries to human hypocrisy and treachery."[4]

The day after Anna finally died, on January 28, 1909, another diary entry reads: "Anna Osipovna died yesterday. She was seriously ill for a long time. During her illness and her life she was always angry with everyone, she was never pleased. She never said anything kind to anyone." And then on February 25, she added, "The death of that awful woman surfaced countless poisoned memories from the bottom of his [Onissim's] soul." Such was the unhappy household in which my grandfather Onissim grew up.

Onissim's brothers possessed the same strong intellect that allowed each to surmount their Vilnius roots but their personalities reflected the general unhappiness of the family. From some 1902 diary entries I learned that John had later married and had a single child, a daughter.[5] Soon after, his wife left him because, as Onissim put it, John was "kind, rigorously honest, but stubborn and narrow-minded."

Onissim's youngest brother, Mischa, was described by Onissim's wife of later years as "rough and harsh."[6] There is information about his university years in Moscow (including a handsome photograph) and a much later reference to both brothers in a letter Onissim wrote in 1918. The letter indicated that brother Misha had had four children and that John's daughter may have been a doctor (or studying for a medical career, as she would have been fairly young). There was also a reference elsewhere indicating that Misha became a chemist. A successful family that had realized their father's ambitions . . . but in many ways, an unhappy one. And perhaps the father was largely to blame.

Onissim's father made sure he went to the best schools; but significantly, he also made Onissim study piano and practice it very seriously. Boris wanted his son to become successful in business or pursue one of the professions that were then opening to Jews. But music as an avocation would show his cultural sophistication. In time, Onissim became an excellent pianist, and music became a lifelong passion, a third clue as to how his life would intersect with the Luboshutzes, who were merely poor Jews from Odessa.

Onissim was sent to Moscow for high school and college and, in 1883, he began his studies at Moscow Imperial University* in physics and mathematics. A year later, he switched to history and philology, and after passing his exams, ended up in law school, undoubtedly under the influence of his lawyer uncle. He was granted a permit to live in Moscow through 1887 as a law student and settled on Milutinskyi Lane, a street that still exists in the city. His uncle, though Jewish, had the requisite permit to live in Moscow and was there to provide help if necessary.

Although there were not yet quotas on Jewish students, Jews still faced discrimination at all Russian universities, so it was a major family event when Onissim entered the law department of the oldest and most prestigious institution of higher learning in Russia. Onissim must have been exceptionally talented to be admitted to Moscow University's intensely competitive law department, and he was fortunate to be exposed to a rich and expansive curriculum, at least initially. Liberal reforms of legal education had led to a broad array of subjects that now included Roman law, international law, canon law, criminal justice, civil justice, and constitutional or state law. And the curriculum went considerably beyond legal subjects; it included statistics, a philosophy course on Immanuel Kant, and a course on Shakespeare's *Macbeth*, taught by Russia's greatest Shakespeare scholar, Nikolai Storozhenko, who would become Onissim's lifelong friend.

---

* This was the name of the institution from its founding in 1755 until 1917. It is now called Moscow State University. Coincidentally, this was the school where my great-uncle Nikolai Shereshevsky studied medicine a few years later. Shereshevsky delivered all of Onissim's children, including my mother.

Thus, by the time he graduated from Moscow University on December 1, 1887, Onissim Goldovsky could boast of being a true Renaissance man with one of the finest educations available anywhere in the world. His education would be one of the most significant influences on his later life and career, and would influence Lea in important ways. His education, his worldliness, his wealth—these were all things that she wanted. But in order to get them, she would pay a price.

Sonate pour Piano et Violon

I

THE MUSIC BEGINS

Allegretto ben moderato

(1885 to 1903)

❧

César Franck returned to the sonata for violin and piano in 1885. Inspi-
ration came immediately this time and the work took only a few weeks to
complete. Franck dedicated it to one of the world's great violinists, his fellow
countryman, Eugène Ysaÿe. The timing was perfect as the sonata was ready
for Ysaÿe to play on his wedding day, September 26, 1886. Legend has it that
rather than prepare for the wedding in a more conventional way, the violinist
spent considerable time rehearsing the difficult piece with one of the wedding
guests, a pianist. The reaction of the bride, Louise Bourdeau de Coutrai, can
only be imagined.

Three months later, the two musicians gave their first public performance
of the sonata as the finale of a long afternoon program. By the time they were
ready to perform it, the hall was so dark that the two performers had to play
it from memory. That did not restrain the crowd. Like so many audiences in
ensuing years, they were wildly enthusiastic. Ysaÿe immediately added César
Franck's sonata to his repertoire and played it in recitals all over the world. It
was during one of Ysaÿe's tours of Russia that Onissim Goldovsky and, later,

members of the Luboshutz family heard the work for the first time. It would change their lives.

The first movement of the sonata has been called "gentle and sweetly reflec-tive." According to Ysaÿe in his letter to the composer, it is "one long caress, a gentle awakening on a summer morning; it is a miracle!"

Lea in the Shimmering City

Katherine and Saul Luboshutz's "miracle" took shape on February 10, 1885, with the birth of a daughter whom they named Lea—my grandmother. Saul was especially ecstatic. By the time Lea was two, the same year my grandfather Onissim graduated from Moscow University, Saul decided without any real evidence that Lea was the musical prodigy he had longed for. Saul and Gitel had not forgotten the 1881 pogrom and their vow to leave. Lea could make their name famous throughout Russia and provide a way out of the Pale of Settlement. Gitel shared Saul's dream, though more practically, she made sure Lea kept Saul distracted and out of the way of the piano business.

There was only one way that Saul and Gitel's dream of getting beyond the Pale to a "better place" could be realistic. Jews who had accomplished this feat had done so through great wealth or extraordinary talent and there was no way a piano business was going to lead them to sufficient riches to impress the authorities. Thus, it was important for Saul and Gitel to learn whether Lea had musical talent as quickly as possible and, if so, figure out how to nurture it. As soon as she could stand on her own two feet, Lea was taught by Saul to hold herself erect, her head tilted slightly up with pride, and to always look her best in every way. Her remarkable deportment and appearance were qualities she retained for the rest of her life. At the same time, she learned to hold a tiny violin and bow and by the time she turned four and Saul was ready to teach her to play the instrument, Lea's posture and hand positions were well established.

She made rapid progress within months. But Saul was relentless. Mastering the music was not enough. If Lea was to succeed, she had to play before audiences so that performing came naturally. Neighbors were summoned to listen. By the time Lea started school at age five, she had enough repertoire to fill a whole program—so her parents organized a concert for her. To prepare, she dutifully memorized little piece after little piece. Gentle Saul, whom everyone loved, was almost unrecognizable as a taskmaster, although my grandmother insists he always criticized constructively.

The conditions under which Lea practiced are almost unimaginable. The family lived in two rooms with windows that opened onto a dank courtyard. As Lea described it fifty years later, "The sun never penetrated, and the rooms were always gloomy and damp. During the winter we had to use a lamp from early in the morning until it was time to retire. The only source of heat was from a little stove which was used with great economy . . . Rising at six I quickly dressed, ate a hasty breakfast, and then practiced although my hands were nearly frozen."[1]

After her early practice and breakfast, she left the cold house for the relative warmth of the outside (even on cold days, outside seemed warmer). She went to school, came home, practiced two more hours, had a one-course dinner, did her schoolwork, practiced another hour, and finally went to bed. That was the routine day after day. The one exception was Friday. On that day, Gitel scrubbed the house, polished the silver candlesticks, cooked a delicious meal, spread the table with a beautiful white cloth, and recited prayers along with Saul before consuming chicken, piroshki (meat-filled buns), gefilte fish with horseradish, and sweet pastries. Even more special was the annual seder (or Passover meal) at which Gitel's father, the rabbi, presided and other family members crowded into their tiny apartment.

Lea's first "concert," as her parents insisted on calling it, was preceded by countless performances in front of visitors. By the time she appeared before her school audience, she was more excited about the new ribbon in her hair than she was nervous about the performance. She played every piece she had ever learned, as people insisted on encores. From that moment on, she decided that she loved to perform. Never again, though, would performing be so easy and enjoyable. The more she learned and the more she mastered her instrument, the harder it became.

Meanwhile, Saul believed that another important component of Lea's training was exposure to great musicians who made their way to Odessa. No matter the cost, Saul either purchased a ticket and held Lea on his lap or stood in the back of the hall holding her high enough to see. According to Lea's memoir, when the world-famous Pablo de Sarasate came to town sometime in the early 1890s, Saul was particularly excited. This man, he told Lea, was considered among the greatest violinists of all time. After the concert, Saul quizzed Lea about what she had heard. Trying to impress her father, she told him that she had heard a false F-sharp in the performance of one of Sarasate's own compositions, and that she was surprised the master could play even one note out of tune.

Saul was enraged. He had expected her to admire and study the divine playing of the great man, not to look for wrong notes. This lesson was not lost on the young child; and for the rest of her life, Lea would admire what was good about performances, avoiding negative criticism. Except with her own students, when critiquing was part of her job, she wanted to be positive. I was always amazed, as I was growing up, by my grandmother's ability to find something to praise, even at concerts that weren't all that great. When a particular performance was awful, I wondered what she could possibly say. She would throw her arms around the dejected performer and remark in an excited voice, "Dah-ling, how you played!"

It was probably during one of Eugène Ysaÿe's concert tours of Russia that Lea and her father heard him play Franck's violin and piano sonata. In later life, she never said when she first heard it, and now I regret that I never asked her. What is certain is that before she was thirteen, she was not only familiar with the piece but also determined both to learn it and someday study it with Ysaÿe.

When my grandmother reached the age of eight, Saul realized he was out of his depth. Lea required both a better teacher and an environment where she would be seen and heard by important people who could help her advance in the fiercely competitive music world. Saul and Gitel were hardly the only parents who claimed they had a "wunderkind" on their hands. Countless Jewish families believed that their children were at least as talented as Lea. The joke in Odessa was: "How do you know which of your neighbors' children will become a successful mathematician?" Answer: "The one not carrying a violin case."

In their attempt to find a great teacher and mentor, the family had extraordinarily good luck. Emil Mlynarski was teaching at the Odessa Conservatory. Mlynarski had studied under Leopold Auer, the greatest living violin pedagogue in Russia. Lea played for Mlynarski and immediately he arranged for a scholarship so that she could study with him. The lessons took place every Sunday in his private home, the likes of which Lea had never even dreamed. The Mlynarskis seemed extravagantly rich. Here Lea not only learned the violin but became fluent in French, the language of the household. Mlynarski's wife and mother both took a shine to the eight-year-old and wanted to give her the polish she would need to complement her violin playing. Special clothes were purchased for these occasions, including Lea's first pair of patent leather shoes. On Sunday mornings at the Luboshutz home, water was boiled for Lea's bath and her mother dressed her carefully and thoroughly brushed her hair. For poor Jews, this connection was too important to be careless.

Thus began the first of Lea's many transformations from a poor Jewish girl to an elegant and refined woman. At the Mlynarskis, she not only studied how to play the violin, she began to acquire the manners, the demeanor, and the sophistication of the wealthy.

Sex and Politics

While Lea was toiling away in Odessa, Onissim was making an alarming discovery in Moscow. There were at least two things that could reliably get a young man in trouble—women and politics—and he had difficulties on both counts. It all began when, still a university student, he decided to spend a summer vacation visiting his fellow student Vasily Rozanov and his wife.

Rozanov was an unusual character. He had been raised by his devoutly Russian Orthodox mother in a tiny town near present-day Nizhny Novgorod. Later, he studied history and philology at Moscow University, graduating

the year before Onissim matriculated. Like many university graduates of his
era, Rozanov was sent by the Ministry of Education to a teaching job in the
provinces. His assignment was Bryansk, a town of sixteen thousand located
250 miles southwest of Moscow in Russia's "black earth" agricultural region.
When Rozanov moved to Bryansk in 1882, he took along his wife of two years,
Apollinaria (Polina) Suslova.

Polina loved men. The more the merrier. She liked them smart, she liked
them dark, and she liked them young. Thirty-eight years old at the time of
her marriage to the twenty-two-year-old Rozanov, Polina was the daughter of a
former serf who had managed to become wealthy as a merchant and manufacturer. She became notorious in the 1860s for her tempestuous affair with
Fyodor Dostoyevsky. She left the novelist for a young Spanish student. After
a short time, she left him for Rozanov. Rozanov's life with Polina in Bryansk
was difficult, to put it mildly. She threw temper tantrums and berated Rozanov
in public, ridiculing his writing and accusing him of having affairs with his
students. She both flirted with and insulted his colleagues at the school where
he taught. She flaunted her wealth, wearing expensive silk gowns and handing
out piles of cash to the locals.

Polina, as it turned out, was good friends with Onissim's stepmother, Anna.
No doubt desperate for company, Polina suggested to Anna that she encourage
Onissim to accept an invitation to visit during the summer vacation. Though
his unsavory stepmother's recommendation was hardly an enticement, getting
out of Moscow was, and Onissim accepted, spending his 1886 summer vacation
in Bryansk. Over the course of those weeks, Onissim and Rozanov developed
a deeper friendship. Vasily, smart, unconventional, and flamboyant, was in the
throes of developing a philosophical system that would make him famous as
an advocate of spiritualism, spontaneity, and free love. How much more could
a young man like Onissim want from a friend and mentor?

Both Onissim and Rozanov were anomalies. Both had been accepted at
Moscow University and both succeeded there because of talent and brains, not
family connections. Although Onissim was comfortably well off, he was still
a Jewish merchant's son from Vilnius, a status far below that of the nobility
surrounding him at the university. Rozanov came from a family of low-ranked
civil servants and had become impoverished when his father died. It was only
natural that these two outsiders were drawn to each other.

Onissim's growing friendship with Rozanov was soon overshadowed by the machinations of the increasingly erratic Polina. Exactly what happened is a matter of speculation.[2] One source says that my grandfather fell in love with a piano student named Aleksandra Petrovna Popova. But Polina also had her eye on Onissim. He was, apparently, exactly her type—young and brilliant, like Rozanov and Dostoyevsky, but darkly handsome, like her Spanish ex-lover. Polina encouraged her husband's solitary writing while imposing herself on Onissim and Aleksandra, taking long walks with them through the woods and fields and once even joining them on an ambitious expedition by boat to the Svensky Monastery, several miles from Bryansk across the Desna River. Despite her efforts, Rozanov's close friend, the poet Zinaida Gippius, reported later that Onissim firmly rejected Polina's advances.[3]

Onissim returned to the university in the fall, ready to focus exclusively on academics. But Polina was not accustomed to being rejected by men and she was angry. She told Onissim's stepmother, Anna, about Onissim's relationship with Aleksandra—"one of those girls who is lovable only in bed." When there was no response, Polina turned up the heat, writing to Onissim's father and accusing Onissim of having made inappropriate advances toward Anna, who had also visited that summer. Boris, knowing that Onissim could not abide his wife and realizing that Polina was not a dependable reporter of facts, did not respond and never mentioned the letter to his son. Polina was now furious and bent on revenge. Fortuitously for her, the perfect opportunity presented itself. She found a letter from Onissim to her husband, criticizing Tsar Alexander III and his university reforms.

This seemingly innocuous letter was dangerous because the political environment had changed in Russia in recent history. Onissim had grown up under the relatively benign rule of the "reforming tsar," Alexander II (reigned 1855–1881). Shocked by Russia's defeat in the Crimean War, Alexander decided that Russia had to be modernized, and he looked to Europe for models. In 1862, he abolished serfdom, ending a way of life that had been fundamental to Russia for centuries. He also established elected councils called *zemstvos*, with some authority over local affairs, and he permitted—within limits—freedom of speech. Numerous political groups formed during this time, including Narodnaya Volya (The People's Will), a radical organization with the express goal of overthrowing the Tsar.

In 1881, a member of Narodnaya Volya assassinated Alexander II, throwing two bombs under his carriage as he drove through St. Petersburg. Alexander II was succeeded by his second son, Alexander III (ruled 1881–1894). The first son, Nicholas, had been expected to assume the throne and had been trained accordingly but died of meningitis shortly before the assassination, leaving Alexander III a role he neither understood nor wanted. Charles Lowe, the Russia correspondent for the *London Times*, described the new Tsar as a "bull" in human form—tall, thickset, and muscular. He was fired by his passionate ambition to impose upon Russia an ideology of nationalism, strict loyalty to the Orthodox Church, and absolute autocracy. Alexander III's thirteen-year reign saw the proliferation of the Okhrana (secret police); the arrest, imprisonment, or execution of thousands of political suspects; and the brutal persecution of ethnic and religious minorities.

Convinced that impressionable students and their liberal-minded professors were behind the wave of political terrorism that had swept Russia and killed his father, Alexander III imposed the iron grip of the police state on all aspects of student life. This included the University Statutes, a set of harsh rules designed to extinguish the slightest spark of campus dissent. Potentially subversive courses, such as international constitutional law, were canceled. Demanding new courses that emphasized rote memorization were imposed on all academic departments. Law was particularly affected, and law faculties were purged of suspected liberals. At Moscow University, two of the most popular professors, Sergei Muromtsev (one of Onissim's favorites) and Maksim Kovalevsky, were forced out and barred from teaching in any Russian university.

These reforms were deeply offensive to the principles of academic freedom. But they were also distressing to the students for more prosaic reasons. New coursework and examination requirements were imposed with no advance notice. The new law school course load, designed to keep students busy and out of trouble, was so heavy that even the Ministry of Justice complained that the students weren't coping. The purge of liberals left faculties short-staffed, and up to a quarter of university teaching positions were filled by poorly qualified temporary professors.

Sometime in late 1886, five years into Alexander III's reign and a few months into Polina's frustrated campaign to ruin Onissim's reputation, the young man wrote the fateful letter to Rozanov, complaining about the university reforms. The Tsar's policies were causing "chaos" [*bezporyadok*] in the universities, he told his friend. Furthermore, according to Rozanov's memoirs, Onissim "sharply criticized the beginning of the tsar's reign" (*durno vyrazil'sya o nachalye tsarstvovaniya*).[4] According to a later police report, the letter closed with the words: "People! Crocodiles! Bryzgalovs [University Inspector of Students]! Rectors! Ministers! Bosses! Hyenas! Scoundrels!; You speak in the languages of slaves!"[5] Clearly this series of insults was directed at the new university administrators and indirectly to the higher-ups whose policies they were carrying out.

Polina now had what she wanted—an instrument of revenge. She sent the letter to the secret police along with an anonymous one of her own, which she signed "An Outraged Mother." She accused Onissim not only of the slanderous crimes against the state that his letter made manifest but also of further abuse of women. She soon got the results she was after. Onissim's letter, based on its contents, was grounds for the police to suspect him of illegal activity and perhaps of belonging to an illegal political society. Accordingly, an official inquiry was launched by the Moscow Regional Gendarmes as to whether Onissim was guilty of a crime under Article 250 of the administrative code.

In the course of the inquiry, a search was made of Onissim's apartment, and it turned up two documents that were banned in Russia—materials for a biography of Tsar Paul I and a letter from Alexander Herzen to the Russian ambassador in London with a response to comments by the political conservative Shedo-Ferroti. Onissim was called in for questioning. His legal skills were already in good form and he presented an articulate defense. Since much hung on who was being criticized, Onissim focused on the text of the letter, particularly on the word *gosudari* (bosses). In older usage, its definition was "feudal lords" and in the singular it could stand for the Tsar himself. In the 1880s, it meant any higher-ups. According to the police report, Onissim explained "that the harsh terms he used with respect to the new system at the university did not refer to the Special Lord Emperor, and that this was evidenced by his use of the plural of the word *gosudari*." As far as the foreign brochures found in his apartment, "Goldovsky said that he found them while sorting out old books and had no explanation of how they had come into his possession." The authorities were surprisingly lenient. Given that "no unfavorable information exists with respect to Goldovsky's political leanings" and since Onissim had no criminal record, he was given what basically amounted to a hand slap—a two-month prison sentence.

For a long time, I wondered how Onissim had been so lucky. Given the political climate of the time, his punishment seemed light, especially for a Jew. Then in 2018, the explanation came in the form of a copy of the actual police report that my Russian cousin Sveta Kuzin, who was helping me with my research, had located in the State Historical Archive in St. Petersburg. In doing their work, the police had made a serious mistake. In the report, Onissim is described as "a student at Moscow Imperial University, of the [Russian] Orthodox religion, and literate." One simple error—describing Onissim as a Christian rather than a Jew—may have been the defining event in his life. But for police incompetence, the world might never have heard of Onissim Goldovsky again.

Despite the light punishment, Polina was delighted. She told Rozanov that Onissim was a dangerous felon and pressured him never to meet with the younger man again; Rozanov refused her demand. Shortly after Onissim's release from prison, Rozanov offered to visit his young friend in Moscow. At first, Onissim rebuffed him, believing that it was Rozanov who was responsible for his imprisonment. When the confusion was cleared up, Onissim and Rozanov were reunited and met in Moscow to discuss the (paltry) sales of Rozanov's recently published book, *On Understanding*. By incredible coincidence, a friend of Polina's spotted the two men dining together and reported back to her. Polina left Rozanov permanently, although she refused to give him a divorce and they remained married for the rest of his life.

Onissim's luck held. Despite the police action, he was not expelled from the university, which was a huge break. He was still a second-class citizen in Russia due to his Jewish roots and, like any Jew, he needed a permit to live in Moscow. If he had been expelled, his permit would have been revoked and he would have had to return to Vilnius, where conditions continued to deteriorate. In 1882, the year before Onissim matriculated, Tsar Alexander III had announced the infamous May Laws, which barred Jews from living in the countryside or owning land. The Jews who had lived for generations in the shtetls were forced to abandon their land, workshops, stores, and inns and move to the cities. Vilnius, already in a severe economic downturn, could not absorb so many internal refugees. The Jewish Quarter became dangerously overcrowded as families took in destitute friends and relatives. Poverty, unemployment, and disease were now the norm.

Jewish existence, even in Moscow, was becoming more precarious. Alexander III's policy of "Russia for the Russians" was so punitive that his top advisor, Konstantin Pobedonostsev (1827–1907), predicted matter-of-factly that "one third [of Russia's Jews] will be converted; one third will emigrate; and the other third will die of hunger."[6] The policies also targeted Roman Catholics, Lutherans, and ethnic Germans, but none were persecuted so violently as the Jews. At Onissim's university, quotas were imposed limiting Jewish students to 3 percent of total enrollment and all the Jewish professors were fired. In 1888, four hundred Jewish secondary-school graduates passed the university entrance exam, but only seventy-four were accepted by Russian universities and none were admitted to Moscow University. Official discrimination was compounded by devastating pogroms carried out by criminal gangs with the tacit support of the police.

The impact of the university reforms on Onissim's academic life, his summer in Bryansk, and his brief but terrifying run-in with the secret police all shaped his emerging political views. He decided early on he would join the opposition, but deciding which branch to join was more complicated. The opposition was divided by one vital question: Was the initial step forward to be economic or political? The far left, which included rural-oriented Social Revolutionaries and the more urban Socialists, believed that the foundational problem in Russia was the unequal distribution of wealth. For them, a revolutionary program would start with the redistribution of property—first and foremost, the redistribution of land from the wealthy gentry and aristocrats to the peasants. The liberals, on the other hand, argued that political reform—specifically, electoral democracy and a rights-based Constitution—had to come first. Economic reforms should be designed by representative political institutions. In the end, Onissim supported the political approach.

As a teacher in Bryansk, Rozanov told Onissim he had been shocked by the terrible poverty of the peasantry. While many intellectuals of that generation idealized the peasantry for their supposed spiritualism, simplicity, and natural egalitarianism, Rozanov was more clear-eyed. He told Onissim that his students from peasant families were utterly lacking in self-discipline and ambition. He was outraged by what he considered the laziness of the locals, complaining that they had no interest in improving their lots in life and spent most of their time gambling, drinking, and gossiping. For Onissim, who was more politically inclined than Rozanov, it must have been clear that rural poverty had to be addressed, but that a sudden redistribution of agricultural land to the brutalized and undereducated peasantry was not the answer. When Onissim returned to Moscow from Bryansk, and then emerged from prison months later, toughened but unbowed, he was already committed to the liberal views about political reform that would define the rest of his life.

My discovery of the emergence of Onissim Goldovsky's strong political views and his commitment to liberal reform answered a question that had remained long unanswered in my effort to understand Lea. Though professing to be apolitical, her autobiography is replete with statements reflecting views similar to those of Onissim. Even her view of the Soviet Union and its political philosophy was evenhanded—quite a surprise to me, given the treatment of the immediate family by the Soviets after the Revolution of 1917. Lea's politics would come to be shaped by Onissim.

On December 1, 1887, Onissim was awarded a Law Candidates degree from Moscow University. It was a precious document. Equally precious was a second certificate stating that, during his time of study at the university, he had never participated in any activities that showed disrespect for the law, the government, or established regulations. Given his recent incarceration during an increasingly repressive political era, he was a very lucky man.

The Luboshutz Trio

At about this time, two more children were born to Gitel and Saul Luboshutz—my great-aunt Anna, on July 13, 1887, and my great-uncle Pinkhus, who later went by the name of Petya or Pierre, on June 19, 1890.[7] Anna's birth was a bit of a disappointment to her parents, according to her sister, Lea. This time they certainly had wanted a boy, but got another girl instead; and the child's ill health did not help matters. Lea continued to be the favored child. Despite Anna's illnesses, Lea admitted in her memoir that she received the best piece of meat at meals, on weekdays sometimes the only piece, along with the undivided attention of their father.

Saul did not even bother to give Anna an instrument to play until she was eight, and then it was a cello, not an instrument at which a girl was expected to excel or become a professional. Her lessons were haphazard, her practice sessions short, and she herself was rather lazy. Nevertheless, Anna surprised everyone by making rapid progress. According to Lea, Anna was the more naturally gifted of the two sisters. Whereas Lea, by dint of hours of practice, had managed to advance rapidly, music came more naturally to Anna. She was born with perfect pitch and had a talent for mastering instrumental technique. In time, Saul realized that he should take more interest in Anna's development, though her lack of motivation infuriated him and after her initial progress he despaired of making her another family genius. Rather, he relied on the fact that she was turning into a beauty, with fiery red hair, black eyes, and a long slender neck. Indeed, it was not unusual for people to refer to the two sisters with the rhyming names of Lea (pronounced in the Hebrew manner as "Lay-ah") and Shayah (meaning "neck" in Russian). Anna's health also improved, and she was practically without illness for the rest of her long life.

With the birth of my great-uncle Pierre, Lea and Anna's brother, the whole family attitude changed. At last, a boy! That was the good news. The bad news was that he was sickly and puny, and the household attention initially revolved around ensuring his survival. Father and mother doted on him; and even as an old man, he was the family favorite. Neighbors took an interest in his health and were free with advice and extra food—a nice piece of fish, some sweets for extra nourishment. Pierre's circumcision was delayed for a long time; and when the day finally arrived and the doctor said it was permissible, the boy almost died from loss of blood. Once his health stabilized, Pierre was a quiet and introspective child. This became a great joke in the family years later when Pierre turned out to be a great ladies' man, a man-about-town.

Pierre too was given an instrument to play. The choice of piano was quite intentional on Saul's part. The family now had a budding violinist, cellist, and pianist—the three instruments that constitute one of the most popular chamber ensembles in classical music. The nascent "Luboshutz Trio" of Lea, Anna, and Pierre in time would become the most famous ensemble of its kind in Russia during the decade before the 1917 Revolution. For now, though, Saul simply had three young musicians of varying abilities and industriousness. Lea remained his treasure—talented and hard working. The other two children were mirror images of each other. Anna had extraordinary native talent but was lazy. Pierre initially showed little aptitude for piano but was industrious. Soon he advanced beyond Anna, fueling further parental hopes.

Meanwhile, in 1893, my grandmother Lea began her three years of studies with Mlynarski. Perhaps more importantly, thanks to Mlynarski's reputation in the musical world, she had occasion to play for every great violinist and musician of importance who came through Odessa. Like today's scouts who search out young sports prospects, these individuals were always looking for the next musical superstar whom they could claim to have "discovered" and, if they were teachers, take on as students. Thus, it was inevitable that Lea would play for the famous Leopold Auer, Mlynarski's teacher, when he came to Odessa in 1896.

The audition was preceded by lunch at the Mlynarski home. Upon meeting eleven-year-old Lea, Auer commented wryly, "Why should a beautiful girl like you play the violin? You should get married when you are old enough." But after hearing her play, he decreed that she should immediately come to St. Petersburg and study with him. Lea was excited at the prospect. But Saul and Gitel faced a dilemma. They had not anticipated that Lea would receive such an invitation at the age of eleven. She was too young to go by herself. The only way she could accept was if one of her parents stayed with her there, and that was impossible. Money was scarce and two parents were required in Odessa, one to mind the business, the other to bring up the younger children. Regretfully, Lea's parents said no.

As they discussed with Mlynarski the impossibility of St. Petersburg, Saul and Gitel realized that Moscow was a possible alternative. There was a fine conservatory there, though some claimed it was slightly less prestigious than the one in St. Petersburg. But Moscow had something St. Petersburg did not—affluent relatives. It was an idea that percolated for a while until the opportunity presented itself when the director of the Moscow Conservatory, Vasily Safonov, came to Odessa. Another event was staged so that Lea could play for him. Though exciting, it was not quite the same as playing for Auer. Safonov was a pianist, a conductor, and a composer, not one of the world's great violin pedagogues. But for Saul and Gitel, it didn't matter. Moscow was the place Jews dreamed about, closed to all but a small number of the most successful. Imagine a daughter, not yet having reached puberty, who might be the first in the immediate family to live there.

Safonov, as expected, wanted Lea as a pupil at the Moscow Conservatory and he generally had good luck arguing with the authorities for more Jewish students. Grand Duke Konstantin Konstantinovich, a poet, lover of music, and cousin of the Tsar, was honorary president of the conservatory, so Safonov was confident that he could get a permit for Lea to come to Moscow. Formal paperwork was prepared and thirteen-year-old Lea signed her own application to the conservatory on January 7, 1899. Acceptance was a mere formality. An October arrival was planned, with Gitel bringing Lea and staying with her until lessons began. Everything was arranged, but Lea contracted yellow fever and the trip had to be postponed, much to Safonov's irritation as he would have to go through the permitting process again. Finally, in January 1900, Lea's health improved and the two set off.

A Perilous Journey

The decision to send Lea to Moscow so that she could become a professional musician could not have come at a better time in at least one respect. A golden age had arrived in Russian classical music and music making. In the 18th and early 19th centuries, what we today refer to as classical music had been produced primarily in Western European capitals. Such places—Vienna, Paris, Venice, Salzburg, London, Leipzig—not only had been home to great composers but also great performers. From the time of Peter the Great (1672–1725), European culture in general and European music in particular were considered part of civilized society in Russia. But Russian music was felt to be the province of the church and of folk traditions.

This view began to change in the 19th century when composers such as Mikhail Glinka (1804–1857), Alexander Borodin (1833–1887), Modest Mussorgsky (1839–1881), Nikolai Rimsky-Korsakov (1844–1908), and a number of others developed a Russian school of composition. While many of the musical forms they employed were those of their European counterparts, a new national style incorporated material that was distinctly Russian. The giant among these composers was Pyotr Ilyich Tchaikovsky (1840–1893), whose works became immensely popular not only in Russia but throughout the world.

As with composers, so too with instrumentalists. While Western European players still overwhelmingly dominated the classical music scene in the first half of 19th century, the formation of the St. Petersburg Conservatory in 1862 and the Moscow Conservatory in 1866 marked the development of two important Russian pedagogical centers which, in time, developed their own highly acclaimed style of teaching and playing. Lea's arrival at the Moscow Conservatory at the turn of the century was well timed since it was a moment when Russian performers were becoming international stars and their country's repertoire was part of their attraction.

But if Lea's arrival in Moscow was fortuitous in certain respects, she still had a major handicap to overcome. She was a woman and, very simply, classical music was a male-dominated world. There was a long-standing French tradition (promoted in painting and literature) of viewing women in the arts—ballerinas, music hall performers, and the like—as "available" to men for something more after the performance. Rich men could become "patrons" of such women, which often translated into setting them up in apartments, bestowing clothing and other finery, and taking sexual favors in exchange. For many of these women, the ultimate goal was marriage. Thus, for Lea to succeed as a great artist, she had not only to become a great player but also overcome these misogynistic attitudes.

But for fourteen-year-old Lea, none of this was part of her consciousness. She was simply excited. She and her mother were taking their first train trip, and for both it would be their first time in Moscow. The idea of the seven-hundred-mile trip filled Gitel with dread. The unknown dangers and uncertainties about what they might encounter were only part of her worry.

She was also concerned about leaving the business and her other children in Saul's hands. But there was no question of letting him take Lea to Moscow. Saul could not be trusted with such a responsibility. She would just have to take her chances and forego the income from the piano business. She felt better about Saul's ability to care for Anna and Pierre. Until his dying day, Saul was wonderful with children.

Traveling third class, Gitel and Lea boarded the train in Odessa, loaded with bundles, packages, pillows, Lea's violin, and a samovar for making tea. The seemingly interminable trip took many days, and they had to sleep on hard wooden benches. The train had a dining car, but purchasing meals was out of the question as the food was expensive and not kosher. Every half hour or so, when the train stopped, Gitel filled the samovar's kettle with water and made tea, often sharing it with other passengers, to whom she told Lea's story. For the travelers in their car, many of them other poor Jews, it was the rags-to-riches story that everyone dreamed about. Gitel reveled in their envy.

Gitel was pleased to see Lea having such a good time, so she did not share one of her greatest anxieties. She had no idea how they would be received by their Moscow relatives. The head of that household, whom Lea in later years referred to as "my uncle," was related to Samuel Polyakov, "the Russian railroad king," who had had business interests throughout the Ukraine and at one time was probably the richest Jew in Moscow. Samuel's brother, Lazar Polyakov, owned a bank and the man Lea called her uncle was a director.

The specific relationship between the Odessa household and the one in Moscow was never fully explained either by Lea or anyone else in our family. I very much doubt that the Moscow family was headed by a brother either of Saul or of Gitel given the extreme difference in their economic and life circumstances. Much more likely is the possibility that Lea was encouraged to describe the man of the family as her uncle in order to claim a closeness which did not actually exist or out of supposed affection.

Whatever the reason, Gitel and her relatives had been out of touch with one another during the several years prior to her letting them know that she was on her way to Moscow with Lea. There had been no definitive response about what she and Lea were to do upon arrival. Not that this was unusual. There were many stories circulating in Odessa about Jews who had become rich, moved to Moscow, and then spurned their poor relatives. The wealthy were often beset by poor family members from the provinces who arrived and sponged off them for as long as they could, and it was against the law to exceed the permitted number of Jews in a household. Gitel's fears increased when two jovial students who accompanied them during the last two days of their journey teased Gitel about her samovar, telling her that she could not possibly arrive with it at the home of her rich relatives, as it would expose her poverty. The students offered to carry it for her and deliver it later. Gitel, trusting no one, decided it could be put in one of the pillowcases and tied with a heavy string.

Sometimes life's events occur just as in fairy tales—both for good and ill. Gitel's fears were fully realized upon arrival. There was no one at the station to meet them. Gitel hired a two-wheeled droshky (open carriage) with a horse and driver and provided the address. At first, the driver was skeptical. Why would third-class passengers be going to one of the most fashionable addresses in Moscow? But Gitel showed him her money, and he seemed satisfied.

Arrival at the house was equally dispiriting. Lea's memory was vivid when she wrote about it almost a half-century later: "[My uncle's] bank was a very rich one, and to have the position of a director meant a lot of entertaining, elegance, and some snobbery. Imagine the picture—the butler opening the door for us, a man with white whiskers, in knee breeches, as stiff as if he had swallowed a stick, standing speechless . . . wondering what to do with us. We were expected to look differently, but our appearance was too much for him. Fortunately for us, a lady covered with jewelry appeared and looked through her lorgnette, first at our shoes, then at our faces. Addressing us in broken Russian, caused undoubtedly by too much knowledge of every other language, she greeted us quite coolly and gave orders to the butler to take care of our luggage and asked us to follow her."

Lea may have been surprised by the halting Russian spoken by the woman who turned out to be her uncle's wife, but it was actually quite normal for someone of the highest social class to struggle with the language of her homeland. Lea's aunt had probably grown up speaking French, the language of polite society. Once she had established her superiority over Gitel and Lea, her Russian "improved," and she led them to a plushly carpeted room with walls of pink silk and a fragrance of flowers. As if this was not overwhelming enough, in the adjoining bathroom were mirrored walls and gold fixtures. Lea's aunt told them that lunch would be delayed owing to the inconvenient time of their arrival and that they should clean up and dress for the meal. Another butler summoned them in an hour's time, and everyone entered an enormous dining room with walls of sumptuous wood paneling and a table so large that Lea thought it could feed everyone she knew at one sitting and still have room left over. Lea's uncle, a small man who seemed quite shy and childlike, apologized that they were not met at the station. His wife interrupted him, saying that he did not have to be so polite to poor relatives. A son, even more awkward than his father, sat at the table and said nothing throughout the meal. Lea decided that she hated all of them.

After lunch, Lea joined the adults in the library. After an awkward attempt at small talk, the aunt asked what was expected of her. Gitel started in an uncharacteristically low voice to tell Lea's remarkable story. Her hostess interrupted, telling Gitel that there was nothing they could do for them, that the family had many obligations already, and that Lea and Gitel's presence in the house was not only an inconvenience but a danger, given how things were going for Jews in the city. They would have to leave. Then Gitel did something that Lea had never seen her do before. She burst into tears. Her relative, showing compassion for the first time, said they could leave their things while they went to the conservatory and until they secured alternative accommodations.

The walk to the conservatory was long, with transport out of the question given their limited funds. On the way, Lea decided she hated Moscow and wouldn't play well so that she could go back to her father, the only person in the world whom she adored. But by the time she entered the large and impressive room of her professor, she had changed her mind. A portrait of the conservatory's legendary founder, Nikolai Rubinstein, hung on the wall. Among the many students, Lea sensed hostility toward her. She began with an unaccompanied Bach prelude and was prepared to go on but Professor Jan Hřímalý[8] simply applauded warmly and told her she would be accepted into his class and should come in three days for her lesson.

Their next stop was the director's office. They were hoping that once Safonov heard about their plight, he would solve things. But as bad luck would have it, he was out of town until the evening. Lea did not want to return to the relatives, but Gitel explained that their situation as homeless Jews in Moscow was dangerous, so they would have to swallow their pride and beg. When they arrived, the butler was now even ruder and initially did not let them in. To

Gitel's astonishment, Lea looked him straight in the eye and lied. "My aunt and uncle insisted that we come back for dinner. Show us to our room please." The butler was even more dumbfounded but did as commanded.

When Lea's aunt returned, she came to their room dressed, as Lea remembered it, like a queen. ("Later," Lea wrote, "when I saw a real queen, I knew my idea of how a queen would dress had been wrong.") Her aunt asked Gitel what had occurred. Once again, Lea took things in hand. "Safonov was away and will not return until this evening at which point we can go back." In the meantime, they would attend dinner.

Two butlers were in attendance for the four diners, as Lea's uncle had joined her aunt and the cousin was not in attendance. Lea's uncle seemed interested in her examination and expressed pleasure when he learned of her acceptance into a famous professor's class. "But how shall you manage?" he asked Gitel in Russian. At this point, his wife spoke to him sharply in French: *"Pas devant les domestiques!"* [Not in front of the servants!] Gitel looked at Lea helplessly, but Lea answered immediately and firmly in the French she had learned in the Mlynarski home: *"Mais pourquoi pas?"* [But why not?] "They know we are poor but honest."

Lea's aunt now paid close attention to this remarkable child. Lea's French was perfect—a surprise, coming from a child of poor relatives in the provinces. Her table manners—learned at the Mlynarski home—were also perfect, her deportment and confidence remarkable for a young person who had had none of the advantages of an affluent home. The aunt smiled and spoke graciously. "It is really too dangerous for Jews to be walking around Moscow at night. Even though it is illegal, you should plan to spend just this night in our house. And, since you are staying, perhaps Lea might grace us with some music."

Lea gained something in these twenty-four hours that lasted for the rest of her life. She had transformed herself from a dutiful daughter into a young woman who would have to take care of herself. She could cope with adversity and often she would have to do so without help. Her certainty that she could convince people to help her was bolstered when she learned that her uncle, who had taken a shine to her, would provide fifteen rubles a month for her support, enough for car fare, strings for the violin, printed music, and lunch money.

The second day and night were still a challenge. Fearing the police at every turn, Gitel and Lea lugged their possessions to the conservatory to meet with

Safonov, who said that they could spend the night in the conservatory library sleeping on couches while he intervened with Grand Duke Konstantin. He was successful, and Lea's permit to stay in Moscow was approved. Meanwhile, some other distant relatives had been located. Their home was modest, but they had no children and were happy to have Lea live with them. Unfortunately, they lived quite far from the conservatory; Lea once again had to rise at six, practice for an hour, take a streetcar as far as Tverskoy Boulevard, and walk for half an hour with her books and her violin.

In school, she skipped two grades in three months and, at the end of the year when she played at the student recital, she received from Safonov a silver coin—a traditional award for pupils who gave the best performances. Years later, she wrote, "I received enough silver coins to make two bracelets."

Superstars in a New Field

While Lea was fortunate to enter Moscow Conservatory in a golden age of Russian music, Onissim Goldovsky embarked on a legal and political career at a time when both professions were abuzz with excitement and fraught with peril.

Alexander II's reforms of the 1870s couldn't be entirely reversed and they shaped Onissim's life in two important ways. First, Alexander II had permitted a cascade of new ideas to emerge in Russia and be imported from Europe. His reign was, in its own way, a golden age of literature and political thought—the era of Fyodor Dostoyevsky, Lev Tolstoy, Alexander Herzen, and Mikhail Bakunin. Among well-educated Muscovites like Onissim's relatives, words like *constitutionalism*, *democracy*, *socialism*, and even *anarchy* were on people's lips.

Alexander III tried to crack down on dissent and he certainly managed to crack down on dissenters. But the thirst for new ideas proved unquenchable. In the 1880s and 1890s, books by Russian and European political philosophers were passed from hand to hand at universities and professional gatherings. Articles by Russians—including some of Onissim's own writings—were published in Europe and then smuggled back into Russia or reprinted in underground journals. Political meetings and organizations were banned, but people like Onissim gathered in private homes to discuss the latest books and ideas. Many defied the risks and joined secret political clubs. The goal of all of this activity: to plan a better future for Russia.

Alexander II's legal reforms proved equally difficult to reverse. The reforms had been announced just months before Onissim's birth in 1865 and they transformed the law from one of the lowest status occupations in Russia—barely a rung above serfdom—to a true profession. Before these changes, at the national level, the Tsar and his circle controlled the imperial courts, while justice in the provinces was meted out by aristocratic estate owners. The job of "lawyering" was the remit of government clerks who did little more than copy and recopy the numerous proclamations, clarifications, and decisions that were issued by various government bureaucracies, supposedly in fulfilment of the Tsar's will. But under the reforms, courts were given independence from the executive branch. Judges were appointed for life. Trials were opened to the public. Juries were introduced for both civil and criminal cases. Finally, judicial discretion was expanded as a way to ensure that everyone was treated equally under the law.

Moscow University was one of the first to promote legal education reform and, subsequently, the university trained a new generation of professional lawyers. Its faculty was the first in Russia to introduce mock trials as a central element in the curriculum. Persuasive argument, elegant presentation, and theoretical sophistication were encouraged. Even after Alexander III's harsh restructuring of universities in an attempt to control students, professors of permitted subjects such as Roman law, the history of law, and European law slipped in radical new ideas about equality under the law, the separation of powers, and natural rights.

Under this new system, much less paperwork was involved in being a lawyer. At the same time, oral argument became more important. Thanks to the presence of a jury and, often, a fascinated and well-informed audience, public opinion played a major role in dispensing justice. From one of his mentors, Prince Alexander Ivanovich Urusov, Onissim learned that one could even ignore the facts of a case, relying instead on public sympathy for downtrodden defendants. It was this ability to convince and persuade that led to Onissim's astonishing effectiveness as a lawyer.

But the reliance on persuasion and oratory was a double-edged sword. In the 1870s, the state had lost several high-profile political trials. Despite overwhelming evidence of guilt, the juries and the public supported the defendants' causes. One of the key protagonists in these systemic developments was liberal jurist Anatoli Fedorovich Koni, a man who in time became part of Onissim's inner circle. Known for his impressive oratorical skills, he believed in the power of words to influence the course of justice: "Words are one of the greatest tools of man. Powerless in themselves, they become powerful and compelling if expressed skillfully, sincerely, and in a timely way. They can become a fascination to the speaker and at the same time dazzle others with their brilliance."[9] But in response to these populist results, Tsar Alexander III decided to reverse course and do away with juries entirely. Onissim experienced this transition directly, which influenced his political activism. Like many Jews and liberal non-Jews, he believed that the law had to be just and consistently applied.

In 1888, when Onissim went to work for the first time, he was accepted into the practice of Rudolf Rudolfovich Mintslov. At the time, the Russian legal profession worked according to an apprenticeship system. A law school graduate had to practice as an assistant to a senior lawyer for at least five years. The Russian word for *patron* was used to describe the senior lawyer, and my grandfather's first patron, Mintslov, was a liberal activist, a celebrated defense attorney, and someone with a lucrative private practice in both Moscow and St. Petersburg. His law practice benefited from the significant railway expansion in Russia; and while Onissim worked with him, Mintslov served as inhouse counsel for the Ryazan-Ural Railway. He was also a prolific writer on philosophy and the law, publishing in both the popular media and specialist legal journals.

But for Onissim, Mintslov's wide-ranging knowledge, interests, and talents were his most impressive qualities. In a book about his legal education, Onissim described his one-year stint with Mintslov as only tangentially focused on the law. "I went to see Mintslov two or three times a week, but mainly—as they say—'for form's sake' since often there were no cases to discuss . . . During the entire time that I was with Mintslov, I worked on only two or three cases, which we took more for the sake of earning some money than for the sake of the cases themselves. But when I was working on a case, Mintslov gave me all the documents to study and he often discussed the cases with me.

"In the absence of any legal problems to resolve, we talked about all sorts of topics. Sometimes we sat at the piano and played four hands. In order to educate me in the art of rhetoric, he recommended that I read Quintilianus [an ancient Roman scholar of rhetoric] in Latin."[10] (Onissim confesses that he never got through Quintilianus, but Mintslov apparently did not insist.)

Mostly Mintslov wanted him to read—sometimes law, but more often other things—to give him a deeper understanding of the philosophical context that infused the law with meaning. Onissim wrote, "He gave me a collection of his articles with the following inscription in his own hand:

> You have come to me as an apprentice, Onissim Borisovich, and I am obliged to teach you our shared profession. What does 'teach' mean in the full sense of the word? It means to bring the student to a full appreciation of the Truth, to encourage him to adore the Truth* and to gradually integrate it into his daily life. Feuerbach said that Truth 'is a woman who cannot be sold, who does not throw herself into the arms of the first person she meets, but rather is a proud beauty who can be understood only in glimpses and only by one who dedicates his whole life to her.'"

Then on August 1, 1889, Mintslov did something that to Onissim was of great value—he gave the young man the catalog to his entire library. In it, Mintslov inscribed the words: "I am giving you the key to what the Egyptians poetically called 'tonic for the soul.'"

After his year with Mintslov, my grandfather's second mentor was the esteemed Prince Alexander Ivanovich Urusov, a famous defense lawyer who took it upon himself to train Onissim rigorously in the application of the law itself. In his approach to the law, Urusov was very different from Mintslov.

---

* There are two words for *truth* in Russian. The word *pravda* means a demonstrably true fact—something that is not false. "It rained today" is an example of *pravda*. The word used here is *istina*, a rather old-fashioned word that means *truth* in a deeper, metaphysical sense. "God exists" or "life has meaning" are examples of *istina*.

According to Onissim, "Urusov and Mintslov shared a love of books and an unshakeable Euro-Philism [i.e., Western sympathy], which ran deep in their blood. But, generally speaking, these two were very different types. Mintslov, by the inclinations of his mind and style of thought, was a scholar, while Prince Urusov was a person who loved life and was a courtroom lawyer by calling."

Onissim came to work for Urusov just as the older man was returning to Moscow after a political exile. Urusov had been arrested, exiled to Estonia, and forbidden to practice law. But after working in local administration and impressing his bosses, he was allowed to return to the law in 1876 as an associate prosecutor in Warsaw. In 1878 he moved to the same position in St. Petersburg. Believing his true calling to be as a defense attorney and wanting to work in Moscow, he returned there just a few days before Onissim came to work for him. Thereafter, his career was meteoric. One assistant recorded Urusov achieving sixty-nine acquittals in a row, many of them for unpopular clients, including peasants. According to Onissim, Urusov "understood a person who was broken, worn out, and defeated—even if the person was from the lowest rung of the social ladder . . . Maybe this came from a deep contempt for conventional morality, but more likely it was a reflection of his great love of life. For him, the individual human being was more valuable than anything eternal." This was something Onissim internalized and believed throughout his life.

Urusov, Christian by birth, abhorred anti-Semitism and endangered himself several times by standing up to authorities over what he considered unfair regulations. According to Onissim, "Racial hatred was so alien to his honorable nature that anti-Semitism evoked in him feelings of both disgust and pity—as with people who are possessed by an obscene lunacy. He felt badly for anti-Semites in the way that you feel badly for someone who suffers from a repulsive illness."

A final trait of Urusov's that Onissim found impressive was the fact that "malice, enmity, and vindictiveness were completely foreign to Urusov's nature and he often admired and complimented the work of skilled opponents, just as a great artist can enjoy paintings by another." Again, this was a trait Onissim attempted to emulate. In his biographical sketch of Urusov, my grandfather recalled a case in Pavlovsk, which his mentor lost after many years of work. As it happened, the opposing lawyer was on the same train going back to Moscow. Urusov invited him to come for dinner at a later date so that they might get better acquainted. "What could I say against him?" Urusov told Onissim. "He found the weak spot in my argument right away. I was stunned. Really he is a genius."

Urusov not only provided Onissim with exemplary legal training but he also treated him as a protégé, letting Onissim try cases himself and develop an independent legal mind. Once the training was completed and just before Urusov died in 1900, he secured an appointment for Onissim to join the law faculty of St. Petersburg University. While there, Onissim's popular but controversial lectures touched not only on the Russian legal system but drew from the legal, scientific, and literary worlds of Western European thought. It was a world both he and Lea would come to know intimately.

Two Fateful Meetings

In later years, my uncle Boris, a distinguished musician himself, claimed that his mother Lea's greatest curse was having been a child prodigy. Prodigies impress because they are so precocious, but only a very few turn out to be the geniuses their parents and teachers believe them to be. Like children learning to read or do multiplication at an early age, most are simply showing aptitude earlier than their peers. If their ability is misdiagnosed, it can pose great problems not only for the ways in which they are educated, but for them as adults. This was my grandmother's fate. "Your grandmother was highly talented, but she wasn't a genius," my uncle told me long after her death. "As a result, her training at the Moscow Conservatory—or lack of it—was a sham and almost destroyed her career."

Lea's own memories weren't much different. By the time she got to the Moscow Conservatory, many of her teachers thought she was among the most amazing talents they had ever come across. Safonov, the director, arranged for a loan of one of the conservatory's finest violins, a 16th-century Italian instrument made in Cremona by a member of the Amati family. Lea was excused from everything except her violin study, including basic subjects in music considered essential to an artist's development. Once again, Lea went through a transformation—this time from an eager and anxious conservatory student to a spoiled and arrogant one.

Lea was favored with the best solo and orchestral performance opportunities. She was immediately assigned the concertmaster (principal violin) position of the conservatory orchestra even though other students were much more experienced and possibly just as gifted. As a result, Lea never learned to be an orchestral section player. When the Moscow Conservatory orchestra traveled to St. Petersburg in 1902 for a major event, Lea was favored once again. The occasion was the unveiling of a statue of Anton Rubinstein, the late founder of the St. Petersburg Conservatory, and she and other students from Moscow were joined in concert by the St. Petersburg Conservatory Orchestra. My grandmother took the concertmaster chair even though most considered the players in the other orchestra superior. Indeed, Efrem Zimbalist, the St. Petersburg Conservatory concertmaster at the time (who years later became Lea's boss at the Curtis Institute of Music in the United States and someone whom I would come to regard as a god of violin playing), was relegated to the fourth stand, according to Lea's recollections.*

Later, in my grandmother's memoir, she was uncompromisingly honest about how damaging all this was. "I now realize how wrong everything was concerning me. My professors overrated my talent . . . The director did the same thing. If a well-known artist came to Moscow, I was the one chosen to play for him . . . When the Moscow orchestra went on tour, I was the soloist with them. Is there any wonder that all this attention from my professor and the director turned my head? I considered myself a very important person, and would not listen to the critical remarks of my pupil colleagues. The more they disliked, the more I pleased myself and I was sure I was right. I blush now when I remember how atrociously I behaved . . . The more I think about it, the more I have to admit that if I had been treated as a normal child, and if I had been told again and again that there was nothing to be so important about, if they had told me that the greater an artist is, the more modest he is, if they had told me to compare myself to someone who knew more, they would not have made the monster they did."

---

* It always amused me that Zimbalist remembered the event differently, telling his biographer that he and Lea had shared the concertmaster chair (see Malan, 210–11).

This was a lesson drilled into my brother and me by our grandmother as we embarked on our own adventures in music years later. But there was a caveat. One should not swagger and boast and behave like a superstar when one was quite ordinary. That we were not permitted to do. But it was equally wrong to hide under a rock (as Lea succinctly put it) and be inappropriately modest and shy. The music world was and is incredibly competitive, and claiming one's place in it is necessary to advance. Being confident and outgoing was not the same as being a blowhard and a braggart and it did not take us long to understand the difference.

Of course, growing up in mid-20th-century America, our challenges were very different from Lea's. We did not have to overcome virulent anti-Semitism. Just as important, we were boys. Lea was one of the only women at the conservatory. Her teachers were all men, as were most of the other students. As an attractive female, there was always the stigma of her sex and, later, the innuendo that Lea was getting special treatment in exchange for sexual favors. All of this must have heightened her sense of "otherness" and isolation. Claiming and building on her talent would be her only viable way forward.

This strategy paid dividends for her in three important ways. First, people gradually stopped belittling her talent because she was female. Quite simply, she was considered the best student in her class, period. The second benefit was that composers began to take an interest in her and to write music for her. One of these was Reinhold Glière, who was just beginning a long and successful career in 1902 when he heard Lea play for the first time. As the composer recalled afterwards, her playing so mesmerized him that he started to dream about her and in one of the dreams the melody for his *Romance* (op. 3) came to him. He immediately wrote it down and asked Lea if he could dedicate it to her and have her play its premiere in 1903. The work was subsequently issued by the Imperial music publisher Mitrofan Petrovich Belyayev and became a standard not only in her repertoire but in that of almost every Russian and Soviet violinist for the next hundred years.[*]

---

[*] This recollection is taken from "The Musical Luboshutz Family" in *Novoe Russkoe Slovo*, August 6, 1987. Sadly, once Lea left the Soviet Union and became an enemy of the state, her name was removed from subsequent editions of the work, so the dedication was largely unknown during most of the 20th century.

Lea's third advantage of unabashedly claiming her talent was that when the world-famous Belgian violinist Eugène Ysaÿe came to Moscow to perform, it was Lea who was chosen to play for him when he visited the conservatory. Like many touring virtuosos, he also was searching out promising students. Ysaÿe was sufficiently impressed when he heard Lea to invite her to his Belgian summer retreat for study after she graduated. Lea was excited about the possibility. She had long been determined to study the César Franck sonata with Ysaÿe. She knew that her tradition-bound professors at the conservatory would not consider adding this piece to her repertoire. But Lea loved what she had heard and decided to try to learn the piece in the event she ever did travel to Belgium.

As Lea's special treatment grew, her fellow students were filled with envy, and one of the students suggested the incredibly daring scheme of disrupting her graduation recital. Everyone understood the importance of this concert, which was to take place on May 13, 1903. At these events, a decision would be made as to whether any student deserved to be awarded a coveted Gold Medal, a rare honor memorialized by the awardee's name being engraved in gold leaf on a prominently displayed marble plaque outside the concert hall. In my grandmother's year, five violin students competed and such was the anticipation of Lea's performance (and Director Safonov's optimism about her success) that the director arranged for Gitel to come from Odessa to hear the program. Saul, the parent most responsible for Lea's musical success, was left in Odessa to tend to the other children.

My grandmother at this point was eighteen years old. Like the other, older candidates, she was to play a full program carefully chosen by her teachers, including an unaccompanied work (the Bach partita containing the devilishly difficult Chaconne movement), a concerto (the brilliant D Major concerto of Niccolò Paganini), and various shorter show pieces. It was her final concert on her beloved Amati violin, which had to be returned to the school, and she wanted the violin to remember her fondly.

This special form of attachment between player and instrument is not uncommon. People say that every player, especially a great one, leaves his or her personality on a string instrument, and that the very cell structure of the wood changes as a result. True or not, my grandmother spent her life playing on some of the greatest instruments ever made, and she regarded them as members of her family, with distinct personalities, character traits, and moods. They had to be treated well if the feeling was to be reciprocated and beauty created.

Before this important performance, a few students bribed the pianist for Lea's graduation recital, convincing him to start the opening of the Paganini concerto a half step higher than it was written, so that when Lea entered with her solo part in the correct key, it would sound as though she had made a mistake, possibly throwing off her concentration for the rest of her performance. Fortunately, like her sister, Lea had perfect pitch and knew the key was wrong as soon as the pianist played the first notes. She turned and said in a loud voice that everyone in the crowded hall could hear, "Now please play it in D major, as it is written." This only added to her triumph. When she was finished, the audience broke into a sustained ovation, much to the irritation of Safonov, since at that time applause was not permitted at these events.

After a long day of recitals, the professors announced the decision. Yes, a Gold Medal would be given to a violinist this year, and it would go to Lea Luboshutz. My grandmother's triumph was complete. Her name would be enshrined in gold on the marble plaque. Lea also received a magnificent certificate, embossed with gold leaf, that she would somehow manage to bring out of Russia all the way to America, where I now preserve it among other family treasures.

The recital was not the only requirement for graduation. My grandmother was expected to pass tests in fourteen other subjects, classes she'd largely skipped, and she was at a loss for how to prepare. Other violin students were studying for examinations in solfège (pitch and sight singing), musical dictation, music history, music theory (including harmony and counterpoint), piano playing, and many other subjects. But the director himself came to Lea's rescue. Based on her performance, Safonov said, she was to be excused from further testing. It was far more important for her to practice her violin, since she was to make an important visit to the home of Lazar Polyakov. Upon graduation in May 1903, Lea received "very good" or "excellent" grades in all the subjects in which she had not participated, many of which she probably would have failed.

The name Polyakov had been in Lea's consciousness from her first day in Moscow. Her uncle worked at Lazar Polyakov's bank. And if her uncle seemed wealthy, the Polyakovs were rich beyond compare. Safonov told Lea to wear her best concert dress and come to his apartment so that they could travel together. While technically the Amati violin was no longer hers to play, she was given special dispensation by the conservatory to bring it, so that she could play for the Polyakovs on a great instrument.

The Polyakov house dwarfed anything my grandmother had seen before, and its contents were dazzling. She wryly remembered how impressed she had been by her uncle and aunt's house. Years later, Lea would say with a smile that she imagined *them* as the Polyakov's poor relatives, which gave her much pleasure. Safonov entered the drawing room first and was greeted with great dignity. He in turn presented Lea.

While the two men spoke, Madame Polyakov quizzed Lea, asking all sorts of questions about her background. Courageously, Lea said she believed they were related and mentioned her Moscow uncle. The older woman was delighted, as she was with all of Lea's answers—except one. It seemed that Madame Polyakov was extremely religious and even had a synagogue in her home. Her food was strictly Jewish; even when the Grand Duke called she did not depart from the menu. Lea admitted that though her grandfather was a rabbi in Odessa, she had been too busy while at the conservatory to go to synagogue except for the New Year's service and the High Holy Day Yom Kippur services. This displeased her inquisitor, though she said she understood how dangerous it was for a young Jewess to walk around Moscow alone. She needed a protector.

At this somewhat awkward point, Lazar Polyakov interrupted to say it was time for music. The large gilt music room into which they moved was particularly grand, with Turkish carpets, European paintings, and a fine piano. Safonov sat down at the piano and asked Lea to give him the piano score to the Paganini concerto. She had never played with the director before and was amazed at his skill. From time to time, Madame Polyakov's eyes closed and she dropped off—she had a sleep disorder—only to awaken when Lea finished a movement, at which point she exclaimed how much she had enjoyed the performance.

After the concert, the men retired to another room. Madame Polyakov returned to the idea of becoming Lea's protector and told Lea that she must come back often. My grandmother told us years later that she fell in love with the old lady. When the men returned, according to Lea's memoir, Safonov said, "You must thank his Excellency. You are now the owner of this wonderful Amati violin. And you can also thank him for the scholarship he provided that made your study at the conservatory possible." Champagne and a cold supper were served. In a daze over the events of the evening, all Lea could remember were the six manservants in attendance.

Growing up, I always loved this story, imagining what it must have been like to be in the Polyakovs' magnificent home. Then in 2014, as if by magic, I found myself there. I was visiting cousins in Moscow and mentioned that I was interested in visiting the old local synagogue, something I enjoy doing when I visit cities with long Jewish histories. As it turned out, there was now a fine kosher restaurant on the roof and, since it was a beautiful summer day, we decided to have lunch there. After passing through tight security—sadly essential for synagogues around the world in an era of terrorism directed at Jews—we were shown into a small, tastefully rebuilt sanctuary that had been constructed using the walls of an earlier synagogue that the Soviets had closed and then reworked for other purposes in 1937. In 1991, with the disintegration of the Soviet Union, the building was transferred to the Chabad Lubavich community, and by 2014 it was serving a resurgent post-Soviet Jewish community with classrooms, a bookstore, a mikvah (ritual bath), lecture hall, and kosher restaurant. If one looked carefully, it was possible to discern the old facade hidden under the glass wall, as well as the hole in the floor in front of the ark, which led to a tunnel used by Jews to escape pogroms.

So far, my interest lay in the aspects of local Jewish history that the building represented. Then, while waiting for lunch to be served, my Russian cousin Sveta, who I was visiting in Moscow, revealed the most extraordinary fact. This building had been part of the Moscow estate of Lazar Polyakov. This was where he had lived, in the mansion with the private synagogue. Indeed, this was the very place where Lea had gone to play. The gilt mirrors and beautiful furniture might be gone, but for me we were on doubly hallowed ground—religiously significant and part of our family's history.

After the evening with the Polyakovs, Lea had to attend one more party before she could return to Odessa and see her father. And this one was in a domicile even more amazing than that of the Polyakovs. The so-called Trubetskoy Palace was considered the grandest residence in all of Moscow and it was now occupied by the textile merchant Sergei Shchukin.[11] Today Shchukin's name is most closely associated with his groundbreaking collection of Impressionist and post-Impressionist art, which he assembled at a time when few Russians knew or appreciated it. Though laughed at by many, Shchukin's collection now constitutes some of the most important period holdings in both the Hermitage and Pushkin museums in St. Petersburg and Moscow respectively. His friendship with artists such as Henri Matisse and Pablo Picasso resulted in important works making their way to Moscow. But Shchukin was also a great patron of music and dance and often hosted performance events at the palace. Indeed, he commissioned two magnificent large paintings, *Music* and *Dance*, from Henri Matisse, who later came to Moscow to help decorate the palace.

Lea, unschooled in any arts except music, had not the slightest appreciation of her host's importance as an art collector or the priceless treasures on the walls. Years later, she described the palace to her daughter, my mother, as "full of those crazy paintings" and in her own memoir seems completely focused on the purpose of the evening, which was to introduce her to wealthy patrons who might be helpful to her career. But Shchukin's name, wealth, and prominence assured her of an audience of other successful businessmen, well-connected professional people, journalists, and prominent musicians. Altogether, fifty people were expected. Lea, who had a premonition that this would be an important evening, dressed carefully.

When most of the guests had assembled, Lea began to play. But during the first number, more guests arrived, and she was distracted by one of the newcomers, a distinguished man, not particularly tall, who looked to be about forty. He seemed to attract everyone's attention. According to her memoir, the shape of his head and the gentle expression in his eyes reminded Lea of a famous painting of Jesus. She was struck by how people seemed to congregate around him. She played another piece and after she was finished, the man came to the piano and asked if she would permit him to play the accompaniment for whatever came next. Lea was irritated—she did not want to perform with an amateur—but felt she could not refuse. She chose an easy, slow movement, which the man played flawlessly. He then looked at her music and noticed sonatas by Beethoven.

"Do you play the Kreutzer sonata?" he asked. Ever since Lev Tolstoy had written his novella *The Kreutzer Sonata* in 1889—a tale of love, jealousy, and murder in which Beethoven's Kreutzer sonata plays a major role—this had become a popular piece in Russia. Lea was torn. She loved the piece but it was difficult—and especially difficult for the piano. "Yes, I do," she answered hesitantly. "Good, let's play it," the stranger said, "with the repeats."

There are many ways to determine whether people are good musicians. The easiest place to start is whether a person plays all the notes accurately and in time. The stranger, who was of course my grandfather Onissim, was apparently remarkably accurate, at least as good as some of the professionals Lea had played with during her years at the conservatory. After that test, the next is whether a person can play musically, with beautiful tone and phrasing. The lyrical beauty of Onissim's playing was entrancing.

But the ultimate test of a good musician, especially in a piece of chamber music (which, after all, is a sort of musical conversation), is to see how well one player can mesh with another. My grandmother and grandfather were playing the Kreutzer for the first time, so there was no way for each to anticipate the musical approach of the other. But once they began, Lea realized why the stranger had suggested they play all the repeats. The first time through, he could get a sense of Lea's musical ideas; on the repeat, he adjusted his playing to match. From that moment, Lea was in love.

After the Kreutzer, the two took a break. Lea learned my grandfather's name and that he was a prominent lawyer. The Kreutzer had been an exhilarating experience and though she talked to many people that night, she could remember almost nothing of who was there or what they said. The guests began to depart and Lea was putting away her violin when Onissim said to her, "I notice you have a sonata by César Franck here. Would you like to read it with me?"

Once again, my grandmother faced a dilemma. Playing the Kreutzer sonata had been a risk, but it was plausible that an accomplished amateur pianist had played it before. But the Franck? It was not commonly played in Russia and the music was not readily available, so it was even less likely that a musician, especially one who did not play professionally, would know it. To make matters worse, it was at least as difficult for the piano as the Kreutzer. Nevertheless, she felt she could not refuse.

And then came one of the most remarkable moments in Lea's life. Onissim played the piano part like a master. How could this be? They played the dream-like first movement, and then the passionate second movement, which derails many accomplished pianists. The fantasy followed and, in a kind of ecstasy, the magnificent finale. It was an extraordinary performance, and an unbelievable one. No amateur pianist—indeed, few professional pianists—could have sight-read the Franck as well as Onissim Goldovsky did that night.

In fact, of course, my grandfather hadn't been sight-reading. He too had been entranced by the sonata when he first heard it played by Ysaÿe in Moscow and had searched out the music when he was in Paris. He had been practicing diligently for months and was excited finally to get to play it with an accomplished violinist. But that was something Lea wouldn't know for years.

Rashel

On a warm summer night in 1903, a few weeks after meeting my grandmother for the first time, my grandfather sat at a piano at Katino, a summer estate on the outskirts of Moscow. The buildings and lavish grounds belonged to his wife, who had invited many of their friends to stay the night. Her name was Rashel Khin. She was famous, having written several successful novellas, stories, and plays, and translated the works of George Sand and Émile Zola into Russian. Her wide literary circle included the celebrated Russian author Ivan Turgenev, as well as many French writers including Zola, Gustave Flaubert, and Guy de Maupassant.

Never in all the discussions of our family's history was Khin's name mentioned, though she was clearly a very important part of my grandfather's story . . . and Lea's. Had Rashel's biography not been published in the year 2000,[12] I might never have heard of her. But when Onissim's name appeared in that book, my siblings and I began to ask questions. And now, many years later, I know enough to lay out her story in full.

The day I am describing was typical of many that summer. There were walks in the morning, political discussions in the afternoon, and a magnificent dinner prepared by Nadine Auer, wife of the violinist Leopold Auer, the very man who had invited Lea to study with him in St. Petersburg when she was eleven. After-dinner entertainment was provided not only by Onissim, an exceptionally gifted pianist, but by the jurist Anatoli Koni, who read poetry or told stories. Koni had been introduced into their circle by Onissim's old mentor Urusov, though Urusov himself had died a few years earlier. Given Koni's connections to the theater world and Rashel's growing involvement in the Moscow theater scene, it was not uncommon for one or more of their actor friends to entertain.

As the guests listened to my grandfather playing Rashel's favorite Chopin sonata, most must have regarded him as a contented man. Like his wife, he was well-known. He was a member of the Moscow bar, respected and feared for his brilliance but also appreciated for his wit. He was well-off financially, thanks in part to his wife's family money. He had traveled outside of Russia and spoke a dozen languages. His writing reflected his broad education, a fascination with the European Enlightenment, and a deep knowledge of the latest scientific and political thinking in the West. He was actively involved in political efforts intended to transform Russia into a liberal constitutional democracy along European lines, and he was welcomed as one of the astute leaders of the movement.

Onissim and Rashel had been married on February 18, 1900. Three years later, they seemed very much in love. She had been unhappily married before and had had a child. Her divorce was acrimonious and the remarriage process legally complicated. But now all of that was behind them. On their third anniversary, Rashel wrote in her diary, "Three years have passed. The price for our freedom was our suffering that is now in the past. Neither Stas [Rashel's nickname for Onissim] nor I feel the least remorse."

But while the marriage might have appeared blissful on the surface, Onissim and Rashel did have their domestic struggles. They did not see eye to eye about family. Now over forty, Khin either could not or would not bear Onissim's children. Further, she had only a casual layperson's interest in music, which for Onissim was a passion. He had been jolted into this realization a few weeks earlier when he had played the César Franck sonata with Lea, and he thought of her now. He had been mesmerized not only by her playing but also by the young woman herself. He must have smiled as he thought about his friend Rozanov, who would have had no problem dealing with two enticing women and justifying philosophically the idea of pursuing both. But hanging around Rozanov had already gotten Onissim into trouble over a sexual escapade. Perhaps this was not a fruitful line of thought . . .

Onissim's road to his current life had been remarkably smooth. Equipped with excellent legal training and a brilliant mind, he taught for a time at St. Petersburg University and also followed in his mentor Urusov's footsteps, defending political dissidents and other unfortunates on the one hand, while building a successful commercial law practice on the other. Law had given Onissim, like many Jews, an entrée to life not only in St. Petersburg but also in Moscow. It had also given him economic security, though thanks to his wife's family fortune, money was not an issue. Indeed, he took on many Jewish clients, both rich and poor, and refused to charge them. To help him with his law practice, he had a slew of assistants. This gave him time to pursue politics—never far from his mind—and his piano playing, which had been a significant part of his life ever since he started taking lessons as a child.

Most of these facts come directly from Rashel Khin's diary, which provides great insight into her life, her relationship with Onissim, and her rivalry with Lea. Ultimately, it also offered a remarkable window into those aspects of Lea and my family that had never been revealed to me. To understand Lea, I soon realized, I would have to get to know Rashel, a woman with few similarities to my grandmother. Though both women were Jewish, they came from wholly different backgrounds. Where Lea was poor, Rashel was rich. Lea was from the provinces, Rashel was born and had lived in Moscow, except when she visited her Paris literary circle. While Lea had no education to speak of, Rashel was among the leading female intellectuals of her day. Lea was twenty years younger than my grandfather (young enough to be his daughter) while Rashel was two years older and provided some of the maternal love toward Onissim that he had lost as a child.

But there was more. Lea was just beginning to embrace her womanhood and wanted to have children, whereas Rashel was naturally more prudish, based on her own admission in her diary, and was through with childbearing. And where Lea was cheerful and optimistic and just entering the most successful period of her life, Rashel was burdened, often unhappy, and feeling as though her most successful years were behind her.

Ever since boyhood, when Onissim had stepped in and taken care of his brothers upon his mother's banishment from the family, he had learned to take care of those in need. Here was a woman, Rashel, who needed him—someone with a fine mind equal to his, someone to whom he could give a modicum of happiness. The fact that Rashel would also be able to advance his career by calling on her extensive contacts and drawing on her wealth was an extra inducement. Onissim had been cautious about relationships with women ever since the Polina episode that had landed him in jail. But by the time he first met Rashel, he was hungry for the company of a woman who offered an opportunity for furthering a rich and productive life. There was a problem, however. She was married.

Rashel met Onissim in 1897 at a public event that he was attending as Prince Urusov's legal assistant. At the time, he was thirty-two and unmarried. He must have been very impressed by Rashel, who was far more worldly and connected than he. She had grown up comfortably in a Jewish family in Moscow; her father, a Merchant of the First Guild, was quite wealthy. But she was also desperately unhappy and had been for some time. She began recording her feelings in her diary in 1891. That diary begins with a *cri de coeur*—a passionate outcry of bitter words that reveals her pain:

> The world doesn't lack for women who don't love their husbands,
> who are worn out by poverty, by wretched, unbalanced, impover-
> ished parents, a coarse, savage brother and three pathetic sisters.
> The assortment in our case is just so conspicuously extreme . . .
> We Khins are a family of losers.

It is difficult to make out from these words that, by the time they were written, Rashel Khin was already a recognized and established writer. She had left Russia in 1880 to study at the Sorbonne in Paris, where she was befriended by two Russian émigrés, the female writer and social activist Evgenia Ivanovna Konradi and the far more celebrated author, Ivan Turgenev, who briefly became her mentor (he died in 1883). Through both, she was introduced to a wide cultural circle, including the leading French writers of the day, some of whose works she eventually translated into Russian. It was in the early 1880s, not yet twenty years old, that Rashel met and married Solomon Feldshtein, whom she very soon grew to detest. To her, the relationship was an imprisonment, and she desired nothing more than to be free. Given her unhappiness, in November 1897 Onissim Goldovsky was like a breath of fresh air. Their meeting involved Urusov, who was one of Rashel's longtime friends.

According to her recollection of the event, some of Moscow's wealthiest noblewomen had taken on a project to establish a new woman's medical college in the city, similar to one that already existed in St. Petersburg. A first step had been to secure the backing of the few female physicians who already practiced in the city. There was huge discrimination toward such women; they were rarely allowed to carry out research on their own or hold important positions. Their support was crucial. Unfortunately, the wealthy matrons had not reckoned with the feelings of another constituency—the wives of Moscow's male doctors, who had not been invited to the group's initial meetings. Deeply insulted, the wives determined to oppose the establishment of a women's medical college in Moscow.

How to proceed? The founders' group decided that the only solution was to find a patron, someone so famous that his or her support of their fledgling organization would carry the day. The ladies approached Rashel Khin, who initially mistook their request as being for *her* patronage—she had, after all, considered a career in medicine and was already well-known, at least in literary circles. She demurred, saying that she was neither rich enough nor famous enough to carry the day. No, explained the ladies, she misunderstood. It was not her support they sought, but that of her good friend Prince Urusov. Rashel agreed to write a letter to the prince; Urusov did become involved and agreed to speak not only to the organizers but to a group of local male physicians and their wives. Rashel described the meeting in her diary:

> Urusov's entrance had an incredible effect. Elegant, handsome, favorably disposed toward everyone, he at once charmed and conquered with his regal simplicity all of the doctors' wives who fell in love with him that morning. Everyone listened with rapt attention, enjoying his every word, delighting in his every gesture. And he was taking obvious pleasure in it as well. Everything was so "serious-serious" but at a certain moments he caught my eye and gave me a wink.

Apparently, Urusov found the whole experience so humorous that "he came to us the next day and acted out the entire ladies' meeting of 'the Pickwick Club of Moscow.'"

The diary excerpt, written tongue-in-cheek, has one other significant entry, written partly in French (like many Russians in her social class, Rashel's writing and speaking tended to flow naturally from one language to the other). She wrote: "The Prince asked permission to bring with him his assistant OB [Goldovsky], 'un charmant garçon qui me secondera' [a charming young man who will act as my assistant]. When I was ready to go home, he [Goldovsky] kindly gave me a lift. I said to him: 'Vous êtes vous assez payé nos têtes?' [You must think we are all out of our minds?] He kindly objected: 'Pas la votre en tous cas, mais j'avoue je me suis amusé.' [In your case not, but I admit, I was amused.]"

The holidays were fast approaching and people were busy. When Onissim and Rashel met again is unclear from this official version of her diary, which had been prepared for publication. On December 31, 1897, Rashel wrote, "I am alone. In an hour and a half a new year begins . . ."—exactly the words that she had written on the same day one year before. Onissim did not seem to be in the picture as yet. But my hunch is that soon after the new year, he started seeing her regularly. There is an uncharacteristic two-month hiatus in her diary before March 30, 1898. But skipping ahead, her next New Year's Eve celebration was quite different from the previous two. She was in the company of two of her closest friends, the jurist Anatoli Koni and the literary critic Nikolai Storozhenko, who had been one of Onissim Goldovsky's professors at Moscow University. And Onissim was there too, playing piano. Without a doubt, Onissim was now the man of her dreams. But she was still unhappy as her husband had made it clear that he would not give her a divorce.

Seemingly, most everything else in Rashel's life had improved following the dispiriting start to her diary. Her financial situation had changed for the better, owing to an inheritance from her father. Her writing was going well and she was widely recognized as a literary talent of the first order. Her estate, Katino, purchased in 1897, gave her much pleasure and she was beginning to develop a reputation as the hostess of a "salon," where the leading figures of the day exchanged literary and political ideas and gossip. And she had the love of a man, Onissim Goldovsky, who was as brilliant as she—talented, handsome, and popular. His politics aligned exactly with hers. Though he was younger,* that did not seem to bother either of them. Rashel wanted a life with him and, in a rather unconventional way, that is what she got. Deciding that she would never change her husband's mind about a divorce, she took a dramatic step—the Jewess, Rashel Khin, converted to Catholicism, thus invalidating her Jewish marriage. Her subsequent marriage to Onissim took place soon after. Immediately following the wedding, the two went to Katino and stayed for a few weeks. Before returning to society and facing a wider circle of friends, acquaintances, and professional associates, they decided to go abroad to Berlin.

Religion

❧

Though my grandmother was not outwardly religious, she never renounced her Jewish heritage, even when others around her were doing so. Indeed, at one point early in her career when it was suggested that she change her name to make it sound less Jewish, she refused. In contrast, I was initially surprised to learn of Rashel Khin's conversion to Catholicism, but this was not nearly as shocking as discovering that my grandfather Onissim had also converted. Rashel's reasons for leaving the Jewish faith were clear—she believed (probably with good reason) that she would never extract herself from her first marriage unless she did so. She also wanted to marry Onissim. While her conversion invalidated her Jewish marriage to Feldshtein, it also made it impossible for

---

* In Carole B. Balin's biography of Rashel, page 89, Rashel's birthdate is given as March 9, 1861, making her four years older than Onissim Goldovsky. The March 9 date is correct, but the year is not. Rashel's diary makes it clear that she was born in 1863. In January 1892 she writes: "I am twenty-eight years old but I am so tired, so afraid of every day as if I were seventy." The 1863 birth year is also confirmed by the Archive of Literature and Art (RGALI) in Moscow. However, to confuse things, Irina Chaikovskaya's article in *Chaika* (see bibliography) cites a book by Mark Averbuch, *Vokrug Yevreev* (Вокруг Евреев), saying Rashel was born either in 1861 or 1863. Rashel's diary would appear to be the most reliable source.

her to marry another Jew. Thus Onissim too needed to convert. According to Khin's biographer, Carole B. Balin, "Theirs was an intermarriage of the most bizarre sort, and, though it appears that the couple remained converts, they became increasingly interested in the well-being of those from whom they had ostensibly severed ties."[13]

I was not the only one surprised by their conversions. At the time, family and friends were stunned, furious, and openly critical. As Rashel observed in her diary on February 24, 1900, just six days after she and Onissim were secretly married:

> Klara [Rashel's sister] is indignant at my 'desertion.' She is cruel, she is rude, she is unwilling to understand. Thanks to Marochka [Mark Mironovich, Rashel's brother], he is clever and is able to see things in a kinder light than the others in such extraordinary situations. He advised me to go to "Katino" immediately and give him the chance to calm the relatives . . . There is still a face-to-face meeting with Maman [Rashel's stepmother] ahead . . . and I can only imagine with what visceral pleasure all these Pharisees will condemn and denounce us.

As if this were not enough, there was Onissim's family—not only the Goldovskys but Onissim's stepmother, Anna, and her family the Garkavis. Onissim had never liked Anna, and her opinion meant little to him. But her extended family was another story. Onissim owed gratitude to them since his Garkavi uncle had assisted him professionally. They treated his conversion like a direct slap in the face, in view of the prominence of the Garkavis within the Moscow Jewish community. Still, as Rashel wrote, Onissim was untroubled:

> Stas [Onissim] doesn't pay attention. He says that after so many years of "servitude" he at last can breathe like a free man. He thanks me again and again, blesses me, and vows to serve me for life and tells me not to doubt him even for a moment. I do believe in his promise of "building our new free home on a solid foundation" . . . I do believe him.

By April 6, 1900, Rashel and Onissim were at Katino, enjoying some peace after the relentless criticism they had endured in Moscow. Among the most critical were Onissim's former Jewish clients—their ostracism stung, considering how generous he'd always been in representing them pro bono.

If Onissim and Rashel encountered a firestorm of criticism from their Jewish friends, family, and professional associates, Christian friends had the opposite reaction. Some even imagined that Rashel and Onissim had been touched by divine light and wanted to come to Christ. This was equally discomfiting.

In reading about my grandfather's conversion, some sources say that Onissim became Protestant[14]—perhaps even Lutheran—though Rashel's diary indicates clearly that the two became Catholic in a single ceremony and that a joint conversion and baptism occurred on their wedding day. From a purely practical point of view, it would have made more sense for both of them to convert to Russian Orthodoxy. The reactionaries in charge of the Russian government detested Catholics and Protestants almost as passionately as they hated Jews. Followers of these religions also faced official discrimination, although their suffering was much milder than that of the Jews. Perhaps the couple simply could not stomach the idea of adopting the religion of their oppressors. They were, after all, only using conversion to marry.

I gradually came to realize that Rashel's and Onissim's conversions were not unusual. During the 19th century, sixty-nine thousand Russian Jews converted to Russian Christian Orthodoxy, twelve thousand to Catholicism, and three thousand to Lutheranism. Like many other Jewish converts, Rashel's and Onissim's Christianity was purely formal. Rashel never mentioned anything about Catholic beliefs in any of her memoirs or other writings. According to the work of one historian,[15] Rashel and Onissim never took advantage of the benefits and privileges that came with their new Christianity. After he converted, Onissim was technically and officially released from the restrictions on Jewish lawyers and could have immediately made the transition from an Apprentice (*pomoshchnik*) to a full-fledged Attorney-at-Law (*prisyazhenyi poverennyi)*. Had he not been Jewish, he would have been eligible as early as 1892. However, Onissim considered it beneath his dignity to benefit materially from his "romantic" conversion and he kept the title of Apprentice (*pomoshchnik*) until the end of 1905, when he officially became an Attorney along with other Jews; a Tsar's Manifesto of October 1905, lifting some discriminatory rules, including restrictions on Jewish employment, made this possible.

Furthermore, according to several sources, my grandfather always embraced his Judaism and, some years after his conversion, in 1906, he published a major work on the history of the Jews in Moscow, courageously documenting in detail the pattern of intense persecution that his co-religionists had experienced over centuries.[16] He remained committed to Jewish causes and Jews in need, providing money and advice when it was requested. He would ask Lea to do the same.

HELP!

෴

One of the specific Jewish projects that Onissim championed came to fruition around the time of his marriage. It was a fund-raising effort to benefit indigent Jews affected by a recent famine. Vladimir Petrovich Potemkin, a younger scholar with considerable interest in Jewish history and philosophy, approached Onissim. Potemkin wanted Onissim's and Rashel's assistance in securing creative work from writers and visual artists for a publication with the simple title *HELP!*[17] Potemkin had recently been rebuffed by the novelist Lev Tolstoy, who told him, "I have to refuse to write anything. If I agree, the public will imagine that I have lost my mind. I am occupied with more important, global questions. Jewish problems are 189th on my list."

According to Rashel, who reported the event in her diary on April 25, 1900, Onissim initially refused to believe Tolstoy could have chosen such words, but Potemkin insisted it was true. Onissim was furious about this blatant anti-Semitism and on at least one occasion when he was invited to meet Tolstoy, he demurred, though he and Rashel did spend a pleasant evening with the writer soon after that.

While Potemkin's effort to solicit material from Tolstoy for *HELP!* was unsuccessful, Onissim and Rashel immediately launched into helping him find other contributors. They had much better luck with the French writer Émile

Zola. Rashel had been close to him ever since her student days in Paris and had been the first to translate some of Zola's writings into Russian. As it turned out, Zola was the perfect foreign contributor to *HELP!* His name had become associated with Jewish causes ever since the January 13, 1898, publication of his article "J'Accuse . . ." [I accuse . . .] In it, he had championed the case of the falsely accused and convicted Jewish French army captain Alfred Dreyfus, who was found guilty of treason despite clear evidence that another individual was responsible. Zola was an international celebrity and his participation in the publication was a tremendous coup.

Zola's contribution to *HELP!* was entitled, "In Defense of Jews." It was translated by Rashel and appeared on page fifteen, after Potemkin's Preface. It is unclear how many of the other fifty-two essays, poems, and stories Onissim and Rashel helped gather, or whether Onissim was the one who persuaded some of the ten distinguished artists to submit drawings. One artist he did approach was Leonid Pasternak (father of Boris Pasternak, the author of *Doctor Zhivago*), who, according to family lore, later painted Onissim's portrait.[18]

Another person Onissim commissioned for the *HELP!* project was Semyon Solomonovich Yushkevich. At the time, Yushkevich was in his early thirties and had not enjoyed much success. Onissim's aid for struggling Jewish men of letters was not uncommon, but on this occasion Rashel regretted it, especially when after the anthology's publication the writer showed up at Katino and wouldn't leave. Yushkevich's appearance in *HELP!* alongside such a distinguished group of writers had convinced him that he too was a writer of masterpieces. He would spend evenings with them criticizing Tolstoy, Turgenev, and Dostoyevsky in Rashel's presence, infuriating her.

Onissim told Rashel to relax, that Yushkevich was only baiting her, that he was in fashion these days, and that if she didn't stop, he would tell people she was jealous. But then it was Onissim's turn to be irritated: Yushkevich began criticizing some of his favorite music. "I am sick and tired of this 'Sub-Gorky,'" Rashel wrote in her diary on June 22, 1903 (Gorky referring to the established author, who had also written for *HELP!*). With the Sub-Gorky nickname, she both dismissed Yushkevich's talent and indicated that his origins were as common as those of the more famous author.

Her mention of Gorky was no coincidence. After the success of *HELP!*, Gorky had invited Potemkin and Onissim to visit in September 1902, as he had a follow-up project in mind. Gorky enjoyed significant fame after some of his stories were published in the 1890s. He was well disposed to the cause of helping Jews; he had personally witnessed and been disgusted by a vicious pogrom against them in his home city of Nizhny Novgorod (indeed, his contribution to *HELP!* was called simply "Pogrom"). As a young writer, Gorky had been influenced by Jewish writings, especially by the 1st century BCE sage Hillel the Elder.

Rashel's initial response to the invitation was dismissal: "What a humiliation [for Jews] always to be an object of charity." Onissim and Potemkin provided a humorous report about the visit when they returned, which she faithfully recorded in her diary:

> In Nizhnyi, they at first could not find the famous writer's house. At last when they did, they mounted the dirty front stairs just as Gorky was descending the back stairs from his porch. Finally, they met and feigned expressions of joy. Potemkin bowed elegantly.
>
> "Who are you? Not correspondents, I hope?" asked Gorky. They introduced themselves.
>
> Potemkin said that they had decided that it was their duty to accept Gorky's gracious invitation and had come to see him. "Oh, damn you," exclaimed the hospitable master of the house, "I didn't realize who you were."
>
> Gorky's proposed project to "help" Jews is a totally unfeasible fantasy. As for the man himself, in spite of some awkward manners, he seemed to make a pleasant impression on them, especially when he smiled. Apparently as a host he is ungracious. As they sat at his untidy table, there were several people seizing slices of sausage with their fingers and all talking at once like a choir. The great writer told OB and Potemkin: "Well, help yourselves," but as there were no extra glasses or cups and the people at the table had snatched all of the bread and sausage, the "guests" went away hungry and had their meal at the railway station.[19]

As for further help for Jews from Maxim Gorky, Potemkin and Onissim came back empty-handed.

Literary Circles

❧

As their relationship developed, Onissim involved himself more and more in Rashel's world of literature and theater. He joined the Society of Lovers of Russian Literature,[20] a group established in 1811 to promote Russian literature as a means of mass enlightenment. Primarily a publishing house with a mission to make Russian literature more accessible to the broader public, it brought out collections of works by Pushkin, Turgenev, and Dostoyevsky, as well as collections of folk songs and transcripts of Moscow State University lectures. Its sociopolitical stance promoting universal literacy and love of literature was totally consistent with Onissim's.

Among Rashel's other important literary friends with a passion for Western literature was Nikolai Ilyich Storozhenko. Like Onissim, he had graduated from Moscow University, where he was both a talented scientist and a literary critic. In the latter capacity, his specialty became British literature and he was among the first Russian Shakespeare scholars. His works were so popular in England that he was elected a vice president of the New Shakespeare Society there. It was Storozhenko who first attempted to get Onissim and Rashel together with Lev Tolstoy. Onissim resisted at first—Tolstoy had made those anti-Semitic remarks when he had been asked to provide a contribution to the Jewish publication *HELP!* and these had stung. Eventually, though, Onissim relented, both out of respect for his old teacher and a realization of how important such a meeting was for his wife. In April 1900, the couple went to Storozhenko's Moscow apartment to meet Tolstoy.

Here is Rashel, writing in her diary on April 25, 1900. In the entry, Onissim is referred to by the initials OB (Onissim Borisovich), Storozhenko as Nikolai Ilyich or Nik Ilyich, and Tolstoy as Lev Nikolaevich. Another guest who arrived with Tolstoy was his longtime friend Count Dmitri Olsufiev, who was also friendly with the Tsar.

As the evening unfolded, it was clear that it was Rashel whom Tolstoy had looked forward to meeting, and that he had known nothing about Onissim prior to this event. Because of the firestorm of protest that had occurred after their recent wedding, Rashel and Onissim were introduced to Tolstoy separately, not as a married couple.

> When I heard [Tolstoy's] first, very simple words: "Well, it is so good that we can finally meet one another . . . I have known about you for a long time," I was so nervous that I couldn't speak. We sat down at the table to have tea. There was mint gingerbread, dried grapes, figs, and pastille* . . . Nikolai Ilyich had brought Tolstoy's favorite sweets. I was touched by N. I.'s tender attention and refined politeness that he brought treats for us, his "common guests," including special Danish dates for Onissim and Kraft chocolates for me.
>
> Lev Nikolaevich smiled when he saw the "treats" on the table and said: "He is spoiling me." He winked at Nikolai Ilyich. "He knows that I have a sweet tooth."

It was inevitable that the conversation would touch on literature—after all, both Tolstoy and Rashel were writers. They discussed Anton Chekhov, a popular writer of plays and short stories, and read one of his stories aloud. The conversation then turned to the question of truth versus falsehood, and the Tsar and his wife, the Tsaritsa, who Rashel describes as "English" and a "Protestant." Actually, Tsar Nicholas II's wife, Alexandra, was Hessian, but most people knew she was the granddaughter of Queen Victoria of England. Alexandra's first language was not English (it was German) and, though raised a Protestant, she had converted to Russian Orthodoxy after her marriage to Nicholas. Nevertheless, many considered her not Russian enough, a foreigner. Her frequent ill health and inability to produce a male heir for many years (son Alexei was not born until 1904, following the birth of four girls), as well as the fact that she did not seem to behave like a true Tsaritsa, simply confirmed their views.

A further context for the conversation that followed are the activities of Sergei Zubatov, the head of the Okhrana, or secret police, who relied on a

---

* This spongy confection is made with apples and egg whites. A recipe (#20) can be found in Tolstoy's wife's cookbook. See Sergei Beltyukov, *Leo Tolstoy's Family Recipe Book* (Amazon Digital Services, 2014).]

network of informers to root out radicals. Zubatov was famous for dressing up his informers as ordinary workers and having them espouse socialist ideology. The informers ingratiated themselves with radicals, who they then encouraged to incriminate themselves.

"You see," said Tolstoy with a chuckle, "There is nobody who can tell the truth to the Tsar and Tsaritsa. On Easter in the church they were surrounded by [Zubatov's] informers who were introduced to them as workers."

"That cannot be true," said Olsufiev.

"Count, it was just so," said Onissim. "They were plainclothes agents of police. They are sent to factories to plant socialist propaganda. It is a clever trick."

"You see!" Tolstoy got excited and looked at Onissim in a friendly way. "We all are wrapped up in a web of lies. Don't you pity the Tsaritsa? She is an English woman, a Protestant, but she is surrounded by Russian Orthodox priests who force her to kiss the 'boards' [i.e., icons].* They say she complained that she is exhausted 'from kissing.'"**

Olsufiev became indignant: "How is it possible to believe such gossip? I know for a fact that the Tsaritsa is fond of the Orthodox Church."

Tolstoy laughed sarcastically. "They will repeat all this nonsense until everyone will believe it. Even the youngster herself will finally believe it."

At this point in the conversation, the host Storozhenko "became concerned that the conversation was becoming dangerously political." To change the topic, he asked Onissim to play the piano. Tolstoy was curious to learn more about who Onissim was.

---

*   Icons, holy pictures, are painted on boards. The truly faithful kiss icons.

**   The words *from kissing* are written in English in Rashel's diary to imitate the words of the English-speaking Alexandra.

Onissim began by playing my favorite Chopin sonata. Tolstoy listened attentively for a while then said: "Nice playing. A professional?" He was very surprised when he was told that Onissim was a high-level attorney [присяжный поверенный]. He looked at me, smiled, and said, "Uh huh, a clever one." I could hardly keep from laughing.

Lev Nikolaevich [Tolstoy] went into the room, sat on a chair near the grand piano, and listened until the end of the piece. Then he asked Onissim: "Do you play Beethoven?"

Onissim answered: "I do, but I thought that you, Lev Nikolaevich, didn't particularly like Beethoven." Tolstoy frowned a little bit, then almost at the same moment smiled and said: "Some Beethoven I like very much." And he added: "And I like that your playing is so musical and doesn't sound like it comes straight from a lesson at the conservatory."

. . . At the end of the evening, Tolstoy parted with us in a very tender way. He told us that he certainly wanted to see us again. He was especially affectionate with Onissim. Tolstoy apparently thinks they are like-minded people who have much in common.

For years, I had heard from older members of my family a vague rumor that my grandfather had played piano for Tolstoy. But it was one of those family legends I could not quite believe. Then in 2015, my cousin Sveta, reading through the hundreds of pages of Rashel Khin's diary, came across and translated the entry quoted above. Even the short segment revealed so much about the people, their relationships, and the times. It was Rashel who had made this meeting possible and whom Tolstoy had come to meet but it had been an occasion for Onissim to meet the great man. When Tolstoy says to her, "I have known about you for a long time," he is referring to her literary reputation. The relationships and interests of Rashel's literary circle enriched Onissim's character, and he owed Rashel a great debt for cultivating them.

I was also struck by the fact that it was Onissim's music as much as his intellect or political views that impressed people, even Tolstoy. The description of the evening taught me so much about the culture of Russia at that time. Even amid oppression and hardship there were such wonderful moments and pleasant gatherings among educated and cultured people. They might spend an evening together reading great literature aloud and playing Beethoven sonatas. And in 1900 at least, liberals in Russia spoke openly, albeit carefully, about the "web of lies" that surrounded their political leaders and the growing socialist activity that would ultimately engulf them. Only Olsufiev was shocked when the conversation touched on the clueless Tsar and Tsaritsa.

One moment in the conversation particularly stands out—the point at which my grandfather assumed that Tolstoy did not like Beethoven. The reference was clearly to Tolstoy's novella, *The Kreutzer Sonata*. While the story was immediately censored after publication, educated Russians such as Onissim had read it and knew that Beethoven's *Kreutzer* Sonata for violin and piano (the very piece that Onissim would play with Lea) figured prominently in the Tolstoy's story as an evil enticement to infidelity and carnal love. However, Tolstoy enjoyed and knew many of Beethoven's works. And he found my grandfather's playing of the great composer quite musical. This was an opinion that, within little more than three years, my grandmother Lea would share.

The Politics of Hope

I had now spent much time learning about Onissim Goldovsky—his life, his work, and his marriage. But as I dug through his past looking for my family, I was frustrated. There was lots written about him . . . and Rashel Khin. But where was my grandmother? Where was confirmation that this brilliant man had led a domestic life with Lea and fathered her children, including my mother? Was I wasting my time? Was it possible that Onissim Goldovsky was not my grandfather after all? To begin with, I needed to understand what had occurred in his life from the time he met Lea in 1903 until her first child who was born in 1907. I knew I could establish his whereabouts and activity in these years since it was well documented in books, articles, and especially in Rashel's diary. Much of his activity and travels related to politics at a critical moment in the history of Russia.

As it turned out, Onissim spent most of the time during these years with Rashel and this added to my confusion. Katino, Rashel's country estate in the outskirts of Moscow, was a key meeting place where prominent professional people—writers, philosophers, musicians, and actors—visited and where politics was often discussed and debated. Onissim was also traveling, writing, and meeting with other activists in the *zemstvos* that had been established by Alexander II. Over the years, the *zemstvos* had become increasingly active in education, health care, and agricultural development. Given the inefficiency of the tsarist bureaucracy, the *zemstvos* were often the only agencies for social welfare and the Tsar himself had been forced to turn to them for help in relieving the terrible famine of 1890 and thereafter.

However, as Onissim grew more engaged, the *zemstvos* were taking on a more overtly political dimension. Though political parties were strictly forbidden, the *zemstvos* offered a forum for debate and activism, especially after councils were established in Moscow and St. Petersburg and a national conference of *zemstvo* leaders was held in 1896. Gradually, the *zemstvos* had come to a consensus in favor of some kind of parliamentary government for Russia, although individual *zemstvo* activists differed over whether the parliament should simply consult the Tsar or enjoy full-fledged legislative powers.

By the end of the century, it had become clear to Onissim that Tsar Alexander III was not going to tolerate even the most modest political reforms, and furthermore, was going to make it nearly impossible for Jews to have any influence. In 1890, the Tsar imposed new rules on the provincial *zemstvo* councils, barring Jews and small landholders from running for council seats. He had given local outposts of the reactionary Interior Ministry veto power over the *zemstvos'* budgets, staff appointments, and legislation. Several *zemstvo* activists were arrested. The national conference of *zemstvos* was shut down shortly after it was created, although its members continued to meet in secret. The liberal intelligentsia was also under threat as Alexander III temporarily closed the universities and arrested dozens of professors and students. A brief spark of optimism when Alexander III died was quickly extinguished; it became clear that his successor, Nicholas II, would be just as despotic. Equally worrisome to a humanist like Onissim was the rise of the radical left, which in 1898 established the Russia Social-Democratic Workers Party—the party that would evolve into the Bolsheviks. To a large extent, he was caught in the middle, politically speaking, at a time when compromise was not sought by either the radical left or the reactionary right.

In March 1903, Onissim wrote to a friend of his and Rashel's in Paris, sharing both good news and bad. "We are all completely caught up in the latest Manifesto. We are extremely happy that *Le Soleil* wrote such a good analysis of it." He was referring to the February 26, 1903, manifesto of Tsar Nicholas II, which contained promises of some reforms and declared "freedom of conscience," or religious freedom. That was the good news. But the letter also spoke of ongoing political repression: "Today, an acquaintance told me that he was in a train car with a Gendarme Officer and the officer told him about a search of Solovyov's place.* On his table was the book *Essays on the French Revolution*—a book that is dangerous to even hold in your hands. It wouldn't hurt for A[natole] France [another writer friend who had written a novel in support of the Jewish officer Alfred Dreyfus in 1901] to hear about this, as I think he has the same book on his table."

Despite the dangers of open political activity, Onissim journeyed to St. Petersburg in November 1904 to attend an historic *zemstvo* conference. By this time, he had met Lea and agreed to become her patron. But he was clearly occupied elsewhere. The Moscow and St. Petersburg district *zemstvos* were hotbeds of dissent, though their influence was limited by a strict prohibition of any kind of national organization. Provincial *zemstvo* representatives were not even allowed to meet with their colleagues from other provinces. Then came an event that changed the ground rules and Onissim wanted to be part of it.

In 1904, the outbreak of the Russo-Japanese War generated an urgent need for war relief. The government, in disarray, proved unable to raise funds or get food, doctors, and medicine to wounded soldiers and displaced civilians at the

---

* This likely refers to Vsevolod Sergeyevich Solovyov, the Russian historian. Though elsewhere in her diary Rashel refers several times to his brother Vladimir Sergeyevich Solovyov, who had been enthusiastic about Rashel and Onissim's conversion to Christianity and had mentioned Tolstoy's anti-Semitism to them, Vladimir had died in 1900 and this event took place in 1903. The two brothers were sons of one of the most famous of all Russian historians, Sergei Mikhailivich Solovyov who tutored the future Tsar Alexander III and wrote a definitive twenty-nine-volume *History of Russia from the Earliest Times*.

front. In desperation, the authorities turned to the *zemstvos*. Their successful war relief effort greatly enhanced the *zemstvos'* popularity and, in October 1904, the head of the Moscow *zemstvo*, Dmitry Shipov, felt bold enough to wring a concession out of the regime. Even he was surprised, however, when the Tsar approved his request to hold a national conference of *zemstvo* representatives in St. Petersburg. No doubt he was less surprised when the Tsar changed his mind two weeks later. By then, however, Shipov had recruited another ally—the new and fairly moderate Interior Minister Pyotr Sviatopolk-Mirsky. As long as the conference participants kept a low profile and there was no violence, Sviatopolk-Mirsky promised to look the other way and instruct the St. Petersburg police to do the same.

The national *zemstvo* conference was held on November 6–8, 1904. Many historians view it as a seminal event on the road to revolution. According to Harvard historian Richard Pipes, "in terms of historical importance [it] may be compared with the French Estates-General of 1789" that led to the French Revolution.[21] More than one hundred delegates attended, representing thirty-three provincial *zemstvos*. Despite their assurances to Sviatopolk-Mirsky, Shipov and the other conference organizers were determined to have a political impact. After much discussion, they decided that the event would culminate in a resolution in the form of an appeal to the Tsar.

With this as background, I was astonished when my cousin Sveta told me that she had found a draft of the resolution marked up in Onissim's own hand in a Moscow archive. Was my grandfather invited to the conference specifically to help draft this crucial document? Rashel's diary confirms that she and Onissim traveled to St. Petersburg to take part in the conference. It is likely that Vasily Alekseevich Maklakov, a friend, fellow attorney, and one of the conference organizers, arranged for Onissim's involvement as an expert on constitutional law and in drafting legal documents.

The Zemstvo Conference Resolution, in a form very similar to the one Onissim had drafted, was released publicly on November 8. It encapsulated the key ideas that he and other liberals had been developing since their student days, calling for state institutions to be subject to the rule of law, eliminating "bureaucratic despotism" and "arbitrary" justice. It called for freedom of speech, conscience, religion, and assembly, and for equal civil and political rights for all citizens of the Russian Empire, regardless of their ethnicity or social status. It declared that the individual and his dwelling place should be inviolable, and that only an independent judiciary should be able to detain or punish wrong-doers. The resolution called for the provincial *zemstvos* to be transformed into independent, freely elected legislatures with authority over all local affairs.

The most controversial point in the resolution entailed the establishment of an elected national assembly. While all the conference participants agreed that some kind of assembly was needed, they were unable to reach a consensus on its powers. As a result, the final resolution contained two alternative pro-posals. Onissim agreed with the more radical majority in proposing an elected parliament with powers to pass legislation, to approve the federal budget, and to oversee the legality of executive actions. However, a minority group insisted on including their alternative proposal—an elected assembly with a purely consultative role.

The impact of the resolution exceeded the conference organizers' most optimistic expectations. It was the first public appeal for a change in govern-ment, from autocracy to a constitutional monarchy. And, remarkably, it had been signed by all the conference delegates, who in turn represented the only elected political institutions in Russia. From the public's point of view, this gave the resolution unique legitimacy. It was widely discussed and reprinted in the non-state media. Sviatopolk-Mirsky personally handed a copy to Tsar Nicholas, and Prince Gyorgy Lvov slipped a copy to the Tsar's mother, Princess Maria Feodorovna.

Determined to maintain momentum, the leaders of a left-leaning group of *zemstvo* activists, the Union of Liberation, followed up by organizing a series of meetings across Russia. Since public meetings were still banned and Sviatopolk-Mirsky was unlikely to look the other way again, the organizers came up with a clever idea. They asked their supporters to hold private dinner parties, either in homes or restaurants, and invite "notables"—important people whom we might today call thought leaders. The Union of Liberation suggested an agenda, which included discussing the Zemstvo Conference Resolution, but local liberals were welcome to speak on topics of their own choosing. In order to disguise the political nature of the dinners, a pretext was invented—the fortieth anniversary of Tsar Alexander II's reform of the judiciary.

Again, the "banquet campaign" exceeded expectations. Throughout late November and early December, forty-seven dinner parties were held across

Russia. Onissim spoke before more than five hundred people at one of the St. Petersburg dinners, at the luxurious Hermitage Restaurant, about the 1864 Judicial Reforms. These reforms were the very actions that had made Onissim's legal career as a Jew possible, and he could celebrate the fact that by the last decade of the 19th century, fully 14 percent of the empire's lawyers and 43 percent of the apprentice lawyers were Jewish. Onissim spoke eloquently, according to Rashel, and the assembled group of five hundred people was naturally roused by the words of one who had experienced directly the impact of these changes. Across Russia, the banquets were encouraged to produce public resolutions calling for political reform, and many did so. But the great majority (thirty-six) opted simply to endorse the Zemstvo Conference Resolution.[22]

These events were sufficiently dramatic that even the Tsar could not ignore them. In early December, he convened a council of top advisors to consider the Zemstvo Conference Resolution. Before he acted, however, Russia became engulfed in violence.

In early February 1905, the police fired on a gathering of unarmed demonstrators near the Winter Palace in St. Petersburg. The massacre triggered a wave of strikes, peasant uprisings, and street violence, and the chaos eventually forced the Tsar to declare major reforms. In October, he announced a manifesto that largely echoed the Zemstvo Conference Resolution, creating an elected legislative body (the Duma) that would share power with the Tsar, legalizing political parties, extending equal civil and political rights to all Russian citizens, and guaranteeing freedom of conscience, speech, and assembly. Onissim and his friends from the *zemstvo* movement immediately created and registered Russia's first legal political party, the Constitutional Democratic, or Kadet Party. Among the first members were Onissim's old law school professors, Sergei Muromtsev and Maksim Kovalevsky—the same professors whose expulsion from the law faculty decades earlier had triggered Onissim's disastrous letter to Rozanov. The Kadet Party was built on liberal ideals, explicitly rejected socialism, and was willing to tolerate the monarchy as long as it was strictly limited by a constitution.

The Kadets' emphasis on civil liberties attracted many liberal Jews as well as Russian intellectuals, and the party strongly opposed anti-Semitic discrimination and, of course, pogroms. The party's platform called for universal suffrage, including women's suffrage, and the immediate convening of a constituent assembly to draft a constitution. Although the Kadets were hardly representative of the population at large—60 percent were nobles and many others were rich businessmen or professionals like Onissim—it won 30 percent of the seats in Russia's first elected Duma, convened in 1906. Onissim was delighted. The Duma, under the chairmanship of Muromtsev, began working on an array of reforms. Thanks largely to Onissim's influence and one of his publications, a law ending the death penalty was passed unanimously by the full house. Another law introducing measures to relieve rural famines was also passed.

The liberals would quickly face bitter disappointment. The Tsar refused to sign their two pieces of legislation. Enraged by the reformist ideas emerging from the Duma, the Tsar sent his troops to disband it. The long-awaited first Imperial Duma had been in session for only seventy-two days.

As Onissim was planning the launch of the Kadets, Rashel was growing more concerned about disturbances in the Russian Empire as a whole. In her biography of Rashel, Carole Balin quotes a remarkable passage from her diary, written just a few months before a family member was to be deported for alleged involvement in revolutionary activity:

> There are student riots in Moscow and St. Petersburg. They say 850 people have been arrested. It's all so extraordinary . . . [The riots have spread] to Kiev and to Kharkov as well. The university in St. Petersburg has been closed since February. In general, Russia is a mess . . . Everything happens at the wrong time, whether too early or too late . . . [the newspaper] . . . reports that students were arrested and exiled to Siberia for five or ten years. I don't want to believe this, though in Russia anything is possible . . . [23]

Fascinating as all this was to me, especially in learning of my grandfather's central role in the events, my reason for tracking his activities during these years had initially been to understand the tangled relationships between Onissim, Rashel, and Lea. Onissim and Lea had met in the spring of 1903 and after that the two must have been seeing each other over the next year or two. Sometime in 1906, Onissim fathered Lea's first child, so a relationship had blossomed in the intervening period. But I was puzzled how that could be, given Onissim's travels and near-constant activities with Rashel. It was almost as if he occupied several places at once.

Looking at the documented record, Onissim and Rashel had spent a great deal of time together in St. Petersburg in conjunction with the Zemstvo Conference and his "banquet speech," so they were clearly together during that entire time while Lea was in Moscow. They were allied in the formation of the Kadets and attended party meetings together. On February 24, 1905, Rashel wrote in her diary: "We have new plans. Stas dreams about a major newspaper. I have already come up with a name—'Free Labor.' Now we need to choose a publishing house." Their discussion of the idea prompted others to start the venture on their own without Onissim, much to Rashel's disgust. This activity was occurring in Moscow, and at this point, Onissim must have been seeing Lea.

In 1905, Onissim and Rashel left for Paris, once again separating themselves from Lea. The reason for the departure seemed connected to the street violence of the 1905 Revolution, and for a long time I wondered whether Onissim was like scores of other fair-weather liberal thinkers, who flew from the nexus of activity when things became violent. That was not the case, but it took me many months to learn the truth.

Arriving in Paris with Rashel, Onissim once again threw himself into political work. He found his way to the *L'École russe des hautes études sociales de Paris* (known in Russian as «Russkuyu vyschuyu shkolu obshchestven-nikh nauk» and roughly translated into English as "The Russian Higher School of Social Studies"). The school was founded in 1901 by Maksim Kovalevsky, Onissim's old law professor, and was located on the rue Sorbonne. It became a center for the opposition in exile. Leading liberals, including the future Kadet leader Pavel Miliukov, as well as some famous socialists (Georgi Plekhanov, founder of Russian socialism, and even Leon Trotsky and Vladimir Lenin) studied and taught there. An underlying philosophy of the school was the unity of human knowledge, something that had appealed to Onissim ever since his days training with the poly-math Rudolf Mintslov.

As revolutionary fervor in Russia settled down after the tumultuous events of 1905, Onissim found himself impatient to return and resume his legal and political work—and his writing. In addition to founding a periodical on psychology and the law, writing a book on the Jews of Moscow, as well as a biography of his former mentor Prince Urusov, he was completing a major new collection entitled *Against the Death Penalty (Protiv smertnoĭ kazni)*; once again he was serving as editor and contributing a central essay.

Was Onissim also impatient to return to Lea? How soon was he able to do so? And where did that leave Rashel? Somehow, I needed to find out.

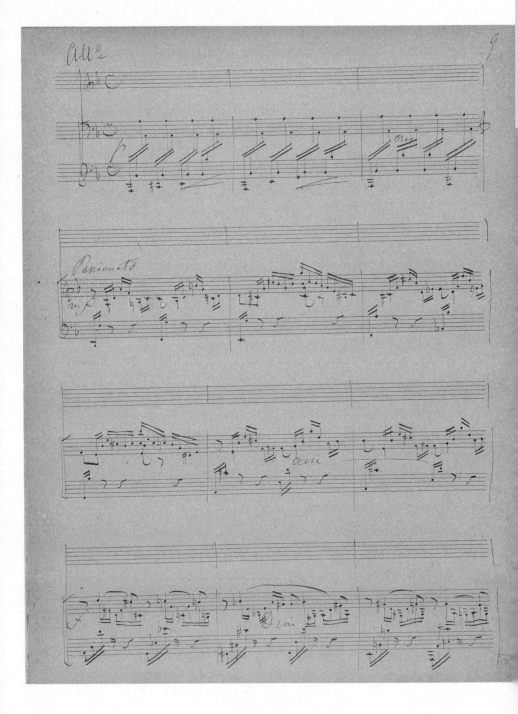

II

THE TEMPEST

Allegro

(1903 to 1921)

◈

During his lifetime, César Franck never enjoyed the acclaim that came to Ysaÿe, who performed his sonata for violin and piano. After the 1886 premiere, it took about a decade for the sonata to be widely known and admired. By that time, Franck had been dead for five years. Ysaÿe, on the other hand, became well-known for the work and kept it in his repertoire for four decades. In time, other performers took up the piece, and it became one of the most popular sonatas for violin and piano ever written.

Ysaÿe taught the piece to my grandmother. Lea taught it to her brother, my great uncle Pierre. Pierre taught it to Lea's son—my uncle Boris. On and on it moved through the family, always resurfacing at important times.

The second movement is a tempestuous celebration of life. It begins with fast finger work on the piano, with the main theme passing rapidly from one hand to the other. The violin enters aggressively and the two are off on a chase. At times, they slow down, reveling in moments of calm, reflective beauty, but these are brief and soon overwhelmed by action, excitement, and events happening at a pace and intensity it's hard to keep up with. "I tell you," wrote Ysaÿe to the composer, "It is simply splendid."

The Relationships

❦

"Simply splendid." Nothing better describes Lea and Onissim's first evening together in 1903. Onissim had never played music with anyone who possessed such intensity, such fire. His relationship with Rashel was cerebral, intellectually stimulating, but deliberate and carefully planned. It appears to have been largely asexual. Ever since his run-in with Polina Suslova, Onissim had been cautious, only rarely allowing himself a loss of control. But here was an exuberant red-headed teenager from the provinces, basically uneducated, whose music revealed a passion he had seldom experienced. He wanted Lea as much as anything he had ever wanted in his life.

For Lea, the attraction was different. She too burned with passion, but that passion was likely for the strong father figure she had never had. The earliest version of her memoir read: "[This was the man who would] guide me for more than fifteen years. It was he who developed the good qualities I had, who improved as much as was possible the indifferent ones, and made of me what I am now. He was to me father, teacher, husband, devoted friend, and critic to the last minute of his life."

All true except for one small detail: Onissim would never become Lea's husband—a fact I didn't learn until I myself had been married for many years and had had my own children.

My grandmother wrote the words "husband" in her memoir in 1936. By that time, she was no longer in Russia. She and Onissim had lived together off and on for fifteen years, and she had three children by him. Now he was dead. Maintaining the fiction that he had been her husband was crucial to her new persona. Though my uncles knew that their mother had never been married and my mother learned the truth well before Lea's death, they too pretended that she was a proper widow. Onissim's photograph remained on Lea's bedside table and when people asked, they were told that the man was Lea's late husband. Only after she died did her children tell us the truth, and then only because things did not add up in the wake of Rashel Khin's biography. It came as a shock that our elegant grandmother, whom I had regarded as a paragon of virtue and proper behavior, had had children out of wedlock. In time, I discovered that the story was far more convoluted than that.

In the 1936 manuscript, my grandmother wrote, "There are things in one's private life that a person should keep to one's self. Certain things have only a deep meaning to the ones concerned. The private life of two people who are very happy and have a great mutual understanding and trust, who were as happy the last minute of their life together as they were at the beginning, has interest only to the two concerned . . . I beg leave, then, of my readers to permit me to refrain from the recording of these, to me, precious memories."

What were those things in her private life she did not want to reveal?

In a later version of the memoir, Lea struck out these passages and removed any reference to Onissim as her husband. She substituted the following: "From that radiant evening, my life began to change character. After that, all my feelings, which had been occupied with music only, began to go into different channels. I found myself day-dreaming while I was practicing. I could hardly spend an hour without thinking of this man . . . He was constantly before my eyes and a desire to see him overwhelmed me. Fortunately, as I later found out, he felt the same way about me. My youth, my talent, my appearance seemed to attract him, as his brilliance, charm, and wit attracted me. The evening was a beautiful one and I will remember it all my life, even as I do now. Onissim Goldovsky appears before me as I write these words, and his picture is beside me on my night table."

Why did my grandmother change her manuscript? My theory is that her brother Pierre confronted her. She had shown him the manuscript and family rumor holds that, upon reading it, he was furious. He felt it was full of lies, including an exaggeration of their childhood poverty. Pierre could be a hot-head when riled, especially if fueled by vodka. Lea probably feared that the revelation that she was not a widow and in fact had never been married might compromise her reputation personally *and* professionally. Better simply to delete any reference to a husband.

The story that my mother told us when Rashel Khin's biography appeared in the year 2000 was simply that Onissim was unable to get a divorce from Rashel, so my grandmother and grandfather never married legally, though in all other respects they were husband and wife. He wanted to leave his wife, so the story went, and had asked for a divorce but was refused. Later, when

I researched this, I found sources that implied Khin used her religion as an excuse to refuse Onissim his request. Rashel used her newly minted Catholicism to divorce her first, Jewish husband only to use it again to refuse a divorce to Onissim. Pure irony. There the story remained.

But it turned out that this was not accurate either. My cousin Sveta found materials relating to Onissim and Rashel, including letters and her diary, which told a different story. I still remember her email to me: "I have been worrying about writing to you and upsetting you. I have learned some things about Onissim that may make you unhappy." We knew that by 1906 Lea was pregnant with Onissim's child, the first of three that they had together, and at some point (I was never sure when) they set up a household together. But then came the bombshell: Onissim never left Rashel Khin. While it is clear that he and Lea lived together, Onissim lived with Rashel as well for most of his life. A decade after my grandmother became pregnant with Onissim's child, and long after they had lived together for extended periods of time, Onissim was still ostensibly a happily married man maintaining another domestic reality.

At first we reconstructed the story in this fashion: Onissim and Lea met in the late spring 1903 and may have begun their affair as early as that fall, when Lea returned to Moscow from Odessa—not an unusual situation for someone of Onissim's class. There were many similarities in culture and mores between this period in Russian history and the American 1960s, when "open marriages" were all the rage. My grandfather probably had many love affairs given Rashel's ambivalence about sex.

Rashel herself had very clear views on the nature of relationships between men and women. For her, the bond that excited her was always intellectual. Everything else flowed from that. Intimacy with men was a function of the marriage of like minds. Carole Balin indicates that Rashel "shared a thirty-year intimacy" with Anatoli Koni during her marriages to both Feldshtein and Onissim, even though the jurist was seventeen years her senior,[1] but it was entirely platonic.

Despite Rashel's moral compass on the nature of relationships outside of marriage, Lea and Onissim's affair was, by the standards of the day, not unusual, though at age eighteen, Lea was fairly young to be involved with anyone, let alone a man almost forty years of age. Her memoir indicates that she was totally mesmerized and felt honored that Onissim had fallen in love with her. But at some point, their relationship went beyond an affair. In one version of her memoir, Lea gives 1905 as the year of her "marriage" to Onissim. If "marriage" is read as "serious affair," this could make sense (she was now twenty years old). She had reinvented herself once again from an arrogant conservatory graduate focused on making a career to a young woman pursuing a deep and serious relationship with an older, married man. The Revolution of 1905 began on January 22; soon after, Onissim and Rashel went to Paris where, amazingly, Lea joined them for a time. Was it before or after the Paris sojourn that he considered making some sort of permanent commitment to Lea?

Certainly, by 1906, the affair was getting serious. Lea, no shrinking violet, may have insisted that the relationship would have to be more; once she was pregnant with Onissim's child, a decision was forced upon the lovers. Perhaps Lea's mother, Gitel, stepped in. She had devoted her life to the development of Lea's career. Now all of that had the potential to unravel. Being a woman was already an obstacle to Lea's success as a major musical star. Pregnancy would complicate things still further. It was important that people's perception of Lea and her career not be overshadowed by the common assumption that women like her were little better than prostitutes. A clandestine affair with a so-called "anonymous patron" that produced children could be catastrophic.

Whatever the cause, Lea moved into a new, larger apartment at 25 Malaya Lubyanka around the time of the birth of their first child in spring 1907. It was from this apartment, just a five-minute walk from where Onissim had lived as a law student, that she signed her brother Pierre's application to the Moscow Conservatory on August 10, 1907. The apartment was large enough so that when Pierre was accepted, he could move right in. It was also large enough to accommodate Saul and Gitel when they visited or should they ever want to move to Moscow permanently.[2]

That same year, Onissim commissioned a giant portrait of Lea with her violin. Six feet high and more than three feet wide, it was painted by Mikhail Shemyakin, the son-in-law of Lea's teacher at the conservatory, Jan Hřímalý. Shemyakin, a pupil of arguably the most important Russian painter of the time, Valentin Serov, was considered a brilliant portraitist and was a member of the Peredvizhniki (Передвижни) group of artists (sometimes referred to in English as "The Wanderers" or "The Itinerants"). He was enjoying considerable fame at the time and had painted a similar large portrait of his father-in-law holding his violin. Once Onissim saw it, he had to have a similar one of Lea. I had always been curious about this portrait, which is now lost, and I was delighted to find a small black-and-white image of it in an exhibition catalog from 1908.[3] In additon, a family photograph shows the gigantic painting hanging on the wall of Lea's apartment behind Onissim, who is reclining on a couch. Shemyakin would later render a much more modest face portrait of Anna Luboshutz, a painting that still exists and was exhibited in Moscow as recently as 2018.[4]

At this time, Onissim was still living with Rashel in their large Moscow apartment and at Katino. Eventually, when Lea bore a second child, Onissim moved her to an even larger apartment at 26 Trubnikovsky Pereulok. Why did Onissim not join Lea and his children full-time in their new home? Did Rashel continue to refuse Onissim's request for a divorce? That is what my mother and her brother maintained. It was a convenient story, but I eventually realized that it was untrue. If it were merely a matter of Rashel refusing Onissim a divorce, why would my grandfather maintain a strong and public relationship with his wife for more than a decade?

A fortuitous accident would eventually turn up the answers I sought. Just as Lea had decided to control her story by rewriting her autobiography, so had Rashel. There were in fact *two* versions of her diary, a relatively short, typed version that she was preparing for publication at the time of her death and a handwritten one running to hundreds of pages and not easy to decipher. Anyone wanting to learn about her life would more likely start with the former—just as my cousin Sveta had done. As I was editing this book, Sveta decided to check the handwritten version to be sure that we hadn't missed anything. And the whole picture changed before our eyes.

Rashel, it seems, had been far more reticent about her personal life in the typed version, leaving out many facts and modifying others. From Rashel's original, handwritten manuscript, Sveta and I learned that Rashel and Onissim's personal life was not at all as we had surmised. There were multiple love triangles of the strangest sort, and much pain and unhappiness. The story came in pieces, and each piece made the saga more bizarre.

Interconnections

❧

Initially, I wanted to know more about Lea and Onissim's first meeting—who might have orchestrated it, how it led to what followed. If Lea knew who had brought Onissim to the musical party on that fateful evening, she never mentioned it, not in any version of her memoir or in conversation with her family. But eventually, I figured it out.

A name in a letter written to Onissim provided the clue. The connecting link between Lea and Onissim was Sergei Taneyev, a well-known pianist and composer whose enduring fame rests on the fact that he played the first performances of Tchaikovsky's piano concerti, as well as the great composer's monumental piano trio and other works. Onissim knew him through Rashel. Taneyev was in great demand as an accompanist to the leading violinists of the day, and among those he toured with was Leopold Auer, the same man who had once invited a small child in Odessa named Lea Luboshutz to study with him. Auer's wife, Nadine, was one of Rashel Khin's best friends, and thus the circle was completed.

Once Nadine met Onissim, she took to him immediately—and he to her. The two loved to gossip. Reading their letters in French is a challenge—they are written idiomatically, and many of the people they gossip about have cute nicknames. Still, their correspondence is one of the few firsthand examples I have of my grandfather's humorous side. And through their letters, I discovered that it was Nadine who introduced Taneyev to Onissim. They bonded quickly over their mutual love of the piano.

Why did Taneyev invite Onissim to the party where Lea played? Onissim had given up his Judaism in order to marry Rashel, but he had remained committed to those of his original faith. With his wife's money, and given her involvement in theater, he had become a patron of Jews struggling to make theatrical careers. But Onissim's first love, culturally speaking, was music, and he probably mentioned to Taneyev, who taught both piano and composition at the conservatory, that he was looking for a young Jewish musical talent to sponsor. Taneyev knew that Lea was the star conservatory talent that year. That year was 1903.

The rest, as they say, is history. Onissim went to the musicale where Lea played, was enthralled, and, very importantly, became Lea's patron. This initial relationship—that of a patron as opposed to a lover—explains later entries in Rashel's diary in which I learned, to my utter astonishment, that she and Lea spent much time together over the next few years with Rashel completely oblivious to Onissim's growing bond with Lea. It also clarifies why Rashel attended Lea's concerts and expressed her opinions on Lea's music making and appearance—her husband was, after all, Lea's patron. The key to the story was now in place.

The Taneyev connection also solved another mystery about the origins of Tolstoy's tale *The Kreutzer Sonata*. Arguably, the piece itself was what brought Onissim and Lea together, and Onissim had indirectly referenced it in his conversation with Tolstoy, so I knew my grandparents were both well aware of the story. To my surprise, as I explored the Taneyev connection, I learned that it was he who had inspired Tolstoy to write *The Kreutzer Sonata* in the first place. Taneyev spent the summers of 1895 and 1896 at Yasnaya Polyana, the writer's home. Tolstoy's wife, Sofia, took a shine to Taneyev, and Tolstoy became seriously jealous. This, Tolstoy's biographers claim, was the love triangle that inspired his tale of jealousy and murder (though happily, Tolstoy carried out the murder only on paper). The Kreutzer sonata had, in its turn, led to Onissim's own love triangle. Here was a clear case of life imitating art.

The First Love Triangle

Rashel's typed diary, the one prepared for publication, turned out to have many omissions. It also contained fabrications. These included Rashel's wonderful description of her apparent "first" meeting with Onissim Goldovsky in 1897 at the event on behalf of a women's medical college, of which Onissim's mentor Prince Urusov was a patron. In it, Onissim is the Prince's charming assistant, the young man who offers Rashel a ride home. Soon after, a romance begins.

In truth, Rashel had known Onissim for almost a decade before that night, and it turns out that Onissim's affair with Lea was not his first. Indeed, he had embarked on the same adventure with Rashel. Two days before their marriage, on February 16, 1900, she wrote in her diary that, "OB [Onissim] has been supporting and protecting me and my child for twelve years." This would indicate that they had known each other since 1888, just at the time Onissim was beginning his legal apprenticeship with Prince Urusov. Though Rashel does not say so explicitly, it seems likely that Urusov introduced them, since the older lawyer represented the Khin family in legal matters. In time, Onissim appears to have taken over much of that legal work. At the beginning of 1895 (January 13), Rashel writes: "Everyone in the family makes use of his services and they all feel that they have the right to do so at any time if they need him. I am amazed at his patience."

It is hardly a surprise, then, that a woman so miserable in her marriage should so quickly transfer her affections to an attractive younger man, one who seemed to be everything that her husband was not. In short order, Rashel and Onissim became close, and she increasingly separated herself from her husband for extended periods and lived with Onissim. Especially important for her were the summer months when she and her son, Misha, could live apart from Feldshtein and she could see Onissim.

This did not please Feldshtein. A very emotional entry in Rashel's diary describes the arrival one night of a carriage that she thought was carrying Onissim, which turned out to be Feldshtein and her father. After words were exchanged concerning her duties as a wife, she came to bed fully dressed and made it clear to her husband that she owed him no conjugal debt. Feldshtein shouted at her, accused her of being an egoist only after her own pleasure. So violent did he become that she rushed from the room and spent the night in her son's bedroom.

From that time on, three things became obvious. Rashel wanted permanent independence of Feldshtein, she wanted her son Misha with her, and she wanted Onissim to be the primary man in her life. Though her father initially had not approved of Onissim, the younger man turned out to be invaluable during the father's final illness when he not only attended the sick man himself but often took care of Rashel's son, as described in her diary entry of February 10, 1896. Though they were willing to battle hard for the right to wed, to do so would require Rashel's divorce from Feldshtein, and in late-19th-century Russia, divorces were not easy to arrange.

Two obstacles stood in Rashel's way. The first was Jewish law, which held that Rashel and Misha belonged to Feldshtein. If he did not consent to a divorce, there was nothing she could do about it if she wanted to remain a Jew. She could live apart from him and often did, sometimes with Onissim, but that meant that he had the right to keep her son from her. Then there was the Russian legal system which—as famously described in Tolstoy's novel *Anna Karenina*—held that only the husband could initiate a divorce proceeding. And Feldshtein, no matter how obnoxious he may have appeared, was not simply being difficult. To divorce, one or both partners had to confess to adultery or prove adultery by the other. Many estranged husbands, especially if they enjoyed prestigious professional or social positions, balked at this kind of public embarrassment. And Russian law threw up another complication. Feldshtein held the identity papers of Rashel and her son, documents which every citizen needed in order to travel within the Russian Empire. He also had Rashel's passport.

Feldshtein was intransigent, but he had not counted on the cleverness of Onissim Goldovsky, who laid out a detailed and bold plan to solve all these problems. Rashel and Onissim would travel separately to the small town of Tolochin where there was both a substantial Jewish community and a Catholic one. According to a complex but tight schedule, Rashel and Onissim would each convert to Catholicism. Once paperwork was completed invalidating her Jewish marriage and she was officially in an unmarried state, they would immediately pledge their wedding vows in a Catholic ceremony. If successful, Rashel would not only get the husband she wanted but she would also get her identity papers and passport issued independently of Feldshtein. If anything went amiss, however, her situation would be worse than before.

Onissim went to Tolochin first and made arrangements. When Rashel arrived several days later, any fantasies she'd had of a lovely wedding ceremony in a romantic rural village were dashed. Recalling the trip a few days later in a diary entry of February 24, she wrote:

> The trip to Tolochin . . . Jewish cab drivers, covered with snow, and arriving in a dreary place, pitiful Jewish village, Jewish children in shabby clothes, squalid Jewish tavern, muddy yards, pigs, a smell of stuffed fish—a Jewish ghetto that I have never seen before but felt

connected to. I was forced to look at this Jewish ghetto at the very moment that I have decided to renounce my Jewishness forever . . .

They quickly proceeded to the conversion and wedding ceremony:

And then there was an old priest, tall, thin, nice, with a kind face and eyes as blue and clear as a child's. There was a room with a low wooden ceiling, wide white-tiled stove, stone walls . . . A primitive statuette of the Madonna with its veil spotted by the remains of dead flies.

We genuflected and an old priest pronounced eternal and sacred words about the Trinity, the union of Father, Son, and Holy Spirit . . . Then there was the marriage ceremony, and the priest intoned the words . . . "In joy and in sorrow, with faith in God in this life and the next . . ." Then I sobbed on the priest's shoulder and he patted my head tenderly. He consoled us and smiled to me and to Stas [Onissim]. And the priest's sister made us some coffee.

The conversion and the dreary marriage ceremony had taken place on Friday, February 18, 1900, without family and friends. But everything had gone according to plan. One can almost imagine the simple storyline "and so they lived happily ever after." But the story of Rashel and Onissim was anything but simple, and the future belied any happily-ever-after. Despite the beginnings of their own relationship, it seems likely that neither of them anticipated the arrival of Lea into the story.

Ysaÿe

Lea returned home to Odessa immediately after her fateful meeting with Onissim and there spent the summer of 1903. Before leaving Moscow, she shared her hope that she might one day take up the invitation that her idol, Eugène Ysaÿe, had extended to her when he was in Moscow: to come to Belgium for advanced study. Among other incentives was her desire to study César Franck's sonata with the master for whom it had been written. Money was the problem. Lea felt confident that she could support herself in Moscow. She had started taking private students soon after her fourteenth birthday and had established a following among ambitious parents. She also had some important concert work lined up, including her first tour of Germany, Poland, and France, playing with orchestras led by Safonov, Arthur Nikisch, and other well-known conductors.[5] But though the tour would be prestigious, it would not be lucrative—fees were quite modest for an unknown talent. On the other hand, the spring concert evening had accomplished its goal. Several influential people had heard her, been impressed, and offered help. Onissim Goldovsky was one of them.

Lea's goal, she told her parents, was to be in a position to take summer 1904 off so she could travel abroad to see Ysaÿe. She would not ask them for their help even though Gitel and Saul's circumstances had improved. They had moved to a larger apartment at 96 Novoselskogo Street in Odessa[6] and had hired a maid. But there was little to spare, especially since Saul had given up teaching and relied on Gitel even for his cigarette money and his charity gifts to beggars. So Lea mentioned that she had asked her Moscow friends to take up her cause and arrange a formal concert for her in the fall. Hopefully, enough additional money could be earned for the trip to Belgium. In the meanwhile, the current summer at home was spent working with her father on a new concerto by Julius Conus that was still in manuscript. Perhaps she could attract attention by introducing Conus's new material before others got hold of it.

Lea recalled the summer of 1903 as one of the happier ones in her life. She hadn't realized how much she missed her father. Despite all the great teaching she had received, she loved working with Saul. "My father was really happy having me again with him," she wrote. "I played a great deal for him, and musically he was still able to help me." About her mother she said not a word. Gitel had played such a prominent role in her life for so long. But, with greater and greater independence as she became a young woman, Lea may have felt that Gitel was no longer such a necessary part of the story. In this, she turned out to be wrong.

Returning to Moscow in the fall, Lea took a room in a boardinghouse that catered to young musicians. There she met another female prodigy from Odessa who had just graduated from the conservatory, a pianist by the name of Esther Chernetskaya, who had won a Silver Medal. When Saul and Gitel learned that Lea was well situated and living with another female, they began to speculate about whether it might be possible to get their second daughter, Anna, to Moscow, where she could also study at the conservatory. Despite Anna's laziness as a young child, she had become serious and had advanced so quickly through the ranks of the Odessa Conservatory that her teachers considered her ready for Moscow. Once again, Safonov, director of the conservatory (who had also been Chernetskaya's teacher and loved the idea of an all-female piano trio composed of Esther, Lea, and Anna), made the arrangements. Saul and Gitel had now accomplished what few if any in Odessa had ever done—not only had they managed to get two children to Moscow, but, more miraculously, both of those children had been girls. For most young women, the only permanent route from Odessa to Moscow was via marriage. Saul and Gitel's daughters made it on talent. Nor did Anna have any less sensational a conservatory career than Lea. In 1908, she too would win the coveted Gold Medal, making Saul and Gitel local celebrities in the tightly knit Odessa Jewish community and, incidentally, boosting Gitel's piano business.

With two children in Moscow, the focus was now on the girls' brother, Pierre. He had worked hard in Odessa and eventually impressed Safonov sufficiently to be admitted to the conservatory as well. But Pierre's talent was more conventional, and his development took longer than that of his "prodigy" sisters. There is a certain irony in the fact that, years later, Pierre's musical career equaled and even overshadowed Lea's, yet his abilities were always considered less than his sisters'. While Anna had been considered lazy as a child when she resisted practice and hard work, Pierre (the boy child) was given credit for his "joie de vivre" and his interest in girls sometimes was given as the explanation for his slower success. A more likely explanation was that throughout his life (and even when I knew him as an established concert artist) he hated to practice. In 1979, when Lea's son Boris wrote his autobiography, he described his uncle Pierre's student days dismissively: "Being a restless adolescent with a marked taste for the fair sex, he spent as much time at the conservatory chasing girls as he did practicing on the keyboard. This proved his 'undoing'—if such it can be called—for when put to the test at the end of his conservatory years, he failed to match the superlative standard set by his two elder sisters, both of whom had been awarded the prized Gold Medal. Dyadya Petya [Uncle Pierre] had to content himself with a distinctly second-class Silver decoration."[7]

In the fall, Lea focused on the concert to raise money for her studies with Ysaÿe. She and her friends had to do everything themselves—book a suitable hall (they gambled on a large one), promote the event, sell tickets, print programs, hire ushers, buy flowers for the stage, plan social events in connection with the concert, invite critics—not to mention, for Lea, preparing the musical aspects of the concert and arranging her attire. Fortunately, Lea's Moscow circle had become large and devoted. The concert sold out quickly and, according to Lea, it was a great success. The reviews were uniformly favorable. There were fashionable gatherings afterward; Lea was feted and met important people. And she earned enough money to take the following summer off to study with Ysaÿe.

Included in Lea's paying concert work was a career-boosting invitation from the most famous Russian basso of the time, Fyodor Chaliapin. He was to become a valued colleague and close friend. At a low moment in her life after the Russian Revolution, when things seemed especially bleak, he would rescue her and use his own fame to put her career back on track. But for now, they simply enjoyed performing together. In addition, concerts were booked for Lea's "all-girl" trio, made possible by the arrival of Anna. It was a novelty ensemble that produced enough interest and concerts to ease the financial burden of another mouth to feed.

But Anna could spare only so much time for concerts. Unlike Lea, Anna was expected to attend all the required classes at the conservatory, and she had to practice and study her instrument rather than coasting on teachers' inflated opinions of her.

Lea's visit to Ysaÿe in summer 1904, her first trip to Belgium, took her farther west than she had ever been. Ysaÿe's summer retreat hosted twenty-five young violinists, among whom Lea was the youngest. Several were wealthy Americans paying exorbitant fees to study with the master. Madame Ysaÿe, the former Louise Bourdeau de Coutrai, was the woman at whose marriage

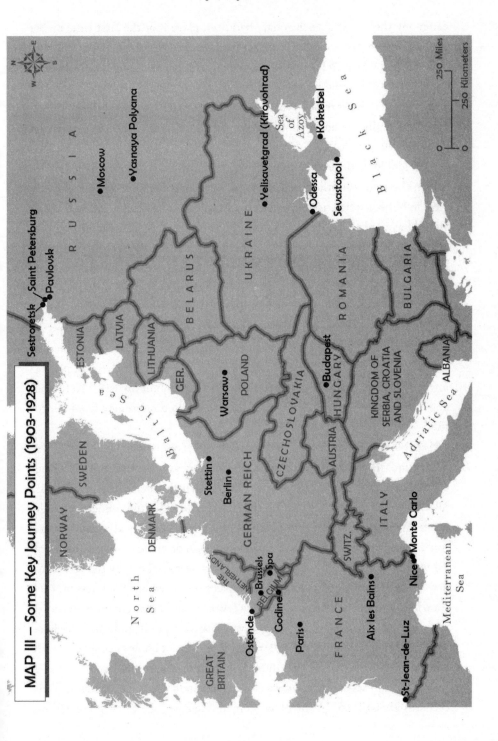

MAP III – Some Key Journey Points (1903-1928)

ceremony the César Franck sonata had been played for the first time by her husband-to-be. By now, the marriage had reached the stage where husband and wife had very different views about many things, including which students should receive priority treatment. Ysaÿe wanted to teach the talented ones. His wife wanted to be sure he gave preference to the rich ones, according to Lea. It was generally the latter view that prevailed, for it was Madame Ysaÿe who arranged the schedule.

Lea had looked forward to meeting Madame Ysaÿe, especially given her role in the genesis of the Franck sonata. But her excitement was short-lived. Lea, to her consternation, learned that Madame Ysaÿe had decided that she would have only a single lesson during her first two weeks, something that her husband did not realize; he assumed Lea had not yet arrived. It turned out that Madame Ysaÿe was by this time a bitter woman who tended to be jealous of pretty young girls, and she had taken an instant dislike to Lea. When Lea's lesson finally rolled around, Ysaÿe asked when she had arrived and expressed surprise when he learned that she had been in town for two weeks. Why had he not seen her sooner? He told her to come back the next day, and soon the lessons became a daily occurrence, with Lea simply following the directions she received from her teacher, not his wife. To further anger the older woman, Ysaÿe told Lea he expected no money from her for the lessons.

Life became complicated. Lea was wedged between two quarreling adults. Each time she received special attention from Ysaÿe, the other pupils, especially the wealthy Americans, whom Ysaÿe took little interest in, made her life miserable—a replay of her years at the conservatory. But the connection to the master made up for everything. Amazingly, when Lea played a concerto or a sonata, Ysaÿe could simulate an entire orchestral or piano accompaniment on his violin. As she put it in her memoir: "I was overwhelmed by the way Ysaÿe played, and how he could accompany a piece on his violin. Each lesson, each time I saw him, when he used to call a few of us in to play chamber music, or when everybody came for a party, it was always a privilege to be associated with him. His personality was so striking that I do not know anyone who could compare with him . . . He was like a lion with the heart of a lamb."

It is hard to say whether he was too affectionate with Lea. Madame Ysaÿe certainly thought so. In the older woman's defense, she often protected her husband from the consequences of his instinctive generosity and willingness to engage with anyone. As Lea put it, "Many people took advantage of him. When we pupils went to hear Ysaÿe at Ostende and Spa . . . we heard the most wonderful playing imaginable. After each concert which, of course, was sold out, as once in Ostende with an audience of ten thousand, he frequently would invite fifty for supper, at least thirty-five of whom would be strangers. They just happened to come into the green room [the artist room backstage] in order to see the great man . . . and he would invite them to join us."

After six weeks, Lea was called in by Madame Ysaÿe, who told her that her husband had a weakness for attractive young women and that, for Lea's own sake, she must leave. Lea broke down and cried. Her time with the great man had been extraordinary, like nothing she had ever experienced. They had not yet studied the Franck together but he had promised that they would. She begged and pleaded with his wife, but to no avail. Madame Ysaÿe told her that she must make an excuse for leaving that would not offend her husband. So Lea went to him and said she had received a telegram saying that her father was sick and that she had to return to Russia. Ysaÿe, guessing what had really happened, was in a terrible rage. But as much as he importuned, Lea did not change her story. She left heartbroken, promising herself that she would return one day.

Two Beautiful Luboshutz Women

This story of suspicion and jealousy was to repeat itself throughout my grandmother's life. Lea was a *krasavitsa* (a remarkable beauty), so the story went, and inevitably men fell in love with her and women were jealous. Lea was always portrayed as the innocent victim. At the time, we had no photographs of my grandmother as a young woman and, by the time I knew her, she was an elderly "grand dame" with perfect manners and high moral standards. It never occurred to me to doubt what I heard, especially as I assumed Lea was the proper "widow" of a man to whom she had been happily "married."

After the fall of the Soviet Union, photographs of my grandmother and her sister as young women finally found their way to the United States. At first these photos seemed to support the stories I had heard of impassioned men and jealous women. There was a woman in the photos who was drop-dead beautiful—the Russian film star kind of beautiful. But as it turned out, it was not Lea—it was her sister, Anna. And from what I could piece together, Anna's life was rather tame by comparison to Lea's. At a young age, Anna married a successful doctor, remained married to him for decades until he died, lived comfortably in Moscow during that time, worked hard as a musician while having a family, enjoyed a successful musical career in the Soviet Union, was beloved by her musical peers, and was feted as a heroine of the Soviet Union at about the time of her eightieth birthday. No drama, as far as I could tell.

But the young Lea in the photographs was not really what one might describe as traditionally beautiful, at least to my eye. Try as I might to adjust for the decades, the most I could say about her was that she was striking. It didn't seem possible that Lea's was the kind of beauty that could have "launched a thousand ships," as the famous expression goes, at least by 21st-century standards. So my theory was that perhaps standards of beauty had changed. Lo and behold, this theory seemed to be confirmed when an article appeared in 2016 in a Russian online periodical. The title of the article, translated into English, was "The Ideal of Women's Beauty—How Has It Been Changing over One Hundred Years?"[8] And who did they use to typify female beauty in 1916? None other than my grandmother. There she was in a photograph, looking (at least to my eyes), somewhat homely in an egregiously large and ugly hat.

Did people consider Lea beautiful in those days? Rashel Khin's snide entry in her diary on May 16, 1906, about Lea was: "She looks too Jewish," referring perhaps to her ample figure and large nose. Lea's teacher, Emil Mlynarski, apparently was concerned enough about her "Jewish" appearance to suggest a name change. Wanting to portray Lea as an "international" young star for her performance with the Warsaw Philharmonic, rather than a poor Jewish girl from Odessa, he had her name changed under the publicity photograph to the less obviously Jewish Elisabella Luboshuzuvna. Years later, in an interview,[9] Mlynarski's daughter, Nela Rubinstein, also joked about Lea's rather well-endowed figure, using the French phrase "bosom du monde al balcon" (meaning literally "a bosom where the balcony is crowded" or less literally but just as caddishly "she was stacked").

As I mulled all this over, and especially when I remembered my grandmother as a musician, I found another explanation for the statements about her extraordinary beauty. It was connected with her music making. By the time I knew my grandmother, she was retired. When she began to teach me and my siblings, she hadn't touched the violin seriously for some years, and by the time I was good enough to play simple pieces with her, she had become quite deaf. Even had she wanted to, she could not have played with the sensitivity required to give me a sense of her skill in her prime. At the time, we had no recordings. Yet when my brother and I started to give concerts in our teens, she began to work with us—and especially to play regularly with him—Mozart sonatas, Beethoven sonatas, the Franck sonata. After dinner on summer evenings, she would take out her violin and play through the repertoire for violin and piano with him. I had a close-up view as she insisted that I turn the pages of the piano part so I could follow along and learn what she was trying to teach. True, she had lost much of her finger dexterity, and her intonation (the ability to play notes in tune) was way off, especially on the high notes. But as I watched and listened, I gained a sense of what had been so mesmerizing about her. With the scroll of the violin held abnormally high, forcing her head back, her eyes seemed to be focused upward as if on some distant star. Looking down from that height, her appearance, even at seventy-five, was striking. She exuded a sense of hauteur—of being untouchable, unreachable. Her haughtiness said, *I know who I am; approach me if you dare.*

Of all people, it was her rival, Rashel Khin, who captured this quality best. Yes, she knew Lea and found the younger woman, for the most part, vulgar. But in a diary entry of January 3, 1908, she admitted: "When she [Lea] is playing, there is a transformation. She turns into a real beauty." And it was precisely this quality of character and beauty that she was trying to teach us when she entreated, "Forget about the notes. Show me what you feel." As I listened to her, it was easy to imagine why men were awed—her music gave off the sense of a near-unattainable and passionate woman. Thinking about it, all the men who had fallen for her—at least the ones I knew about—were either professional musicians or men like Onissim, for whom music was central to their lives.

Domestic Problems and a Revolution

❧

It seems extraordinary to me that, after years of strenuous efforts to marry Rashel, my grandfather started pursuing another woman, my grandmother, only a few years later, though I realize it is hardly unheard of. Putting aside his motivations for a moment, the sheer complexity of what he had been through with Rashel would, one might think, justify a period of calm happiness with his new wife. And perhaps that happiness existed for a time. But after Onissim and Lea met in the spring of 1903, everything changed. Their relationship (whether sexual or not at its inception) probably began the following year, when Onissim became her devoted patron. Given the amount of time he and Rashel were spending together in connection with all of his political activity, people probably did not even notice that he was also spending time with Lea, including inviting her to his and Rashel's apartment in Moscow and to Katino, the country house that Rashel had purchased and where much of the summer was spent. Onissim often attended Lea's concerts, occasionally accompanied by his wife, and he sometimes followed her when she went on tour.

The tumultuous events of 1905 complicated everything. When revolution broke out in St. Petersburg, triggering strikes, riots, army mutinies, peasant uprisings, and pogroms across the country, Onissim and Rashel needed to make a decision about what to do. The violence persisted for months. By fall, Moscow was besieged with street violence, and in October, the battle was literally on Rashel and Onissim's doorstep. The 1905 Revolution began in

January when troops guarding the Tsar's Winter Palace in St. Petersburg fired on a crowd of unarmed protestors. Known as Bloody Sunday, the massacre unleashed a wave of strikes and riots across the country.

That same month, Moscow's deeply conservative "metropolitan" (the title for archbishop of the Orthodox Church in the city) wrote an epistle to all believers. The epistle called upon the Orthodox faithful to repudiate the revolutionary movement and assert their loyalty to the Tsar, the church, and the Russian nation. In thinly veiled language, Metropolitan Vladimir blamed Russia's economic ills on Jews and atheist intellectuals. The epistle was read aloud in Moscow's churches on Sunday, October 17. On that day Onissim and his assistant, Akim Ginsberg, were relaxing in Onissim's study, discussing political events. Rashel was also at home. It probably never occurred to these three—people who cared deeply about the plight of Jews—that the metropolitan's anti-Semitic views were being expounded just a few steps down the street, at the venerable St. Pimen Church. A few moments later, two young brothers who spoke out against the priest were chased into the street.

As she described the events in her diary the next day, Rashel was the first to hear the commotion. Looking out of the window, she saw a frenzied mob kicking a young man on the ground, while his brother, bleeding from a deep facial wound, tried to pull him to his feet. When Rashel screamed for the crowd to stop, a shower of rocks shattered the window and crashed into the room. Rashel's son, Misha, rushed into the fray, dragging the two injured men into the house. Meeting Onissim at the front door, Rashel found him, "pale as a corpse," with the two bloodied young revolutionaries. Onissim and the servants barricaded the door with furniture. But the crowd continued to shout threats, bang on the doors, and throw rocks. Rashel wrote in her diary that "the mob was just about to burst into the house and finish us off" when the police arrived—led by a brave neighborhood cop whom Onissim had occasionally tipped. The police managed to disperse the crowd. The young men's mother arrived to take her injured sons to the hospital. And a glazier was summoned to patch up the broken windows.

Onissim and Rashel were thoroughly shaken. Too nervous to stay at home, Onissim, Rashel, Misha, and a servant left before dark to go to Rashel's sister Klara's house. Rashel recalled in her diary that Klara was ecstatic to see them, having heard a rumor that they had been killed. The next day they learned of the Tsar's October Manifesto, creating Russia's first parliament, the Duma, and granting civil and political rights to all citizens of the Russian Empire. "Oh, my God, I don't know what to begin with," Rashel wrote. "We have come through a lot of things. I am surprised my heart did not burst! A Constitution. Yes, yes! In Russia we have a Constitution signed by the emperor."

Rather than flee from danger, at first Rashel and Onissim stayed in Russia during most of 1905 and attended party meetings despite the risks. When violence came to Moscow, Rashel had, after all, shouted down an unruly mob and Onissim had rescued two young men who might otherwise have been killed. They had shown genuine bravery. But upon reflection, in the wake of this incident and with great uncertainty about what could occur next, Onissim said that they should go to Paris for a time, and Rashel agreed. Unbeknownst to her, Onissim was not only worried about Rashel with whom he lived, but he was also worried about Lea, whose actions he could not track so closely. Fortunately, Lea was planning to leave the country temporarily. Vasily Safonov, Lea's mentor from the conservatory, had once again been kind and invited her to come to Paris with him when he guest-conducted the Lamoureux Orchestra in a Sunday matinee on December 17, 1905, at the Nouveau-Théâtre at 15, rue Blanche. Lea would serve as the soloist in the Beethoven violin concerto. Now Onissim saw a way to protect both women he loved.

Onissim told Lea that she should stay with his family in Paris. Rashel was unaware of the invitation and was thus surprised and dismayed by Lea's arrival. "She [Lea] appeared in Paris and we are stuck with her. She is not spiteful but she is very sly and smooth-tongued and so very different from us. But . . . she is a pauper! It is not fair to turn our backs on her at such a difficult time and in a foreign country."[10] Of course, by this time she was much more in Onissim's eyes, but Rashel did not yet have a clue of the intensifying relationship.

Rashel generally found Lea to be a typical Odessa Jew—vulgar, loud, uneducated, though admittedly, in Lea's case, quite talented. But when it came to young attractive females, Rashel was far more distracted by another woman threatening family harmony, another Odessa-born conservatory student with whom Rashel's son Misha was infatuated—the pianist Esther

Chernetskaya (Lea's old roommate). Though Onissim dismissed the idea, Rashel was terrified that her nineteen-year-old son would do something rash, like run off and marry Esther. The woman was attractive and Rashel had to admit that, though she was uneducated and socially unacceptable (as were most Odessa Jews to an affluent Muscovite), Esther had a certain charm. This in contrast to the Luboshutz girls, Lea and Anna, who were simply "vulgar and loud."

Once Lea came to live with Onissim and Rashel in Paris, she consoled young Misha, who was heartsick over separation from his beloved Esther. According to Rashel, Lea did nothing but slander her Moscow roommate. Rashel could not decide whether to be happy at this effort to belittle Esther in Misha's eyes, or incensed at Lea's crude behavior. She became so depressed by the whole situation that she lost her appetite. At the same time, Lea asked Rashel if she might borrow some money. She told Rashel that she had not packed for a long stay and did not have enough clothing. "L. Luboshits[11] asked me to lend her twenty francs so she could purchase 'the most simple change of underwear' because she 'had nothing at all' and then instead [of buying an inexpensive pair] she showed me in wild ecstasy a pair of transparent pink panties that she bought 'for next to nothing' on sale."

Lea's Paris performance went off without a hitch. A review from the December 24, 1905, *Le Ménestral* reported that while Safonov's approach to "the Beethoven Violin Concerto was a bit lacking in energy, Mlle Luboschitz played its difficult solo parts and the long cadenza by Joachim with great accuracy, a lovely and solid technique, a pure and sober style."* Yet, Lea's delight in the review was mitigated by her worry about things in Russia. According to Rashel, "Lea began to groan about what is 'going on' in Russia."

Admittedly, things had deteriorated in Russia, and Lea had every right to be concerned. Though the Tsar had finally compromised with the

---

* Another review from *La Revue Musicale* of January 1, 1906, says almost nothing about Lea. Rather, it complains about Safonov's expansive orchestration of a Mozart serenade using sixty-five players (including eighteen violins) instead of single strings (one per part). The article then says with tongue-in-cheek French humor: "And we might have feared that the same system would have been applied to the Beethoven Violin Concerto, which came afterwards, such that Mlle Luboschitz's part would be doubled by half a dozen first violins. In fact nothing of the sort happened, and common sense thus suffered only one attack."

opposition, issuing the October Manifesto, Russia's increasingly influential radical wing was unimpressed. In November, the Bolshevik leader Vladimir Lenin returned from exile and called for an armed uprising. St. Petersburg, exhausted from months of unrest, hardly reacted. But Moscow Bolsheviks called a general strike and the city was once again engulfed in violence. The so-called Moscow Uprising lasted for almost a month and killed more than one thousand Muscovites, including hundreds of civilians. And the writer Maxim Gorky, with whom Onissim had collaborated on his publication *HELP!*,[12] was at the center of the action, supplying the rebels with money, guns, and explosives.

Rashel and Onissim, still in Paris and still playing host to Lea, learned of the tragedy on January 5 (December 23 according to the Russian old-style calendar), when they received a packet of mail, including newspapers, from home. Rashel's female companion and sometime servant/helper, Nadezhda Ivanovna Ivanovskaya (whom she referred to as Nadenka), had sent the mail. Rashel was devastated:

> In Russian newspapers there are lists of those killed, wounded, arrested, and lists of bombed houses. They have killed people who had no connection to the Revolution, they killed children. Nadenka said that Moscow is demolished. Now I know what revolution means. Chaos, blood, fratricide . . . the whole nightmare of a Civil War.

In the same entry, Rashel wrote that in spite of everything, the family would take their chances and return to Moscow. Clearly, Onissim was anxious to get back. And not a moment too soon—Lea had gotten on Rashel's last nerve:

> I am sick and tired of everything here. This Odessa violinist who is clutching at us irritates me. She is vulgar, grasping. One can stand her only when she is playing her violin with frenzy. She fawns on me, she is obsequious with Misha, she ingratiates herself with OB [Onissim]. Or suddenly she starts to cry hysterically and tell us what a miserable creature she is, what a poor background she comes from, how strongly she loves her parents, what a musical

genius her brother is—and it is all accompanied by wild gestures, tears, crying. In these moments I pity her immensely and I want to help her . . . and then to go far, far away from her.

Upon first reading this passage, I imagined Rashel was simply exaggerating and that the grandmother I had known could not possibly have been as obnoxious as the older woman had described. But I can now see it differently. Here was young Lea, for the first time living with her lover . . . and his wife. Moreover, this wife was not just any woman—it was the famous Rashel Khin, an intellectual, a successful writer, a woman who grew up among the rich and famous. She was old enough to be Lea's mother and probably treated Lea like a spoiled little ignorant girl from the provinces—all of this in front of Onissim. Is it any wonder that Lea appeared to be acting out?

The Second Love Triangle

Home once again in Moscow, life began to settle down to something approaching normality. Rashel was relieved on two counts. The streets seemed safer, and Lea was out of her hair. But from time to time, the two women would run into each other. Rashel's ambivalence toward Lea—pity, disgust, envy—surfaces off and on in her diary until eventually it evolves into sheer anger and hate. But, remarkably, the full process took more than a decade. For years, Lea was little more than an irritant and distraction, and Rashel found that she had some good qualities. On September 27, 1907, Rashel wrote about how wonderful Lea had been with her son, Misha: "Lea . . . admires his education, his intelligence, and so on. And I notice that every time that Misha appears near Lea she becomes very 'sweet' and Misha begins to joke and make witticisms." But then Rashel cannot help herself: "He doesn't understand that Lea is a cunning old fox, a real predator."

During this period, Onissim was arranging business trips that just happened to coincide with Lea's concert tours. In the same September 27 diary entry, Rashel recorded that she and Misha were seeing Onissim off on a trip to the Crimea. "By coincidence," Lea; her sister, Anna; and their pianist, Esther Chernetskaya, were on the same train going on a concert tour in Yelizavetgrad[13] and Odessa—so Onissim had decided to attend their concerts.

How could Rashel not have suspicions? In some ways, it was natural for a patron to take an interest in the individual he was supporting. Beyond that, perhaps it was Rashel's Puritanical nature. She simply could not conceive of Onissim being different from herself. While she herself had been in an adulterous relationship with him prior to their marriage, that was somehow different. She had hated her first husband, lived apart from him, and wanted a divorce. In this case she and Onissim had a loving and intense marriage. Each took interest in people outside the marriage. She loved men like Urusov and Koni as intellectual sparring partners and correspondents, but she was faithful to her husband and had no wish for intimacy beyond that. Even so, her assumption that Onissim shared these views strains credulity. He and Lea already had a child, my uncle Yuri, born on March 15, 1907.[14] Had Onissim not yet publicly acknowledged this son as his own? At first, this seemed far-fetched; thanks to Onissim's patronage, Lea had moved into a large apartment with servants to help care for the boy. But there is at least one clue that perhaps Onissim did not make a public display of his fatherhood at the time of Yuri's birth. It would have been customary for him to name his firstborn son after his deceased father, Boris Goldovsky, just as he, the firstborn son, had been named for his grandfather. But it was not until Onissim and Lea had a second son fifteen months later that Onissim chose to do so. On the other hand, cousin Sveta located a copy of Yuri's birth certificate. At least legally, Yuri was listed as the son of Onissim Goldovsky and Lea Luboshutz who were in a "civil" (гражданский) marriage.

It is true that in Rashel's mind, there was growing uncertainty. She complained on October 8, 1907, that Onissim was home so rarely that he seemed a guest in their house. A week later, she wrote about the two of them seeing Lea off on her first tour of America. Though none of the three knew it yet, Lea was already pregnant with Onissim's second child. Rashel writes: "How lucky she is! Her life, in spite of its inevitable obstacles [literally 'thorns'], is nevertheless so interesting. She is a very good violinist, but such a rude person . . ." And then Rashel admits, after watching Lea perform, she had come to regard Lea as a beautiful rival. "Lea played Tchaikovsky's 'Serenade Mèlancolique.' Her face really is quite beautiful. When I came home I cried. I feel desperate. My heart is being squeezed. It seems that nobody loves me . . ."

From the beginning of 1907 until the birth of my uncle Boris Goldovsky some eighteen months later, Rashel experienced deepening turmoil. The peaceful married life she had anticipated after her wedding to Onissim in 1900 was anything but, and she began to admit to herself that her world was tearing apart.

At the end of the year 1907, Lea discovered she was again pregnant and cut her American tour short. Whatever she may have told Rashel about her earlier-than-expected return from America, Rashel's diary entry of December 3, 1907, shows only admiration for her young rival: "Lea came from America joyful, vivid, gorgeous. . . . She is a talented, healthy young girl, who knows how to forcefully make her way. She knows the value of her talent and she knows how to make others realize it. She is brave with people. And she never misses any opportunity."

A few days later, Eugène Ysaÿe was in town. Lea was thrilled to invite Onissim and Rashel to his concert and to host them all afterward at her apartment. Rashel's warm feelings were nowhere in evidence when on December 8, she wrote in her diary, ". . . yesterday Stas [Onissim] and I were invited to Lea's to have breakfast with Ysaÿe. We were invited 'pour faire les honneurs' [to pay our respects] and to speak French. Lea and Anna were so loud that it was difficult to speak over their hubbub. Moreover, they spent so much time ingratiating themselves with Ysaÿe. It was disgusting." Many years later, returning to this page in her diary, Rashel is furious: "How unkind it was [for Onissim] to deceive me and force me to be a guest of this licentious, vile creature."

At the very end of 1907 on New Year's Eve, Lea visited Rashel and Onissim at Katino. It was the last time that she would be welcome there. Four days later, Onissim left abruptly with Lea for Moscow. He had, most conveniently, received an urgent telegram from a client.

When precisely was the veil of uncertainty lifted? This was a question my cousin, who was translating key passages in Rashel's diary, and I knew was critical to the entire story of the love triangle. Sveta dutifully trudged off to the Moscow archive again and again to review more pages of difficult-to-decipher handwriting. After weeks of searching, Sveta wrote to say that though Rashel had suspicions and people told her repeatedly of Onissim's treachery, nothing in her dated diary describes a sudden breakup with Onissim. Was something amiss in our research? How long could Onissim live a very public double life with Rashel convincing herself it wasn't so, in the face of mounting evidence and the warnings of friends? Onissim and Lea's family were requiring more of his time. "Business trips" (code for living with Lea) became so frequent that Rashel despaired. Her long solitary stays at Katino were only occasionally interrupted by Onissim's presence.

From March 18 to 26, 1909, Onissim was in London, conducting business with a client, Artyemii Ivanovich Derov. Onissim took Rashel with him, but they would have no time to resume marital intimacy. Derov, a millionaire industrialist who had discovered one of world's richest coal deposits in Ekibastuz, was eager to build railways to deliver the precious fuel to cities and industrial centers, and he needed Onissim's help in the intricate art of structuring and financing railway construction deals in tsarist Russia. Onissim was "working constantly" and he and Rashel spent little time together—she complained that there was no mutual sightseeing or recreation. Onissim was going through the motions of being a husband while extricating himself emotionally. Meanwhile, his dual lives were becoming public knowledge. Onissim and Lea entertained a great deal, and inevitably there was overlap between those who'd met Onissim and Lea as a couple and those who were friends with Rashel.

Joachim Says No

Starting in 1904, Lea's career had been on a sharp upswing. She was away from Moscow frequently, giving concerts throughout Russia and elsewhere in Europe. Though at age nineteen she was an increasingly well-established performer, she had a nagging worry that she was not fully developed as an artist, a feeling not unusual in those who have enjoyed easy success as children.

A silver *podstakannik* (tea glass holder) that Lea Luboshutz gave to Onissim Goldovsky around 1915. It was made by the German silversmith Feodor Rückert. The two young boys on the front are Lea and Onissim's sons Yuri and Boris Goldovsky. *Photo: Allan Green.*

CÉSAR FRANCK
1822-1890

ABOVE: César Franck, the Belgian composer who presented his great sonata for violin and piano to his countryman, the violinist Eugène Ysaÿe, in 1886. *Copyright © Lebrecht Music Arts/Bridgeman Images.* BELOW: The Ysaÿe brothers, Eugène (violin) and Théophile (piano) playing the Franck sonata in a painting by Servais Detilleux. *Copyright © Lebrecht Music Arts/Bridgeman Images.*

Rabbi Sergei Katzman, Lea's grandfather. He agreed to give his daughter
Katherine's (Gitel's) hand in marriage
to the violin teacher, Saul Luboshutz,
when the girl turned sixteen.

Katherine (Gitel) Katzman
Luboshutz, Lea's mother. A domi-
neering woman, she ran a piano
business and was universally
looked to as head of the family.

Saul Luboshutz, Lea's father and first violin teacher. Religious, quiet, and shy, he was adored by his children and grandchildren.

Lea with her beloved Amati violin, a gift from the Polyakov Family, circa 1907.

Title page from a German edition of the Romance by Reinhold Glière, written for Lea when she was still a conservatory student, with the dedication to her at the top. The work became popular worldwide and was a favorite encore piece by Russian violinists for decades.

RIGHT: Anna (left) and Lea Luboshutz in a publicity photo from around 1907. Anna had such a beautiful neck that people used to refer to the two women as Lea (pronounced "Lay-ah") and Shayah (which in Russian means "neck"). BELOW: Lea's gold medal graduation certificate from the Moscow Conservatory. Somehow, the family managed to carry this magnificent document from Russia to Berlin to Paris and ultimately to the United States.

ABOVE: In a characteristic pose, Anna Luboshutz looks to her older sister, Lea, for guidance and leadership. In time, Lea's extramarital relationship with Onissim would drive the sisters apart. BELOW: The marble plaque at the Moscow Conservatory with Lea and Anna's names enshrined as gold medal winners (Lea in 1904, Anna in 1909).

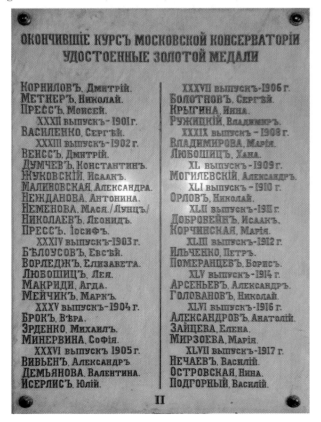

ОКОНЧИВШІЕ КУРСЪ МОСКОВСКОЙ КОНСЕРВАТОРІИ
УДОСТОЕННЫЕ ЗОЛОТОЙ МЕДАЛИ

КОРНИЛОВЪ, Дмитрій.
МЕТНЕРЪ, Николай.
ПРЕССЪ, Моисей.
   XXXII выпускъ - 1901г.
ВАСИЛЕНКО, Сергѣй.
   XXXIII выпускъ - 1902 г.
ВЕЙССЪ, Дмитрій.
ДУМЧЕВЪ, Константинъ.
ЖУКОВСКІЙ, Исаакъ.
МАЛИНОВСКАЯ, Александра.
НЕЖДАНОВА, Антонина.
НЕМЕНОВА, Мася. /Лунцъ/
НИКОЛАЕВЪ, Леонидъ.
ПРЕССЪ, Іосифъ.
   XXXIV выпускъ - 1903 г.
БѢЛОУСОВЪ, Евсѣй.
ВОРЛЕДЖЪ, Елизавета.
ЛЮБОШИЦЪ, Лея.
МАКРИДИ, Агда.
МЕЙЧИКЪ, Маркъ.
   XXXV выпускъ - 1904 г.
БРОКЪ, Вѣра.
ЭРДЕНКО, Михаилъ.
МИНЕРВИНА, Софія.
   XXXVI выпускъ 1905 г.
ВИВЬЕНЪ, Александръ.
ДЕМЬЯНОВА, Валентина.
ИСЕРЛИСЪ, Юлій.

   XXXVII выпускъ - 1906 г.
БОЛОТНОВЪ, Сергѣй.
КРЫГИНА, Инна.
РУЖИЦКІЙ, Владиміръ.
   XXXIX выпускъ - 1908 г.
ВЛАДИМИРОВА, Марія.
ЛЮБОШИЦЪ, Хана.
   XL выпускъ - 1909 г.
МОГИЛЕВСКІЙ, Александръ.
   XLI выпускъ - 1910 г.
ОРЛОВЪ, Николай.
   XLII выпускъ - 1911 г.
ДОБРОВЕЙНЪ, Исаакъ.
КОРЧИНСКАЯ, Марія.
   XLIII выпускъ - 1912 г.
ИЛЬЧЕНКО, Петръ.
ПОМЕРАНЦЕВЪ, Борисъ.
   XLV выпускъ - 1914 г.
АРСЕНЬЕВЪ, Александръ.
ГОЛОВАНОВЪ, Николай.
   XLVI выпускъ - 1916 г.
АЛЕКСАНДРОВЪ, Анатолій.
ЗАЙЦЕВА, Елена.
МИРЗОЕВА, Марія.
   XLVII выпускъ - 1917 г.
НЕЧАЕВЪ, Василій.
ОСТРОВСКАЯ, Инна.
ПОДГОРНЫЙ, Василій.

II

ABOVE: Onissim Goldovsky at about the time he met Lea for the first time. LEFT: Rashel Mironovna Khin, Onissim Goldovsky's wife. She was considered one of the great intellectuals of her day. A writer and translator of major French works, she also hosted a salon in Moscow and at her country estate.

LEFT: Lea in a publicity photo from around 1909. BELOW: Lea and Onissim's sons [Boris (left) and Yuri] around 1912. The enamel portrait on the front of the *podstakannik* was based on this photograph.

ABOVE: Katherine Luboshutz with children [Lea (left), Pierre, and Anna] and her grandchildren [Boris (left) and Yuri] around 1911. RIGHT: Onissim Goldovsky in a formal portrait.

RIGHT: Onissim Goldovsky at his most informal. According to his son Boris, "I don't recall ever having seen him dressed in anything except formal suits." BELOW: Eugène Ysaÿe, the violinist to whom the Franck sonata was dedicated. This inscribed photograph of Lea's teacher hung on her wall until the day she died.

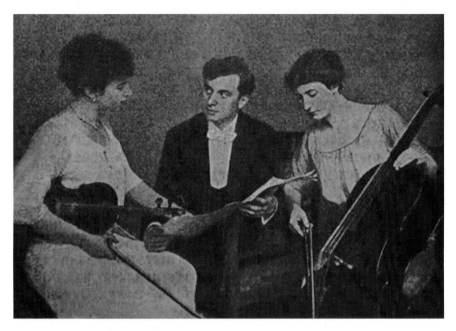

ABOVE: The Luboshutz Trio (Lea, Pierre, and Anna) in a newspaper clipping from 1913. BELOW: Onissim relaxing in his study in Lea's apartment. The giant portrait of Lea, painted by Mikhail Shemyakin, hangs on the wall to the left.

ABOVE: Anna Luboshutz and Dr. Nikolai Shereshevsky on their wedding day in 1913. BELOW: Portrait of Pierre Luboshutz by Yvonne Doguereau, a "lady friend" in Paris (1914).

ABOVE: Onissim's motorcar circa 1915. Onissim driving, Lea beside him, Pierre in back seat closest to foreground; Yuri and Boris in front of car. BELOW: Irina Goldovsky in 1922 preparing to leave Russia. Her grandmother Katherine to her right has just sewn a winter coat using upholstery fabric from the couch.

RIGHT: Yuri Goldovsky as a student at Moscow University (1923) at the age of sixteen. Such was his brilliance that he was coddled by the Soviets and enjoyed the patronage of his famous uncle, Dr. Nikolai Shereshevsky. BELOW: Irina Goldovsky (age five) in Paris. When she arrived from Moscow, Lea was shocked by her appearance and began to dress her stylishly.

ABOVE: The Nemenoff family (from right: Aaron, Marie, Mounia, and Genia). Marie's family, the Jacobses, had been furriers in Russia and had emigrated to Germany. Later, their son-in-law Aaron Nemenoff opened a shop for the family in Paris, where this photograph was taken around 1909. BELOW: Pierre Luboshutz and his second wife, Genia Nemenoff. Genia had been Pierre's piano student in Paris and became his musical partner in what became the internationally acclaimed duo-piano team Luboshutz & Nemenoff.

Lea wondered whether she should get more training. Having been frustrated in her attempts at advanced study with Ysaÿe, she thought about connecting with another of the great violinists of the time, Joseph Joachim. She especially wanted to study the Beethoven, Mendelssohn, and Brahms concertos with him.

As a twelve-year-old, Joachim had made a sensational debut as soloist in the Beethoven violin concerto, with Felix Mendelssohn conducting the orchestra. Mendelssohn was so impressed that the two performed together again, debuting Mendelssohn's new violin concerto. The composer Johannes Brahms also became close friends with Joachim and dedicated his violin concerto to the violinist, leading the orchestra with Joachim both debuting the new concerto and playing the Beethoven in the same concert. Joachim wrote his own cadenzas—or traditional solo sections, often written by an instrumentalist to show off a dazzling technique—for both. He would complain later that there was an awful lot of D major on the program, since both concertos were in the same key. Lea had been playing Joachim's cadenza to the Beethoven concerto for some time. This was something else she wanted to study with the master.

Lea was honest enough to admit in her memoir, "I think how lovely it would be if I could say, 'Lea Luboshutz, pupil of Joachim.'" She had not had an opportunity to study with Leopold Auer, who was regarded more and more as the greatest pedagogue in Russia. And pedigrees, as far as the person one studied with, counted for a lot. People might say, "She's Russian, so why didn't she study with Auer?" Studying with Auer's teacher, Joachim, would silence those critics.

Lea contacted Joachim in Berlin on one of her tours. While her memoir does not give the year, it may well have been 1904. She secured an appointment, and asked whether he would consider teaching her. "I shall never forget his figure or his face. I had an impression of great height and great benevolence and he looked like some Germanic deity with white hair, a long white beard, and wrinkles of kindness all over his face. He had extraordinary beauty of person and a wonderfully gentle face. I asked whether he would give me lessons on Brahms and Beethoven concertos.

"'First I hear you play,' he said.

"I chose a Beethoven sonata and, after he heard me, he put his arm around me and said, 'I am an old man and teaching for me is hard. You can play these concertos without my help.'" It is true he was over seventy and only had a short time to live (he died on August 15, 1907), so one can certainly take these words at face value. But Lea did not. It was the first time in her life that a great man of music had rejected her, and she took it hard. It was something she never forgot.

Even years later, she said that Joachim undoubtedly regarded her as a student whose technique required reteaching from the ground up. He simply did not approve of her training. This theory may not have been off the mark, even given how advanced she was as a player and how much success she had achieved with a technique that differed from Joachim's, one of the exemplars of a German school of violin playing.

At the time and for decades thereafter, until recordings came to produce a more uniform "international" style, there was a clear difference in approach between the leading schools of playing. Much of it focused on bow technique, which in turn affected the tone. Lea had been trained according to Ysaÿe's technique, which used the right forearm with little movement of the wrist. Ysaÿe believed that this produced the most beautiful and unified tone. Joachim, on the other hand, used a wrist technique that produced a more articulated approach, which some claimed allowed a player greater flexibility in being faithful to the composer's wishes. Critics of Joachim's technique said it produced jerkiness and less continuity (and elegance) of tone. Interestingly, Joachim's pupil, Leopold Auer, had still a third bow technique in which the player used the whole arm. That too was intended to produce a beautiful tone and in time this emphasis on beauty of sound became a hallmark of the so-called "Russian school" of violin playing. Lea may not have studied with Auer and her bow technique may have varied somewhat from his, but her playing was truly Russian when it came to sound production.

As she thought about why Joachim had rejected her, Lea may have considered another difference in her technique. To give expression to the sound, she used plenty of vibrato, or pulsating pitch. This had become more exaggerated under the influence of Eugène Ysaÿe, who used an intense vibrato. Many of the German school, including Joachim, used almost none. There are few things more disconcerting to a musician than the perceived overuse of vibrato.

Though the feelings of antipathy between these schools of playing diminished in time, they were still quite intense when I was growing up in the 1950s and 1960s. I can recall many harsh words spoken by my musician relatives about the merits (or lack thereof) of musicians from what they would refer to as "the German school." One summer during a lull in activities, I asked my grandmother whether I should attend a concert at a place called Kneisel Hall in Maine, where some well-known string instrumentalists were scheduled to play a chamber music program. The venue had been established in the little town of Blue Hill in 1902, when a violinist, Franz Kneisel, who had served as concertmaster in Berlin and Boston, turned his summer vacation home into an instructional mecca for string players. Though Kneisel had been born in Romania, his father was a German bandmaster, and he had studied in Vienna with Jakob Grün (a close colleague of Joachim)—a pedigree that would have been impressive to many, but not to my Russian family of musicians.

Though Kneisel was long dead in 1960 (he died in 1926), when I made the suggestion of going there to attend a concert, Kneisel Hall still had a reputation for being influenced by Germans and their approach to string playing. My grandmother's reaction was withering. While she was never critical of performers in public (a trait for which she was well-known and respected), she could be caustic within the family. "Why would you go there? Ugly, ugly!" When my brother was invited to perform at Kneisel Hall several years later, eyebrows were again raised. But this time there was a dilemma. We were told repeatedly never to turn down concert opportunities. So a kind of truce was arranged in our household, and it was assumed that the family's approach to playing had at last triumphed over the other camp. I am sure no one at Kneisel Hall had the least idea that their invitation had been anything but flattering.

As part of their focus on beautiful sound production, Russians had (and still have) a reputation for playing fast and loose with the composer's instructions, often allowing themselves leeway to demonstrate both virtuosity and elegance in their playing. Russians defended themselves by claiming that when players like Joachim stressed fidelity to the score over all other considerations, they were often being unmusical and lacked finesse. "Those people," I was told, "think too much." A student of the Russian violinist Efrem Zimbalist told me a story about once coming excitedly to a lesson after hearing a concert by the Polish violinist Bronislaw Huberman, who was particularly known for his interpretations of great works of the repertory based on his individualistic analyses of the musical score. But, as most people acknowledged, there was a certain roughness to his playing and his sound could hardly be described as beautiful.

"Mr. Zimbalist," the student exclaimed, "I have just heard Huberman. He is so amazing. You can tell that at every moment he is *thinking* when he plays."

Zimbalist's reply was classic and caustic. Unable to pronounce an English *th* with anything but a *t*, he said calmly, "You tink he tinks. I tink he stinks."[15]

At one point in my own musical development, I returned home from a summer spent at the Marlboro Music Festival in Vermont where the Viennese-trained pianist Rudolf Serkin presided. I spoke to my Russian musician relatives about how I now knew for the first time how really to interpret music, declaiming with the passionate intensity of an adolescent who has just come across the holy writ. After talking to Serkin and others whom I perceived to be musical gods, I had come to the conclusion that many Russian musicians were sloppy and did not study a score carefully enough. I was not smart enough to consider what it might mean to say this in front of Lea; her brother, Pierre; her musician son, Boris; and others of their camp. Basically, it was sacrilege. The anger fomenting around our dinner table was palpable. Much as they admired Serkin's playing (most of the time), they told me that his approach—putting the instructions in printed music ahead of making music "beautiful"—would, with lesser artists, produce a terrible result. Then I was told something truly radical, as far as I was concerned: Often the composer himself didn't really know what was best and at other times simply made mistakes and depended on performers to make appropriate changes.

"You mean change notes?" I asked in horror.

"Of course" was the reply. It was heresy—and I was hearing it from my own family. The fact that my own relatives would say such a thing—go against the composer's wishes—was something I kept secret for a long time.

Balancing Domesticity and Career

Once Onissim had moved Lea to a large apartment with space for children and servants, they began to establish a domestic arrangement in which they lived whenever possible as a true family. Lea could not legitimize her position by taking the Goldovsky name, but it was not unusual for female musicians to retain their maiden names as stage names, a lucky break for her socially. No one questioned the fact that she still went by the family name of Luboshutz (pronounced Luboshitz in Russian). In their apartment, they were soon entertaining lavishly and growing a family. Their first son, Yuri, was born in March 1907. Fifteen months later, on May 25, 1908,[16] Lea gave birth to a second son, Boris, named for Onissim's father. Almost nine years later on November 23, 1917,[17] came a daughter, Irina (my mother), who in later life claimed to have been "unplanned." All of the children went by the surname of Goldovsky.

During her pregnancy with Yuri, Lea had been invited to perform in America—the very tour that Rashel documented in her diary. The invitation came from Modest Altschuler, a Moscow Conservatory graduate who had emigrated to New York in 1893 and established the Russian Symphony Orchestra there in 1905. The group specialized in Russian music and featured big-name Russian soloists. Altschuler invited Lea, Alexander Scriabin (who is best known today as a composer but at that time was more famous as a pianist), and others to perform that season. Vasily Safonov, the man who had brought Lea to the Moscow Conservatory, was to conduct the orchestra (he was in New York anyway as music director of the New York Philharmonic that year, so it was quite convenient). Lea would appear as violin soloist in the Tchaikovsky concerto. Onissim urged her to accept, as this would be Lea's first concert in the United States and with very prestigious musicians. Yuri's birth was relatively easy and there were nurses to care for him while Lea was away. So despite the fact that she was a first-time, young mother, she felt few pangs upon embarking for the United States—as few Russian musicians had done by late fall 1907.

Sailing on the French liner *La Touraine*, it turned out that Fyodor Chaliapin was on board. The famous singer was also to appear in New York at the Metropolitan Opera. He had come with his wife and four-year-old son, Boris. So the crossing was replete with gossip about music and musicians, philosophy, and family. The group arrived in New York on November 10, 1907, just four days before Lea's Carnegie Hall concert with Altschuler's Russian Symphony Orchestra. It would be the inaugural concert of the organization's fifth season.

Though many people were looking forward to hearing this young female phenomenon from Russia (if one believes contemporary press accounts), Lea's family name was posing a challenge for the Americans. The ship's manifest had spelled her name Lubochitz. The October issue of the *Musical Observer*, heralding her arrival in America, spelled it Loboschiz. The *New York Times*, announcing the arrival of her ship on November 10, botched her name completely, spelling it Lubackitz. The same paper, in its review of the concert four days later, referred to her as Laya Luboshiz. For a musician trying to establish a career and a name for herself in America, this was nothing short of a disaster. Something would have to be done to make Lea's last name easier for those in Western nations to pronounce and spell. And for English speakers, that new name should avoid any scatological connotations that the actual phonetic rendering of the Russian Luboshits might suggest. Happily, by the time Lea returned to the United States some years later, she had become Lea Luboshutz.

Lea's concert at Carnegie Hall was a triumph. Eleven encores and a twenty-minute ovation, according to Lea; even allowing for exaggeration, it must have been a tremendous ego boost. Indeed, she felt quite grown up, at twenty-two years of age. But afterward Altschuler was concerned that she was too young to go around New York unescorted, and so requested that two women—Mrs. Sidney (Tessie) Prince and Mrs. Hetty Frankel—serve as minders. Their aid proved invaluable when Lea became nauseated and weak after the concert. She was pregnant (with Boris), and the women insisted that Lea forego the stress of the tour and return home. Lea reluctantly agreed.

Once home, she felt frustrated to be in such good shape instrumentally only to miss so many important performances. As luck would have it, there was to be a competition among the twenty best violinists in Moscow. To qualify, each contestant had to have won a graduation medal from the Moscow Conservatory. Lea entered her name and, as she put it somewhat dismissively in her memoir, "Since I had done almost nothing but practice in the weeks I was away I felt prepared." She won first place.

But after the trip and the competition and after the birth of her second son, Boris, Lea decided to spend less time performing and more time with her children. It was an occasion to reinvent herself once again as a happy "wife" and mother and it was a welcome change. Music had dominated her life since she was a young child, and she was excited by the novelty of a comfortable life, made possible by the apartment and domestic help that Onissim was providing. She felt inadequate in light of Onissim's great erudition. While his linguistic abilities were dazzling, she spoke only Russian, French, and Yiddish and she was culturally unsophisticated except for her music. She knew nothing of the visual arts; and when she performed at the homes of the great Russian collectors like Sergei Ivanovich Shchukin (whose palace she had appeared in when she met Onissim) and Ivan Morozov (who also had extraordinary holdings of Impressionist and early modern painters), she had no idea what to make of what she saw on the walls. She decided to undergo a program of self-improvement, studying languages, history, and literature. She sat in as her children were tutored, ostensibly to supervise the instruction. Her French improved and she became fluent in German.

She also wanted to understand Onissim's legal work and persuaded him, as much as possible, to explain to her the details of his cases. Yet it seems they never discussed politics, and Lea remained largely ignorant of this aspect of Onissim's life. Perhaps his intention was to separate the calm of domestic life from the dangers of political activism. It was also true that political activity involved his wife, Rashel, from whom he still had not separated.

During her time off, Lea began to travel for pleasure—something she had never done before. Onissim often paid for extended vacations for her and the children, which gave him time to spend with Rashel. On one of these trips, Lea took four-year-old Yuri, three-year-old Boris, and a governess to southern Europe for a two-month holiday to get away from Moscow's intense winter cold. They stayed in a little village near Monte Carlo. While the governess took the boys for long walks, Lea indulged her love of gambling. Onissim had been prescient. He knew it would be difficult to keep Lea from the gaming tables, so he gave her money in exchange for a promise that she would quit—if and when it ran out. Not only did Lea win more than she lost, she was able to add to her jewelry collection with the winnings, a fact she deliberately included in her memoir.

Lea's reinvention as an upper-class woman who had earned a life of ease and had time for an intellectual self-improvement program was short-lived. Once Onissim moved in, he became more insistent that she return to the concert stage. In public, he was still her patron, and her career was important to the way the two of them were perceived. But it was far more than that. Lea was now a high-profile artist. This was not the time for her to rest on her laurels. Furthermore, Onissim loved her for her music and he had always imagined a home with music playing constantly. If he had wanted a life companion who was his intellectual equal and who could closely track his political and legal work, he could have stayed exclusively with Rashel.

Because Onissim was teaching in these years at the university in St. Petersburg and going there on business trips, he often took Lea along. His appointment to the law faculty at the university had been made possible by his mentor, Urusov, just a few months before the older man's death in 1900. Onissim's popular but controversial lectures touched not only on the Russian legal system but also drew from the legal, scientific, and literary worlds of Western European thought—subjects that would become central to his writing and political activity. In addition to his teaching, his legal practice required him to meet with wealthy St. Petersburg investors, who he represented in railway deals.

Lea loved these excursions and described the train trips, including the quality of the linens and goose-down pillows in the lavishly appointed first-class sleeper car and the large suite permanently reserved for Onissim at the Hotel Europa. Initially, Lea used these times to further her self-improvement program by going to museums, especially the Hermitage. But Onissim made clear that she too should treat these times as opportunities for developing her career. He introduced her to the distinguished Petersburg journalist Arkady Veniaminovich Rumanov,[18] who was following not only her career but those of her younger siblings. There still exist several letters she wrote to him in these years, including those from cities where she was touring.

When Lea took up the violin in earnest again, she was surprised to discover that Onissim could be a taskmaster, making sure, like a scolding parent, she put in her practice hours. She had once told him that she needed to practice four hours a day to be in concert shape. This became the minimum requirement. When Onissim came home in the evening, his first question was, "Leitchka, did you practice your four hours today?" If she confessed to only practicing a couple of hours, he was displeased, treating her like a child. Gradually, she got the message and worked as hard as she had in the old days. To Onissim's great joy, the house was again filled with music—not only Lea's practicing but also the rehearsals of the Luboshutz trio—Lea, Anna, and Pierre. The previous all-female trio ensemble had disbanded upon Esther Chernetskya's marriage and it seemed only natural for Pierre to take her place.

There was another reason why Lea's career was important to Onissim. Her constant travels gave him time to spend with his wife. According to later biographical information about Lea,[19] one of her tours through Russia and Siberia included more than one hundred recitals. Other concert tours in these years included various European capitals and the Far East. She was in great demand as a soloist, often introducing new works written especially for her. At home, as a major figure in the music world, Lea was encouraged by Onissim to appear in benefit concerts. This would enhance her reputation, he explained, silence some of their critics, and he could afford to support her. He was especially concerned that she appear on behalf of Jewish causes, for which he insisted that she never accept a fee, just as he had never done in his legal work. This, too, was important for him among his Jewish friends and family who had never forgiven him for his conversion to Christianity. He could claim that his patronage of the young superstar was a boon to those of the Jewish faith.

Lea's solo career, as extensive as it was, was only a part of what made her unusually successful. The Luboshutz Trio quickly became nationally prominent and popular. It did not hurt that the highly respected violinist and pedagogue, Pyotr Solomonovich Stolyarsky, told people he could not name a better ensemble—that this one was truly the very best, achieving "inaccessible heights."[20] According to a September 1913 magazine article,[21] the trio was touring to nearly fifty cities during a five-month period in 1913–1914; the following map gives some idea of their placement. Even by 21st-century standards, this would be a strenuous and difficult tour, especially with so much of it coming in the middle of winter. In 1913, it seems hardly possible that the three siblings could have played so many concerts and covered so much territory (almost eighteen hundred miles north to south and a similar distance east to west) in such a concentrated period of time.

The September 1913 article included one other point that must have made Lea even more beloved: "One cannot but mention the generosity that this talented violinist has always shown toward the many charity societies in Moscow in taking part in concerts for their benefit."[22] Such behavior was only to be expected of a great artist—especially one under the patronage of Onissim Goldovsky.

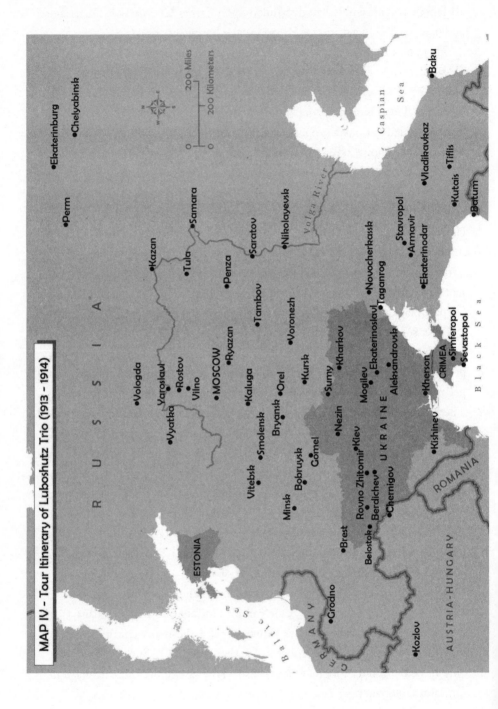

MAP IV - Tour Itinerary of Luboshutz Trio (1913 - 1914)

The Jewish Historian

⁙

The stories I heard about the Goldovsky and Luboshutz families often mentioned how fortunate they had been as Jews in Russia to survive peacefully in
the provinces and, later, to live in Moscow free of persecution and fear. My
impression had always been that while anti-Semitism was a constant threat—as
it was almost everywhere in the world to some degree at this time—if Jews
were careful, successful, or both, life in Russia could be relatively trouble-free.
As I finally discovered, nothing was further from the truth.

Onissim Goldovsky's conversion had been an act of convenience designed
to let him marry Rashel. Accounts of the conversion often stated that Onissim
never used his change of religion to hide his Jewish roots and that he remained
steadfastly active in Jewish causes. But until I found a mention in a bibliography, I did not realize that he had written about the oppression of Jews in the
Russian Empire at a time when to do so put him at considerable risk. Onissim's
article "The Jews of Moscow" was included in a collection called *Jewish Moscow*
published in 1906—not in Russia but in Berlin, presumably because it would
have been blocked by the censors in Moscow. Onissim's article was reprinted
in the widely circulated Russian political journal *Byloe* in September 1907.
While the book covered centuries of history, Onissim's contribution focused
on a recent event—the expulsion of the Jews from Moscow. Onissim himself
would have been living in Moscow in April 1891 when Grand Duke Sergei
Alexandrovich, the governor of Moscow and brother of the Tsar, suddenly
ordered the police to round up Jewish artisans and merchants in Moscow and
put them on trains to the Pale of Settlement.[23]

Discovering this article felt to me like a striking coincidence. My father's
first cousin Edwin Wolf II had published his classic *History of the Jews of
Philadelphia* when I was old enough to remember it as an important family
event.[24] Now I was learning that my mother's father had done the same for
the Jews of the city in which he lived.

Like much of his writing, Onissim's "The Jews of Moscow" is very scholarly,
a contrast to the polemical political writing at the time. Onissim made a point

of always loading his work with specific examples and evidence. Although he was clearly angry and distressed by the terrible event he described, Onissim nonetheless wrote like a lawyer, resting his case on solid facts. Somehow he was able to get access to secret official documents about the government's policies toward Jews, which he cited at length. The regime's persecution of the Jews had been covered up by censorship or by the outright lies of senior officials, but Onissim's work tore down the official veil of secrecy.

During the century following the establishment of the Pale of Settlement in 1791, Jewish residency rules had been gradually relaxed, and exemptions were carved out for "valuable" Jews. Starting under Tsar Nicholas I (ruled 1825–1855), Jewish doctors were allowed to move out of the Pale, and out-standing students were allowed to enroll in Russian secondary schools and universities. This seems to have been the route that Onissim took to Moscow. Merchants who ran successful businesses in the Pale for at least five years and who achieved First Guild status were also allowed to move out of the Pale into other parts of Russia—hence, the Moscow residency of Lea's aunt and uncle. If a Jewish merchant managed to keep his First Guild status for twenty-five years, he could become a full-fledged Russian citizen and pass on his residency rights to his descendants, as was the case with Rashel's family.

The largest migration out of the Pale was brought about by Tsar Alexander II. In 1865, Alexander opened Russian residency to two social classes—the *remeslenniki* and clerks. *Remeslenniki* is usually translated as "artisans," but the term is much broader, embracing anyone who was not a university graduate but who had some kind of specialized skill or training *(see table)*. Tailors, midwives, skilled factory workers, silversmiths, distillers, and flour millers were all *remeslenniki* and thus eligible to leave the Pale under this reform. Alexander's reforms allowed merchants who left the Pale to take with them as many Jewish clerks as they needed. Clerks were white-collar workers such as accountants, bookkeepers, managers, specialized traders, and salespeople.

Approximately one million Jews left the Pale following Alexander's reforms, settling in Moscow, St. Petersburg, Nizhny Novgorod, and other Russian cities. More than 70 percent of them were *remeslenniki* and most of the rest were clerks. Merchants and university graduates were a tiny group, never numbering more than a few thousand throughout Russia.

Remeslenniki Professions Typically Held by Jews

Tailors	Photographers
Dressmakers	Lithographers
Midwives	Glaziers
Skilled factory workers	Watchmakers
Railway engineers	Silversmiths
Mechanics	Street pavers
Cooks	Flour millers
Bakers	Shoemakers
Butchers	Distillers
Vinegar makers	Publicans

I have already described the political repression that swept Russia under Tsar Alexander III and his successor, Nicholas II, underpinned by the xenophobic policy of "Russia for the Russians." Alexander and Nicholas were not solely responsible for codified anti-Semitism—both were probably more oblivious and incompetent than venal. But they surrounded themselves with some of Russia's most fanatical reactionaries.

The lowest point in this dismal period came in early 1891 with the expulsion of Jews from Moscow. Onissim was in his mid-twenties, living in central Moscow and learning the legal profession under the tutelage of Urusov. While Onissim was not directly affected, his article provides a detailed and heart-wrenching description of exactly what happened.

In February 1891, Grand Duke Sergei Alexandrovich was appointed governor-general of Moscow. To welcome him, Moscow's police chief arranged an especially vicious roundup of "illegal" Jews. In the middle of a freezing night in March, Cossack horsemen, under the command of Russian police officers, surrounded a poor Jewish neighborhood called Zaryadye, a stone's throw from the Kremlin. House-by-house document checks were conducted and approximately seven hundred men, women, and children were carted off to Moscow's transit prison, an infamous establishment where hardened criminals were held to await transportation to Siberia.

On April 9–10, the first days of Passover, a worse blow fell. An imperial decree stripped the *remeslenniki* and clerks of their right to live in Moscow. Approximately twenty-eight thousand Jews living legally in the city, many for decades, were given deadlines ranging from three to twelve months to leave. Within that time, they were expected to sell their belongings, wind down their businesses, and set out with their families on the five-hundred-mile trip to the Pale of Settlement. Anyone who missed the deadline was considered "illegal" and risked arrest and forcible deportation on the transport trains.

As Onissim recalled in his article, the local police enforced the new rules with terrible vigor. They barely differentiated between "legal" and "illegal" Jews, rounding up whole communities and deporting them en masse. Babies, young children, pregnant women, the disabled, and the ill were loaded onto the transport trains without mercy. According to Onissim's article, an order was issued to postpone this deportation but it was intentionally held back until after the trains had departed.

The most dreaded aspect of the deportations was the *etap* (этап). There is no simple translation of the word. It denotes a group of prisoners who are being moved on foot, usually tied together or manacled. In tsarist Russia, this was a common way of moving criminals from one prison to another or to the train station for exile to Siberia. When a transport train was ready to take Jews to the Pale, they were marched to the train station in *etaps*. Onissim's article cites evidence from official documents confirming the use of these techniques.

The expulsions continued until about 1895, when only a handful of Jews were left in Moscow, and during 1891 and 1892 similar expulsions were carried out in St. Petersburg, Kiev, Kaluga, Podolsk, Ryazan, Riga, Tomsk, Tiumen, and Liepaja. Historians estimate that between 300,000 and 400,000 Jews were deported to the Pale of Settlement during this period.

Like all Jewish catastrophes, this one somehow resulted in a new strain of Jewish humor that was quickly embraced by Jew and Gentile alike. Rashel's great friend, the jurist Anatoli Koni, recounted one of these jokes to Rashel and Onissim:

A Russian, an Englishman, and a Jew are talking politics. They are dreaming about catching Germany's Kaiser Wilhelm and making him a prisoner.

"I will break his bones," said the Russian.

"I will put him in the pillory and let everyone beat him," said the Englishman.

Said the Jew: "I would not beat him. I would give him my passport and send him to Russia."[25]

What did all these events mean for Onissim and his family? In principle, Onissim was protected from expulsion by his status as a university graduate and lawyer and, later, by his conversion to Christianity. But then in 1893, the Minister of Justice announced that no more "non-Christians" would be admitted to the legal bar without special permission. In Odessa, all practicing Jewish lawyers were promptly disbarred. Additionally, the Russian government was less enthusiastic about Jewish converts than it had been under earlier regimes. For centuries, the government had encouraged conversion to Orthodoxy. The process was simple, and converts became full-fledged members of the Russian Orthodox community. But in 1890, it was announced that converts would still be considered Jewish for the purpose of school and university quotas. The conversion process was made more difficult, requiring a six-month waiting period during which the church examined the candidate's intentions and qualifications.

The handful of Jews who managed to stay in Moscow found it increasingly difficult to practice their religion or even survive in what the Russian Orthodox referred to as their Holy City. The Moscow Synagogue was closed in 1890. All of the rabbis and kosher butchers in Moscow were expelled at the same time. In the summer of 1892, the city government closed all Moscow hospitals to Jews.

Popular anti-Semitism, encouraged by official anti-Jewish policies and racist newspapers like *Novoye Vremya*, became ubiquitous throughout Russia. Street thugs targeted anyone with Jewish features or a Jewish name. Jews were routinely forced to give up their seats on buses and trams to non-Jews. Gangs put out the word that Jews should tip their hats to military officers and civil servants, and they stood ready to assault anyone who failed to do so.

Onissim exposed all of this in his extraordinary history. His work was something new in Russia—not a collection of stories and poems and drawings like 1901's *HELP!*, but a well-researched work of history, an exposé based on secret documents. It was also a remarkable act of political courage. Not a single descendent in Onissim's children's generation (or mine) learned about the book for more than one hundred years.

Ysaÿe Again and a Full Family Life

One summer between 1910 and 1913 (accounts of the exact date vary), Lea had a second opportunity to study with her idol, Eugène Ysaÿe. Somehow, Lea and Madame Ysaÿe got over their antipathy, perhaps because Lea traveled as a "married woman"—her identity when she traveled outside of Russia. Her early memoir states: "What a glorious time we had! I was much older and in love with my husband . . ." She also mentions that Ysaÿe was in love with a pupil of his, whom he later married, so perhaps Madame Ysaÿe saw Lea as the lesser threat. Whatever the case, at long last, she had a chance to study the Franck sonata with the man for whom it was written.

Ysaÿe was always complimentary and she had no way of knowing what he really thought. But several years later, Lea learned that she had made a very positive impression. She was scheduled to perform in Brussels. Ysaÿe told her he was coming to the performance and that he had a surprise for her. He had asked Queen Elisabeth of Belgium, his pupil and a very competent violinist, to be present at the concert. "After the concert," Lea wrote, "I was introduced and invited to the Palace for several occasions." Indeed, some years later when she was living in Europe, she played on multiple occasions for the Queen.

Onissim was mostly living with Lea at this point, and while he was, from all reports, a happy man, his children remember their father as somewhat daunting. From his son Boris's autobiography: "With his graying beard, thinning hair, and piercing dark eyes, my father . . . was a most imposing figure. I don't recall ever having seen him dressed in anything except formal suits that looked like morning coats . . . There was something magisterial about Father which may unwittingly have influenced my later life, for he was an erudite person with a well-stocked library who always gave the impression of having vast funds of knowledge to impart."[26]

Since music was so important to Onissim, he insisted that the boys each learn to play the piano. To him, even at their early age, their success in music was far more important than any other achievements. As Boris recalls: ". . . oddly enough, there was never any question in those early days of our following in Father's footsteps. It was taken for granted that like Mother, Aunt Anna, and Dyadya Petya [Uncle Pierre]—who gathered almost daily in our living room for their trio rehearsals—Yuri and I would be 'artists' and thus beings of a higher order."[27]

But the boys' cultural education did not end there. They were introduced to ballet (even briefly taking dance lessons) and went to operas and the theater. Friends of the family made these events special; the dinner table was replete with artist guests who appeared in the various performances. One of Boris's first exposures to opera—a field for which he would later become world famous—was a great disappointment to him. Lea's friend, the famous basso Chaliapin, was to appear as Tsar Boris Godunov in the eponymous opera and little Boris assumed that meant Chaliapin would be on stage most of the time. But the opera dragged on with no appearance of the great man, and the little boy eventually fell asleep and missed Chaliapin's appearance—probably the most famous Boris Godunov of all time! Other operas were a disappointment as well. "It struck me as being a singularly ponderous and stilted art form,"[28] Boris wrote in his autobiography, an amusing comment for the man who later became known in America as Mr. Opera.

Boris's disappointment was heightened by comparison with Moscow's theater scene, which was enjoying a golden age. Here Onissim's two lives converged, as many of the theatrical friends he had made through Rashel became dinner guests at his and Lea's apartment. Lea remembered these evenings as much more fun than the ones that involved primarily musicians. Though there were exceptions like Chaliapin, many of the musicians were more subdued and left at an early hour. The theater people stayed into the wee hours—and drank—becoming boisterous and giddy.

Onissim's devotion to the theater strongly influenced my uncle Boris. One of the frequent visitors to the house was Ivan Moskvin, an actor in Konstantin Stanislavsky's celebrated Moscow Art Theatre. Moskvin loved music, especially Bach, and often came early for dinner parties so he could listen to the young boy practice. Boris was at the time studying Bach's *Well-Tempered Clavier*, and each week he would play for Moskvin the latest prelude and fugue he was preparing for his lesson. In appreciation, Moskvin gave him tickets to the theater. "I didn't realize it at the time, but these were worth a king's ransom," Boris wrote in his autobiography.[29]

In the end, Boris did end up pursuing a career in opera, determined to make the art form more like the great theater he had witnessed as a boy. He trained singers to think and behave like actors. "Don't look at me," he shouted from the orchestra pit in rehearsals. "Look at her. She is the one you are in love with. Tell her, not me. Make it believable." Boris's stagings were famous for the believability of the dramatic action. Only a few of us knew that this derived from his earliest experiences of opera and theater as a young boy in Moscow.

Anna Emerges from Her Sister's Shadow

"Let's better begin from the very beginning," says Anna Luboshutz in an article that appeared in the Soviet Union just after her eightieth birthday. The article—written by Nina Zavadskaya—was from a magazine called *Muzykalnaya Zhizn* (*Musical Life*) and the year was 1969. For decades—ever since the mid-1930s—there had been no communication between the two sisters. Now, more than half a century later, for the first time, I could almost hear Anna—my great-aunt—speaking in her own voice.[30]

"I spent my childhood in Odessa. My father was a violinist, a music teacher who dreamed that his children one day would form a famous trio . . ." Anna recounted the part of her life I already knew from Lea's memoir—the three children of Saul and Gitel Luboshutz, their musical studies in Odessa, the discovery of Lea and her extraordinary Moscow Conservatory career, which paved the way for her siblings, Anna and Pierre. But when Anna discussed her own experiences, everything was new. This woman had remained a cipher throughout my childhood, the name Anna a virtual placeholder. No one I knew had spoken to her since the 1920s. I never really knew what caused the break. At last, here was her story.

At seventeen, Anna joined Alfred von Glehn's cello class at the Moscow Conservatory in fall 1904. She also studied piano with Dmitri Veiss. Although she was recognized first and foremost as a cellist, her piano playing was good enough that she accompanied some of the great artists of the day. In the article, she says she once played the piano accompaniment for Eugène Ysaÿe (presumably at the time he visited Lea while concertizing in Moscow). Anna advanced quickly and, after two years, began performing in public.

"I was very lucky. I lived at my sister's apartment after she had come back from abroad . . . There, she had made friends with Eugène Ysaÿe, Pablo Casals, and other outstanding musicians; and whenever they came to Moscow, they would visit my sister's apartment on Myasnitskaya Street. Once when Pablo Casals gave performances in Moscow, he stayed the whole three days at our apartment. And he never put aside his cello—he mainly played Bach while I sat behind the door, all ears, trying not to miss a single sound."

"What amazed you about Casals?" the interviewer asked.

"Well, first of all I realized that he was so great, one could not imitate his playing. But it was his bearing, his presence that influenced me the most. So many cellists come on stage and tune the instrument, turning the pins endlessly, dampening the audience's anticipation. Casals did none of that. He came on stage, took his seat, cast an eye at the conductor, and started to play. I decided to behave the same way."

At her final graduation recital, Anna played the Dvorak cello concerto, "the very concerto I heard Casals play when he was in Moscow." This recital was similar to the event at which her sister, Lea, had triumphed five years earlier, winning the Gold Medal. Despite her excitement, a cloud hung over Anna.

Six months before, an instrument collector, Evgenii Frantsevich Vitachek, had been so taken with her playing that he had loaned her a beautiful Italian instrument, a Guadagnini. Many people today consider cellos by Guadagnini superior to those of Stradivarius. "I truly fell in love with that cello," Anna remembered. "The closer the day of my exam came, the lower my spirits, because I knew that after the concert I would have to return the instrument."

When Mikhail Ippolitov-Ivanov, the conductor of the orchestra, saw her long face, he called her into his office. In the magazine interview, Anna uses a Russian translation from Shakespeare's *Romeo and Juliet* to describe the scene. "For never was there a story of more woe . . ." When he closed the door, she burst into tears. Upon hearing the reason, Ippolitov-Ivanov promised to do everything possible to get the cello for her. And he kept his promise. At the graduation ceremony, she was rewarded not only with the Gold Medal (the first cellist ever to have been awarded one) but also with the Guadagnini. Ippolitov-Ivanov had raised a large sum of money and persuaded Vitachek to sell the instrument, which was presented to Anna. Like Lea and her Amati violin, Anna left the conservatory with a great instrument. And she, too, would see her name in gold on the wall of honor at the conservatory.

More than a century later, in 2014, I visited the wall of honor at the conservatory with Anna's great-granddaughter. Together, we paid homage both to Anna and to Lea. The gilt lettering on the marble plaques was shining as brightly as ever. There were so many names I recognized—the pianist and composer Sergei Rachmaninoff (1892), the composers Dmitri Kabalevsky (1929) and Aram Khachaturian (1934), the cellist Mstislav Rostropovich (1946), who became Anna's close friend and colleague before emigrating to the United States in 1974, and the pianist Sviatoslav Richter (1947).

That June day in 2014 that I visited the U-shaped building of the conservatory was perfect and sunny. The rose garden was in full bloom and the great statue of Tchaikovsky gazed down benevolently. I had wanted to see the hall where the competitions took place but, to my frustration, we had come on the very day that vocal competitions occupied the same room, so it was closed to visitors. As we pondered what to do, there was great applause from inside—someone had just finished their series of songs—and the doors opened for a short intermission.

Without asking anyone, I walked through the crowd, entered the hall, and sat down, taking in the beautiful venue while wondering whether someone would realize I didn't belong and toss me out. I should have known better. This wasn't some refined, uptight American classical music audience but a typically noisy, effusive group of Russians, who hugged, kissed, and shouted to one another across the room. They couldn't have cared less about a stranger in their midst. Indeed, everyone was all smiles and, perhaps because I looked like someone familiar, several people waved before the competition started up again. It was not difficult to send myself back a century and imagine what the experience must have been like for Anna and her sister. They too must have had their audience of partisans, with bouquets and bravos heaped upon them.

In addition to touring with her siblings as the Luboshutz Trio, Anna performed alone during summer seasons in Sestroretsk, Pavlovsk, Warsaw, and other cities. She was particularly fond of appearing at the grand annual benefit concerts organized by Leonid Vitalyevich Sobinov in Moscow to support needy students. The concerts were held from 1910 until 1916. "Oh, those were memorable and famous concerts!" she told the interviewer. "The Hall of Columns was crammed full. Some students could get standing room but for the most part the tickets were very expensive! As for the playbills, the most beautiful ballerinas from the Bolshoi Theatre sold the playbills at a fabulous price."

In the article, the interviewer cannot help asking Anna whether she knew Chaliapin, a name familiar to any Russian who knows even a smidgen about opera. "About a year after my graduation from the Conservatory," she said, "I visited the Koussevitzkys. Feodor Ivanovich (Chaliapin) was there with his accompanist, Feodor Feodorovich Keneman, who knew me well. During one of their conversations, Chaliapin mentioned that he needed a violinist or a cellist for the next day's concert at the Bolshoi Theatre. 'Well, here you are! Here is a cellist sitting right in front of you,' said Keneman . . . Chaliapin was surprised. But nevertheless he invited my brother [Pierre was Anna's accompanist] and me and wrote a pass for us to get backstage the next day.

"Standing on stage in the Bolshoi Theatre I peeped through a small hole in the closed curtain. The auditorium was full—even the standing room section was crowded with people. Suddenly I got cold feet and I said aloud, 'Good Lord, I am scared!' Chaliapin laughed and told me to look in the mirror!

127

'Who would dare to offend you?' He took a chair for me and carried it out on the stage himself. He addressed the audience and told them that the first Russian female cello graduate from the Musical University who had won a Gold Medal was going to perform for them . . . Everything went well and Chaliapin celebrated the triumph. Later Chaliapin engaged my sister and me to tour France. We went to France twice and performed with him in Monte Carlo and Nice."

Having read Anna's account of Chaliapin, when I visited Moscow for the first time, I was curious to see the house where Chaliapin had lived, which is now a museum. When the two ancient female guides learned that Sveta, Anna's great-granddaughter, and I were related to musicians who had performed with the great basso and rehearsed in this very house, they showed us every nook and cranny. In time, we were ushered into the beautiful music room and told to sit and listen to a remarkable historic recording of Chaliapin. I marveled not only at the great man's vocal sound, but at the warm and friendly acoustics, which Anna and Lea must have loved.

When the recording was finished, I looked more closely at the piano. The guide opened the keyboard—it was a Bechstein. To my amazement, she kept pointing at the keyboard, saying, "Play!" At first, I felt it would be a sacrilege. Then, thinking of Anna, who had probably sat with her cello less than five feet away, listening for the introduction from this very instrument, I closed my eyes and played some chords. It was the closest I would ever feel to my great-aunt.

In later life, Anna was not modest when it came to her critical reviews. In her eighties, when she was being interviewed, she recalled that they were uniformly positive and that critics commended her for her heartfelt, strong manner; style; and special artistry. An article in *Voice of Moscow* mentioned a cello competition in 1911, at which Anna ended up being part of a controversy. The writer said that Anna's playing stood out against the other participants, noting that since her previous performances, she had become more mature and had developed a distinct musical personality. When she didn't win, the *Voice of Moscow* writer was incensed, blaming the organizers of the competition and the bias of the jury, which had all been chosen by the then director of the conservatory. Happily, the controversy only enhanced Anna's reputation.

Anna's marriage to Dr. Nikolai Shereshevsky must have pleased her family, especially her parents. Here was a Jewish professional man who was well-known and well established economically, dogged by neither political controversy nor marital complications. And they were a handsome couple. Their wedding picture shows Anna, beautiful as always, with a tall, elegant, mustachioed bridegroom. Their marriage took place on August 16, 1913, and lasted until his death in 1961. Anna gave birth to twins in 1915—Nadezhda and Sergei (the latter named for Anna and Lea's grandfather, the Odessa rabbi Katzman)—and despite the economic security and relative comfort the family enjoyed, the woman whose father had once complained of her laziness continued to be a workhorse, playing concerts and touring for decades thereafter.

The Shereshevsky marriage strained the relationship between Lea and Anna and eventually severely curtailed the activities of the Luboshutz Trio, although not before the very long, strenuous tour in 1913–1914.[31] Anna must have realized that this tour would mark not only the end of the family chamber ensemble but perhaps some of the closeness she had enjoyed with her sister. After her marriage, the two women led very different lives with men whose views on domestic matters and politics were poles apart. Shereshevsky, who ran a hospital, was considered a paragon of probity. Onissim, of course, was the father of Lea's children but married to another woman, with whom he also lived and maintained a public life. And he was politically active at a time when such behavior had grown increasingly risky and could have posed dangers for other members of the family, not to mention Shereshevsky's professional position. Anna and her siblings spent less and less time together.

Against the Death Penalty

I had become so focused on trying to understand my grandfather's domestic situation between 1903 and 1907 that it came as a surprise to realize how professionally active he had been in those years, and how much time he devoted to publications related to his legal and political analysis. In 1905, two years after he met Lea, he helped to start a journal devoted to psychology and contributed to it by writing an article on the psychology of witness testimony. Drawing extensively on the research of German psychologists as well as French writers and a series of lectures he had given at St. Petersburg University, the article argued that witness testimony could be extremely unreliable as a guide to truth. The article turned out to be so influential that it was still being reprinted nearly a century later.[32]

The next year, 1906, Onissim fathered his first child, Yuri, with Lea. But this was also the year that he saw the publication of a major work, *Against the Death Penalty* (with a second edition a year later), a book for which he served as editor and contributing author. The timing of the child may have been accidental, but not so the book.

Against the Death Penalty is a collection of fifty essays, solicited by Onissim and his colleagues. Some of the contributors are Russian (including his old friend Rozanov), but many are by Western European writers, and they represent a variety of liberal and enlightened views. Onissim's own essay[33] is a tour de force—a review and discussion of the essays received from European scholars, writers, and political leaders. I was thrilled when I was finally able to track down a copy of the book.

The book was explicitly political, an attempt to persuade the new legislative assembly (the Duma), which had been permitted by the Tsar, to outlaw the death penalty. Onissim's article in particular was not intended to be scholarly, abstract, or legalistic. Designed for a popular audience, it was a simple summary of the main points of the European essays—the editors knew Duma deputies were unlikely to read the entire volume. Onissim's piece exhibited his vast knowledge and erudition, and his mastery of ideas from many places and legal traditions.

It is less clear why the editors, a group of respected legal activists, chose to focus on the death penalty. The most pressing issues facing the new Duma were land reform and rural poverty. Unemployment, too, was a daunting problem made more urgent by the soldiers demobilizing from the Russo-Japanese War. The "Jewish question" was also on the agenda, and Onissim had already written about that in his book documenting the difficult history of the Jews in Moscow.[34] However, it was typical of Onissim to see a bigger picture and, while most Russians were focused on bread-and-butter issues, Onissim was concerned about the long-term implications of executing even a few thousand prisoners.

The death penalty had been abolished for criminal offenses in Russia under Catherine the Great. But it could still be applied in political cases and its increasing use at the time may have been the key motivation for Onissim's book. According to an appendix in *Against the Death Penalty*, the ultimate punishment was used rarely throughout the 19th century—a handful of cases per year, at most. However, at the turn of the century, application of the death penalty for political crimes became common. Between 1896 and 1900, twenty-four death sentences were imposed. Between the end of 1900 and the beginning of 1905, the death penalty was imposed five times. But by the time of the Revolution of 1905, fifty-four political prisoners were on death row and, in 1906, the number rose to an astonishing thirteen hundred.

Anti–death penalty activists saw an opportunity in the first Russian Duma. Onissim explicitly states that *Against the Death Penalty* was intended to persuade Russia's newly minted parliamentarians to abolish the death penalty entirely. His efforts both succeeded and failed—succeeded when his anti–death penalty position was adopted by the Duma but failed when the Tsar proceeded to ignore the newly minted law and then dissolve the Duma itself. The regime continued to mete out death sentences as vigorously as before.

One final impression of Onissim's essay, aside from its obvious learnedness and the expansiveness of its arguments, is just how much his personality is revealed in his writing. At a time when much political writing was polemical and vitriolic, my grandfather comes across as tolerant, open-minded, and reasonable. While his disgust at the tsarist regime cannot be hidden, his writing is calm, respectful of alternative points of view, and focused on justice rather than power. He also clearly has a sense of humor, as evidenced in wry comments about the various Russian political factions.

The demands of Onissim's legal work, his writing, his political activism, his social and domestic life with Rashel, and his relationship with Lea must have been almost overwhelming. Then came news of Lea's pregnancy. Clearly, something had to give. Yet, as long as the system could hold, Onissim would soldier on.

The Unraveling

⥊

By 1909, Rashel's colleagues had begun to suggest that she needed to be more aware of her wayward husband's relationship with Lea. She was incensed, and they backed off. But in 1910, her longtime companion, Nadenka, put it a slightly different way: Onissim was not worthy of her, she said. Again, Rashel was furious. A diary entry of April 26, 1910, questions Nadenka's motives:

> I don't know why Nadenka has decided to dethrone Onissim Borisovich. She has started almost with a hunger to do so and seemingly with pleasure . . . glorifying me at the same time. It seems she has always been surprised at how two people like OB and me—who are so different in intellect, in brains, in tastes, in nobility, in our whole make-up—could have become a couple.
>
> "OB is a very good person, but you (she means me) are on such a higher plain, cleverer, deeper . . ."
>
> Listening to her words makes me feel unbearably bitter. Not because it can belittle Stas [Onissim] for me, but because it disparages Nadenka herself.

In spring 1912, it was her friend Nadine Auer's turn. Nadine had endured the humiliation of a routinely unfaithful husband of her own, the violinist Leopold Auer, and she gingerly brought up the subject of Onissim's infidelity. Rashel calmly answered that she had heard such rumors for at least three years—when she had asked Onissim about them, he told her they were untrue.

On May 4, Rashel confronted Onissim. He denied everything, calling it "vicious slander." But by May 15, 1912, something had snapped in Rashel's thinking. She wrote:

> Is it possible, is it really possible that SUCH a betrayal, such a dirty, dishonest and cynical deceit could have been done by a person who

was to my mind the most faithful and safe haven and irreproachable knight for me?

Is it possible that these eyes, these lips could lie so
monstrously . . .

Oh Lord! Can I go on living knowing all that? I convince myself
that it could not be, that I must BELIEVE, that if I don't believe
I will ruin the life of my family, there will be an abyss ahead. It's
my DUTY to believe.

But my soul is burning with doubts every minute.

At last, I thought. Here was the moment for the ultimate break. And
yet, on May 18, Rashel backtracked—once again, she blamed her so-called
friends for misleading her. She wrote in her diary that she and Onissim
were trying to put a good face on things. "I believe that we both are victims of malicious slander. I shall do everything to repair our life. But I
feel terrible. Why did Nadine alarm me? What a fatal role the Auers have
played in my life."

What did Rashel suspect at this point, and how much could she tolerate?
How could she not know that Lea's two sons, with the surname Goldovsky,
were Onissim's children? Such ignorance seems implausible in Moscow's
small intellectual and cultural milieu. But if she did know or suspect, what
was left? Was it the slander she couldn't accept or simply the accusation
that Lea had usurped her place and that Onissim had abandoned her?

Whatever it was, Onissim realized that if he wanted to save his
marriage—and obviously he did—he had to do something dramatic to
restore Rashel's faith. He agreed to spend two weeks during the summer of
1912 with Rashel at Katino and then remain there off and on for much of the
summer. "The nightmare has disappeared," she wrote. "Let's hope that it has
disappeared forever."

The following fall and winter, their old feelings for each other seemed to
have returned. On February 25, 1913, Onissim surprised Rashel by purchasing
one of the great mansions in downtown Moscow. "Stas [Onissim] came and
told me that he had bought Rafalski's house. I can't believe it! I love that house
so much! An old mansion, without pretentious decorations, on Starokonyush-
ennyi pereulok, near the Arbat. I like that location too."

Did Rashel know that the location of their new home was only a fifteen-minute walk from the apartment that Onissim shared with Lea?

Regardless, no sooner had they moved in than Rashel realized the intimate, quiet life she dreamed about with Onissim was pure fantasy. She was lonelier than ever. On April 6, 1913, she wrote:

> Who is to blame and how to change it—I don't know. The only thing I know—it has to change otherwise we will all die exhausted and embittered. One cannot live like this. It is a constant rush, a kaleidoscopic change of events that became chronically crazy. There is no doubt that the main reason is our huge expenses.

To simplify life and reduce expenses, Rashel sold Katino for nine thousand rubles. She was now committed to remaking her life in Moscow with Onissim, the man who had rescued her from a terrible marriage, who had helped raise her son, and who she claimed in her diary only a few weeks earlier was generous beyond measure. But it did not take long for Onissim to decide that Rashel needed to have a place to go for the summer. In 1914, he rented a dacha (country house) for her; and by May 14, she was already moved there. Onissim visited occasionally . . . and continued to spend time with Lea in her own dacha, just as he had when Rashel was at Katino.

Pierre Makes His Way

On the surface, no two men were more different than Onissim and Pierre, Lea's brother. Onissim was serious, learned, articulate in both the spoken word and the pen, and courageous in his actions. Pierre was funny and light-hearted. He hated school and was a self-proclaimed coward. And yet, there were many similarities. Both were pianists with an extensive knowledge of solo and chamber music literature. Though music was not Onissim's profession, he played at a professional level and admired those who played better than he. Both were passionate about music and literature. Both were attracted to beautiful women. And both enjoyed a good joke.

Indeed, despite their differences in age, economic status, and temperament, the virtual brothers-in-law respected each other and enjoyed each other's company. Pierre told me once, "Your grandfather was the most brilliant man I ever knew. He could convince anyone of anything. If it was raining outside, he could persuade you that the sun was shining." Onissim turned to Pierre for pianistic advice, especially when it came to the musical education of his two sons, both of whom Pierre taught for a while and then continued to guide after he passed them on to other teachers.

Pierre had much to thank Onissim Goldovsky for, not the least of which was his conservatory career. Both Lea and Anna had thrived in Moscow, and Pierre's acceptance to the school was essentially a fait accompli. The problem was not getting in but staying in. Pierre began his piano studies with Konstantin Igumnov in October 1907, and Rashel reported in her diary on October 24 that anti-Semitism was raising its ugly head. Pierre and twenty-two other new Jewish students were to be expelled from Moscow. But Onissim "pulled strings" and somehow Pierre remained. After graduation, based on a June 11, 1886, law, Jews who graduated from the conservatory received a permit to live and travel anywhere in the empire. From then on, Pierre seemed to lead a charmed life.

Pierre and Onissim loved jokes, the dirtier the better, and as her young sons were growing up, Lea was concerned that they might inadvertently repeat unsavory words or phrases they had overheard. It was Pierre who came up with the convenient "drink of very cold water" device. According to Lea's son Boris, when Pierre wanted to tell a very off-color joke, he would say to Boris and his brother Yuri, "Your father wants a very cold drink of water. Go to the kitchen and be sure to hold your finger under the faucet for a long, long time to make sure it is very, very cold." Boris recounted in later life that his finger would turn blue, so determined was he that the water be ice cold, and he never could figure out why the adults laughed so uproariously while he was doing so.[35]

Despite Pierre's feigning the character of an unschooled moron, he read widely and loved to discuss literature with Onissim. The educational system in Russia at that time used memorization and public speaking as a way for young people to learn great literary works. Everyone had to memorize famous passages from important novels and poems. One such passage was the scene in Tolstoy's *War and Peace* in which Prince Andrei Bolkonsky is wounded at the Battle of Austerlitz. In his seventies, Pierre could still recite the scene word for word, and he quoted it loudly to distract me when we were playing Ping-Pong, a game at which he excelled. Occasionally he would break off from the Russian to proclaim, "Your cook is goosed,"—his unique version of "your goose is cooked."

Pierre's exploits with women were legendary. Rashel Khin knew Pierre and his reputation. In early 1909, inviting him to try out a new Bechstein piano that Onissim had purchased for a thousand rubles, she referred to Pierre as *otorva*—a Russian word that combines the meaning of womanizer, libertine, and reckless daredevil.[36] Because of his exploits, Pierre would get into scrapes. His favorite story was about a woman he jilted who told him that she would shoot him and then herself at Pierre's next concert: "When you come to the funeral march in the third movement of the Chopin sonata, I will kill you. I have already purchased the gun."

Pierre did not take her seriously and forgot about the threat until he came on stage, at which point his blood ran cold. There was the young woman, sitting front row center, a large handbag in her lap. "All I could think about was her shooting me in the head. So I raised my right elbow as I played and bent my head practically to the keyboard to protect it from the bullet. I had convinced myself that the bullet would lodge in my arm and I would be saved." Pierre played through the movement, expecting a gunshot at any moment. But it never came. When the final strains of the funeral march had at last died away, the woman got up and noisily rushed out of the hall. Pierre gradually straightened, smiled, and played the final movement, the *presto*, faster and with joyful abandon. Arthur Rubinstein, a famous pianist of that era, was said to have remarked about that final movement that it was like "wind howling around the gravestones." Never had truer words been spoken.

Despite his happy-go-lucky demeanor, Pierre had inherited his mother's practicality. He realized from an early age that he would probably never be a great soloist. Even in Odessa, he sought out established performers for whom he could serve as a piano accompanist or with whom he could collaborate in chamber music ensembles. One of those performers was Pawel Kochański (later known as Paul Kochanski), an Odessa-born violinist who, like Lea, had begun studies with his father and then moved on to study with Emil Mlynarski. Of all of Mlynarski's students, Lea and Paul were almost certainly the two for whom he harbored the greatest hopes of success, and he was delighted when Pierre offered to be Paul's accompanist. The two became close friends and performed often together over many years and in many countries. It was with Kochanski that Pierre first performed the Franck sonata. It was also with Kochanski that Pierre got some of his first tastes of America and of performing in Carnegie Hall.[37]

Following one of his trips to Paris in 1914, Pierre, now in his early twenties and fancying himself something of a Lothario, brought back a portrait of himself rendered by a nineteen-year-old artist named Yvonne Doguereau. According to Pierre, Yvonne had been hopelessly in love with him. Evidence suggests that Pierre may have heard something of Yvonne's talented younger brother Paul, a pianist, and possibly even been asked by Paul's ambitious parents to hear the boy play. But the tales Pierre brought home to Moscow were not of a young male pianist but of a lovely female artist who not only signed and dated the pastel portrait but included her address, perhaps suggesting ever so subtly that Pierre might want to return and rekindle their romantic liaison. Sadly for Pierre, by the time he relocated to Paris permanently, Yvonne had decamped to the United States. And unfortunately for me, the portrait remained in Russia and when I finally learned of it a century after it had been drawn, it was much too late to ask my great uncle to recount the backstory.[38]

Pierre's decision to focus on chamber music served him well when he got to Moscow. Soon after his arrival, Lea and Anna's piano partner in the all-female trio, Esther Chernetskaya, married. At first, Lea and Anna sought another female partner. An older Odessa pianist, who had made a major sensation as a girl but had dropped out of the concert scene, was willing to help out. Her name was Rosa Isidorovna Kaufman Pasternak,[39] the wife of the portrait painter Leonid Pasternak. Onissim knew him, as it was Pasternak who offered an illustration for *HELP!*, the publication Onissim had helped assemble to aid destitute Jews. Rosa Pasternak had given birth to four children, starting with her son Boris (later the famous Nobel Prize–winning poet and novelist) in 1890. The two eldest children fell ill in early childhood, forcing Rosa to devote herself exclusively to their care. But by the time Lea and Anna approached Rosa, her children were older and healthy, and Rosa was willing to perform again. Given that chamber music was less strenuous than solo playing, what had been an all-girl trio seemed like a good fit. But Rosa's participation was brief—it turned out she had a weak heart and could not stand the strain of public concerts. Meanwhile, Pierre had already started playing with his sisters and the three of them gelled musically, as have so many other sibling ensembles. It was only a matter of time before the brother and sisters established their chamber group.

Once Pierre joined, the ensemble was rechristened the Luboshutz Trio and the two groups—one with Pierre and the other with Rosa—coexisted for a time, with Pierre going out on a long tour in 1909 but Rosa playing with Anna and Lea in Moscow. Indeed, it was Rosa and not Pierre who ended up playing at an important event in November 1910—Tolstoy's memorial service at the Moscow Art Theatre.[40] Pierre was still a student, two years short of graduation; it was only fitting that the more experienced (and far better known) Rosa should be the pianist. In addition, her husband, Leonid, had known Tolstoy—he painted him and drew his portrait numerous times, and was the first speaker at the memorial service.

The Tolstoy memorial event was a long one—the trio's involvement alone lasted almost an hour. The Art Theatre Chorus opened with a rendition of "May His Memory Live Forever." It would have been fitting for Rashel and Onissim's old friend, the theater administrator Alexander Ivanovich Sumbatov-Yuzhin, to act as master of ceremonies, but he had been dispatched to Tolstoy's estate, Yasnaya Polyana, to attend the funeral and lay a silver wreath on Tolstoy's coffin. The responsibility fell to Pasternak. Pasternak had just returned from Yasnaya Polyana, and in his speech, he not only extolled the great writer's virtues but also mentioned his recent conversations with the devoted peasants who had attended Tolstoy during his final seven days while he lay dying at a railway station at Astapovo. Two speakers followed, one of whom recited a Tolstoy short story. It was only then that Lea, Anna, and Rosa played the monumental piano trio in A Minor by Tchaikovsky subtitled "To the Memory of a Great Man" (the piece was originally dedicated to Nikolai Rubinstein). Even after their extended performance, there was still another speaker. As great as this honor must have been for the Luboshutz sisters, it is strange that no one in the family ever talked about it to my generation.

The trio's growing success bolstered Pierre's fledgling career. His connection to Onissim Goldovsky continued to be valuable. It was Onissim who introduced him to the well-known musician Serge Koussevitzky, who began providing Pierre with performance opportunities. Koussevitzky was a double bass player, a conductor, and an impresario who eventually moved to the United States to become the much-heralded music director of the Boston Symphony Orchestra. In 1902, he had married the dancer Nadezhda Galat. After only two years, he tired of her and sought a divorce to marry Natalie Ushkov, the daughter of an extremely wealthy tea merchant. Galat told Koussevitzky's lawyers that under no circumstances would she agree.

It was Onissim who ultimately persuaded her. According to Lea in later years, in addition to Onissim's extraordinary powers of persuasion, a great deal of money changed hands. Koussevitzky's gratitude was lifelong, and he performed with Pierre and presented him and his sisters in many concerts in Russia, France, and the United States. One long tour in Russia in 1915 included a trip down the Volga River on a barge, with Pierre appearing as piano soloist with Koussevitzky's orchestra and accompanying him in double bass and piano concerts. A century later, it is possible to purchase Koussevitzky and Pierre's double bass and piano recordings from the 1920s. In a biography of Pierre, written a few months after his death in 1971, the writer (his nephew Boris) claimed that Pierre had also studied conducting with Koussevitzky and served as his assistant.[41] When Koussevitzky became the head of the Boston Symphony Orchestra, he not only selected Pierre and other members of the Luboshutz family to appear as soloists, he appointed Lea's son Boris to head the Opera Department of the Berkshire Music Center at Tanglewood, the Boston Symphony's summer home, which Koussevitzky established in 1940. In doing so, he invoked his friendship and gratitude toward Boris's late father, Onissim Goldovsky.

No career choice of Pierre's turned out to have more important consequences for him, both immediately and later in his life, than his decision to become the accompanist for the American dancer Isadora Duncan. And the decision was definitely his to make—Duncan was desperate and had no alternatives. By the time she came to Russia in 1905, she was already famous, some might say infamous. She had, in her own mind, reinvented dance, seeking what she described as the divine expression of the human spirit through the medium of the body's movement. Eschewing the rigidity of ballet technique, she danced barefoot in loose-fitting tunics, using a free-flowing physical approach that became the forerunner of modern dance. Only in her music was she conservative—she loved classical works, especially those with free-flowing melodies.

Isadora's reputation was based on more than her onstage persona. Her private life was notorious, her philosophy of free love reminiscent of Rozanov's. When she arrived in Russia, a country she came to adopt as her own until well after the Revolution of 1917, she needed a pianist, one who knew the classical repertoire. But, according to her biographers, none of the established pianists was willing to play for her. People accused her of degrading the masterworks of the classical repertoire with her unseemly dancing, and pianists were unwilling to risk their reputations on her.

Pierre Luboshutz had no such qualms. As a very young pianist in Moscow, he had little reputation to lose, and he saw an opportunity to make money. He volunteered, was accepted on the spot, and played for Duncan for many years, in Russia and in Europe. Indeed, it was Duncan who eventually made it possible for Pierre to emigrate to the West after the Soviets took over, and he realized he had little future in the Russia of his youth. Pierre's association with Duncan also enhanced his reputation as a lady's man. Though Duncan never had any romantic interest in Pierre—her autobiography is replete with lists of lovers, and Pierre's name is not among them—mere association was enough.

Onissim the Mason and the End of Politics

For a long time, I thought that, given the pressures on his professional and domestic life, my grandfather had stepped back from his political activism after he returned from Paris following the Revolution of 1905. Then my cousin wrote me from Russia with some interesting news: "I have a surprise for you. Did you know your grandfather helped establish a Masonic lodge in Moscow?" She had been poking around the State Library in Moscow, chasing down references, translating letters, locating Onissim's university register, and then this fact turned up. After learning all I could about Freemasonry in Russia, I realized what had happened. Open political discussion had become too dangerous, and people like Onissim had to find a way to communicate in secret with people they trusted. Freemasonry, with its emphasis on secrecy and careful vetting of members, was the answer. If anything, Onissim was even more politically active than before.

At first things went well. But in time, as happened so often during this period in Russia, the Masons split over beliefs and tactics, and after this, Onissim's involvement in Masonic activity diminished.

Although his son Boris remembers Onissim as remaining optimistic about political change well into 1917, Rashel's diary describes Onissim as falling into periods of exhaustion and despair over the deteriorating political situation. His sense of purpose had always been rooted in his work toward a more just society. Now his aspirations were being slowly but inexorably destroyed by extremism both on the right and left. The dissolution of the Duma (the legislative body that was to herald the change to a more representative form of government), the failure to abolish the death penalty, and the collapse of his Kadet Party were terrible blows. It seemed there was no longer a place for thoughtful liberals in Russia.

But few events felt more devastating to Onissim than the arrest of his friend Aleksei Aleksandrovich Lopukhin in February 1909 and the man's ultimate fate. Onissim and Lopukhin had been law students together at Moscow University, and Lopukhin had married Ekaterina Urusov—a cousin of Onissim's mentor, Alexander Urusov, and sister of his fellow Mason Prince Sergei Urusov. Like Onissim, Aleksei Lopukhin was committed to the rule of law, believing that the keys to reform in Russia were equal justice and limited state power.

While Onissim was a specialist in civil law, Lopukhin focused on criminal law. When cases demanded both types of expertise—as they often did—Onissim and Lopukhin worked together. United by a shared philosophy and common business interests, these two famous lawyers also maintained a close friendship. Both believed that change in Russia should come about by making major reforms in existing institutions. In Lopukhin's case, neither money nor prestige motivated him—he had no need for either. It was his conviction that appropriate reform could only come about if leaders from his background and social circle worked assiduously for it. As a result, he took on a very difficult job—head of the Russian police—between 1903 and 1905, a time of extreme revolutionary foment. It was this job that eventually landed him in serious trouble years later.

The tale is typically Russian in its involuted complexity, but the first spark that ignited this tinderbox came with the assassination of two government officials, Interior Minister Vyacheslav von Plehve and the governor of Moscow, Grand Duke Sergei Alexandrovich. Unfortunately, their deaths occurred under Lopukhin's watch as chief of Russia's police at a time of increased political violence. Lopukhin was told to do whatever was necessary to root out the radical element—legally or otherwise.

Lopukhin did not believe in extralegal justice and to complicate matters, he was trying, unsuccessfully, to rein in police abuses, weed out anti-Semites, and prevent pogroms. His appeals were ignored. One of the things he had tried to do was fire a man by the name of Yevno Azef, who worked clandestinely for the department and served as a spy. Lopukhin felt Azef was an especially nasty agent and worried that the man was too erratic. However, higher-ups in the Interior Ministry protected their agent. After eighteen frustrating months in office, Lopukhin resigned and returned to his law practice.

In 1908, a police officer from Warsaw revealed information about Azef the spy to Vladimir Burtsev, a journalist for the liberal journal *Byloe*. Yevno Azef had been hired while Lopukhin was heading the police, he said, ostensibly working for them. But Azef was actually a double agent, the source claimed. It was Azef who had been behind the assassinations and, thanks to these successes, he was now in charge of the terrorist wing of the Social Revolutionary Party. Azef's ultimate ambition, the officer said, was to kill the Tsar.

Burtsev did not publish anything right away—he held his fire until he could confront Lopukhin. As fate would have it, soon after, he found Lopukhin on a train, traveling to meet Onissim, who had summoned him to help with an urgent railway deal. The reporter confronted the startled former police chief, demanding to know if a man named Azef had worked for the secret police while Lopukhin was in charge. Did he know that Azef was a double agent? Lopukhin recognized the name instantly, of course. According to some versions of the story, he actually admitted that Azef was a police agent; in other versions, the look on his face revealed all.

It took Lopukhin a few weeks to grasp the full implications of what had occurred. Burtsev went straight to Paris to warn the exiled leaders of the Social Revolutionary (SR) Party that Azef was a spy, and began pressing Lopukhin to travel to Paris personally to confirm the story to the skeptical revolutionaries. On the other side, a top secret police officer and, a day later, Azef himself showed up at Lopukhin's St. Petersburg apartment threatening violence unless Lopukhin denied any association between the police and himself.

By December 1908, a desperate Lopukhin fled St. Petersburg for the refuge of Onissim's home in Moscow. There, he told Onissim the whole story and the two talked through the dilemma. On the one hand, Azef had to be stopped, especially if he intended to kill the Tsar. But there was no proof he was a double agent, and if Lopukhin confirmed to the Social Revolutionaries that Azef was working for the government, the spy would probably be executed. Onissim advised making a decision soon. As long as Burtsev's story was neither confirmed nor denied, it was Lopukhin's life that was in danger.

No one knows exactly what path Lopukhin chose, but the SR leadership announced on December 26 that it had sufficient evidence to condemn Azef as a traitor to the revolutionary cause and expel him from the party. Azef narrowly avoided execution by escaping to Germany. Therefore, it was not he but rather Lopukhin who faced the punishment. In February 1909, he was arrested, accused of treason, and of revealing state secrets. Onissim and Prince Sergei Urusov both testified in Lopukhin's defense, but the result was a search of Onissim and Rashel's apartment by government authorities. A day after the trial ended, the police arrived after midnight and began looking for incriminating documents. The search lasted several hours and was significant enough that it was reported in the February 22,

1909, issue of *Russkoe slovo*. The article suggests that though nothing incriminating was found, certain banned books were removed (a fact Rashel disputes in her diary).

On April 30, Lopukhin was pronounced guilty of treason. Rashel wrote: "[Lopukhin] was sentenced to five years of penal servitude . . . Stas [Onissim] came in the morning and he told me that it had not been a trial, it had been a massacre, a nightmare, a most cynical violation of the Law. Oh, God, how terrible!" Another good man ruined.

A Fiftieth Birthday and a Sad Ending

On January 6, 1915, Onissim turned fifty, and Rashel threw him a big party. But his heart wasn't in it, and it was not a success. Less than a month later, on February 1, Lea's old roommate and Misha's old flame Esther Chernetskaya, paid a call on Rashel and Onissim. Now married and a respected pianist and teacher, Esther wanted to visit her old friends who had been so generous to her when she had been a student. Onissim asked her to play. As Rashel wrote the next day in her diary: "[Esther] played the piano for the whole evening and while listening to her music I thought about the Fata Morgana [mirage] of my life. Suddenly I got very upset. I went to OB [Onissim] with the silly hope that he would console me. Again and again I realize how merciless generous people can be when they have decided that all their actions are pure and irreproachable." Many years later she would add to this entry: "Now I know why he was so terrible to me." His emotional loyalties were now entirely with Lea.

By this time, Lea's two boys were seven and six years old, and Onissim's life was increasingly complicated. Lea must have known the details of Onissim's continuing relationship with Rashel, though nothing is revealed in Lea's memoir. But my sense is that Onissim had been clear from the outset about the "arrangement," and that Lea had agreed. It was probably kept from their children, at least for a time. My mother, born in 1917, claimed that the first she heard the name "Rashel Khin" was when Carole Balin's biography was published in 2000—a remarkable fact, if true.[42] As for my uncles (nine and ten years older than my mother, respectively), I am less sure what they knew.

I also wonder about the reaction of Lea's family. From what little we know of their attitude toward their eldest child, Lea could do no wrong. For her mother, Gitel, differences in age, social considerations, and religion probably counted little in her calculations. She had fought hard to lift the family out of poverty. Onissim was rich, and his patronage had already made an enormous difference in Lea's life. As far as Lea's career was concerned, on balance Onissim's assistance had been a positive. His wealth and influence counted for a great deal. That point of view was part and parcel of who Gitel was and what she believed. Even a generation later, Gitel, now in America, approved a marriage proposal made to her fifteen-year-old granddaughter (Lea and Onissim's daughter, Irina—my mother) by a wealthy Philadelphia businessman. Irina married a year later at age sixteen, the same age as Gitel had been for her own nuptials.

We do know that Anna Luboshutz disapproved of Lea's lifestyle. While still a student, Anna had benefited from Onissim's patronage as well. But she began to lose patience when she was dragooned into deceiving Rashel about Lea's and Onissim's "coincidental" trip to Crimea in 1907. Things only deteriorated from there and after Anna's marriage; her husband strongly objected to Lea and Onissim's "arrangement." Not only did it compromise Lea's reputation, it was potentially bad for Anna's as well.

In 1915, Anna gave birth to twins. Now a mother herself, she became increasingly concerned for Lea and Onissim's children, and over the years she conveyed her disapproval to her family. Many decades later, Anna's daughter, Nadezhda, well into her seventies, spoke about Lea at a family gathering in the 1990s. The recollections of her mother's words were still fresh. "Onissim was a great divorce lawyer without a divorce." The words were patterned on the Russian expression "Сапожник без сапог" (he is a boot maker without boots), or the English expression "the cobbler's children have no shoes." If Onissim had wanted a divorce in order to lead a proper life, implied Anna's daughter, he was certainly smart enough to figure out how to get one. To Anna, Lea's situation was inappropriate and absurd. This attitude led to a rift between the sisters that would have serious consequences in their later lives.

In the end, Rashel did finally acknowledge what had occurred—that Onissim was living dual lives and that she'd had clues for years. She acknowledged it fully and with incredible bitterness. This seems to have happened around the time of the 1917 Revolution. Rashel's only companion at this point was Nadenka, who had lived with her for twenty years and been through so many of Rashel's ups and downs. Nadenka loved Rashel and would perform various personal tasks such as washing Rashel's hair. Now she was witnessing her friend's profound suffering. She had written to Rashel's dear friend, the jurist Anatoli Koni, to express her concern, and a 1919 letter in response from him shares that concern: "I am not writing to Rashel Mironovna because I don't want to disturb her. But I do worry about her health . . . My heart aches for her."[43]

Koni had never liked Onissim and had warned Rashel about him on numerous occasions. The two men had clashed professionally after Onissim had written his high-profile article about the unreliability of witness testimony and the difficulty of determining "truth" in law courts. Koni was a traditionalist when it came to testimony. He found Onissim's arguments about the importance of psychological factors to be counterproductive to the smooth workings of the law. But there was personal animosity as well. The two men were not friendly to each other. Rashel believed this was simply jealousy on Koni's part, as Onissim was a rival for her affections on the one hand and a professional rival on the other. But now Koni's warnings had come home to roost.

In 1920, Rashel recovered somewhat. She decided to go through her diary, extracting passages for a memoir focused on world events and important people she had known. Again and again, as she pored through the handwritten diary, Rashel came upon passages that made her realize how naive she had been. When feelings of outrage overcame her, she penned a few choice words in the margins, making it clear that she now knew what Onissim had done and she could never forgive him. Some of these marginalia are associated with entries that go as far back as 1906.

One of the marginal notes that accompanies the entry for February 19, 1910, reports on a literary charity event attended by Onissim and Rashel at which

Lea was also present. Despite her antipathy, Rashel had gone with Onissim out of politeness and engaged Lea in pleasant conversation. Ten years later, looking back, the humiliation of that moment shook her. Three people had stood together and talked. Two were aware of the deceit. She, the wronged woman, had been clueless. As she wrote in 1920: "Now I know that it was OB's [Onissim's] impudent mistress at that charity event. How dare he take me to that event, what a disgrace! And he watched my conversation with that vile creature . . ."

Once she gained momentum, Rashel no longer needed previous entries to inspire her rage. On a clean page after the dated entries end in this her most personal of diaries she wrote: "With what a stench of treachery did OB [Onissim] fill my life. Behind my back, he arranged another life in that disgusting Odessa circus . . . Mon chevalier 'sans tâche et sans reproches' . . . O . . . La suprême ironie des affections humaines. [My knight 'without blemish and without reproach' . . . Oh . . . The supreme irony of human affections.]

Of all the materials in the Rashel Khin archive, perhaps none is more revealing than a collection of undated literary sketches for a play she never finished. The play features two successful people, and the male character carries on a relationship outside the marriage.[44] In one sketch, the husband is busy and has no time to speak to his wife (it feels as if it could be a quote from her diary)—there are calls, clients, meetings, lectures, trips. The wife is upset; she wants to start living "a real life together." In pursuing this "always busy" life, she says, they are losing what is most important. Days pass, months flash by, autumn, winter, summer . . . Their children grow up and go away, their friends abandon them. The wife says, "It is a crime, do you understand it, we committed a crime—we missed out on life . . ."

Further along, a second excerpt from the sketches deals with the help-lessness that accompanies infidelity. Rashel writes: "When a person who is still in love expresses furious indignation against another who has been unfaithful—this is a sign of the final (and usually the vain) hope of keeping love alive."

Finally there are the husband's words in her written draft of the play that I am certain Rashel heard directly from Onissim: "I love you and I love her. I need you both for the complete fulfillment of who I am. One woman simply cannot satisfy my complex emotional and intellectual requirements."

And so, with these new materials from the hand of Rashel Khin, my search for the truth about the love triangle ended. Rashel's diary provided a timeline and a description of key events, but it was the marginalia from 1920, her unfinished play, and Koni's letter that revealed the emotional fallout. Rashel was a broken woman. During the years remaining to her, she wrote nothing more in her diary. After the Revolution, she published no more plays, stories, or translations. Though she did not actually die until 1928, nothing is heard from her again. Her life was essentially over.

Contemplating all of this, I assigned blame to Lea and Onissim, though I had to acknowledge that I did not have their side of the story. But I did have enough facts to know that Lea and Onissim had dissembled and lied; and in Lea's case, the lying went on for decades until her death in 1965. Rashel had tried to tell the truth as she had experienced it. Her words were not easy for me to read and take in. Rashel had written so many things in various manuscripts and they had lain in silence within a Moscow archive, some for a century or more. They waited, it seemed, for my cousin Sveta and me, relatives of those who had done her so much harm, to discover them.

The Railway Prince

What goes through a man's mind when he decides to turn from a secure lifestyle to an uncertain one? One can speculate about the emotional reasons why Onissim Goldovsky eventually turned to Lea and away from his wife. But the economic angle had me puzzled. How could he afford it? Onissim's career had advanced partly on the basis of talent and superb training. But his wife's money also played a role, at least initially, as did the contacts her family afforded him. Onissim came from a comfortable but not affluent background. In the years prior to his marriage, he economized by living with Rashel's brother, Mark Mironovich Khin, and the two shared a single servant.

By the beginning of the 20th century, though Onissim was well-known in legal circles and had a commercial clientele, much of his practice was not lucrative, based as it was on idealistic principles. He represented Jews for free and he took political cases and indigent defendants. In this, he followed in the footsteps of his legal mentors. But where they had had independent means, he had none. After his marriage, that changed, thanks to Rashel's inheritance from her father. Onissim was now able to taste the ease and pleasures of an opulent lifestyle. While his own income became considerable as his commercial practice grew, the expenses of maintaining two households where everyone lived well must have been considerable. In one way or another, Rashel's money was helping make possible his life with another woman.

An event in 1903 crystalized his dilemma. That year, Nadine Auer had asked his advice on how to invest thirty thousand rubles. Onissim told her of a "sure thing," an investment that would pay well. But it didn't pan out, and Nadine lost her money. Onissim was furious with himself, and insisted to Rashel that they pay Nadine back the entire thirty thousand rubles, borrowing what they did not have. It wiped them out of ready money for a time, according to Rashel's report in her diary of September 22, 1903. But as a woman who had grown up with plenty of money, Rashel was amazingly blasé about the entire affair. Things would right themselves. Onissim's response was completely different. He had been stung by the experience with Nadine. They needed to be rich, he explained. Rashel wrote in her diary that:

> Stas [Onissim] told me: I WANT TO BE FAMOUS AND RICH FOR YOU. I answered that I want simply to live quietly and realize that we are actually living together instead of rushing around. Stas answered: "In order to be able to afford this kind of life, I have to be rich. And to be rich I have to become famous."

There was too much in Onissim's life that required significant funds, including feeling comfortable with the circle of crucial connections that Rashel had provided. In her diary she mentions the extraordinary sum Onissim shelled out in 1909 to support their lifestyle—thirty-three thousand rubles. At the same time, he was maintaining Lea and her children. Both women enjoyed summer country houses at his expense, and Onissim purchased the Rafalski mansion for Rashel in 1913. As I tried to puzzle things out, I concluded that something must have occurred in Onissim's professional life to provide him with the money he needed to become very wealthy. But I was hard-pressed to figure out what.

Then cousin Sveta found the clue I had been searching for in a Moscow archive during the summer of 2014. We wound up referring to it as the "railroad letter," a missive sent to Onissim that revealed just how deeply he had become enmeshed in the highly profitable business of railroad development. At exactly the time Onissim met Lea, he was in the process of attaining his own comfortable fortune.

Tsar Alexander II issued the first order to start building railways in 1857. By 1862, two thousand miles of track had been laid. By 1878, that figure increased to fourteen thousand miles and by 1900, when Onissim apparently became involved, Russia had thirty-three thousand miles of railway line. Continued expansion seemed inevitable. The first priority for Russia's railway planners was linking Moscow and St. Petersburg. Next, they built lines to areas of military significance, such as Crimea—where memories of Russia's humiliating defeat by England, France, and Turkey were still fresh (during the war, as historian Loren Graham writes, Russia's beleaguered soldiers relied on horse-drawn wagons to bring supplies from the northern cities). Once lines to the Western borderlands in Crimea, Poland, and the Baltics were completed, the Tsar's aspirations became even greater. In the 1880s, plans were drawn up for lines to China, Central Asia, the Persian Gulf, and the Indian Ocean.[45]

Railways had assumed a mystical significance in the Russian imagination as a symbol of progress, and a "Great Siberian Railway"* was the most stirring idea of all. To Russians, Siberia symbolized freedom, endurance, and unlimited potential, much as the West did in American popular consciousness. A railway to Siberia would finally open access to the natural beauty and vast resources

---

* Many English speakers are familiar with Trans-Siberian Railway but Great Siberian Railway is a more accurate rendering of the Russian language descriptor during the period being described.

of this fabled region. The challenges of building in the harsh weather, formidable mountain ranges, and vast rivers only added to the project's appeal. If Russia could lay forty-five hundred miles of railway track across one of the world's most remote territories, then at last it would have to be recognized as a "great power."

A railway stretching from Moscow to Peking was to be the symbol and mechanism for Russia's imperialist ambitions. In 1891, a special Siberian Committee was established, reporting to Minister of Finance Sergei Witte but closely monitored by the Tsar. The committee quickly settled on a route for the Great Siberian Railway, running from Moscow through Chelyabinsk and Irkutsk and terminating at Vladivostok on the Pacific Ocean. Witte even persuaded the Chinese to let the line from Irkutsk to Vladivostok pass through Manchuria, an arrangement that significantly reduced the cost while giving Russia a toehold on Chinese territory. The railway would have a branch line to the strategically vital Chinese city of Port Arthur. Construction began in late 1891 and, given the challenging terrain and weather conditions, proceeded with remarkable speed. The railway was completed in 1916, but it was usable by 1899—as long as passengers didn't mind traversing gaps in the route by horse-drawn wagon, sleigh, or ferry.

One challenge in the rapid construction project was that the Russian government was perennially broke throughout the 19th century; huge sums were spent on the military and debt, while most of the population was too poor to pay much in taxes. Thus, it was decided from the outset that railway construction in Russia would be a public-private partnership. The government would build large trunk lines, such as the Great Siberian Railway, but save costs by bypassing cities and towns, allowing private entrepreneurs to step in and build the smaller connecting lines.

Railway building by private entrepreneurs thus became a booming business in the late 19th century, and the "railway kings" were Russia's first self-made millionaires. But the attraction of the railway business was not in its operating profits. Freight tariffs were capped at a low level to stimulate industry, and the Russian public was unable to pay much in passenger fares. Most railways had operating losses. But crucially, the state would guarantee any debt incurred by private citizens building railroads, backing both the principal repayment and also a fixed rate of interest, usually 4 to 5 percent, payable in gold.

Railway promoters reaped huge gains by essentially embezzling government funds. Construction costs were routinely exaggerated so that the government would authorize too much debt. Expenditures were minimized by cutting corners on safety and equipment, and the railways' shareholders hoarded the excess cash for themselves. When that cash ran out, the government was usually willing to authorize more debt to keep construction going. In some cases, the government even purchased financially troubled projects, resulting in another windfall for shareholders. By 1906, almost half of Russia's eight-billion-ruble national debt was due to foreigners who had lent money to insolvent railway ventures.

Despite the strain on the state budget, there was an additional burst of railway building in 1906. After its defeat in the Russo-Japanese War (1904–1905), Russia lost control of Manchuria and the intended route of the Irkutsk-Vladivostok stretch of the Great Siberian Railway. An alternative route, farther to the north through Russian territory, had been planned and the Tsar was eager to get this line built as quickly as possible. The concession process, which had been dominated by a handful of wealthy insiders, was opened to new entrepreneurs. Those who proposed to build in East Siberia received favorable financing terms and above-average tariffs.

This was where Onissim's letter came in. We don't know who wrote the "railway" letter as it is not signed, but its purpose was to pass along information obtained by Onissim's Siberian client, Artyemii Derov, to Onissim and his friend Aleksei Alexandrovich Lopukhin. Lopukhin (who could not possibly have foreseen his eventual downfall and treason conviction) was looking for investment projects. Derov had learned that a well-known railway investor, Pyotr Nikolaevich Pertsov, had decided to build a line connecting the Great Siberian Railroad to the Siberian city of Pavlodar (Derov was both the founder and mayor of Pavlodar). If the Pavlodar line was built, the writer suggested, then branch lines to other smaller towns would also be needed. Lopukhin could gain an edge on the competition by applying immediately for one of those concessions—a line from Pavlodar to the agricultural town of Minusinsk, for example. The concession would then qualify for excellent terms. The writer included a hand-drawn map, which was crude but fairly accurate (compare his hand-scribbled rendering to map V following it).

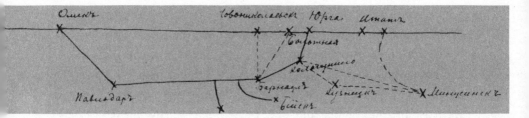

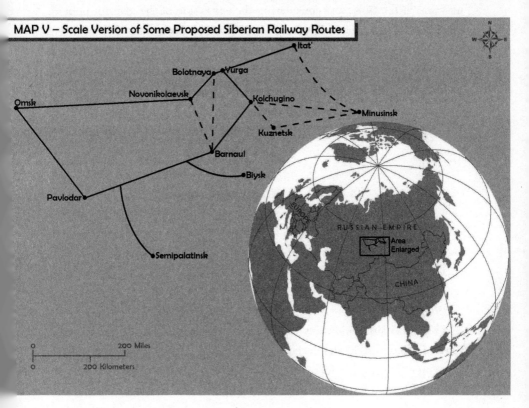

MAP V – Scale Version of Some Proposed Siberian Railway Routes

When I first read the railway letter, I realized some people were preparing to make a great deal of money, and Onissim was involved. I wondered whether he was being cut in as an investor on this deal or any similar ones. In the end, I concluded that he probably was not. The industry was still monopolized by a few hugely wealthy "railway kings" (one of the most famous was Samuel Polyakov, the older brother of Lea's earliest patron, Lazar Polyakov) and a handful of others who controlled a good deal of cash. Also, personal railroad speculation did not seem to fit Onissim's personality or his lack of ready capital.

On the other hand, business was business, and attorneys of rich men generally made large fees. Onissim's first employer, Rudolf Mintslov, had gotten immensely rich on railway deals, and Onissim may well have picked up some expertise and connections from him. In view of how active the railway business was at the time, and considering the expansion of the investor pool in this period, Onissim may have worked on several railway transactions—even while his main interest was the defense bar. The railway business offered astonishing returns for investors, and their attorneys clearly did well. So well, in fact, that Onissim Goldovsky was probably wealthy enough to maintain two expensive households—one for his wife and one for my grandmother and their children.

The Revolution

By 1915, Onissim Goldovsky was a very rich man. In a short time, though, he would find himself and his family in very difficult straits. It is not unusual for people to lose their fortunes. But what I had always found strange was that Onissim and Lea had so little inkling of what was coming. In Lea's case, it was easier to understand. She was a performer who left the interpretation and response to world affairs to her "husband." But in Onissim's case, why did he not better prepare himself for the inevitable fallout from the coming revolution?

On a spring day in 1990, during a trip I made to Warsaw with my wife, Dennie, something occurred that brought home to me the reality of what must have occurred for my grandparents and why they were so unprepared for it. At the time, I was not really thinking about my Russian family. I was interested in learning firsthand about the disastrous fate of Poland's

Jews during World War II. Unfortunately, what I initially saw in Poland turned out to be so completely foreign to my own experience as a Jew in America that I wasn't able to take in the experience of those who had lived and died there.

I had grown up in a big house in a lovely suburb of a major American city. Our house was in a parklike setting, and I had walked on shady lanes and in kempt woods much of my life. The men in my community, mostly Jews whose families had emigrated from Germany generations earlier, worked in the city as doctors, lawyers, judges, and businesspeople. Though most of them attended synagogue occasionally, they were not particularly devout. Indeed, they were so assimilated that I wondered whether the elite Gentiles with whom they worked even realized that many of them were Jewish.

On the third day of my visit to Poland, I went to a conference center where Dennie was to speak. It was part of an old estate, located in a park outside of the city. I decided to explore the tree-shaded lanes, strolling by large and lovely houses that reminded me of the one in which I grew up. Gradually I felt more at home. At lunch, I asked our host about the neighborhood. "Oh, that's where the wealthy Jews lived before the war. They worked in Warsaw as professionals . . . They were completely assimilated, working side-by-side with city leadership. They probably could not imagine in their worst nightmares what would happen to them when the Nazis came to power because they had been part of the upper class for so long."

Suddenly, everything changed for me. The trip had become painfully relevant. These Jews—the ones turned out of their houses by the Nazis and later sent to the gas chambers—were my people, or at least very like them. They lived comfortably in large houses. They worked as part of the power structure of Warsaw. Some did not even practice Judaism. Is it any wonder they did not have the foresight to anticipate the horror that was coming to the Jewish people in Poland? If I had been one of them, would I have done the same and turned a blind eye?

It was then that I thought about my grandparents, Lea and Onissim. They had faced something eerily similar. Although the crisis in Moscow after the 1917 Revolution was different from the one in Poland, there were too many parallels to ignore. Onissim had been a successful, wealthy Jew, totally assimilated. Technically, he was a Christian, but he could never shed his origins and his history, just like those with a Jewish background in Poland in the late 1930s. And in Onissim's case, his long-term political activism made his situation completely untenable.

Ironically, it was the outbreak of World War I that had alarmed Onissim and Lea the most. Yet for them, it turned out to be a false alarm. They were vacationing on the Côte d'Azur, the French Riviera, that August. On hearing about the outbreak of war, they rushed home, concerned about the well-being of the children. But when they arrived in Moscow, things were surprisingly calm. Onissim did suggest that Lea stop appearing at public concerts in Moscow and that she give up touring, at least until the war ended. He returned to his law practice and political work and continued to thrive. In 1916, Boris and Yuri were in school until May, after which the family went to their dacha for the summer. There were beautiful gardens, woods with mushrooms and berries, a river to swim in, tennis and croquet courts. Lea, disappointed that she hadn't borne a daughter, bought a cow from a peasant family and jokingly named the animal Dochka (daughter). At least this provided fresh milk every day even if it was only for Lea's male offspring. Social calls were made to the textile magnate Grigory Krestovnikov. Any troubles seemed far away.

But in fact, a cataclysm was approaching that would sweep away everything Onissim had built, including his family. In January 1917, after an especially harsh winter and years of the Tsar mismanaging the economy, food shortages began to develop in Moscow and St. Petersburg. By early February, Onissim, still unaffected, wrote a calm letter to his theater-administrator friend Sumbatov-Yuzhin requesting four first-row season tickets to the Malyi Theatre—a gift for a friend visiting from St. Petersburg. Soon after, he traveled to St. Petersburg and found the city in foment; the so-called February Revolution was at hand. He returned to Rashel's at the end of the month, excited about developments. As she wrote in her diary on March 1:

> OB came back from Petrograd . . . He is awfully excited, cheerful, and younger looking. He said that he had lived for this—how lucky that his life coincides with these great events. It is his greatest

happiness. He says that the excitement in the city is impossible to describe.

In March, Tsar Nicholas II abdicated—a development that Onissim believed "promised an end to the somber palace intrigues and the machinations of half-educated charlatans like Rasputin," as his son Boris wrote sixty years later.[46] Political authority in Russia was handed over to a Provisional Government made up of leading members of the current Duma—the fourth one formed since Onissim and the Kadet Party's years-ago failure.

Learning more about these events and Onissim's response to them was a total surprise to me. I had studied the Russian Revolution and assumed that by 1917, it would be clear to any intelligent person what was really happening. But my liberal grandfather, confident in Russia's future as a constitutional democracy modeled on Western political ideals, remained optimistic through the summer 1917. He spent time with his family at their dacha. Several of his liberal friends were running the Provisional Government, which was expected to rule Russia until a Constitutional Assembly could be elected. Perhaps there would be a role for him.

Onissim knew that the Bolsheviks were active during summer 1917, organizing factory workers into *soviets* or committees, and spreading communist ideas among rank-and-file soldiers garrisoned in St. Petersburg. But like other members of the middle and upper classes, he viewed Bolshevism as a fringe movement. They hadn't even bothered to field candidates for the Duma. Their leader, Vladimir Lenin, had been in exile in Europe until recently.

Then on November 7 the Bolsheviks seized power, backed by soldiers and armed workers. Overnight, Onissim and his family found themselves in deep trouble. The Bolsheviks were known to be ruthless, and they particularly detested liberal political activists and members of the prerevolutionary "bourgeois" elite. Though Onissim had not been politically active for some time, he was brought in for interrogation.

Years later, Boris recalled the changes to the family's domestic life after the November 1917 Revolution: "Father lost his right to employ a cook and a maid . . . The *shveitsar*—which is to say, the janitor—was likewise freed from his menial occupation and disappeared overnight. Not content with that, the

authorities closed the front entrance of [our apartment building],* thus con-
demning the elevator. We were no longer permitted to use the front stairwell;
instead we had to use the back staircase, climb five flights, and enter the
apartment through the kitchen door . . . The apartment . . . was declared too
spacious for a family of six (two parents, three children, and one governess).
We were thus required to take in a family of complete strangers . . . The meals
too grew steadily meager . . . For the first time in our lives we learned the
meaning of permanent, unremitting hunger."[47]

Anna's situation was totally different from Lea's. Her husband, Shereshevsky,
was one of Moscow's leading physicians and he had demonstrated loyalty and
support for the new regime. Because loyal doctors were initially in short supply
to the Bolsheviks, he and others like him were treated well, their bourgeois
backgrounds conveniently overlooked. Nothing made this more obvious than
the family's living situation. New laws required that most apartments throughout
Moscow were to be shared between former wealthy and educated occupants
and families from less prosperous classes. The bathrooms and kitchens were for
general shared use by these families. This was not only true in Lea and Onissim's building but in Anna's as well . . . with one exception. The Shereshevsky
apartment—even larger than Lea and Onissim's—remained for a single family
due to a Certificate of Protection (охранная грамота) signed by the Bolshevik
Soviet People's commissar, Anatole Lunacharsky.[48] Anna continued to live in
luxury. The frayed relationship between Lea and Anna continued to deteriorate.

As he so often did, Pierre decided to take the easy way out. Considering the
living situation in Moscow intolerable, Pierre decamped for his parents' home in
Odessa. The grim life was not for him, though others in the family were prepared
to wait out the situation and hope for the best. Later correspondence indicates
that Pierre's departure was sudden and that he may have simply walked away
from some of his regular concert commitments.[49] But Odessa was still free of

---

* Boris gives the address in his autobiography (which was written in 1979) as 15 Trubnikovsky Pereulok, which is across the street from where the family actually lived. Yuri's
university application lists the actual address as 26 Trubnikovsky Pereulok, Apartment 24.
While in Moscow, I confirmed that Boris could not have been correct, since the building
he mentions has only two floors and the family lived on the fifth floor. The building Yuri
mentions has seven stories. It is most likely that Boris remembered the number on the
building across the street.

Bolsheviks, and food was plentiful there. Pierre, a self-admitted coward in later years, decided it would be easier to maintain his leisurely bachelor life in the south. But neither the bachelorhood nor the easy life would last for long.

The Civil War and Red Terror

The Goldovsky family's experience was in no way unique. Once in control, the Bolshevik regime set out to transform government, society, and the economy—the faster, the better. While Lea would eventually be able to reinvent herself once again as a breadwinner, Onissim was at sea in this new world. Within days of taking power, the Bolsheviks nationalized Russian industry, banking, and trade, rendering his commercial law practice irrelevant. The criminal courts were dissolved and replaced by "revolutionary tribunals," in which peasants and workers acted as judges and anyone could serve as a lawyer. People accused of political crimes faced the summary justice of the CHEKA, a secret police force established in December 1917 and charged with "defending the Revolution." Onissim was able to find occasional work. In 1920, he served as a consultant to the Northern Timber Industrial Cooperative enterprise in St. Petersburg; in 1921, he did additional work for Rabkrin (RKI), or the Workers' and Peasants' Inspectorate (Рабо́че-крестья́нская инспе́кция, Рабкри́н, РКИ), a governmental establishment responsible for evaluating state, local, and enterprise administrations.[50] But it was a far cry from his former professional life. His robust income evaporated almost completely.

It was not just his career that had gone up in smoke. Onissim's political dreams were shattered. The Kadet's vision of liberal democracy in Russia had lost even a modicum of public support and polled only 5 percent in the November 1917 elections to the Constituent Assembly. Emboldened by the liberals' poor showing, the Bolsheviks outlawed the Kadet Party and arrested its top leaders, two of whom were murdered in the prison hospital. Although Onissim survived the initial political purges, he and his family were under constant threat and clearly in danger. A central premise of Marxism is that a person's socioeconomic circumstances dictate his political beliefs; therefore, workers ("the proletariat") are natural allies of Communism, and members of the bourgeoisie its natural enemies. The revolution, as Lenin made clear, could only be secure when the bourgeoisie was destroyed. As a successful lawyer, Onissim was a bourgeois and an enemy of the Bolsheviks by definition, regardless of whether he actually engaged in political activity. The fact that he also had a written record of support for the liberal cause only made things worse.

One of the leaders of the CHEKA explained the Bolsheviks' novel approach to justice: CHEKA officers were "not to look for evidence as proof that the accused has acted or spoken against the Soviets. First you must ask him to what class he belongs, what his social origin is, his education, and his profession. These are the questions that must determine the fate of the accused."[51]

The Bolsheviks also waged economic warfare against their class enemies. As mentioned, middle- and upper-class families, including the Goldovskys, were forced to share their living space with proletariat families, who often stole their belongings and spied on them for the CHEKA. When professionals like Onissim were barred from employment, they survived by selling their possessions. Members of the "bourgeoisie" were also charged special taxes and conscripted for manual jobs, such as sweeping the streets, clearing snow, or pulling carts. They received third-class ration cards, which entitled them—in the words of one Bolshevik leader—"to just enough bread so as not to forget the smell of it."[52] Encouraged by Bolshevik slogans such as "Death to the Bourgeoisie," petty street criminals targeted those who looked or spoke like the bourgeoisie, especially if they were Jewish.

Onissim found himself increasingly isolated as his friends fled or succumbed to the stresses of the era. Sergei Urusov was arrested and forced into military service with the Red Army. Onissim's law school professor, Sergei Muromtsev, died in 1910 after spending almost a year in prison. Aleksei Lopukhin, his partner in the railway venture, served out a prison sentence and emigrated in 1920. Artyemii Derov, the source of the original tip for the railway deal, died bankrupt in Moscow in 1920. And Dmitry Shipov, who had organized the 1904 Zemstvo Conference, went to prison, where he died in 1920. And on it went.

While the tsarist-era elite suffered the most, the aftermath of the Revolution brought hardship to almost everyone. Industrial production ground to a halt after the Bolsheviks fired factory managers and technicians, replacing them with workers' committees who were often inexperienced and ineffective. In the countryside, peasants refused to sell their produce for rubles, which were rapidly losing their value due to inflation. The government recommended barter, but city dwellers had virtually nothing to trade. When the government started forcible food requisitions in January 1919, the peasants hid or destroyed their harvests. The small amount of food that was available was sent to the Red Army, which was fighting first the Germans and, later, the White Guard anti-Communist forces.

A severe shortage of food in Russia's cities resulted. Russians ate horses, dogs, cats, and zoo animals; instances of cannibalism were even reported. It was not unusual for people to die from starvation on the streets of Moscow; bread rations were reduced to only a thousand calories per day, and according to historian Orlando Figes, the population of the city halved between 1918 and the end of 1920—more than five million deaths all told.[53]

The Revolution broke up the Russian Empire and launched wars that periodically cut Onissim and Lea off from their relatives in Vilnius and Odessa. Ukraine declared independence immediately after the Revolution, falling under a Ukrainian nationalist leadership allied with Germany. Over the next few years, Ukraine was a battleground among Ukrainian nationalists, anarchist partisans, former tsarist officers trying to overthrow the Bolsheviks, anti-Communist (and anti-Semitic) Cossacks, the invading Polish army, and the Bolshevik Red Army. The leaders of all of these factions "rewarded" their troops by permitting them to plunder and destroy local Jewish villages. The Red Army finally triumphed and Ukraine was reincorporated into the Soviet Union in December 1922. Vilnius was occupied by the Germans and then by the Red Army before being annexed by Poland in 1922.

Amid this wave of hardship, Lea rose to the occasion by relying on the survival skills she had learned during her childhood in Odessa. "Every day death was as close as life," she wrote years later. "People never knew which one would claim the day. In our time we had had sufficient comfort and luxuries; then overnight nothing . . . Everything we possessed except our personal clothing and bare necessities for maintaining life was taken from us . . . People reacted to the disaster in different ways. Some began fighting for their possessions as if they were worth something and ended up losing their lives. We postponed our feelings and fought for nothing, for we were concerned only for the personal safety of our family. Nothing interested us now but the protection and care of our children. We did not try to be splendid or brave; we were only practical. There is a time to die but it was not then, at the convenience of the government."

However, out of necessity Lea hoarded jewelry and traded possessions like her fur coats for food. Though their beautiful silver flatware was taken, the family was able to retain the *podstakannik* (the tea-glass holder eventually given to me decades later by my mother), a Fabergé cigarette case, and other small items that could be safely hidden.

As for Onissim, Lea was generous in describing his inventiveness—apparently he cobbled together a little stove from various articles they scrounged. But in truth, it was she who rescued the family. The gravest immediate problems were water, heat, and food. With no heat in the apartment, the pipes froze and water had to be carried up five flights of stairs. As for food, most stores were closed, and Lea was particularly concerned about milk for the children. She made a deal with her former milk delivery woman, who was not supposed to provide milk to the bourgeoisie. Lea traded her fur coat for a daily delivery of milk, which could be hidden under the coat the peasant woman now wore. Early in the mornings, out on the street, Lea pawned or traded other clothing (of which she had a lot) for butter, eggs, and cheese.

"I hated both my fear and deceit," she wrote, "but hunger knows no patience and makes no friends." Her forays were successful, but Lea knew it was only temporary. She needed a more permanent solution to the food problem. She would have to be the primary breadwinner. And indeed, "breadwinner" in a literal sense is just what she was. She became a member of VSORABIS, the All-Union Society of Art Employees (Всорабис Всесоюзное Общество Работников Искусства), and later persuaded Pierre to join (Lea's membership number was 13394, Pierre's 17115).[54] Her concerts, now mostly in factories and at other workers' gatherings sanctioned by the Soviet authorities, were played in exchange for food. Lea's first concert—arranged with government approval "for the cultural entertainment of the workers" in 1917—produced ten pounds of bread, five pounds of sugar, and two pounds of herring. Other concerts generated wood and coal, potatoes and apples. Yuri and Boris came along to help haul the "fee" home. Onissim was not welcome at these events and stayed in the apartment.

My mother's birth on December 6, 1917, complicated Lea's life. She had performed concerts right up until the baby was due. But afterward, milk poured from Lea's breasts whenever she played the violin. In the past, she had taken time off to nurse her children, but now she needed to work. Irene was handed off to a wet nurse and eventually, Lea stopped producing milk. During the short period between the Revolution and his departure for Odessa, Pierre served as Lea's accompanist and was also paid, though far less since he was not the soloist, but it still meant more food for the family. At the same time, Pierre sought his own solo appearances since they paid him more.

On the occasion of one of Lea's early factory concerts, Pierre had a happy conflict—a solo engagement. Who should fill in for him? Nine-year-old Boris immediately pleaded for the spot. He often practiced with Lea and had learned some of her simpler pieces. But since he was still regarded as a beginner (though a talented one), his offer was met with laughter—one of the few occasions for it in those days. Another pianist by the name of Semeon Samuelson was engaged and began rehearsing with Lea. But Boris was not to be deterred. For the next twelve days, he practiced Lea's repertoire feverishly. It turned out they were lucky to have him as backup, as Samuelson came down with influenza. Now Lea had no alternative—it was Boris (a risky option) or no concert (an unthinkable option). Boris was dressed in a sailor suit and pressed into service.

The concert caused a minor sensation—Boris stole the show. The factory supervisor re-engaged them on the spot, insisting that Boris return with Lea. Then came the clincher—if Boris would play a solo or two, the group would not only pay him his accompanist "fee," but would throw in some candy for the boy and some extra herring and apples. Years later, when Boris played piano recitals, family members insisted that he retell the story of his solo "debut" and play the work that caused such a sensation when he returned to the Soviet factory as a soloist—Mendelssohn's delightful (and not easy to play) Rondo Capriccioso, op. 14. For Onissim, this must have seemed bewildering, to see his son working at such a young age to help out the family. But for Lea, who had the sharp business acumen of her mother and who had survived against all odds as a child alone in Moscow, it was nothing new.

Meanwhile Onissim spent most of his time on correspondence and meetings. The political and economic situation was increasingly unstable, and it was unclear who was best positioned to help whom in the jockeying for power, or in some cases, the simple need to survive. Onissim was still considered by some a distinguished jurist and many people turned to him for advice, not aware of just how precarious his own situation was. In spring 1918, Onissim received a letter from someone in trouble—Vasiliy Rozanov.

Onissim and Rozanov's long friendship would have survived Rozanov's later conversion to Christianity (after all, Onissim himself had converted) but it had been accompanied by virulent anti-Semitism. As a result, the two hadn't spoken in years. But now Rozanov, desperate, wrote, asking my grandfather if he remembered their youthful friendship. Onissim answered: "You ask me if I remember you, Vasily Vasilievich? Of course I do. You were my first friend when I was young and in those times I admired you with rapture. But you in your turn dealt a blow to me that left indelible wounds for long years . . . To tell the truth, I have been full of indignation and anguish toward you who was such a close friend. I don't want you to think that I am arrogant. I am not scolding you. I do not have the right to do so. But indeed at our age relations must be truthful . . . That is why I didn't soften these words with smooth lies."[55]

Then, lightening his tone, Onissim did offer to set aside an evening or holiday so they might meet. There is no way to know whether this meeting took place, but there was little Onissim could have done to help Rozanov. The philosopher was loathed by the Bolsheviks and he did not have an intrepid wife like Lea to fend for him. Broke and unemployable, Rozanov starved to death the following year.

During the worst of the post-revolutionary chaos in early 1918, Lea's parents were able to reach them suggesting that she bring the children to Odessa. The Treaty of Brest-Litovsk had been signed between the Bolsheviks and the Allied Powers on March 3, 1918, ending Russia's involvement in World War I. But Germans still occupied Odessa and large parts of the Ukraine, a rich agricultural region where food was still plentiful. The conditions were far better than in Moscow and this had already enticed Pierre to return to his parents' home. Once there, he had immediately secured conventional concert work and teaching assignments.

Onissim agreed that taking the children to Odessa was a good idea and he encouraged Lea to go. But he decided to stay in Moscow, as events were unfolding daily that might affect the family's future. After a factory concert at which several officials were present and seemed in good humor, Lea asked permission to leave with the three children, saying her parents were old and needed care. They authorized a small cattle car to transport Lea, the children, and her former governess, Katya Rigert, who was loyally staying by them. They were to bring their own bedding as well as pails and brushes for cleaning their space in the cattle car.

Comparing the two accounts I've read of the trip—Lea's and Boris's—is almost comical. For him, it was an adventure. Boris describes a train trip that ends abruptly at "no man's land"—a part of the country controlled by neither the Russian nor German side. Though the war was technically over, no trains crossed this territory. Passengers were bundled into horse carts and carried to the other side to resume the trip with another train on the German side. For the boys, it was great fun.

Lea describes a more harrowing trip. In retrospect, it is amazing that she risked the journey at all. Perhaps she did not realize what she was undertaking, or maybe it indicates just how desperate she was. Railways were the main means of transportation in a country coping with both a civil war and a famine. Traders inundated passenger and cargo cars, trying to acquire food in the country to sell at huge profits in the cities. Since this kind of activity was illegal, the traders were usually armed. Riding side by side with the traders were Bolshevik "food brigades," who were also armed. The food brigades were heading to the countryside in search of food, although they forcibly requisitioned it from the peasants rather than buying it. And preying on everyone were starving mobs of criminals, eager to attack anyone who seemed to be carrying anything of value. At the same time, the railways were being used to transport the various soldiers and irregulars who were battling each other in the Civil War. Both the Whites and Reds in Ukraine frequently blew up the railway lines to try to prevent enemy troop movements.

Years later, Lea recalled that their car was often sidetracked and delayed, waiting for repairs or for another train to carry them further. At each stop, hordes of people who had been waiting days or weeks pushed onto the car. Lea's permit for the family's space meant nothing, and she feared for the safety of the children, especially the baby Irina. The family was afraid to move from the little space they had and were thus shut in for days with limited water. They ran out of food. There were no bathroom facilities. Years later, Lea would say that memories of the trip, and her fear for the children, gave her nightmares for the rest of her life.

At last they arrived at their destination, exhausted, hungry, and dirty. Odessa was an oasis. Food was plentiful and the children gradually relearned how to eat slowly until they were no longer hungry, rather than guzzling as much as they could and making themselves sick. Milk, meat, eggs—it was heaven. Lea was impressed with Pierre, who spent more and more time caring for the children. They adored him, and thus Lea felt confident that she could leave them to his care and return to Moscow and to Onissim—now her greatest concern. Although the return trip was equally terrible, at least Lea was not worrying about her children. But when Onissim saw her, he was shocked at her appearance. The journey had taken a lot out of her and she had eaten almost nothing.

One thing did complicate Lea's journey to Odessa. Pierre had married a local girl, much to Gitel's surprise and displeasure. The new family member, Elena Mikhailovna, joined the ménage, adding to the tension in their already crowded home. Fortunately, the apartment was often empty, and she must have been some help taking care of Irina when Gitel was busy with the piano business. Saul often took Yuri and Boris to the synagogue. He wanted his grandsons to learn how to lead an exemplary life of piety and generosity. For them, the Jewish services were a novelty. Though their father supported Jewish causes, he was technically a Catholic and more accurately a political liberal and agnostic who did not go to shul. The boys did not understand Hebrew and had not learned even the most basic prayers, so it did not take long for them to become bored. But their boredom was mitigated by the fact that Gitel encouraged them to become Boy Scouts. Years later, Boris proudly bragged about all the medals he had earned.

Gitel also insisted that the boys continue practicing piano. To placate her and make up for the fact that she was still angry at him for his marriage, Pierre agreed to oversee their musical instruction. Everyone knew Boris was the budding musician, but Pierre did not neglect Yuri. He believed that playing piano competently would always come in handy. In this he was prescient. Though Yuri studied mathematics and would eventually become a professor in that field, in time Pierre helped him join the musicians' union back in Moscow, and so Yuri was able to partly support himself with the piano during the difficult 1920s.

Lea was back in Moscow in the fall as the concert season began. Programs in major halls were re-established but they no longer involved patronage of royalty, the aristocracy, or the bourgeoisie. Rather, they were open to all. Lea was engaged for a series of five concerts in the Grand Hall of the Moscow

Conservatory with her good friend Fyodor Chaliapin.[56] The last of these concerts was to be the grandest, with the two soloists appearing with an orchestra conducted by another valued colleague, Serge Koussevitzky. Lea was relieved that she was still considered important enough to be featured so visibly. It might serve as some measure of protection for Onissim.

In Odessa, Boris had badgered his uncle Pierre into teaching him the piano part of the César Franck sonata for violin and piano. Boris knew it was his mother's favorite piece and an important part of her repertoire and he wanted to demonstrate that he could play it once they were reunited. Pierre knew the Franck sonata well, of course, from his concerts with Paul Kochanski, but he felt it was much too difficult for a prepubescent youngster. Boris reminded Pierre that he had already proven his abilities in the factory concerts. His mother might need him again, he argued. Pierre finally agreed to teach the piece, though it turned out that the second movement was beyond Boris's ability to play without mistakes. Even so, another member of the family had been initiated into César Franck's magical music.

Beginnings and Endings

⋘⊗⊗⋙

Within eighteen months of the children's arrival, it became clear that sending Yuri, Boris, and Irina to Odessa had been a mistake. At first, Odessa had been like a world away from the upheavals of the Revolution, but the port city soon became as turbulent and dangerous as Moscow and St. Petersburg. Between 1917 and 1921, the city changed hands six times, falling to Bolshevik sympathizers, Ukrainian nationalists, the French army, pro-Soviet Ukrainians, Russian forces loyal to the Tsar and, finally, to the Red Army. The city was in virtual anarchy during these years, and the brunt of the violence fell on the Jews. A 1921 census found that one-third of Odessa's Jews had lost at least one family member in the Civil War and, of those, almost half were children who had lost one or both parents.[57]

Lea, heartbroken, decided to bring back everyone, including her parents, so that they could all be together in such uncertain times. She once again made the perilous trip to Odessa. In planning their return north, the group split up. Lea left first with the boys. Pierre and his wife would bring Saul; Gitel would bring Irina, the nurse, and the jewels and other valuables that could be pawned in Moscow. Ever resourceful, she began sewing them into her featherbed coverlet and pillow, which she could feign were necessary because of her frail condition.

The valuables made Gitel's trip the most dangerous. Her ruse of the coverlet and pillow worked for a while. But Red Army soldiers traveling on the train noticed that she took them with her whenever she got out to stretch at train stops. They began to hound her, "Why do you need to take that with you? We will watch it for you. Are you carrying something valuable?" Gitel became terrified—not only about losing the jewels and other valuables but about being branded a counterrevolutionary, trying to cheat the state. At the next stop, she took Irina and the nurse into the station. She gave them the coverlet and pillow and told them not to move or talk to anyone until she came back. With that, she got back on the train and it took off—without Irina, the nurse, or the jewels. Once the train started up and was well away from the station, she raised a ruckus: "Get the train to stop, get the train to stop, I've lost my granddaughter." Taking pity on her, the conductor told her to get off at the next station. He gave her a pass to return to her granddaughter and resume her journey on a later train. The soldiers even handed down her belongings, and thus she was eventually reunited with Irina, the nurse, and her jewels.

The terror Irina experienced that day—watching a train depart with the only relative left to her—was deeply traumatic. It constituted the first of several severe shocks that would affect her psychological stability years later. When she was nearly forty, Irina had what at that time was called a "nervous breakdown"; the collapse was so debilitating that it left her incapacitated for many months and required five years of intense daily therapy. We, her children, didn't understand it at the time—she had always struck us as unshakeable. But we learned years later that the horror of the train trip and various traumas that followed were responsible.

With the family reunited, there was a brief period of happiness. But it was short-lived. Food shortages were the greatest immediate concern, especially when little Irina became very sick. In her oral history years later, my mother reminisced: "Uncle Pierre always reminded me in later years that he walked miles to get a chicken because I had whooping cough and [Gitel claimed] that only chicken soup would cure me."

Onissim finally acknowledged that his hopes for a return to political stability were no longer realistic. He and others of the liberal bourgeois class were now targets for the new regime. Twice Onissim was called in for questioning and though he was released both times, it was clear that his life was at risk. By 1920, he acknowledged that the only solution was for the family to leave the country. But because he had delayed far longer than many of those who were in similar circumstances, it would now be complicated. He could not just pick up the family and depart. To make matters worse, it was not even clear whether everyone in the family was willing to go.

Onissim and Lea assessed their options. The Bolsheviks had imposed restrictions on travel and emigration. Only citizens or permanent legal residents of foreign countries were permitted to emigrate, and even those cases were reviewed individually by the People's Commissariat for Internal Affairs, the successor organization to the CHEKA, popularly known as the NKVD. Obtaining a passport to travel abroad required the approval of the NKVD, the People's Commissariat for Foreign Affairs, and the People's Commissariat for Military Affairs.

Securing permission, like almost everything else in Russia at this time, was unpredictable. Simply applying could be risky. People who wanted to emigrate or travel abroad might find themselves under suspicion of being "enemies of the state." And if they were not granted permission, their lives became even more untenable. In the early years of Soviet power, things were so chaotic that quite a few people did manage to escape by obtaining travel visas. But by 1921, the Soviets had consolidated their control over the government apparatus, including border control and emigration agencies.

Onissim believed he might be able to emigrate because of his Lithuanian background. During the years 1917–1919, Lithuania was occupied by the Germans, then the Soviets, and then the Poles. But the Lithuanians managed to expel all those invading armies and, in July 1920, the Soviet Union recognized an independent Lithuania. At that point, anyone who could document Lithuanian citizenship was legally a "foreign national" and thus eligible to emigrate. The procedures were formalized in the Russian-Lithuanian Peace Treaty signed in 1922. Since Onissim had been born in Vilnius, he might well have qualified as a "foreign national," despite his many years' residence in Russia. But if he were denied permission to emigrate and labeled an "enemy" of the Soviet regime, again, this would count even more against him.

Getting Lea and the children out was the highest priority, and thanks to Lea's musical career, she and Boris had a good excuse to leave the country, at least temporarily. Lea's parents and her brother, Pierre, were also enthusiastic about leaving when the situation allowed it and they agreed to do all they could to follow once Lea got established in Berlin. Onissim had many contacts there and Lea was well-known as a performer. It was a center of culture where a great artist should immediately be welcome. Onissim must have believed that, as soon as the others were out and the danger of retribution to the family overcome, he could play his "foreign national card" or come up with another plan for himself, Yuri, and Irina.

For Anna and her husband, the situation was different. Shereshevsky was a physician, too valuable to the nation to get permission to leave. The fate of the Shereshevsky family had transpired in a way quite unlike that of Lea and Onissim's. In part because of his usefulness as a doctor and his reputation in the medical world, Anna's family continued to keep their large apartment and still lived well. They had also been champions of the new regime. While there was not a lot of communication between the two sisters, Lea realized that Anna and her husband had no intention of leaving. Lea and Onissim's eldest son, Yuri, was also beginning to resist the idea. According to Boris's autobiography, Yuri had begun to show sympathy for the new Soviet state. The tensions between his love of family and his personal ambitions and beliefs did not augur well for the future of family harmony.

But for the time being, the easiest part of the plan turned out to be getting Lea and Boris out of the country. Onissim arranged some concerts for them in Germany through his contacts at the German Embassy in Moscow. Once they were safe, he would figure out a way for the others to follow. Initially Lea was reluctant to separate, but she finally applied for a visa to Germany. Since Boris had already played concerts with her and she was leaving her other children in Russia, the visas were approved without delay. Before they left, Onissim asked Lea and Boris to play the Franck sonata for him. Boris was extremely proud that he had learned it in Odessa and was excited about showing it off. Lea had other feelings. As she wrote in her memoir, "The day of separation came and once again the future betrayed me. Could I have foretold it, I would never have gone." It is one of the few times I ever knew of my grandmother looking back with regret.

It was 1921 when Lea and Boris departed for St. Petersburg. There they found a boat about to leave for Stettin. Although the boat was full, Lea explained to the captain that she had a recital to give on a certain date. The goodhearted man agreed to take them on, but explained that the only place for them was under the stairway leading from second to third class. Once again, Lea and Boris had a horrendous trip, though this time it lasted only three days and two nights.

Lea held on to her precious Amati violin at all times. Boris was in charge of the fifty American dollars Onissim had given them, a veritable fortune since one dollar could provide nice lodgings for a week. The money seemed ample—Lea would collect concert fees in the meantime and Onissim would follow shortly. Lea had also sewn many jewels inside her clothing and used other jewels as buttons on various pieces, all of which would be transported surreptitiously.

After an auspicious beginning for Lea and Boris with successful concerts in Berlin, things went wrong—badly wrong. For one thing, Yuri was now actively resisting the idea of leaving Moscow to join his mother and brother. He was a promising mathematician, about to enter university, and was being treated well by the authorities despite his father's reputation. He saw a future for himself in the new Soviet state and began writing ominous letters to Boris about his younger brother's bourgeois tendencies, though it took weeks for them to get through, given the poor communications between Russia and Germany.

More troubling was the fact that Onissim himself wasn't well. The political and emotional strain had taken its toll and his stamina was giving out. For a third time, he was called in for interrogation and this time, things looked more serious. Rumors circulated that he would soon be arrested. Then there was the physical strain of having to walk up five flights of stairs every time he entered his apartment building or helping Yuri carry water upstairs. Onissim had led a life of ample food and drink and he had put on weight. He was a smoker. His heart was weak.

Ultimately, it was a cerebral hemorrhage that killed him. By the time his brother-in-law Shereshevsky arrived at the apartment, three-year-old Irina was standing by her dead father. So soon after her first trauma of abandonment on the train from Odessa, Irina felt this second shocking loss deeply—something I learned from my father only years later.

Onissim Goldovsky died on September 7, 1922, at the age of fifty-seven. He had been a man devoted to ideas, a man influenced in part by Western Europe and the Enlightenment, but also by a host of Russian thinkers, his teachers and mentors, and others who had established a tradition of progressive ideas and utopian visions for the country's future. These ideas included freedom for all, a government responsive to the will of the people, the emancipation of women, religious freedom, universal education, the rule of law, the importance of reason and rationality over dogma and superstition, and a belief that through political effort there could be progress toward a better tomorrow.

While Onissim's views aligned with those of other "Westernizers" and liberals in Russia and progressive thinkers in Western Europe, they were also heavily influenced by Judaism. Ironically, while he had undergone a conversion of convenience to marry and had spent the majority of his adult life technically as a Christian, he never lost contact with an essentially Jewish system of beliefs. At the center was his respect for the law, a basic tenet of Judaism. Indeed, Jewish "beauty of holiness" is rooted in the idea that good men live by the precepts of Torah (the Hebrew word for law) and Talmud (a later codification of Jewish law). He also subscribed to what the Russian-American literary critic and essayist Philip Rahv has described as the Jewish character trait of "feeling for human suffering on the one hand and for a life of value, order, and dignity on the other."[58]

Onissim had read and rejected the works of many contemporary writers in which nihilistic characters led lives without meaning, intention, or value—writers like Turgenev in *Fathers and Sons* or Dostoyevsky in *The Possessed*. He replaced nihilism with a faith in the human potential to change the world. In a characteristically Jewish manner, Onissim, as Rahv put it, "transcend(ed) all sectarian understanding of suffering, seeing it as the fate of the whole of mankind, which can only be mitigated when all men assume responsibility for one another."

How important was Onissim in the history of his time and place? Given the fate of Russia, with the triumph of extremism after 1917 and the virtual elimination of all those who shared Onissim's views—not very important. His name appears in many histories of the time, but he was a side player, mentioned in footnotes, if at all. In his day, however, many believed his views would prevail. This was true not only in Russia, but also abroad. In June 1908, the Russian-born investigative American journalist Herman Bernstein, who covered the Russian Revolution for the *New York Herald*, came to Moscow to interview Onissim as one of the emerging political leaders of Russia.[59] To outsiders, there was a strong possibility that he would be on the winning side.

In terms of his personal life, I am the first to acknowledge that Onissim Goldovsky was not a perfect man. Even by the standards of the time, his treatment of his wife was in many ways cruel, and she suffered profoundly by his deceit. In addition, perhaps a trace of arrogance prevented him from imagining a world in which other, more extreme views of political change might trump his own. But in the end, I admire his vision, his intellect, and his courage. Most of all, I admire what he wished for all mankind. Years before his death, the French writer Émile Zola—one of many whose life was touched by Onissim—wrote him a letter whose closure expressed these grand sentiments almost exactly:

> You have included me in a great project and I am very grateful to you for this. If we hope to overcome human misery and build God's Kingdom on earth, it is essential that we reach out our hands in a fraternal handshake that extends from one end of the earth to the other.[60]

It is the perfect eulogy for Onissim Goldovsky.

Lea did not learn of Onissim's death for some time. Communication was difficult and news trickled in sporadically. As she prepared for the reunification of her family, Lea was more optimistic than she had been for some time. Berlin was the center of music and culture in Europe, and she felt free and safe there. A large Russian émigré community knew her name and came to her concerts. But when she learned of Onissim's death, Lea broke down and wept. She had worked so hard to ensure that their plan would succeed. Now, she did not know what to do.

Lea could not go home to bury Onissim—it was too dangerous. That was left to other members of the family, as was the plan for family reunification in Western Europe. All that remained for her was a photograph of the man she had loved—a photograph that would rest on her bedside table, in the many places she subsequently lived, until her own death in 1965.

III
THE LONGEST JOURNEY
Recitativo-Fantasia:
Ben moderato

(1921 to 1930)

෧෨෮

At some point in its history, a great piece of music takes on a life of its own. Neither the composer who gave birth to it nor the person for whom it was written can do more than claim their role in its history. For Eugène Ysaÿe and the Sonata in A Major for Violin and Piano by César Franck, this moment was near.

By 1921, Ysaÿe was sixty-three. He had been playing the violin since age five. Physical ailments were beginning to trouble him, as they do many violinists in their sixties. Ysaÿe decided to accept an offer to become conductor of the Cincinnati Symphony Orchestra, a position much less strenuous than that of a touring violin soloist. There he became increasingly close to Jeanette Dincin, a violinist forty-four years his junior, whom he married two years later. She cared for him during the ten years until his death; afterward, she would fight to keep his legacy alive.

The third movement of the Franck sonata is a "fantasia" or fantasy—a musical form that invites improvisation. Ysaÿe found it to be profound. In his letter to the composer, he wrote, "The [third] movement, that sentimental declamation . . . is the most gripping part of the work."

There are no set rules for a fantasy; it is a form in which classical composers feel they can operate more freely. For his part, Franck decides to go on a musical journey of exploration. The intensity of the second movement is spent. The tempo is more subdued and moderate. It is time to take stock, explore the melodic material, and figure out where he wants to go . . .

Berlin

❧

If there was one thing Lea didn't know in 1921 after arriving in Berlin and in the months afterward, it was where she wanted to go. There seemed to be no good alternatives. Returning to the family in Russia was out of the question. Western Europe was in postwar turmoil. The United States was too far away and, aside from her brief trip there in 1907, it was unknown territory.

My grandmother's state of mind is difficult for me to imagine. Two of her children, Irina and Yuri, were still in Russia and she desperately wanted them with her. The family was to unite in Europe but this depended on Soviet exit visas that were difficult to secure, and the fact that Lea eventually overstayed the time limit on her own visa would only make it more so. Berlin had been decimated by a world war and Germany's economy was wrecked. Communication with her relatives was difficult, slow, and dangerous, since letters were routinely opened and read by the authorities. And it did not take long for her to realize she was running out of money.

Yet remarkably, Lea did not despair. She reinvented herself once again. She would now aspire to take her place as a top musical star in the firmament of a preeminent European musical capital. The weeks and months following her arrival in Berlin had actually had their share of encouraging success, and on that basis she was determined to stage a major concert after her initial run that would cement her reputation. After many attempts, she secured a meeting with one of the leading impresarios of the time, Louise Wolff, who managed careers for the most important musicians of the day and organized concerts for the Berlin Philharmonic. Wolff's concert agency, the most powerful in Germany, was started by her husband, Hermann, in 1880. Upon his death, Louise took it over with the help of a partner, Erich Sachs—hence the name of the agency, Wolff and Sachs.

Lea proposed an all-Russian concert, in which she would appear with the Berlin Philharmonic. Wolff demurred until Lea mentioned thirteen-year-old Boris, whom she described as a prodigy. Boris was now studying with Leonid Kreutzer, a popular pianist and conductor whom Wolff respected, who vouched for the boy's talent and offered to conduct the concert. Wolff couldn't resist. The program would open with Lea playing a concerto by Alexander Glazunov—a work still considered fairly new since its first performance in Russia in 1905. Boris would follow with a piano concerto by another contemporary Russian composer, Sergei Lyapunov, and Lea would close with the Tchaikovsky violin concerto, already one of the most popular in her repertory.

Wolff was shrewd. Given the huge number of Russians who had recently fled to Berlin, an all-Russian concert promised to be remunerative. Still, Wolff was unwilling to shoulder the risk by herself. At her request, Lea deposited many of her jewels as collateral. Now she and Boris needed the four weeks before the concert to prepare. She went to friends of Onissim's—Georg Wertheim, founder of the Wertheim chain of department stores, and Frau Schlesinger, whose husband, Moritz, was a German diplomat. They helped sell tickets while Lea invited music critics she knew in Berlin, writing personal letters to each. Since she had no jewelry to wear (Mrs. Wolff had prudently made sure everything was in her safe), Lea, according to her memoir, went straight to Lanvin in Paris and convinced the manager to sell her a magnificent gown on credit to complement her bright red hair. This was a long trip for a mere dress but, as always, her "look" was part of the show. A runner was rolled out from the backstage door to the spot on stage where she stood and played. She would march out trailing her gown which, thanks to the runner, never touched the floor.

The concert took place in January 1922 and was the talk of the town, according to both Lea's and Boris's accounts. Tickets sold out quickly. In addition to the expected Russians, who shouted and cheered their enthusiasm as only Russians can and who insisted on many encores, most of the important critics came, as did several distinguished musicians. One was the pianist and most sought-after piano pedagogue in Germany, Artur Schnabel, who was so impressed with Boris's playing that he in time would become his teacher—a great honor. Financially the concert was also a success—Lea got all her jewelry back, plus much welcomed cash. The reviews were positive. And Boris stole the show; his blue sailor suit, short pants, and shiny black shoes made at least as great an impression as Lea's ballgown, and more ink was devoted to him than to Lea. For the moment, Lea didn't care. After all, Mrs. Wolff agreed to serve as their agent, which meant Lea was now represented by an experienced impresario with connections throughout Europe.

Boris's recollection of how the concert came about differs from Lea's. His autobiography makes no mention of Lea's Herculean efforts, but gives much of the credit to Leonid Kreutzer. Kreutzer had been a well-known pianist and composer in St. Petersburg and now was a professor at the Berlin Hochschule für Musik (Conservatory). When Lea asked Kreutzer to take on Boris as a student, he was flattered. He immediately decided that Boris, like Lea, was a genius.

At one of their early lessons together, Kreutzer was surprised to learn that Boris had never played any works by Frédéric Chopin. He suggested that the young pianist bring the composer's Preludes to the next lesson. As Boris recalled, "When I inquired at the music store, I was told there were twenty-four Chopin Preludes. Since my teacher had asked me to bring them along, I decided to learn the lot. So I turned up at the next lesson prepared to massacre all twenty-four Preludes—an act of idiocy if there ever was one . . . 'The darling boy!' he kept repeating, almost clapping his hands in delight. 'Isn't he marvelous! My, what ambition! What industry! What talent!'"[1]

According to Boris, Kreutzer was so excited with his new pupil that he decided himself to organize the concert with the Berlin Philharmonic—an orchestra which at that time was available for hire—with Boris and Lea as soloists and himself as conductor. Perhaps there is some truth to both accounts. Boris's memoirs are often more reliable than Lea's, though I certainly do not think Lea would have made up the important role that Louise Wolff played or the necessity of using her jewelry as collateral.

Lea grew more optimistic after this important concert. She had money to upgrade their living situation and decided to move to more comfortable lodgings on the Hohenzollerndamm, closer to Boris's Russian school. She also started conservatory teaching,[2] a source of much-needed cash, and planned more concerts. Lea realized she needed to be patient about the family joining her. The Soviet government was very likely displeased with her deception—leaving on a concert tour and never coming back.

One morning, as Lea was preparing for a rehearsal, she was summoned to what she refers to in her memoir as the "German Consulate" (probably the Ministry of Foreign Affairs). She added: "Terror came over me completely and at once. I could hardly move." When she arrived, a telegram was presented to her. It stated that Onissim had died of a cerebral hemorrhage. There had been only a four-minute interval for Onissim between normal life and death.

"Sorrow, like hunger, changes the human form," Lea wrote in her memoir, "and I cannot tell you how long I remained stunned and inert. I could neither think nor act. Now I can shorten the bad to a moment, but then it was a lifetime."

A brief memorial service was held for Onissim in Berlin and many of Lea's new Russian acquaintances attended. Several promised funds and other help if necessary. As she always had, Lea soon pulled herself together. "Never look back," her mother had counseled her. "Always look to the future." That is what Lea now did.

Complications—Familial and Romantic

Though she was overwhelmed with sorrow, Lea's first concern was getting her two other children—Irina and Yuri—out of Russia. If she had to make a choice, Irina would be her immediate priority. Reunification of the family would always be her long-term goal, but the fate of her three-year-old child—without a parent and in a hostile city—was her major focus. She could not simply go to Moscow and retrieve Irina. That bridge had been burned. But the emigration rules did offer another option. Foreign nationals could travel to and from Russia. In a brilliant but risky plan, Lea approached Herr Schlesinger, the diplomat who had been Onissim's good friend and whose wife had been so helpful in promoting the recent concert. She explained her situation and made a simple request: Could he or some other gentleman, on his next trip to Moscow, pick up Irina, claiming she was his daughter, and bring her to Berlin?

Schlesinger agreed to help, though as consul General, he himself was too well-known in Russia to pull off the deception. The ideal person was one Gustav Hilger, a man only a year younger than Lea who had been born and spent his youth in Russia. According to his official résumé, Hilger was serving in Moscow as delegate general of the Red Cross and Germany's Nansen representative, part of a committee charged with distribution of food and supplies from foreign governments. But there was much more to his résumé of a clandestine nature that I was to discover decades later. According to a U.S. government file on Herr Hilger from 1948, prepared as part of the Nazi War Crimes Disclosure Act and declassified by the Central Intelligence Agency in 2004, Hilger was involved in clandestine activities throughout his career, including well after Lea knew him, for Nazi Germany. He had the perfect physical appearance for undertaking Lea's project. Quoting from the file: "There was nothing about him, pale and quiet, with dull brown hair and thick-rimmed glasses, of average size and middle age, and lacking in any color, to attract public attention." Even more important, as a person traveling on a diplomatic passport, he would be subject to less scrutiny at the border.

After Hilger arrived at the family apartment in Moscow and somehow convinced the family to trust him, Irina was told she must prepare for a long trip with Herr Hilger, and that she must say that he was her father. This was the third great psychological trauma my mother experienced before her fourth birthday. After having believed herself abandoned in a train station by her grandmother on the trip from Odessa to Moscow and then standing beside her father when he was stricken and died, she was now being sent away with a stranger she had never met, a man whom she was to call Father. This, too, haunted her for decades, as we, her children, learned, in bits and pieces much later.

At first when Lea went to pick up Irina in Berlin, she didn't recognize her. The child was pale and thin, with a strange lack of color. She seemed smaller than Lea remembered, a little shrunken. Irina's once beautiful hair, deloused before the trip, was arranged in short, straggled braids tied with strings. And she was wrapped in a heavy, peculiar-looking coat made out of upholstery fabric from the sofa in the Moscow apartment. In Gitel's usual practical fashion, since she was unable to purchase material to make a warm coat for Irina, she simply tore fabric from the furniture. The terrible scratchy coat was the only thing Irina could recall about the trip years later.

But Irina clearly remembered her reunion with her mother in Berlin. "Mother gave one look at me, took me to a store, dressed me, took me to a hairdresser, had my hair cut and put a large bow on the top of my hair and this was a sign that I was to be stylishly dressed from that moment on."[3] The "official" version of what happened next—the version told by Boris in his autobiography and generally accepted by the family—was that soon after Irina's arrival, Leonid Kreutzer, who had been providing every kind of support and affection, decided their relationship should become something more. In time, their connection progressed into what Boris described as "a hot and heavy affair."

"Romances of this kind are not easy to conceal," Boris wrote in his book, "and Kreutzer was evidently less than expert in the art of amorous dissimulation. All I knew was that suddenly, without warning, my piano lessons were terminated. Why? There were embarrassed explanations. Frau Kreutzer, it seemed, had put her foot down. 'No, you are *not* going to teach this boy any longer and you are *not* going to see that woman again!' . . . 'That woman' of course was Mother, who in early 1922 was still a relatively young and attractive widow of thirty-seven years."[4]

After Boris's death, I began to wonder about his version of events and whether he either may have misremembered things or was too young at the time to know what really was going on. The chronology as he presented it seemed off. He talked about his mother being an attractive widow in early 1922. But this was not quite correct. Onissim did not die until September 7 of that year and very little time would have elapsed between that date and when her affair with Kreutzer was discovered. A more likely version is that Lea's affair with Kreutzer began well before she got news of Onissim's death—perhaps soon after she arrived in Berlin. Could this explain why Kreutzer had done so much for Lea, and why he had been so enthusiastic about Boris for so many months? It appears that Lea too could have more than one romantic partner.

In spring 1923, after their breakup, Lea and Kreutzer played one final concert together on March 24 at the Beethoven Saal. It was a major event for Lea. She was appearing in a famous concert hall of over two thousand seats with one of the most distinguished pianists in Berlin. A concert guide from the period displays Lea's name prominently and includes excerpts of her glowing reviews, mentioning her consummate technique and her large and beautiful tone. Kreutzer, whose name is shown in smaller type, appears to be playing only a supporting role.

They chose to play the Franck sonata. The very work that had cemented Lea's love affair with Onissim now marked the end of her affair with Kreutzer. Though they were appearing in public as a happy duo, their relationship, both romantic and professional, had ended, thanks to the intervention of Kreutzer's wife. The good German woman, it seemed, was more important to the distinguished pianist than the poor, Russian immigrant violinist, no matter how talented or attractive. There is, of course, a further irony to the story and it is in the name Kreutzer itself. It is part of the title of Tolstoy's famous novella of infidelity, *The Kreutzer Sonata*. Here again, life was imitating art.

The discovery of Lea's affair with Kreutzer resulted in far more than the loss of Boris's teacher. Concert engagements began to disappear as news of the affair spread, and the patronage of both Kreutzer and Louise Wolff was withdrawn. Growing anxious, Lea had to consider whether her attempt at reinvention as a reigning doyenne of the musical world of Berlin was going to work out. Perhaps it was not the best place for her.

Boris and Schnabel

When I think of Lea and Boris in Berlin and all that occurred there, I sometimes find it hard to believe that Boris had barely reached puberty when they arrived. During that first year, he went to school, took piano lessons, served as his mother's accompanist, played solos with orchestras and in his mother's recitals, and began to find ways to supplement the family's income. It helped that he had come to Berlin speaking fluent German—in Russia, he and Yuri were tutored in the language by their Latvian governess, Katya Rigert, the same woman who had accompanied Irina on the fateful trip from Odessa to Moscow.

More than a year had passed since Boris's initial success as a soloist. Now, after his mother's unfortunate love affair with Kreutzer, he had to find another piano teacher. The most influential one available was Artur Schnabel. Roughly the same age as Lea and trained in Vienna by the legendary Theodor Leschetizky, Schnabel had been teaching in Berlin since 1898. Lea and Boris paid him a visit. Reminding them that he had already heard Boris play at their concert with the Berlin Philharmonic, Schnabel agreed to take him on as a student without requiring an audition and at no fee, in honor of Lea's great eminence as a colleague. Apparently Schnabel was either unaware of her affair with Kreutzer or it was of no particular interest to him.

For Boris, the lessons with Schnabel were a completely new experience. The pedagogue was not interested in the usual exercises and études that a young pianist at Boris's stage of development was generally expected to learn. Rather, he assigned Boris the massive and complex masterworks of Beethoven, Brahms, and Schumann. Once Boris came to his lessons, Schnabel did most of the playing. The pupil was there to listen and absorb. To Boris, Schnabel's studio became a shrine to great music making, where he was exposed to playing the likes of which he would never forget.

Like many Germans, Schnabel believed that the most obvious way to play a piece of music was never the right way. One had to spend years in deep study of the score to know what the composer really intended and how to bring out the profundity of his musical ideas. Boris's previous teachers—all Russians—were not bound by ideas like "composer's intent" and "sanctity of the score." The score was only a starting place in a performer's personal search for beauty.* But

---

*   As an example of the Russian approach, some years later, when Boris was in Cleveland, the great pianist Sergei Rachmaninoff appeared with the orchestra there. When asked about a tempo in a Beethoven concerto, he took an obvious swipe at Schnabel: "I am not a Beethoven expert. I just play ze right tempo." See Honigberg, 82.

under the influence of Schnabel's powerful personality, Boris began to believe that they had all been wrong. Schnabel was a god and his way—that is, the composer's way—was the right way.

During this period, Boris sought ways to earn money to purchase printed music for his own personal library. He persuaded a friend of Lea's who worked for the League of Nations, and on whose piano Boris practiced, that he needed a better instrument. Boris offered to act as his agent and was given forty American dollars—a great deal of money in the only stable currency available in the country at the time. Boris haggled with a piano dealer, something he had witnessed in his grandmother's piano shop in Odessa. He was interested in a lovely Bluthner baby grand. When he mentioned that he might consider paying in dollars if he could arrange a side deal of 10 percent commission, the transaction was completed at the forty-dollar price. Boris spent his extra four-dollar commission on forty volumes of the complete works of Bach, Mozart, Beethoven, Schubert, Brahms, and Liszt—music I would see sitting on my uncle's piano in Boston decades later.

Gitel Again Rules the Roost

⌘

No one ever told me how my great-grandparents, Gitel and Saul Luboshutz, managed to leave Russia. I only knew that they arrived in Berlin soon after Irina, likely in late 1922 or early 1923. Gitel once again successfully sewed and hid valuables in her featherbed, as she had during the train trip from Odessa to Moscow. Lea's memoir lovingly lists many of these items, including silver and enamel sugar tongs, Onissim's cigarette case by Fabergé, the *podstakannik* (tea-glass holder), and various jewels. Yuri remained in Moscow with his aunt and uncle, the Shereshevskys, with whom he was close. It seemed he had no immediate desire to leave the Soviet Union.

One explanation for why the Soviets granted exit visas was that Saul was old and had little to offer the new state. The Soviets were adapting their guidelines for those wishing to enter or leave the country. People of economic value (like Dr. Shereshevsky, Lea's brother-in-law) were encouraged to come to the Soviet Union—or were prevented from leaving. Those of little value were sometimes permitted to leave. These policies were eventually incorporated into Lenin's so-called New Economic Policy or NEP. As early as 1922, a policy change allowed people who were not economically valuable to depart if they had been disabled by a "calamity." Onissim's sudden death possibly qualified as such.

Another explanation might be that the Luboshutz family was from Odessa. During the period from 1918 to 1920, Odessa had been controlled in turn by Ukrainian nationalist rebels, the Red Army, the White Army, and the French army. In 1920, it even briefly declared itself independent. Could Gitel have made the somewhat farfetched argument that she and her husband were technically foreign nationals, and therefore should be allowed to go abroad according to existing travel policies? Or possibly the overall confusion of the time meant that some individuals were treated differently, especially when bribes lubricated decisions. The Luboshutz family had always assumed that bribes were a fact of life. Indeed, so ingrained was the habit that years later Gitel attempted to bribe a saleslady at the John Wanamaker department store in Philadelphia in exchange for a better price on underwear (the attempt failed and Gitel was ushered out of the store).

Here is my favorite possible explanation for their successful departure: Gitel was so obstreperous that officials were simply glad to be rid of her. She was fearless, and she was persistent. Throwing her into jail was simply too much bother. "Give them exit visas," I can imagine an official saying, "before I tear my hair out."

Saul and Gitel arrived just in time. Almost immediately after their arrival, Lea began to cough convulsively. A doctor was summoned, and the diagnosis was a very serious case of pneumonia. Gitel as was her wont simply took over. Ignoring the advice of the doctor, she applied the old-fashioned remedy of heated suction cups on Lea's back, which did the trick as she knew it would. After a few weeks, Lea recovered, returning to work. By now, Gitel was in charge of their domestic life again. Lea had two more mouths to feed, but she rejoiced in her restored health, the gradual reuniting of the family, and, more practically, the help she was receiving with Gitel running the household. Lea needed to spend her time practicing, chasing down people who could engage her for concerts, rehearsing when other musicians were involved, traveling to the concerts themselves, and preparing for the family's next big move—to Paris.

Certainly Berlin had been closer to Moscow and to Yuri. Lea still believed her eldest son would remain loyal to the family and would ultimately join them. She could not seem to understand that the young man was taking his own path, establishing himself as a star in the new political firmament. She was pleased at his apparent success as a brilliant student and budding mathematician but she did not realize that given the importance of his profession to the new Soviet state, he was being treated far better than he had ever been before.

Staying in Berlin was a way to stay closer to Yuri, but her attempt at reinvention there had not worked out and life had proved difficult. In the French capital, a growing community of Russian émigrés was settling in and Paris was another important European musical center from which Lea could advance her career—albeit perhaps with more realistic expectations this time. Many people there had known Onissim from his visits with Rashel. Others had met Lea in 1905, when she had concertized and enjoyed Rashel and Onissim's hospitality. So just months after her parents' arrival in Berlin, Lea took them and Irina to Paris, leaving fifteen-year-old Boris in Berlin to continue his studies. The family moved into a large modern apartment building at 16 Rue Raynouard in Passy. Located in the 16th arrondissement, the area boasted plenty of artists, writers, and musicians, as well as affluent Russian émigrés. Their beautiful building had been completed in 1913 by architect Albert Vêque and was part of a complex, built in a U shape around a square or courtyard where Irina could play, while still in view of their upper-story flat. Lea might not be a reigning musical queen, but she could at least attempt to live well and gradually rebuild a musical career.

On the one hand, life in Paris felt like such a relief after Moscow, and even after Berlin. Yet it was far from easy. Lea had to support a large family as a performing artist at a time when the economy had not yet fully recovered from the world war and there was much competititon for paying opportunities. Lea was determined that her family would behave not as poor recent immigrants but as people of quality who belonged in the highest of society. Part of this was making sure one comported oneself properly in public. As Irina recalled in her oral history: "Even though life was hard, Mother's philosophy was that you stood up straight, dressed attractively, held your head high, and behaved perfectly. I was taught to curtsy and to be charming at all times. Mother was very strict about behavior."

Lea enrolled Irina in a fashionable elementary school connected with the Lycée Molière. Saul dropped Irina off and picked her up each day. The two would walk home and Saul would give her her favorite snack—a piece of chocolate wedged into a baguette and a glass of diluted red wine. Afterward, in nice weather, they proceeded a few blocks to the Trocadero Gardens. On other days, they would detour, walking down the rue Beethoven (Irina loved the name) to the Seine to watch the boat traffic, or, crossing the river at the Pont Neuf, they would walk under the Eiffel Tower to enjoy a stroll on the Champ de Mars. These were among Irina's fondest memories of Paris. Later, when the longer walks across the Seine became too much for Saul and on those occasions when Boris was living with the family in Paris, the two youngsters would run to the Eiffel Tower, take the elevator to the top, and race down to the ground. Boris always won the race and, to Irina's frustration, he reminded her that he always got better marks in school. "But at least I am prettier than you," she insisted. She couldn't wait for him to leave home.

In Paris, Gitel was again put in charge of cooking and shopping. Though she spoke only Russian and Yiddish, she could, according to Lea, make herself understood in any market or any shop anywhere she traveled. Lea marveled at how Gitel would leave in the morning and come back with everything on the shopping list.

Soon after settling in, Lea took a chance and booked the prestigious thousand-seat Salle Gaveau for a concert on December 11, 1923. She had learned about the venue from Eugène Ysaÿe, who played there during the hall's first season in 1907–1908. Her friend the cellist Pablo Casals, who had stayed in the family apartment on one of his trips to Moscow, had also performed at the venue and spoke highly of it. Built in the early years of the 20th century, the hall was a perfect location at which to introduce herself to Paris audiences. Lea summoned Boris from Berlin and chose her pieces carefully, deciding to reinforce her reputation as one of the more important Russian artists by including, among others, the *Romance* of Reinhold Glière, which had been written for her.

Arriving at the concert hall that night after taking longer than usual to dress, Lea and Boris rushed out of the cab, leaving their printed music on the seat of the vehicle. By the time they realized the disaster, the cab was gone. What to do? Someone was immediately dispatched to their apartment to find other music they could play, albeit unrehearsed. In the meanwhile, Lea and Boris decided they would open the concert with the announced piece—a Handel violin sonata both could play from memory. After it was finished, with new printed scores that someone had fetched from the apartment now safely backstage, an announcement was made that the program would have to be changed as the printed music for the original program had been left in a cab. At that moment, a well-dressed gentleman walked up to the stage and handed them the lost music. He had been the next passenger in the cab in which Lea and Boris had been riding and had been on his way to their concert. Seeing the music, he wondered whether it was theirs and brought it to them. For Lea, this could only mean that her luck had changed.

The event, with all its attendant incidents, had captured the interest of musical Paris and was described in its full drama in *Le Ménestrel* on December 21, 1923—a great break for Lea. The article was her first full-fledged review in Paris. It praised the "many aspects of Mme Luboschitz's talent: her ample sound, expressive richness, delicacy, and strength . . . These qualities were particularly in evidence . . . above all, in the Concerto in A Minor of Vieuxtemps, whose style the artists fully understood and communicated." Lea was especially happy with this latter comment. Henri Vieuxtemps had been the teacher of Eugène Ysaÿe. Having studied the concerto with Ysaÿe, Lea knew she was practically receiving guidance from the composer himself. Boris was happy as his playing was also mentioned positively, albeit briefly, and the fifteen-year-old had now been reviewed in yet another major European capital.

Even with this successful concert evening behind them and the promise of more concerts and more income, Lea told Boris that it was simply too expensive for him to return to Berlin. Boris was enraged. There were no teachers in Paris who could compare with Schnabel, he insisted. When Lea made it clear that her decision was firm, Boris took out his hostility by teasing Irina mercilessly and playing sloppily in rehearsals. At one of their rehearsals, an exasperated Lea took off a shoe and threw it at Boris, hitting a vase instead and smashing it. When her rage subsided, Lea realized that she was dealing with an adolescent. Shoe throwing was not the answer. She needed her brother, Pierre, and she wrote him a letter, asking whether he now might come to Paris. She asked that he do everything possible to convince her elder son, Yuri, to come as well.

For his part, Pierre had been trying to figure out how to leave Russia for more than a year. But he wanted to be sure that if he left for Paris, he would have work. Unbeknownst to Lea, he had written to Serge Koussevitzky, the musician who had given Pierre some of his earliest performing opportunities in Russia. He was now well-known in Paris as a double bass player, conductor, and impresario. Though he had often provided work for Pierre in the past, their relationship had frayed when Pierre fled Moscow for Odessa in 1917, abandoning his concert schedule and leaving Koussevitzky and others in the lurch.

My great-uncle had always been a happy-go-lucky, funny, and confident man. Yet this letter, written in anguished and impassioned Russian, is serious, apologetic, and fawning. It is addressed both to Koussevitzky and his wife—perhaps gently reminding them that his brother-in-law Onissim Goldovsky had made their marriage possible by arranging Koussevitzky's complicated divorce from his first wife. Pierre wrote:

> There is not a day that I do not think about you. It is so obvious. All my best memories, all the hopes of my youth, all the beautiful things in life—everything came from you . . . My thoughtless departure to the South, the hard times, all the last years I tried to make ends meet—under these circumstances there was no opportunity to study seriously. And that is why I didn't write you. I thought that before writing I had to become worthy once again of the attention and regard you had toward me.
>
> . . . If in your heart there is still a shadow of your former kind feelings toward me, please write me regardless of whether you can

give me any employment. Don't forget that I will never decline any musical job. And I want you to know that I have saved enough money that I can afford to live near you and to wait for a job.[5]

Koussevitzky may have wanted to help Pierre and in later years he did—often, and in many ways. But for now, Pierre was still in Russia, and there was nothing Koussevitzky could do. That task would fall to Pierre himself or someone who held more clout with the Soviet authorities.

Meanwhile, given the strain on the household in Paris, Saul, now in his late seventies, was continually pressed into service in any way he could be useful. He had a way with children, and Irina adored him (after his death, Irina would keep a photograph of him on her bedroom wall until her own death, three-quarters of a century later). Their walks continued, but on cold or rainy days and as Saul's mobility diminished, they stayed in the apartment, where he taught Irina various card tricks and games. They played for hours, with Irina delighting in the fact that Saul let her win more often than not. Quietly Lea fretted about Saul's health and tried not to think of what life would be like without him.

Queen Elisabeth's Dress

In my family, after-dinner entertainment was often a mix of music and stories, and the best stories generally had Lea as a main or supporting character. Both the music and the stories would be performed over and over again. Like a favorite piece of music, a good story deserved to be shared whenever an occasion called for it. And like musical performances, there were many different ways to render a good story—and loud arguments over which version was best. Given Lea's penchant for reinventing herself, stories could evolve to suit the needs of the moment.

One of the all-time favorite family stories was the tale we called "Queen Elisabeth's Dress." There were two competing versions—Lea's and Uncle Boris's. Here is what they could agree upon: The Queen Elisabeth in question was Queen Elisabeth of Belgium, who had studied violin with Ysaÿe and had accompanied him to one of Lea's concerts in Brussels. The two female violinists, Queen Elisabeth and Lea, had met after the concert and enjoyed each other's company so much that an invitation was extended to Lea for her to come to the palace for a dinner and to play for their majesties and guests. This must have been sometime during 1923.

Here the stories deviate. According to Boris's version, in Lea's letter accepting the queen's invitation, she asked whether she might bring her teenage son as her accompanist. The queen's response was gracious. She wrote back and said that Lea should by all means bring Boris, and that the royal family would be pleased if he played a solo piece or two. Lea ordered him to write to Ysaÿe and learn the queen's favorite composers. When he learned that she loved Chopin, he immediately got to work on some preludes and nocturnes, compositions that he had studied with Kreutzer.

According to Lea, none of this happened; she used a different accompanist, and Boris wasn't present for the performance.

Whichever version is true, the other essentials of the story remain the same. Lea spent much time preparing her wardrobe. She made the rounds of various *salons de haute couture* in Paris, explaining that she needed a simple but elegant gown for a very important concert. In the end she settled on something from Lanvin. The pianist (either Boris or someone else) was also fitted with new formal attire, including a tail coat, white tie and vest, pants with a velvet stripe, cummerbund, and a dress shirt with studs and cufflinks. The clothing represented a large financial expenditure, as did the considerable time Lea spent at the hair salon.

Lea and her pianist arrived in Brussels the day before the concert. On the night of the event, a magnificent Hispano-Suiza motorcar was sent from the palace, first to pick up Ysaÿe, who was elegantly dressed and weighted down with medals, and then the evening's performers. Inside the palace, they were directed to a chandelier-lit salon with many guests already assembled and awaiting the king and queen. Eventually, doors opened into a series of rooms leading to the private chambers of their majesties. The king and queen were announced. When they appeared, Lea was horrified. The queen was wearing a dress identical to Lea's.

Lea felt her knees giving way. According to Boris, she gripped his arm, turned pale, and whispered, "Look, look!" Boris could not figure out what was so strange about two women wearing the same dress. "This did not strike me as particularly unusual, since many of the gentlemen present were dressed exactly as I was. But the effect of this similitude of dress on Mother was so staggering that for a moment I thought she would faint. Nevertheless, Her Majesty, ever gracious, simply smiled as they greeted one another and said, 'Aren't fashions becoming this year? And isn't it the nicest model of the year? How becoming it is to you!'" That, according to Lea, put her at her ease. According to Boris, this was not the case. "The comforting words had no effect, and when the time came to start the concert, Mother had barely enough strength to tune her violin."[6]

Boris's version of the story ends rather abruptly. His mother played one piece, pleaded a headache, and they left soon after, never to be invited back to the palace. He was greatly disappointed that he never got to play his Chopin for the queen. For the rest of his life, in many of his recitals, he charmed audiences by telling the story and saying, just before sitting down at the keyboard, "So now I will play for you the Chopin I never got to play that evening for the queen." Audiences always loved it.

In Lea's version, though, she was not going to remain defeated by circumstance. According to her, after she recovered her composure, they sat down to dinner, she to the left of the king and to the right of a prince. Ysaÿe was between the queen and a princess. The king talked about his last visit to Russia for the coronation of Tsar Nicholas II and what a cruel tragedy the Tsar's assassination had been, taking him away from a people who adored him. The king was a wonderful conversationalist, and, according to Lea, "You almost forgot that you were in the presence of royalty."

After dinner, the king conducted Lea to the concert hall, where she played a full concert. She began with serious pieces, which bored the king and prince but fascinated the queen and the princess, who was a fine pianist. Only when Lea began to play little show pieces did the king and prince perk up. After the concert, the queen said she wanted to give Lea something in memory of the occasion and presented her with a signed photograph. Her accompanist, she said, received a beautiful gold cigarette case.

I have never known what to make of these two versions, both credible. I have seen the signed photograph of the queen, which sat on a table in Lea's living room throughout her life. And I am certain that she played for the king and queen on multiple occasions. A 1925 review in a New York newspaper, *The Sun*, states that Lea was "appointed solo player to the King and Queen of Belgium, a post she still holds, during her sojourn abroad."[7] But perhaps Boris's story also has merit; he swore until his dying day that he was there when the dress disaster occurred.

For me, the story says something else about my grandmother. Here was the woman who had grown up poor and yet had played for a royal dynasty in Russia. That Tsar and Tsaritza were no more. Yet such events never held Lea back. She simply ingratiated herself with other royals in another land.

Promises to Keep

⁓⦂⦂⁓

By the beginning of 1924, Lea was working very hard. Concerts for royalty were all well and good, but there were the expenses of maintaining a family, and Lea wanted them to live in comfort, with a modicum of the old elegance from the Moscow days. Despite a good deal of professional success—she was finally playing with orchestras throughout Europe again and teaching at the Paris Conservatory[8]—she worried that her career had plateaued. Such thoughts are not unusual from time to time even for a very accomplished musician, but Lea's were based on concrete facts. Though she was living in Paris, she had not yet appeared at the most important venue, the grand opera house, Palais Garnier. And she had not yet been invited back to America, which, increasingly, was the land of opportunity and big fees.

She decided to give a major recital in Paris in another of the modest-sized halls—the Salle des Agriculteurs—on June 16. She played an old standby, Beethoven's Kreutzer sonata, but she also showed her varied repertoire by selecting works from six different countries, many of which would be unfamiliar to Parisian audiences.[*]

But this still left the much more important question of how to appear at the Palais Garnier, and once again, Lea took matters into her own hands rather than wait for something fortuitous to happen. At almost two thousand seats, even with great effort and with the support of many friends, she realized she could not take on the project of a concert in this venue on her own. Even with the help of a commercial promoter, she knew realistically that she was not famous enough to fill the venue. The alternative was to appear with an orchestra, but so far none had booked her as a soloist there. So she appealed to her old friend Fyodor Chaliapin, who was now living in Paris and was one of the most famous vocalists in the world.

When Lea called on him, he was delighted. They chatted about the past and gossiped about friends and fellow artists. Then she got to the point. With Onissim's death, she had to play more important concerts and be noticed by the right people so that she could command higher fees. A concert at the Palais Garnier would propel her to the next level. As it happened, there was an open date (July 9, 1924) after the main season finished. She couldn't pull it off by herself, especially since many concertgoers would be out of town for the summer. But if Chaliapin appeared with her in a joint recital, the event would be a sellout. "I knew full well that he did not need the concert," Lea recalled in her memoir. "That audiences the world over jammed the doors every concert he played. Chaliapin looked at me and smiled.

"'For you,' he said, 'I do it. We will give a recital in the grand opera house.'"

Lea was thrilled. As so often when she had an important concert, she went shopping. She would never again wear the dress she had worn for the event at Queen Elisabeth's palace. But she did go to Lanvin, this time with no money, and explained the situation, saying that she felt confident she could pay after the concert. The manager, who knew her well, agreed to sell her the gown on credit.

---

[*] The program for that concert is in the family archive. The musical selections in addition to the Beethoven include works by Schumann, Weber, and Simon (German), Nardini (Italian), Bloch (Swiss), Rode and Le Borne (French), Scriabin and Juon (Russian), and Burleigh (African American).

The day of the concert, Lea received a call. Chaliapin was not well and could not sing. This was the worst possible news. The hall was sold out; if people arrived and found he was not appearing, it would be worse for Lea's career than no concert at all. She took a cab to Chaliapin's apartment and pleaded with him, explaining what was at stake. Remarkably, for a singer who was not in full voice, he relented. He told Lea that for her he would sing that night, even though he would not do such a thing for anyone else.

Chaliapin went on stage first with his longtime accompanist, Fyodor Keneman, and was greeted with tumultuous clapping, bravos, and stamping. It didn't seem to matter that he was not in good form; people loved him too much to take notice. Then Lea and her pianist took the stage. They opened with a Vivaldi violin concerto. The contrast was palpable. Chaliapin was a world celebrity. Even his accompanist, Keneman, was a Gold Medal winner from the Moscow Conservatory and a recognized composer as well as an accomplished pianist. And Lea? She was one of many newly arrived Russian émigré musicians on the French musical scene. While she too had received a Gold Medal and was relatively well-known in Russia and Berlin, she had had only a few appearances in Paris. Her accompanist—a gentleman named Latinsky—was an even lesser light. The applause they received for the Vivaldi concerto was far more subdued than what Chaliapin had gotten—"In spite of my beautiful Amati violin and Lanvin gown, the audience turned cold," Lea later wrote. But as she continued to play, she sensed a rising warmth in the hall.

Intermission came. Chaliapin and Lea were sitting together backstage when a gentlemen approached, greeting Chaliapin as if the two knew one another well. Lea gave them some privacy for a while. Then the gentleman turned to Lea and said in Russian, "I am Sol Hurok, and you are Lea Luboshutz. You belong in America, and if you will come, I will promise to be your manager."

Chaliapin smiled, wished her well, and promised her great happiness and success. Lea then returned to the stage for her finale. She had chosen the piece that had always been associated with change in her life, a work she was confident her French audience would love—the sonata for violin and piano by César Franck.

In Lea's memoir, she is rather dismissive of her own playing that night—the focus is first on Chaliapin and then on her meeting with Sol Hurok. Based on that, I had always assumed that her performance might have been lackluster.

But press coverage of the concert indicated Lea's success was considerable. Strangely, though I never found a review of the actual concert, words describing it can be found in a subsequent review of another young female violinist—a Mademoiselle Jelly d'Aranyi. It had been written some six months after Lea's concert. In it, the writer lavished far more praise on his recollections of Lea's performances, especially that one in July.

> Yet, while this young woman is an excellent virtuoso, I hope I may
> be allowed to say that I prefer, and by far, the remarkable Russian
> violinist Madame Lea Luboschitz, who, in her recital at the Salle
> des Agriculteurs, proved once again, as she did at the Opera on
> the evening of the Chaliapin concert, where she certainly had a
> triumph, that she is now all but unrivaled. Her bow is a thing of
> beauty, her virtuosity incomparable, her expression of rare accuracy,
> and her style of absolute perfection. My goodness![9]

Why would Lea say nothing about this wonderful response to her playing? It was partly, I think, characteristic of the low estimation in which she held music critics, a view shared by the rest of the family and many of her colleagues. There was no question that good reviews were important in furthering one's career—artist managers and promoters needed them, especially if they were from well-known writers and publications. But as an accurate guide to one's playing, they were worthless.

Hurok, on the other hand, offered something that was well worth crowing about—an American tour. Chaliapin told Lea a bit about Hurok after the concert, repeating that the impresario had the ability to make her famous in America. Hurok was a few years younger than Lea, but he was already a successful promoter and manager. He offered her an initial group of concerts in the United States, beginning in January 1925, less than six months from their meeting.

Solomon Izrailevich Gurkov, or Sol Hurok, as he renamed himself in America, did not grow up around music or musicians. He never studied an instrument. He grew up in a small Russian village and after coming to America as a teenager in the wake of the 1905 revolution, Hurok tried a variety of ventures in Philadelphia and New York, none related to music. But in 1907, a friend convinced him to go to a Chaliapin performance in New York. After that night, Hurok decided on his life's destiny—to become a promoter and presenter of great performers.

His first attempts to "get into the business" were modest events featuring local talent. His breakthrough came in 1912, when he presented the Russian violinist Efrem Zimbalist in a concert so successful that Hurok convinced Zimbalist to let him become his personal manager in the United States. Zimbalist turned out to be Hurok's first "international" star attraction. Still a young man and not nearly as famous as Chaliapin, Zimbalist realized that, though he was a rising star, he had strong competition in a crowded field. The idea of a hardworking local promoter—especially a Russian who knew his way around America—was appealing. Hurok's successes with Zimbalist soon led to other musicians joining the Hurok roster including, eventually, Chaliapin himself. By 1919, Hurok had branched into dance, presenting a troupe organized by none other than Isadora Duncan (and affectionately called the Isadorables) for six performances at Carnegie Hall. By the time Lea joined Hurok's roster for the 1924–1925 season, he was making many people's careers.

As plans for her initial tour developed, Lea at first told Boris he should go with her to America as her accompanist, but Boris wanted to return to Berlin and Schnabel. If he did not go to work with the great pianist, he told her, he would commit suicide. (*Ah*, I think now, *the frustrations of raising an adolescent!*) Lea patiently explained that with high living expenses in Paris, she did not have money to give him an allowance in Berlin. The sixteen-year-old then made a brash promise: He would take only enough money to cover travel costs and two weeks' living expenses. Thereafter, he would either make do on his own or come back to Paris. The Schlesingers and the Hilgers promised to help, including initial housing. And the Bluthner piano company offered Boris free use of a piano, as it did to every Schnabel student in exchange for their playing Bluthner instruments in their concerts. Schnabel's lessons would continue to be free, out of respect for Lea.

Lea gave her consent along with the initial funds Boris requested, and no sooner had Boris arrived back in Berlin than he secured a job playing in a café. But this good fortune was short-lived, as German laws forbade foreigners holding jobs without proper permissions. Since the café reported his earnings, the government soon caught up with Boris and he was ordered to leave the country within twenty-four hours. This punishment seemed harsh, but there was an additional reason for it—irregularities with his papers. "How many times were you born?" asked the police.

Apparently Boris's birth certificate gave his birth date as May 25, according to the old style Julian calendar in use at the time of the Tsars. His passport gave the new style Gregorian calendar date of June 7. Once again, Herr Hilger, the man who had rescued Irina from Moscow, was pressed into service. Explaining the calendar discrepancy and pleading Boris's ignorance as a youthful mistake, Hilger managed to secure permission for Boris to remain in Germany as long as he did not work for wages. Furthermore, he convinced the officials to bend the rules and allow Boris to take on a few paying pupils. This small income was sufficient to allow Boris to move into his own lodgings. He depended on many meals in the homes of Russian and German friends. But he kept his promise and did not ask his mother for any more money—a point of great pride.

As for Lea, she arrived in New York in January 1925. It was the second time she had set foot on American soil, after her first abbreviated visit some seventeen years earlier. Hurok arranged a suite for her at the Great Northern Hotel, half a block from Carnegie Hall, the hall where Lea had played in 1907. At that time, she had been one of many musicians appearing with Altschuler's orchestra. Playing a recital at the famous hall or being the featured soloist with an American orchestra there would be different. Hurok promised that if she did well on this first tour, she would soon be appearing at Carnegie Hall regularly. It was a promise he would keep.

But first, Lea needed to establish a strong reputation in America, garner favorable reviews, and impress orchestra conductors. On Hurok's say-so, many would engage her a first time. But the name of the game in America, Hurok explained, was re-engagements and that would depend on her. As Lea recounted proudly, her track record for re-engagements in America turned out to be impressive. By 1930, according to one published report, she had been re-engaged almost everywhere she had played and in some American cities had done so every year since 1925.[10]

Lea's New York recital debut took place at the Aeolian Hall on January 23, 1925. At eleven hundred seats, the venue was about the same size as the Salle Gaveau, where Lea and Boris had played their first concert in Paris. With great anticipation, Lea awaited the judgment of the critics. Happily, the reviews the next day, though brief, were favorable, including, importantly, one in the *New York Times* that claimed Lea was a student of Leopold Auer. It was not true, but all famous Russian violinists touring America at the time were Auer pupils, or so it seemed, so it only enhanced her reputation. She was, the review said, "a player of vitality and verve . . . the mistress of many moods." The *New York Sun* praised her excellent intonation and added that, "her expression of emotions [was] delivered by a warm and fluent style."

Lea played a second, equally successful concert at the Aeolian Hall two weeks later. Hurok could now confidently promise a more extensive American tour and a Carnegie Hall "debut" the next season. Happy with these results, Lea looked forward to returning home to Paris. But there was one more concert to play—unplanned, unrehearsed, and not in a concert hall—or even on American soil. This performance would prove to be one of the most fateful events of her life.

On May 2, 1925, Lea embarked for Europe on the SS *Majestic*. Who should be on board but two great pianists, Josef Hofmann and Dame Myra Hess. As reported a year and a half later in the *Musical Courier* (January 27, 1927), the captain prevailed upon the three musicians to play a concert to benefit the Seamen's Charities. On May 6 at nine o'clock in the evening, people gathered in the Lounge on B deck. Lea opened the concert with Hofmann. She sensed that something special was going to happen that night and she decided to play the César Franck sonata. It was a huge success and while it may have been an impromptu concert, Hofmann seemed to have enjoyed it sufficiently to suggest that he and Lea consider concertizing together in the future.[11]

Two promises were made on shipboard after the concert. First, Hofmann told Lea that he would make arrangements for an initial concert tour. Such was his prestige that a year and a half later, the duo would be playing in Carnegie Hall, after debuting together in London. Second, Lea made a promise to Hofmann. When she had come to the United States in 1907, she told him, she had been pregnant with her second son. Now an accomplished pianist himself, Boris could brag that his first appearance on the Carnegie Hall stage had occurred while still in his mother's womb. "The next time I come to the United States, he will be with me and you will hear him." The promise, though kept, was one she later regretted.

Isadora to the Rescue—Twice

❧

Lea's sons, Yuri and Boris, had begun their musical training at age five, on their father Onissim's insistence. Now that their sister, Irina, had reached that same age, Lea, Saul, and Gitel decided she should start piano lessons. The results were not happy, as Irina was miserable and appeared to lack native talent. But perhaps dance was a possibility. In the apartment above theirs in Paris lived a former Russian ballerina by the name of Madame Olga Preobrajenska,[12] with whom Irina had become friends. Preobrajenska's career had included not only acclaimed performances throughout the world but distinguished teaching, including at one time running the ballet school at La Scala in Milan.[13] Such a pedigree was enough for Lea. She walked Irina over to Preobrajenska's Paris studio one day to observe a class and, when her child seemed enchanted, Lea enrolled her, imagining that Irina could become a prima ballerina.

Actually, Lea had another reason for the arrangement. She did not believe that Preobrajenska's apartment, where Irina had been spending much time, was a healthy place for a child. It had a strange odor of decay and animal droppings, as the aging ballerina kept a Scottie dog and a large turtle. She also had a companion—a hawk-eyed lady with dwarfism and a hunched back—whom Lea found frightening. Not so for Irina, who had formed a deep friendship with both Preobrajenska and her companion, the latter of whom told Irina seemingly endless stories and allowed her to touch the humpback for good luck. Lea was concerned about cleanliness as well as her young daughter's growing sense of living in a fantasy world. Perhaps a rigorous ballet program would be an antidote.

Coincidentally, Pierre was also becoming more involved in dance back in Moscow. Having served for several years as Isadora Duncan's pianist, he was now helping the glamorous star with the dance school that she had opened in Moscow in 1921. It promulgated Duncan's philosophy about the proper training of youngsters—free form, emphasizing fluid and graceful movements of bodies clothed in loose tunics, very different from the classical style favored by Preobrajenska. As she was setting about training young dancers, Duncan was also preparing for more solo performances, working late into the evening in her so-called red studio to the strains of Scriabin, Liszt, and even Beethoven's Fifth Symphony.[14] Pierre, who was living in Lea and Onissim's apartment, made himself available whenever he was needed. Pierre was also helping Yuri, who was studying mathematics and hoping to go to Moscow University (where his father had initially also studied mathematics before transferring to law). Though the young man had no interest in a musical career, his early piano training proved useful. Pierre helped Yuri join the musician's union, and the budding mathematician's playing was good enough to earn money from occasional concert work. Yuri was also able to get a job helping Pierre with piano duties at Isadora Duncan's dance school. Indeed, on his university application, Yuri listed his occupation as "pianist at a choreographic college."

Yuri was determined to stay in Moscow, as he felt he had a real future in the new Soviet Union. But after Saul and Gitel departed, Pierre's desire to leave grew more urgent. Yuri was in good hands as his aunt Anna and her husband had promised to look after him. As a mathematician, Yuri had more in common with Uncle Nikolai Shereshevsky than he did with Uncle Pierre, and Lea was urgently encouraging Pierre to join the family in Paris as soon as possible. Though Boris had returned to Berlin to study piano and Lea no longer needed Pierre to help her manage her unruly son, she did need him as a replacement accompanist. Besides, Gitel and Saul were no longer young. It was a lot to ask for them to run the household and be responsible for Irina's child care, and if Pierre came, he could help there, too.

With Yuri admitted early to Moscow University (he had advanced astonishingly as a mathematician and was admitted at the age of sixteen), Pierre knew the time had come. Having failed with Koussevitsky, Pierre appealed to Isadora Duncan. Such was her popularity with the Russian authorities that she secured exit visas for Pierre and his wife, Elena, and they were able to join the family in Paris in 1925. They stopped in Berlin to see Boris, but Pierre had promised the family he would come as soon as possible to help out, so the visit with Boris was brief. Pierre's arrival was welcomed by everyone. He could be as practical as his mother and always seemed able to find work. His personality was also the perfect antidote to the stress and the doom and gloom that often surrounded the family. His marvelous sense of humor was much needed after the many years of difficulties.

A few months after Pierre's arrival, Irina was in her first dance recital. The whole family attended. Lea was enchanted; her newest dream of a star-ballerina daughter was seemingly being realized before her eyes. She took some of her spare cash and had a very short squirrel fur coat made for Irina, considered very fashionable at the time. With a similarly short skirt underneath and low socks, much of Irina's skin was exposed during the cold winter months. Gitel, who always had a fear of drafts, complained that this was unhealthy. When Irina caught her first cold of the season, Gitel was incensed. "In stepped the powerful Babushka [grandmother]," wrote Lea. "The stylish coat went down; the short socks came up and, in no time at all, under concentrated Russian authority, Parisian chic left Rue Raynouard."

One evening soon after Pierre's arrival, Isadora Duncan, who was herself in Paris, came to pay a visit. Lea had just returned from a concert and was making a late supper. She mentioned that Irina was an extremely gifted dancer and Isadora perked up—she was always looking for young talent. She asked when she could see Irina dance. Irina had been asleep for hours, but the two women were so excited that they decided to wake her up. A sleepy Irina was told to put on her tutu and her ballet slippers and perform.

Lea should have known better. She had seen Isadora dance on several occasions. In one concert at the huge Bolshoi Theatre in Moscow, she saw an entire solo evening of Isadora dancing, free-form, to the accompaniment of a full orchestra playing an uncut version of Tchaikovsky's Pathétique Symphony. Irina's teacher Preobrajenska, on the other hand, had been an internationally known prima ballerina with the Russian Imperial Ballet whose rigorous, rule-governed movements had been taught carefully to Irina. Before the young girl danced a step, it should have been clear that this was not going to be a good match. Irina began, and Isadora watched carefully. As Lea recalled years later, "To my great surprise and astonishment I heard the following sentence which I have never forgotten."

"'My dear idiot, this child has no talent whatsoever.'"

Once Lea heard that Irina had no talent, the dance lessons ended. For a time, Lea was angry, especially since Irina had been reduced to tears and wanted to continue in the dance class. But ultimately, Lea believed that Isadora Duncan had done the family a favor. She had rescued Irina from a life as a struggling performing artist—a life Lea knew well. From then on, the course of Irina's life was simple and straightforward, and Lea's task (and Gitel's) was clear. They needed to find this six-year-old a rich husband—not immediately, of course, but sooner rather than later.

The Prokofiev Violin Concerto

Soon after Lea returned to Europe from America in 1925, she started to plan a family summer vacation. It was the first time since the Moscow days that she could afford one, and she wanted to pay more attention to Irina. The seven-year-old, now free of piano and dance lessons, had to be brought up properly and nurtured carefully if she were to snag a wealthy husband. Lea employed a governess—an Englishwoman called simply Miss B who was, according to Lea, "a 'lady' in the strictest Victorian sense." Miss B taught Irina the most elegant English language, as well as proper manners. My mother's mastery of English made her immensely happy, particularly once Boris rejoined the family. Irina's arrogant brother had always teased her about how ignorant she was. Now she knew a language that he did not.

Miss B convinced Lea that Paris was no place for a young girl in the summer, so Lea rented a house in the resort town of St.-Jean-de-Luz, a location popular with other musicians including Chaliapin, the composer Maurice Ravel, the violinist Jacques Thibaud, the pianist Arthur Rubinstein (who a few years later would marry Nela Mlynarski, the daughter of Lea's Odessa teacher), and many others. Boris, whose lessons with Schnabel were suspended during the summer months, returned to France to join the family. He had kept his promise to his mother and had survived in Berlin for eight months without her help. But it had been a Spartan existence and he had often been cold and hungry. The comfortable apartment in Paris and the even nicer house in St.-Jean-de-Luz were like paradise to him. When Lea again offered him the opportunity to go to America as her accompanist, he jumped at the chance. Lea promised Hurok that she would premiere a new concerto by Prokofiev in the United States on her upcoming fall tour. She could work on the solo violin part alone, but it would be very helpful if Boris could play the orchestra parts on the piano during the summer so that she could become familiar with the full score.

The story of how Lea ended up playing the New York debut of such an important new work had its origins some months earlier, just days in advance of Lea's setting off on her first Hurok-sponsored American tour. The impresario had told Lea that she should bring new Russian repertoire with her that would impress American audiences and critics. As one of many Russian violinists vying for attention, such music would make her more marketable. Lea knew of one such piece—Prokofiev's first violin concerto. It had premiered in Paris in October 1923 but was unknown in America. Lea got in touch with the composer, who was in Paris at the time. She asked whether she might play the work for him and get his suggestions. They met on the last day of 1924. According to Prokofiev's correspondence, he was bowled over by Lea's playing and agreed to help her in any way he could.

Two days later the composer wrote a letter to their old friend Serge Koussevitzky, who had conducted the world premiere of the concerto in Paris on October 18, 1923, with Marcel Darrieux as the violin soloist. Subsequently, Koussevitzky had moved to the United States to become the music director of the Boston Symphony Orchestra. He had received the composer's permission to present the first performance of the violin concerto in the United States. It had originally been scheduled with the Boston Symphony's concertmaster, Richard Burgin, as soloist. But the music had not arrived in time, so the concert had been rescheduled for April 24, 1925. Now, in his letter, Prokofiev wondered whether Koussevitzky might consider substituting Lea for Burgin. The stars were aligned, he said, since Lea had just left for the United States on New Year's Day and wanted to play the piece.

> Two days ago Lea Luboshutz came to me and played my Violin Concerto. She played it better than Darrieux. Yesterday she left for America where she is going to play the Concerto in different places but the first performance she would like to play with you.

If the playing of the concerto by Burgin hasn't happened, maybe it would be very good for Lea to play it.[15]

When I first learned of this letter, I was of two minds. On the one hand, I was not thrilled to learn of Lea's plotting to replace a respected colleague. For though the letter indicated that the idea was Prokofiev's, Lea undoubtedly had a hand in suggesting it. Even in the competitive world of classical music, this was not proper behavior. Burgin was a fine player and a decent man—who, incidentally, became a longtime family friend. On the other hand, I was pleased to learn that Prokofiev had liked Lea's playing so much. To be honest, I had never known just how good a player my grandmother was. It was well-known that she was a child prodigy, but those are a dime a dozen, most flaming out or becoming ordinary as adult players. And there was no arguing with the fact that she had been scrappy, possessed of street smarts, with energy and grit. This counted for a lot given the chaos around her and it contributed to her ability to secure concerts and attract audiences. But this was different from true artistry. Until I located a rare recording, there were none available at the time to help me judge her talents. So learning that a composer as important as Prokofiev wanted to entrust the U.S. premiere of his concerto to Lea meant a lot to me. She must have been awfully good.

Much as Koussevitzky liked the Luboshutz family, dumping Burgin in favor of Lea was not something he would consider, though he promised her she could perform the piece with his orchestra three years later. In lieu of this, Prokofiev told Lea he would allow her the first performance of the concerto in New York, which was, he claimed, a more important cultural center than Boston in any case. Before New York, Prokofiev said, Lea should play the concerto in Paris, as he felt local audiences should hear her rendition of the piece.

Sol Hurok was thrilled with the news. He started making tentative arrangements for a New York performance to take place in fall 1925. He pulled off something of a coup, convincing the distinguished composer, pianist, and conductor Ernst von Dohnanyi to lead the orchestra in an all-Russian program (consisting of works by Rachmaninoff, Tchaikovsky, and the Prokofiev) with Lea as the featured soloist. Meanwhile, with Boris assisting her, Lea spent the summer mastering the concerto for her Paris concert.

Lea's Paris performance of the Prokofiev concerto (a "warm up" for the New York concert) took place on October 11, 1925. According to the music critic Theodore Lindenlaub, writing in *Le Temps* on October 15, 1925:

> Sunday saw the triumphal success of the one and only Mme Léa Luboschitz. This violinist is unique in every sense of the word . . . Especially in her manipulation of the bow, now ample and strong, now of an unbelievable lightness and airiness. But one also feels, behind the astonishing power of this young woman, a deeply superior musical intelligence.

The New York premiere on November 10, 1925, was also important to Lea's later career. It made such a great impression that one local critic would recall the concert almost a decade later.[16] More immediately, the effusive accolades in the next day's *New York Times* review offered new material for Hurok's publicity mill:

> Interest centered in the concerto, which was fortunate in finding an interpreter like Mme. Luboshutz. She stood invincible, imperturbable, master of the instrument and the intricate lines allotted to her bow.

"Invincible and imperturbable." Lea was now forty years old. During the four decades leading up to this event, no words could more aptly describe her character and spirit. This would be her new persona.

Boris and Lea Come to America

In fall 1925, with Irina back in school and under Gitel's supervision in Paris, Lea and Boris set out for New York for Lea's second Hurok-sponsored tour. Hurok had arranged an extensive itinerary of performances, highlighted by the

New York premiere of the Prokofiev concerto at Carnegie Hall on November 10. Lea's Carnegie Hall recital debut (violin and piano) would follow on November 21, with seventeen-year-old Boris as her accompanist.[17]

Once again, Lea's suite at the Great Northern awaited her. There was an upright piano for Boris in one of the rooms. An early caller was the pianist Josef Hofmann, who had agreed to hear Boris play. Boris sat at the upright—hardly a great piano—and played the long and difficult Liszt B Minor piano sonata from beginning to end. As Boris described him, "Hofmann was on the shortish side, and he had the squat build of a mountaineer . . . The one thing about him that might have led one to suspect that he was an artist was a certain moodiness which would often descend on his brow and sit there like a cloud."[18]

As Boris played, that cloud seemed to descend. It was clear that Hofmann did not like what he was hearing. Again, Lea should have known better. Hofmann and Schnabel, Boris's latest and most influential teacher, took very different approaches to the piano. Boris was aiming to encompass the profound metaphysical meaning of the score. In so doing, as he himself later admitted, he allowed sloppy technique—he was totally unconcerned with the delicacy of touch and beauty of sound that was one of the keys to Hofmann's own playing. Not wanting to offend Lea, Hofmann simply demurred. But Boris got the message: "To have my playing brushed aside by someone like Josef Hofmann, for whom mother had an almost limitless admiration, was a humbling experience."[19] For the rest of their lives, the two men cordially detested each other.

The disappointment engendered by Hofmann's brush-off was soon supplanted by the reaction of Ernst von Dohnanyi, the orchestra conductor for Lea's New York performance of the Prokofiev concerto. Though the concert was only two weeks away, the distinguished-looking gentleman had not yet heard the piece or even seen the score. He came to the hotel and once again, Boris sat at the piano in the presence of one of the finest pianists in the world—this one also a noted composer and conductor. Boris and Lea played through the difficult work with Dohnanyi sitting on the sofa and listening. He closed his eyes and did not bother to follow the printed music, which surprised Boris. He seemed to be soaking it in.

When they finished, Dohnanyi (who "combined the informality of a country squire with the grace of a diplomat,"[20] according to Boris) seemed pleased. "'It is a fine piece and I am particularly intrigued by the scherzo movement . . .

Madame, would it trouble you too much to play the middle movement over, and this time I will accompany you?'" Boris was amused. It was an extremely difficult and tricky movement with lots of syncopation and changes of key. He had practiced it for weeks and still made mistakes. As only an adolescent could, he had anticipated with great excitement the likelihood that one of the world's great pianists would stumble through the music that Boris had just played. But far from struggling, Dohnanyi played the movement better than Boris ever had. "Not only was this somewhat dilettantish-looking man a keyboard virtuoso, he was a sight-reading magician!"[21] wrote Boris. In an instant, loyalty to Schnabel was out the window. Boris wanted to study with Dohnanyi. For the rest of the long tour, Boris did nothing but badger Lea about his need to study with his new great god.

At the same time that Lea and Boris were writing letters home to Paris about their success in America, Gitel was dealing with Saul's deteriorating health. My great-grandfather died of a heart attack on January 13, 1926. The ever-practical Gitel decided not to try to reach Lea. She knew how important the American concerts were, and she suspected that if Lea knew about her father's death, she would want to return home before the end of the tour. Lea had canceled concerts on her 1907 tour when she discovered she was pregnant. Gitel felt that she could not risk doing so again. Cancelations were and are an anathema in the concert business. Presenters shy away from performers who are "easy to sell but hard to deliver."

For Irina, the death of her grandfather was yet another blow—one more loss in the tiny circle of adults who had nurtured her. At some expense and considerable effort, Gitel made all the arrangements for a proper Jewish burial and located individuals who would help her sit shiva for the required seven days, according to Jewish law. Saul had been a good Jew, an extraordinary father, and a loving grandfather. Mostly, he had been a good man. As difficult as he had made her life, Gitel had been devoted to this life companion who had chosen her as a young girl, made her his wife, and given her extraordinary children.

When Lea and Boris at last returned to Paris, Gitel told them of Saul's death. For Lea, the shock was simply too much to bear, and she fell seriously ill. It appeared that Gitel had misjudged—perhaps it had not been wise to withhold information while Lea and Boris were abroad. Lea's current identity was of a woman who was strong and could always cope, and even Gitel had been taken in by it. But there was something about her relationship with Saul that touched a part of Lea that she hid and protected from everyone else. And there was a practical side to the loss. As Boris recounted years later, "For years this sweet, soft-spoken, pious, somewhat scholarly, and abominably hen-pecked husband had served as a kind of lightning rod for the electric storms touched off by Babushka's [Gitel's] volatile temper. From now on Mother [Lea] would have to bear the full brunt of these discharges."[22]

Unable to eat, Lea became weak and lost weight. As she had no concerts lined up for a while, Gitel insisted that she take some time in the spa town of Carlsbad for a rest cure. At first Lea demurred, but eventually she agreed to go for three weeks. When she returned, she wrote to a friend that she was feeling much better, "like a new creature."[23] But she continued to have nagging worries about Boris's determination to go to Budapest to study with Dohnanyi. Now more than ever, she did not want him leaving her again.

Dohnanyi

❧

I am always amused when people say, "No wonder you are a musician. You inherited your family's genes and their musical talent." If they only knew how little genes and talent figure into the process! No matter how much I try to explain, they remain unconvinced. People seem to like the simple idea that musical talent is inherited and that this explains how and why people become professional musicians.

It is true that there is some element of talent in being an accomplished musician. But most professional musicians are not great, they are merely very good, and one can be a reasonably good journeyman professional without much talent at all. I should know, as I fit that category! And any skill benefits from excellent early training. Musicians tend to start training their children and grandchildren very early. The adults are able to provide superb training either themselves or by persuading relatives and colleagues to take up the task. Many young people who are not from musician families start learning an instrument relatively late or start with poor training that they have to unlearn . . . or both.

Moreover, adults in musical families generally make the youngsters practice, long and well. Appropriate practice is not only about a certain number of minutes or hours—something any parent may require. It is also about working correctly. Without guidance, many young people practice poorly, waste time, and develop bad habits. But a professional musician knows what a child should work on and *how* that child should work on it. He or she has attentive ears when the practicing goes awry. When I started on violin, my grandmother practiced with me every day to be sure I was working correctly.

A third element that musicians can offer is what might be called musical social capital. Young family members get the best teachers, they get proper instruments (and beginners especially need good-quality instruments), they get early performance opportunities and connections to those who work in the business and can promote them, and they get good practical advice on how to negotiate the perilous paths of advancement, whether it is audition technique, attire, selection of works for different audiences, or ways of working a crowd. In some cases, they also get financial support.

All of this is important in considering Boris's quest to become a great pianist. This should have been no problem. He was gifted. He had had very early training from his Uncle Pierre and a rigorous practice schedule overseen by his mother. He had learned not only the solo piano literature but had played sonatas with his mother and was concertizing with her well before puberty. In Germany, two great teachers—Kreutzer and Schnabel—had taken him on as a student for no fee and, in Kreutzer's case, coached him through important concerts. And through Lea's association with Sol Hurok, Boris had access to a leading American promoter and manager.

Even so, there was a problem. In a short period of time Boris encountered two great and famous pianists who refused to teach him. Josef Hofmann probably would have hated any Schnabel student on general principle, but Dohnanyi was a more open-minded musician, and he also turned down the request to take Boris on. How was this possible?

It was not that Boris wasn't a good musician—everyone could see that he was superb. Musically speaking, Schnabel's tutelage had positively influenced his ability to grasp the shape and meaning of great works for the piano. But Boris's approach to the keyboard, partly because of Schnabel's influence, was "unpianistic" and sloppy—he was a banger who used his muscles in what both Hofmann and Dohnanyi considered antimusical ways. Neither wanted to retrain from scratch an adolescent who had acquired what they considered bad habits. Schnabel could get away with a certain muscular approach to the instrument because he was a genius. Many of his imitators could not.

Boris greatly admired Dohnanyi and, in a very short time, he came to agree with the older man's assessment of his technique—an astonishing admission for a young man who had already played in many of the world's greatest concert halls. When Dohnanyi first demurred, Boris kept pushing. And finally Dohnanyi relented—somewhat. He told Boris that, out of respect for Lea, he would recommend the young man to one of his assistants in Budapest whose specialty was piano technique. If Boris progressed properly and was able to master a completely different approach to the keyboard, Dohnanyi would take him on.

There was one remaining problem—money. Lea told Boris that she could not support him in Budapest. Once again, Boris complained incessantly. Wasn't she making lots of money? And besides, his life was at stake. Lea reminded him that not long before he had been threatening suicide if he could not continue his lessons with Schnabel.

One of their arguments happened to occur when they were attending lunch at the New York home of Sidney and Tessie Prince, whom Lea had met on her first tour of America in 1907. Tessie, a pianist, had cared for Lea upon discovering Lea was pregnant with Boris, and they remained close friends. The Princes were wealthy (he served as a governor of the New York Stock Exchange and had made a lot of money in bonds) and they were philanthropic, especially toward musicians. They also had a more personal reason for being affectionate toward Boris. In 1915, the Princes' only son, Leonard, died of pneumonia soon after completing his studies at Williams College. They were devastated. The Princes now considered Boris an adopted son.

At the Princes' apartment during their fall 1925 tour, Lea expressed her frustration to her host and hostess. "You know what my crazy son wants to do now? He wants to go to the Franz Liszt Academy in Budapest and learn how to play the piano. It is a place where he does not know a soul, and he can't even speak the language."[24] Tessie was sympathetic to Boris's point of view; as a fine pianist herself, she admired Dohnanyi. For his part, Sidney said that he and Boris needed to have a private talk. They went into the next room, and Prince leveled with him. He had lost his son who had been planning to join the family business. Why didn't Boris just give up the piano and come work for him? In time, he could become rich.

Boris thanked him, but explained that he had his heart set on being a musician. Prince continued to try to talk him out of it. Finally he said, "I will take this up with Dohnanyi, and if he says you should go to Budapest, I will pay your way and give you an allowance. Let's say $100 per month."[25] For Boris, who had subsisted on eight dollars a month in Berlin, this sounded like a fortune. Indeed, at the time, it was. When he ultimately did get to Budapest, Boris lived so well that he was referred to as "the rich American," though this was a laughable description: His visa had run out and he would not have been able to return to the United States even if he had wanted to.

Boris spent four transformative years (from age eighteen to twenty-two) in Budapest. He progressed rapidly with Dohnanyi's assistant, who taught him an entirely new hand technique, one lighter and more graceful. While Boris could still play as loudly as ever, his touch was more delicate and controlled. After a single year of remedial training, he was one of four pianists admitted to Dohnanyi's class at the Franz Liszt Academy of Music.

Several things about musical study with Dohnanyi were new to Boris and all of them served Boris well in his later musical career. All of Dohnanyi's piano students were required to study conducting. This gave them a grounding in musical score reading, how other instruments were played and balanced in an ensemble, and it served as an introduction to the great symphonic literature. Students also had to attend opera performances and study opera scores to understand the human voice—the most perfect of instruments, according to Dohnanyi—and the remarkable dramatic musical repertoire housed in opera. Boris's later career as an opera conductor, stage director, and impresario owes a great deal to Dohnanyi.

Finally, Dohnanyi's students were told to learn a large number of compositions, primarily to familiarize themselves with the works. It was Dohnanyi's opinion—in this regard, not unlike Schnabel's—that a seventeen-year-old was not yet mature enough to study a late Beethoven piano sonata or other deep works at the necessary level. But if that student was comfortable with a piece and could play it at a superficial level, he or she would be better prepared on returning to the piece later to forge a deeper understanding and interpretation. Boris went through all thirty-two Beethoven sonatas with Dohnanyi. The experience transformed his understanding of music for life.

One of his favorite memories was when he brought the huge and difficult Piano Sonata no. 29 by Beethoven (the Hammerklavier op. 109) and played the slow third movement for Dohnanyi. The master, as usual, did not interrupt. Boris had edged up the tempo just slightly, because of the great length of the piece. Dohnanyi asked whether Boris felt that seemed right. Boris said that he realized he wasn't playing it as a true *adagio sostenuto,* but this way he could shave ninety seconds off the performance time, getting it down to fifteen minutes exactly.

"Tell me," Dohnanyi said quietly, "do you think it is better to play a piece wrongly for fifteen minutes or play it right for sixteen and a half minutes?"

In such ways Boris came to respect Dohnanyi's impeccable taste and his quiet but firm approach to music and teaching. Indeed, there was only one moment when the teacher became angry enough to threaten to drop Boris as a student. Boris had joined the local chess club to meet people his own age and practice the Hungarian language, which he was learning from scratch—his fifth language after Russian, German, French, and English (later he added Italian and Spanish, for good measure). But what started as occasional visits turned into obsessive hours watching others play and asking them to teach him the fine points of the game.

In time, Boris started playing chess competitively. On one occasion, it was announced that the chess grand master, Géza Maróczy, would be coming to the club and would take on anyone who wished to play. So many people signed up that they were assigned to teams of two. Boris happened to be paired with the club's finest player. Of the fifteen matches, theirs was the only one that Maróczy lost, not because of Boris but because of the skill of his partner. Still, the local newspaper carried news of the match with Boris's name listed first as part of the winning team. Dohnanyi saw the article and was not pleased. At the next lesson, he told Boris that he now understood why his recent lessons had been so poorly prepared. Boris could choose between piano and chess, but there was not time for both. Thus ended Boris's short-lived chess career.

In later years, Boris claimed that his final instructional session with Dohnanyi was perhaps the most useful lesson he received from any teacher. The four pianists from the class were invited to Dohnanyi's home. After dinner, to their surprise, they were ushered into his bedroom. The older man went to his closet, took out his concert clothing—tailcoat, vest, pants, and other paraphernalia—and showed the astonished students how to lay it out, properly fold the clothing, and place it in a suitcase so that it would not be crumpled when the suitcase was opened at the end of a long trip. "This was Dohnanyi's very special manner of indicating that we had now made the grade."[26]

Le Rossignol

During Lea's American tour in fall 1925, she began to have second thoughts about her violin. She was no longer convinced that the Amati was right for her. She had fallen in love with this remarkable 17th-century Italian instrument as a teenager in Moscow and by an almost miraculous set of circumstances, her rich patron Lazar Polyakov had made it hers. And though for years thereafter, she had been ecstatic about owning and playing such a fine violin—she was now no longer sure.

To experienced musicians, this should not come as a surprise. An instrument is like a spouse with whom one hopes to develop a deep, long-term relationship. Sometimes that relationship is "'til death do us part." Often, though, it is not. One can fall madly in love only to fall out of love later. This was not a case of another love object. Lea had not found another violin she loved more. But she knew she wasn't satisfied with the Amati. Perhaps she had matured enough as a musician that it did not seem the soulmate it once had. Maybe it was the halls and the orchestras in America. Whatever the reason, Lea was questioning the long-cherished violin.

For a while, she experimented with another instrument from the golden period of Italian violin makers. She had played the Amati for many years and had briefly had the use of a Stradivarius in Moscow so there was no question in her mind that these Italian instruments from the 16th, 17th, and 18th centuries were the finest violins in the world. She chose an instrument ascribed to a member of the Bergonzi family of Cremona. Experts believed that Carlo Bergonzi had apprenticed either with Hieronymus Amati or Antonio Stradivari, so Lea anticipated that this violin would feel familiar and comfortable. Later there was some question about the violin's precise provenance though there was agreement that it was a golden period Italian instrument. But for Lea provenance was not the main consideration. She was not an investor or a collector. She was a performer and what she was looking for was an instrument that she loved and that, in a manner of speaking, loved her back. Ideally that violin would allow her to produce a beautiful and full sound and at the same time would facilitate a near flawless technique. Unfortunately, with this instument, she once again began to have doubts.

Those doubts were confirmed by a complete stranger who was not a musician but was someone who would change her life and bring her the instrument of her dreams. The stranger's name was Aaron Naumburg and he had come backstage at Carnegie Hall with his wife, Nettie, to congratulate Lea and to invite her to their apartment at 1 West 67th Street for a frank discussion about her career. They were very interested in women artists, he said, and wanted the opportunity to know her better. When Lea visited soon after the Carnegie Hall concert, she marveled at the Naumburgs' fourteen-room, six-thousand-square-foot triplex with its paneling, ceilings, and arches—Jacobean, Tudor, and Gothic treasures imported from England. The apartment was crammed with paintings by Rembrandt, Rubens, El Greco, and Franz Hals, as well as Flemish tapestries, carved jade, stained-glass windows, and much more. Its main room was forty-five feet long with eighteen-foot ceilings—ideal for concerts. And everywhere, fresh flowers, which Lea loved.

Despite the lavishness, Lea felt comfortable with what she described in her memoir as the simple and generous hospitality of the couple. Interestingly, though the Naumburgs were Jewish, their apartment was full of Christian images and iconography. There were several representations of Madonna and Child, a painting of the Holy Family by Murillo, tapestries with Christian imagery, and a series of 17th-century Swiss stained-glass windows based on the Christ story and Jesus's teachings. Aaron's father, Lazarus (Louis), and Lea's grandfather Sergei Katzman had both been rabbis who preached first and foremost the beauty of holiness. Lea's father, Saul Luboshutz, had lived his life according to this precept. But clearly for the Naumburgs, as with Lea, it was the other way round. They believed in the holiness of beauty, whatever its content and wherever its origins.

Soon they got down to business. Naumburg told Lea they were much impressed with her playing—quite remarkable, he said, especially for a woman. But they had agreed that the tone quality of her violin was a handicap. "As you see, Madame Luboshutz, I am a collector of paintings, but I would like you to look for a first class violin which I will buy instead of another painting," he said.

It was not the first time wealthy patrons had offered to help Lea secure an instrument. She knew an important but sensitive question had to be asked: "How much would you like to spend?"

Aaron Naumburg answered. "The price is of small importance. I want it to be a violin of great quality."

Lea thanked him and said she would find out what instruments were available. While she was open to any great violin, she was particularly interested in a Stradivarius from the luthier's so-called golden period, 1700 to 1725. She had once briefly had the use of such an instrument during her Moscow years when the so-called Wieniawski Strad, made in 1723,[*] had been loaned to her by its then owner. But though she loved the instrument, she was unable to acquire it. Now with Naumburg's backing, things might be different.

Lea's search, which had been rather casual up to this point, took on new intensity and purpose. She visited violin shops in New York, Chicago, San Francisco, London, Paris, Vienna, and Milan. Everywhere the answer was the same: nothing of that quality available. Finally, after a concert in London, Lea was told that the Wurlitzers of Cincinnati, a family in the instrument

---

[*] This instrument is now in the State Collection of Unique Musical Instruments of the Russian Federation, Russian National Museum of Music. On April 21, 2018, several rare violins, including this one, were featured at a concert at the Moscow Conservatory. A printed program included photographs and descriptions of each of the instruments, including musicians who had played them. Lea's name is included with the "Wieniawski" Stradivarius.

business that had stores in several American cities, had recently purchased a Stradivarius that they intended to keep in their New York shop. Upon her return to the United States, Lea immediately went to New York and asked the manager, J. C. Freeman, a distinguished violin expert who had greatly enhanced the company's reputation among serious violinists when he joined the company in 1920, whether she could try it.

Le Rossignol, or The Nightingale, was the most extraordinary instrument Lea had ever seen. So named for its beautiful tone, it had been built in 1717 by Antonio Stradivari himself. Before playing it, Lea admired its physical beauty. Unlike the backs of many violins, which are made from two pieces of wood, the back of this violin was a single piece of maple cut on the slab. Lovely striations showed through the varnish—one of the elements that makes the sound of Stradivari's instruments so superior. Everything about the violin's appearance was lovely, including the beautifully cut F holes and the scroll—both important features. According to one of the world's greatest authorities on fine violins, Alfred Hill, of the distinguished London firm W. E. Hill & Sons, "I look upon this 'Stradivari' as one of the supremely fine existing examples of the maker's work, the beauty of which cannot be surpassed, its purity and condition to be equalled by few!"[27]

As Lea examined the violin, she saw that it was in remarkable condition. One of the reasons why may have been that it had been in storage, unplayed and untouched by human hands for quite a while. This news was a temporary setback. While keeping a violin in a museum or a bank vault for an extended period may be good for its appearance and condition, it is not ideal for sound or ease of playing. Wood, as Lea knew from her experience with the Amati, is living material and is more responsive when the vibrations created by a player stimulate the cell structure on a regular basis.

Initially, Lea found the instrument difficult to play, but gradually she became accustomed to it, and it to her. All in all, she played for six hours straight in the Wurlitzer store, going from room to room to check different acoustics until it was closing time. In the end, the relationship between Lea and the violin progressed from affection to an out-and-out love affair. And as luck would have it, Lea knew the Wurlitzers in Cincinnati personally. She had played with the orchestra there under the conductor Fritz Reiner, and had even been entertained at their home.

Now she called Rudolph Wurlitzer to say that she had her upcoming annual concert with the Cincinnati Orchestra and would love to play the Stradivarius there. He was intrigued, having never heard it played at a concert, and gave his consent, inviting Lea to stay at his home when she came to perform. Before she left the New York store, she had to sign for the instrument in a large book that contained the signatures of many famous artists. As she recalled, "It turned out to be one of the most important signatures in my life." Determined that the violin would never return to that showroom, she called Naumburg to make sure his offer to purchase an instrument was still good. He assured her it was and told her to keep him informed.

Wurlitzer initially told Lea the Strad (as musicians often refer to these instruments) was not for sale, but after an all-night marathon intense discussion which followed the after-concert party at his home, he at last relented. "If you personally purchase this instrument for your own use," he told her, "I will sell it to you for the exact price that I paid for it." Lea was excited—until she heard that price. One version of her autobiography cited $35,000 though she had reasons to depress the figure to make it credible that she could have purchased it; another source put the price at $50,000.[28] Whichever it was, never before had Lea heard of a violin selling for so much. The price was extraordinary at the time, though it was actually ridiculously inexpensive given contemporary prices for Strads. Allowing for inflation, today Wurlitzer's price would have been between half and three quarters of a million dollars depending on which figure one believes; on the current market, such a violin would well sell with an eight-figure price tag.* Sadly, such instruments have become commodities, like fine art, with many of them kept in storage and never played.

Lea thanked Wurlitzer and told him she would think it over. A few hours later, she boarded the train for New York and upon arrival, reluctantly returned the instrument to the shop. Perhaps in time, Wurlitzer might lower the price. She went to the Naumburgs and reported the conversation. Aaron Naumburg

---

* Boris, who inherited the violin in 1965, sold it for $40,000. At the time, this was considered a fair price, though he probably could have sold it for more had he not been interested in seeing it go to one of Lea's former students. Still, even if he had sold it for double the price, the amount would have been paltry compared to the millions of dollars such instruments sell for today. The extraordinary rise in prices for fine Italian string instruments began in the last quarter of the 20th century and has continued unabated.

heard the news impassively. "Far from collapsing, he was not even surprised. The blessed man went straight to his desk, wrote a check in my name, and presented it to me."

They struck a secret deal: Lea would be the individual purchasing the violin, per Wurlitzer's condition, but she would write a private letter to Naumburg, which no one else would see, indicating that the instrument belonged to him. He, in turn, would insure the instrument. Lea immediately purchased the violin, showed it to the Naumburgs for their approval, and wrote the letter. She had been the violin's legal owner for less than two hours.

Now a story had to be put out to the rumormongers in the music world about how Lea could have possibly afforded what may at the time have been the most expensive violin in the world. Wurlitzer had insisted that Lea be the purchaser and that the violin be for her own use. The clear implication was that the violin must not be resold to a collector. Yet in a sense that is precisely what Lea had done. So she told people that she had found a patron who lent her the money, which she would pay back over time[29]—a somewhat outlandish notion, given her earning capacity. But this was the 1920s. Everyone was rich, it seemed, and other Russian violinists like Zimbalist, Mischa Elman, and Jascha Heifetz were making a great deal of money in America. Lea seemed to be emerging as a high-profile artist. Maybe, people speculated, she was making a lot of money as well. The Wurlitzers were also happy that Lea was playing their instrument. In several concert programs, including those from Carnegie Hall, a Wurlitzer advertisement for its fine violins listed Lea as one of the distinguished artists playing an instrument they had handled. And in 1928, at J. C. Freeman's request, she inscribed a photograph to him, which he could display in the Wurlitzer showroom: "To my dear Mr. J. C. Freeman in grateful appreciation of my Strad. Lea Luboshutz, New York, 1928." Happily, the photograph is now in my possession.

Lea's delight with the Nightingale was complete so long as she did not think about what would happen when the instrument had to be returned. As a special favor to the family, she agreed to serve as a judge for the Naumburgs' International Solo Artist Competition. The competition had been established by another family member in 1925 and would become, per the *New York Times*, "in its quiet way, the most prestigious [classical music competition] of them all."[30] But just as the 1928 prize was to be announced, a day of reckoning arrived. Aaron Naumburg died unexpectedly. It was a devastating blow. Lea now assumed that the Strad would pass to one of Naumburg's heirs.

But when Lea paid a condolence call to Aaron's widow, Nettie (with whom Lea had become close), she received some welcome news. An attractive woman with big brown eyes, a full figure, and beautiful skin that set off her pearl necklace, Nettie was dressed simply and elegantly. She soon got down to business. Since there were no instructions in Aaron's will about the violin, Lea should continue to use it until Nettie's death, at which time the violin would return to the family and become part of her estate. Lea continued to stay with Nettie whenever she was in New York and Nettie went to Lea's concerts in the city. But on March 6, 1930, Nettie too died. Lea's reprieve had been so short, the happy years with the Nightingale so few.

On March 10, 1930, Lea attended Nettie's funeral. A nephew, James N. Rosenberg, spoke of Nettie's spirit: "A gentle and gracious lady lies at peace beneath this bank of flowers," he began, and the eulogy continued in kind.[31] If Lea was moved by his speech, she did not say so in her memoir. My hunch is that my practical grandmother had little patience with such Victorian purple prose.

A few weeks later, a large envelope arrived, containing a generous sum of money ($10,000) that had been left to Lea in Nettie's will.[32] As welcome as it was, there was no news of the violin. What Lea did not realize was that, as central as the Stradivarius was to her life, it was a small detail in a complex estate, including, most prominently, Nettie's gift of the apartment and its contents to Harvard University. That gift had been finalized in Nettie's will on January 22, 1930, but her death came so soon afterward and so unexpectedly that many details still had to be worked out.

At long last, Lea heard from Rosenberg. As she wrote in her memoir, "He told me that the entire family was aware of the regard and affection which the Naumburgs had for me both as an artist and a woman and that he felt he could best carry out their feeling by presenting me with the violin." Enclosed was the paper she had signed plus an insurance policy from Lloyds in London dated one year ahead.

I have often contemplated Lea's amazing good fortune in life. So many patrons took her on and provided money and other forms of help, not only to her but to other family members including her sister Anna, her brother Pierre, and her son Boris. This luck began when Lea was a child and continued for decades thereafter. Was Lea so special? Or was it simply a different era, one in which such acts were more common? Upon reflection, I think it's a little of both. Lea was fortunate to have been a successful woman violinist at a time when such a thing was rare. Her story of triumph over adversity was compelling. And she had great charm, as did Boris, who reflected her glory and was also blessed with patrons throughout his life.

But I believe there was something else at work. Lea lived at a time when philanthropy was more personal—before the age of foundations with their armies of professional giving officers, or government agencies checking off guidelines in grant proposals. Today, there are many who believe the old days of patronage were unfair and ineffective; that it favored the lucky few with access to the rich, and relied overly on the whims of wealthy donors who lacked knowledge, sophistication, and skill. In some cases, these criticisms may be valid. But, for the most part, I think they are unfair. Many patrons were not only more enlightened, but were far more knowledgeable than the professionals who give away money today. Furthermore, they gave with a kind of boundless enthusiasm that now seems rare. What they may have lacked in strategic planning, policy development, and rigorous accountability, they made up for with joy.

Josef Hofmann, Mary Curtis Bok, and the Curtis Institute of Music

It is the fate of many great composers to be largely ignored during their lifetimes. Many work in obscurity and poverty, and are celebrated only years or generations later. But if such is the destiny of composers, the reverse is true for performers. Most who achieve great celebrity in their lifetimes are forgotten soon after they leave the concert stage. Their names become virtually unknown after a single generation. Ask classical music lovers how many

19th-century composers they can name and they will reel off a practically endless list: Beethoven, Brahms, Chopin, Mendelssohn, Schubert, Schumann, Verdi, Wagner. Ask these same individuals to name famous 19th- or even early-20th-century classical music performers who were not also recognized composers, and you are likely to get blank stares.

Which perhaps explains the fate of the pianist Josef Hofmann, the man who arguably had the greatest impact on Lea Luboshutz's life and career in America. A century ago, his celebrity was immense; he was considered possibly one of the greatest pianists of all time. Olin Downes, an important critic of the era, writing for the *New York Times*, described him as "the master who forges beauty linking the mighty past with the living present."[33] The greatest of musicians were inspired by him. Composer Igor Stravinsky, conductor Bruno Walter, pianist Glenn Gould, and opera singer-philanthropist Alice Tully all wrote in their memoirs that they decided to become musicians after hearing Hofmann.

As a five-year-old prodigy, Hofmann was compared to Mozart. As an adult, he was considered without peer. Olin Downes's eventual successor as chief music critic at the *New York Times*, Harold C. Schonberg (his book *The Great Pianists* is a standard reference work on the subject), wrote that Hofmann was the most flawless and perhaps the greatest of pianists in the past hundred years. Rachmaninoff dedicated his third piano concerto to Hofmann and crossed a Chopin work off his own repertoire list after hearing Hofmann play it. Hofmann's musical memory was legendary. In 1912–1913, during a tour of Russia, he played twenty-one successive concerts (two with orchestra and nineteen solo recitals) in St. Petersburg that included 255 different works all performed from memory.* By the end of World War I, Hofmann was at the height of his fame and could draw audiences as almost no one else could.

It was to this superstar of the music world that the Philadelphia philanthropist Mary Louise Curtis Bok turned when she wanted to create the greatest music conservatory in the world—the eponymous Curtis Institute of Music. The two met in 1898 on Hofmann's second tour of America and became

---

* Schonberg, Harold, "The Greatest Pianist of his Time," *New York Times*, April 18, 1976. The opening concert with orchestra alone would have been beyond the ability of other pianists. It featured not a single concerto nor, as sometimes occurs, two, but five concertos by Beethoven, Chopin, Liszt, Rubinstein, and Tchaikovsky, all played by memory.

immediate friends. Mrs. Bok was the daughter of Cyrus Curtis and the former Louisa Knapp, who had made a fortune publishing the *Saturday Evening Post*, *Ladies Home Journal*, and other magazines. Daughter Mary's husband, Edward Bok, was also part of the company, having succeeded Mary's mother, Louisa, as chief editor of *Ladies Home Journal*. The entire family had an intense love of music, and Mary herself was a fine pianist. Hofmann quickly became part of the inner circle. Edward Bok convinced Hofmann to write articles for the magazine beginning in 1901, and in 1907 he began writing a regular column on piano playing. Mary turned to him regularly for advice about music. A rich correspondence sprang up. In time, Hofmann was persuaded to move to Philadelphia, but long before he did, Mary had broached the subject of a new conservatory in the city that would be the envy of all others in the world.

Having inherited a large fortune when her mother died in 1910, Mary Curtis Bok's philanthropic activities already included many musical ventures, including the support of a local neighborhood music school. But this larger ambition of the world's greatest conservatory was always in the back of her mind, and she sought the advice not only of Hofmann but of another famous musician, Hofmann's close friend, the conductor of the Philadelphia Orchestra, Leopold Stokowski. Stokowski's enthusiasm was immediate, his advice practical . . . and self-serving. A Philadelphia-based conservatory could become a feeder for his orchestra, with faculty drawn from the principal positions of each instrumental section. In this way, new recruits to the orchestra would immediately understand how the unique sound of the ensemble was created, and would thus contribute to his musical vision. And once they joined her faculty, his players could supplement their income at Mrs. Bok's expense.

Hofmann, on the other hand, was cool to Mary Bok's idea, particularly her suggestion that he take a prominent role. Hofmann had had experience teaching in some of the great conservatories in Europe and Russia, and he may well have had doubts that America could produce anything of such quality. He also had enough experience with Mary to know that she would take an active hand in running the school. As a rich woman who knew her own mind and was not a great musician, she could be an obstacle.

The extensive correspondence between Bok and Hofmann, preserved in the Curtis Institute of Music archives, reads like a game of cat and mouse. Bok knew what it would mean to capture Hofmann as director of the school, or barring that, at least head of the piano department. When he refused both offers, she asked at least for his public endorsement, which he also politely refused, saying that it would be unfair to other institutions. Mrs. Bok's enticements became ever more tempting, and at last Hofmann said he would consider a ten-week appointment at the beginning of 1925. Mrs. Bok offered him $50,000 (three-quarters of a million dollars by today's standards and an extraordinary sum). When a great deal more was subsequently added to the pay package (rumors range from between an additional $25,000 to $50,000), Hofmann accepted the Curtis Institute directorship for the 1927–1928 academic year.

From the start, it was clear that Hofmann was going to be his own man, as far as faculty and school policy were concerned. He began by rapidly replacing local faculty members with individuals he believed would bring international renown to the school. One of his first appointments would turn out to be the violinist he had met and performed with on board the SS *Majestic* in 1925, Lea Luboshutz.

A Controversial Appointment

⚜

Though Hofmann and many of the other people he was recruiting were well-known to the Curtis community, Lea was not. So as part of Hofmann's plan to hire her, he decided to introduce her by playing a joint recital with her at the Institute, billing it as a warm-up concert for their joint appearance at Carnegie Hall a few days later. The concert was only the beginning of the controversy surrounding Lea and the Curtis Institute. She was not yet a member of the faculty (though Hofmann had assured her she would be), and this event would mark the first time an outsider would be invited to grace the Institute stage.[34] This was bound to enflame the envy of existing faculty members for whom an appearance in front of Mrs. Bok and their colleagues was a prestigious opportunity. They also knew that the fact that Hofmann was personally appearing with Lea would be a huge endorsement and would greatly impress Mrs. Bok. Hofmann felt that, in Lea's case, Mrs. Bok's approbation was crucial. Though in theory, he had carte blanche to hire whomever he chose, he already knew that Lea's appointment would be problematic because he suspected it would be opposed by the then head of the violin department, Carl Flesch. As a result, he had decided not to consult Flesch, which was itself completely contrary to normal practice in such situations.

Lea and Hofmann's Curtis concert took place on January 23, 1927.[35] And what a show it must have been! It included three major works, any one of which might have been the featured piece on a standard program. The concert opened with Lea's old standby, the César Franck sonata, just as the concert with Hofmann on shipboard had. But at this recital, instead of small short works to follow, the program continued with a Brahms sonata and ended with the Bruch violin concerto, with Hofmann playing the orchestra part on the piano (as was common practice in those days). As Lea wrote to Mrs. Bok afterward (ostensibly to thank her for a gift of flowers), "I believe the success was a genuine one, and it quite thrilled me . . . If the success at Carnegie Hall will be one half of that at the Institute, I will be very pleased."[36]

Lea's appointment to Curtis was finalized soon after the concert. The first written reference I can find is a note from Hofmann to Mrs. Bok on April 4, 1927: "Since Madame Luboshutz is to become a member of our faculty, I enclose a letter . . . which may be of interest to you." The letter Hofmann refers to is one that Lea had addressed to Mrs. Bok who had offered to pay for hospital expenses incurred by Lea when she had became ill sometime in the previous couple of weeks. Lea expressed heartfelt gratitude but wrote that other friends (presumably the Princes) had paid the bill. Three days later, Hofmann wrote again to Mrs. Bok to assure her that Lea had completely recovered, had resumed practicing, and would definitely be healthy enough to start teaching in the fall.

The careful orchestration of Lea's official appointment to the Curtis faculty might have been unnecessary had it not stirred up the anticipated controversy. Hofmann was prescient in anticipating the objections of Carl Flesch, an internationally known performer and pedagogue. Indeed, Flesch was incensed—Lea had no teaching experience, he claimed, which was just one of his problems with her appointment. He hinted that there were nonmusical reasons why Lea was being invited onto the faculty. As he wrote many years later in his autobiography:

> Amongst the numerous Russian emigrants in that period, there was Lea Luboschütz [b. 1889], who tried her luck in America . . . In New York, she was at first supported by beneficent art lovers, until she met Josef Hofmann, who took an interest in her and gave a few sonata recitals with her. Although she had never taught before, he decided to engage her as a teacher for the Institute. For this purpose he required my consent as head of the violin department, which he obtained after our lady president [Mrs. Bok] had exerted some pressure on me. I now had definite proof that the future of the Institute would be determined by personal relationships and intrigues of all kinds, and I firmly decided to leave.[37]

The passage is rife with errors, some minor, others more serious. Lea was born in 1885, not 1889. She had taught students in the three countries in which she had lived and worked—Russia, Germany, and France—and had actually been appointed a professor of violin at conservatories in Berlin and Paris prior to her appointment to Curtis.[38] True, this was not her primary source of income, but Hofmann himself had made it clear that he wanted people who were great artists first, and teachers second. As to being supported by beneficent art lovers, it *was* true Lea had patrons, but she had always earned her way, and with the many concerts Hurok booked for her, she was supporting herself and her family with concert fees.

The passage quoted is also dripping with innuendo, stopping just short of directly implicating Hofmann and Lea in a romantic liaison. Such an accusation would have been risky. But others carried out the scandalmongering on Flesch's behalf. Accusations of an affair between Lea and Hofmann began circulating even before Flesch officially departed. People were looking for reasons why a woman like Lea should succeed in a male-dominated world. Sleeping with the boss was an easy explanation.

What did Lea make of all this? She ignored it. She behaved as though Flesch was one of her most beloved colleagues, writing him warm letters after he moved to Germany, and even attending his concerts when she was in Europe. As a result, whatever anger Flesch may have felt, he could only return the courtesies and he maintained a cordial though distant relationship with Lea, even inviting her to visit him and his wife in Baden-Baden in a letter sent to her in January 1931.[39] Indeed, this was one of Lea's secret weapons and one of those characteristics people most admired about her and that astounded me growing up. Some called it hauteur, others described it as aristocratic (amusing for someone who grew up a poor Jew in Odessa). Still others said Lea could "kill with kindness," though that was not her intent. She never gossiped about colleagues, always treated them with respect, and simply traveled on another plane (my mother called it "gaining altitude"). In the case of Flesch, she said only nice things about him for the rest of her career. In an article she wrote in Curtis's school magazine in 1936, she was still talking about meeting him abroad: "In London, I had the pleasure of meeting my old friend and former colleague Carl Flesch, whose performance of the Beethoven concerto is always a great event there."[40] This despite the fact that she actually hated the way he played the Beethoven concerto.

Flesch's unhappiness with Lea's appointment went far beyond the reasons cited or hinted at. Lea had supplanted him as a recital partner with Hofmann, and this must have been a major blow, given Hofmann's fame. And there was something else working against her in Flesch's eyes, which became apparent when Hofmann subsequently appointed Efrem Zimbalist and the legendary Leopold Auer to the Institute faculty. Quite simply, these violinists represented an approach to music that Flesch disdained. In many respects, Flesch's approach was not unlike that of the detested Artur Schnabel. His teacher in Vienna had been Jacob Grün[*]—a protégé of the same Joseph Joachim who had refused to teach Lea in 1904. More than two decades later, the issue was the same: Joachim's students developed a style of playing that the Russian violinists found unmusical. About Grün, whose name means "green" in German, Lea's Russian colleague the violinist Efrem Zimbalist quipped: "Green is good for the eyes but not for the ears."[41]

But the feeling went both ways. Flesch did not think much of Zimbalist either. Indeed, the feeling was reciprocated in spades. Flesch's style of teaching

---

[*] Franz Kneisel, another violinist who was detested by the Russians, was one of his students. Kneisel was the violinist who started the summer school in Maine about which my grandmother had remarked privately to family members, "They play so ugly there."

was Germanic to the core. He liked to be addressed as "Professor" and wanted students to offer a slight deferential bow when greeting him. He favored a tradition of pedagogy, with everyone attending a class in which one person played and the others listened and observed. Flesch, like Boris's teacher Schnabel, believed that deep score analysis was key to learning to play well. According to the recollections of Orlando Cole, a cello student at Curtis at the time, Flesch "was very severe . . . He would say, 'You have a beautiful tone, and you have fine technique, but no brains.' He just murdered people."[42]

"Beautiful tone . . . but no brains." Here, Flesch might have been giving his assessment of Lea and Zimbalist. How the Russians' focus on tone must have frustrated him! The German master Joachim, who Flesch idolized, used very little vibrato and had a tone described by historians as "dry, inexpressive, and hard," while the Russian pedagogue Leopold Auer, who replaced Flesch as head of the violin department at Curtis, was known to stress expressive vibrato and preached to his students, "Sing, sing, sing on your violin—it is the only way in which to make its voice tolerable to the listener."[43] If one had to take liberties with the score to accomplish this, so be it! Lea, herself, would make clear this philosophy in her class yearbook of 1929–1930 where she wrote, "What is the most wonderful thing about violin playing? It is the beauty of the tone! It does not come just from the fingers, it comes from our whole being."[44]

In leaving Curtis, Flesch also cited irreconcilable differences with the director's (Josef Hofmann's) teaching philosophy. As he wrote: "Hofmann showed little understanding of my teaching methods. I have always tended to occupy myself even more intensely with the average pupil than with the *elite*. A teacher who is only interested in great talents is like a man who only seeks the company of rich people."[45] Take that, Mr. Hofmann, *and* your friendship with one of the richest women in America. Indeed, Flesch himself had approached Mrs. Bok, going behind Hofmann's back, to give her advice on how to run the school. This move backfired badly, as Flesch recalled later.

I saw the catastrophe coming and tried to prevent, or at least to delay it. In a detailed memorandum addressed to Mrs. Bok, I branded as unsocial the Institute's addiction to star-breeding, and recommended that preparatory classes should be introduced in order to educate talented pupils from the elementary level onwards. My suggestions met with complete incomprehension.[46]

Bok gave Flesch the cold shoulder and ignored his advice. He responded years later by portraying her unflatteringly in his autobiography. It was reported that when she learned of the many passages in Flesch's autobiography that criticized Hofmann and herself, she had it removed from the Curtis Institute's Library.[47]

To Hofmann, to Mrs. Bok, and to Lea, the quality of the students mattered most, and everything else flowed logically from that premise. After Hofmann took control of Curtis, one of his earliest decisions was to reduce the size of the student body, thereby improving its musical quality. At one point in the school's first year, according to the annual report, enrollment reached 317. In Hofmann's annual report for 1927–1928, enrollment was down to 218 due to, as he put it, "greater selectivity." This policy continued over the next decade along with the growing prestige of the school; by the end of 1940, the number of students was down to 195. The percentage of local students in 1927–1928 diminished from 62 percent to 38 percent and the percentage of students from outside the United States increased sixfold as Hofmann and his faculty scoured the world for talent.

There were two additional conditions that Hofmann laid down when he took the Curtis Institute job that made Lea's move to join the faculty propitious. First, tuition must be free to ensure that Curtis could attract the very best students. Mrs. Bok needed to create an endowment sufficient to guarantee free tuition forever for all students. Indeed, once the policy was implemented for the 1928–1929 school year, free tuition became one of its greatest drawing cards, especially during the Depression years in the 1930s. Hofmann's second condition was that Mrs. Bok must provide for those students who required year-round instruction, which meant paying for travel and housing for teachers and students away from the hot, humid Philadelphia summers.

For this latter requirement, Mrs. Bok asked whether it made sense to send students and teachers to Europe. Hofmann replied on January 31, 1925, that, "Your idea to send the 'exclusive pupils' abroad is a grand one! Let us hope that it will be worthwhile doing it. All depends on the pupils, of course, for, as someone said: 'There are no good teachers. There are only good pupils!'"

This was a mantra Lea would repeat for the rest of her life. Only reading Hofmann's letters years later in 2015 did I learn its source.

Was It Music . . . or Something More?

⟨♔⟩

Hofmann began concertizing regularly with Lea a few months after their shipboard meeting in 1925. A London concert at Wigmore Hall on June 25, 1926, may have been the first and it was sold out well before it took place, not surprising for any program involving Josef Hofmann. The program included a Grieg sonata and both the Beethoven *Kreutzer* and the Franck sonata—pieces often associated with turning points in Lea's life. The review praised Hofmann and was only lukewarm about Lea's playing, complaining that her big tone was "not always honey to the ear" and that her phrasing was "decisive if not always subtle."[48]

It may well be true that Lea did not play especially well at this concert, as she had much to be nervous about. Her recital partner was one of the most famous musicians in the world and expectations would have been high. Further, Hofmann was playing, as he always did, without printed music—he had a phenomenal memory and found the printed score a distraction. This was unheard of in joint recitals (both musicians always used printed music in such ensemble playing though they played by memory when they performed with orchestras). Now it forced Lea, who was always nervous about memory slips when she played with orchestras, to undergo the same pressure in a recital with piano, to memorize all this music for the first time in her career.

Hofmann and Lea were back in London at Wigmore Hall on October 9, 1926, and there are two reviews of that concert, in which Lea played a very ambitious program consisting of Beethoven's op. 24 sonata, the Brahms G Major sonata, and the Bruch concerto (with Hofmann playing the orchestra part on the piano). As so often happens, when it was clear that the famous

Hofmann had made Lea a regular recital partner, the critics changed their tune and praised them both.

During the next season (1926–1927), Lea and Hofmann played in Phila-delphia on November 7, 1926, on the prestigious *Atwater Kent Radio Hour,* one of the first multistation classical music programs anywhere, with concerts broadcast on both CBS and NBC. The series was sponsored by an important manufacturer of radio receivers, Atwater Kent, and had its own orchestra for certain programs (indeed, Lea would solo with that orchestra just over a year later).[49] By January 30, 1927, they were more than ready for their Carnegie Hall concert and the sixteen-concert tour that followed in the spring.[50]

During the 1927–1928 season, the duo played at least another eleven concerts in the United States.[51] At one of the most important—in Chicago on November 27—music critic Edward Moore made it clear that Lea was a musician entirely on Hofmann's level:

> Something quite out of the ordinary in violin and piano recitals took place yesterday afternoon when Lea Luboshutz, who is new here, combined forces with Josef Hofmann, who is not, though absent for some time. She would seem to be much the same sort of violinist that he is a pianist, that is, polished, suave, learned, and always in the best of taste. Therefore when two such intelligences join on a work like the Grieg sonata in F, it is quite likely to sound better than it ever did before.[52]

Then, there it was—the phrase I had been waiting for: "The César Franck Sonata sounded even finer . . ." Of course, it would be part of such an important program and a highlight for those who attended.

This was the review Lea had hoped for—a nationally known critic in a major city who vouched for her greatness—playing on the same level as that of Hofmann. It was powerful ammunition against those who dismissed her appearances with Hofmann as no more than charity work on his part. One of these was Flesch student Henri Temianka. Years later, recalling Hofmann and Lea's first concert together at the Curtis Institute, Temianka felt that the results did more to harm than to help Lea, since Hofmann did not know how to be an accompanist and couldn't keep his playing under control. "Josef

Hofmann, the titan of the piano, once generously tried to help an excellent but lesser-known violinist," Temianka wrote. "He accomplished the exact opposite, for the gasping audience concentrated exclusively on the thundering piano *tutti*."[53] Other musicians continued to believe that this was no more than Hofmann's quid pro quo to keep Lea in his bed.

On the other hand, critics poured on the praise, while Lea and Hofmann were booked for more and more prestigious concerts. In that same touring season (1927–1928), in addition to New York, domestic performances took place in Philadelphia, Cleveland, and Pittsburgh, with an additional appearance at the Ann Arbor Festival in the spring.[54]

All of this would suggest Lea and Hofmann were spending considerable time together rehearsing and touring internationally. It seems that they gelled musically from the start. According to the London *Observer*'s review of one of their early concerts: "Only the finest players can thus leave music to itself and yet give such an interpretation as these artists did."[55] The next day, the *Daily Chronicle* added its praise: "A new violinist of striking quality, Mme. Lea Luboshutz . . . has a very fine tone and technique (and) took her share in a splendid performance."[56] Soon afterward, according to Lea's recollections, she was surprised to learn that Soviet authorities had invited her and Hofmann for a twenty-concert tour. Despite the fact that her son, Yuri, was still in Moscow and there were plenty of other family members she would have dearly enjoyed seeing again, there was not the slightest possibility of accepting.[57] It was far too dangerous.

Had Lea and Hofmann met before the chance encounter on shipboard in 1925? Rumormongers believed the relationship had gone on for years before. It is quite possible that Lea had gone to his concerts in Russia—he played there off and on from 1895 to 1913, with an extended stay in 1907. On one of those visits, Hofmann may have heard her play as well. He would have met and taken account of her—attractive young women rarely passed Hofmann's notice, and there were not many who played at her level. Could Hofmann also have gone to Lea's 1907 Carnegie Hall debut? Maybe, though Hofmann rarely went to others' concerts unless he had to.

The question of when Hofmann and Lea first met interested me because so many people seemed to assume that when they started playing concerts together, they had been lovers for some time. As Hofmann was a well-known womanizer who conceived a child out of wedlock with a young girl in late 1923 while married to his first wife, I wanted to see if I could establish whether there was something to these rumors.

It is true that Hofmann was not known for seeking out other musicians with whom to play recitals or chamber music, so playing with Lea was an uncharacteristic gesture. He was primarily a soloist, though he had played a few concerts with other violinists—Jan Kubelík in Russia (presumably at the request of those organizing concerts there) and Fritz Kreisler in America (a short-lived collaboration). He had also appeared with Carl Flesch while they were colleagues at the Curtis Institute, but it is reported that he did not think much of Flesch's playing and it did not last long.[58] Indeed, when Hofmann appeared with Lea at Carnegie Hall in 1927, the critic Olin Downes commented that it was the first time in many years that Hofmann had been heard in any capacity other than as a solo recitalist or soloist with an orchestra.[59]

People who had seen Hofmann and Lea on shipboard commented upon an obvious romantic connection. One of the rumors that surfaced immediately and was still circulating decades later was that Lea—whose full-length fur coats were a characteristic feature of her wardrobe—had arrived in Hofmann's stateroom one night draped in her furs with nothing on underneath.[60] And when it came to the appointment of Lea to the Curtis faculty, raised eyebrows were rampant. Why would Hofmann insist, particularly over Flesch's objections, if there was not something going on? Were their concerts together no more than opportunities for trysts on the road?

In Lea's early days at the Curtis Institute, a rumor even spread that my uncle Boris was Lea and Hofmann's love child. This was completely absurd, as Lea was in Russia with Onissim at the time Boris was conceived. But people had played with the math and decided that Boris was conceived by Hofmann during his tour of Russia in 1907 (Boris was born in 1908, so it was remotely possible). Those gossipers never examined the photos of Boris and Yuri when they were four and five years old, respectively. The brothers looked practically like twins, and there is no way, chronologically or geographically, that Hofmann could have fathered both boys.

Were Lea and Hofmann lovers, as so many people claimed? I was able to review some of their letters, many of which are in German, a language that Hofmann's wife, who reviewed much of his correspondence, did not speak. Some letters between Lea and Hofmann concern details of concerts and finances, but in others there are occasional glimpses of a relationship that goes beyond the professional. What to make of a letter that Hofmann signs "Voluptuously, sweet hope, devotedly, I remain with best greetings, your devoted Josef Hofmann"?[61] Or a telegram from Lea: "I AM SO TIRED I JUST DIDN'T THINK I AM ASHAMED OF MYSELF PLEASE FORGIVE ME YOU KNOW I LOVE YOU".[62] (The telegram goes on to express concern and affection for Hofmann's son, perhaps as a way to mask the deeper meaning of the message.) Does any of this constitute a smoking gun? Perhaps not, but when I read these missives for the first time, there was certainly enough there to fuel my curiosity.

Then there are Hofmann's letters to others, including one in German to the pianist Sidney Silber on October 15, 1927, that talks about the possibility of the two getting together when Hofmann arrives in Chicago. But Lea will be with him, Hofmann explains, and he needs to see what she wants to do first: "(It) will not be much of a rest because, as you know, the ladies today are very demanding!! . . . We will blow out at the Congress Hotel. You can get in touch with me there and then we can arrange an appointment. As for my lady-partner, I don't know if she has any plans for these two days; we will see it then (honny soit . . .)."[63] The "honny soit" is clearly a reference to the French phrase *"Honi soit qui mal y pense"* or "Shame be to him who thinks evil of it." Was Hofmann suggesting that there was every possibility that he and Lea would likely spend intimate time together and Silber should not think evil of him?

There is one other intriguing passage in the letter. Hofmann refers to Lea as "Mrs. Lea Luboschutz (fortunately not Miss any more . . .)" Lea, of course, had never been legally married and had arrived in the United States portraying herself as a single woman. Was the decision now to describe herself as a respectable widow a joint decision she had made with her lover, Josef Hofmann?

Boris, in his autobiography, dismisses the idea of a sexual liaison between Hofmann and his mother, writing that Lea was simply Hofmann's "cover" for his affair with the teenager he later married. Hofmann's first concerts in England with Lea, Boris claimed, gave the pianist an excuse to take the young woman abroad, where she could have his child. The woman was his private student and became pregnant when she was legally underage. Lea was instrumental in helping Hofmann avoid a public scandal. That young woman became Hofmann's second wife, Elizabeth "Betty" Short.

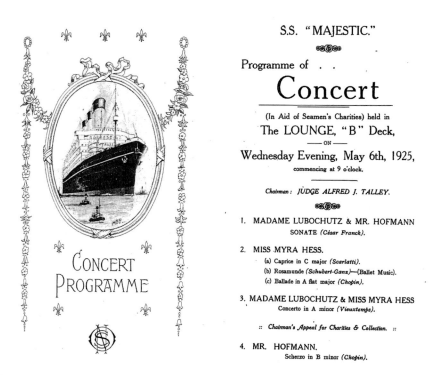

S.S. "MAJESTIC."

Programme of . .

Concert

(In Aid of Seamen's Charities) held in

The LOUNGE, "B" Deck,

— ON —

Wednesday Evening, May 6th, 1925,

commencing at 9 o'clock.

Chairman: *JUDGE ALFRED J. TALLEY.*

1. MADAME LUBOCHUTZ & MR. HOFMANN
   SONATE *(César Franck).*

2. MISS MYRA HESS.
   (a) Caprice in C major *(Scarlatti).*
   (b) Rosamunde *(Schubert-Ganz)*—(Ballet Music).
   (c) Ballade in A flat major *(Chopin).*

3. MADAME LUBOCHUTZ & MISS MYRA HESS
   Concerto in A minor *(Vieuxtemps).*

   :: Chairman's *Appeal for Charities & Collection.* ::

4. MR. HOFMANN.
   Scherzo in B minor *(Chopin).*

Printed program from Lea's first concert with Josef Hofmann on May 6, 1925, playing the Franck sonata aboard the SS *Majestic.*

Lea in one of her many fur coats. Rumors circulated that Lea arrived in Hofmann's stateroom with nothing on underneath the furs.

To an inspired Artist, Madame Lea Luboshutz, with best compliments and wishes of Josef Hofmann

New york Nov. 20th 1926.

Hofmann's earliest inscribed photograph to Lea, who he called "an inspired artist," November 20, 1926. They toured internationally together for the next several years.

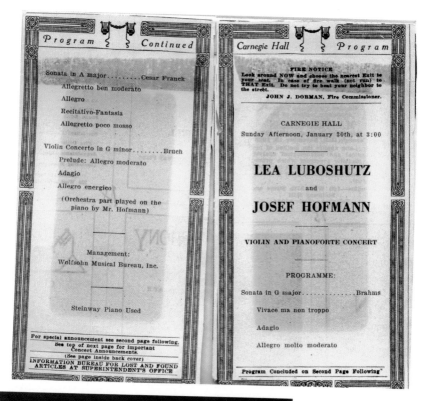

ABOVE: Lea and Hofmann's first joint appearance at Carnegie Hall (January 30, 1927). They played the Franck sonata (of course). LEFT: Lea's first official portrait with the Nightingale Stradivarius (1928).

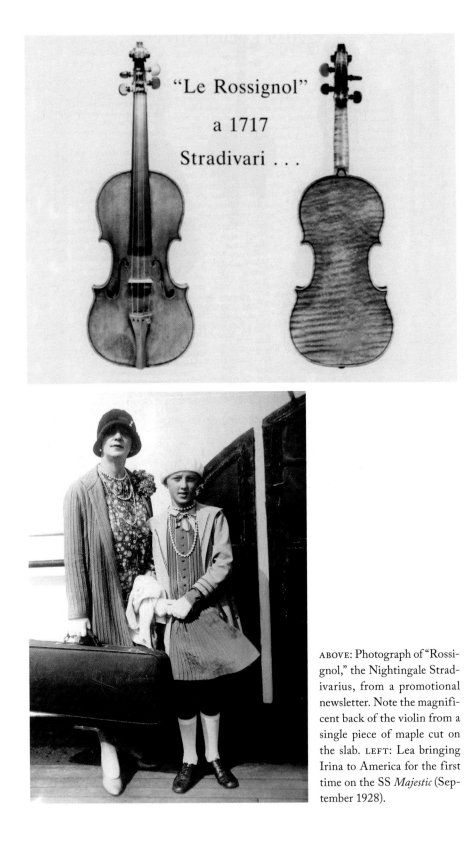

"Le Rossignol"

a 1717

Stradivari . . .

ABOVE: Photograph of "Rossignol," the Nightingale Stradivarius, from a promotional newsletter. Note the magnificent back of the violin from a single piece of maple cut on the slab. LEFT: Lea bringing Irina to America for the first time on the SS *Majestic* (September 1928).

ABOVE: The Town of Rockport, Maine (circa 1930), when Mary Curtis Bok established the summer colony for her Curtis Institute of Music. BELOW: The view from Mary-Lea Cottage (Lea's summer home in Rockport, Maine). Note the lighthouse in the far distance to which a teenaged Irina (now named Irene) rowed daily to have a meal with the lighthouse keeper and his wife.

ABOVE: Yuri Goldovsky, aged twenty-three, in Moscow in 1930. Well situated as a university associate professor, he had no intention of leaving the Soviet Union despite Lea's pleas. BELOW: Lea proudly driving her first car in Maine (circa 1931).

Walter (Billy) Wolf at about the time he met fifteen-year-old Irene Goldovsky (1932). He was nine years older and completely smitten.

Lea and her mother were impressed by Billy Wolf's wealth. Irene was impressed that he was a horseman who regularly participated in local fox hunts.

Irene on her wedding day (May 16, 1933). Lea made sure the event was memorable, including the wedding dress and the flowers. Josef Hofmann played the wedding march on a Steinway that he later gave to Irene and Billy.

ABOVE: Lea with son Boris Goldovsky rehearsing in Maine (circa 1935). LEFT: Four generations of first daughters: Katherine (Gitel) Luboshutz, Lea Luboshutz, Irene Goldovsky Wolf, Alexandra Wolf (1936). BELOW: The Goldovsky family (Boris, Margaret, Michael, and Marina) at their home in Brookline, Massachusetts (circa 1940).

ABOVE: Adrian Siegel's iconic portrait of Lea rehearsing with the Philadelphia Orchestra. *Copyright © Philadelphia Orchestra (1945).* BELOW: Al Bendiner's sketch of Lea that appeared in the *Philadelphia Bulletin* (November 3, 1945). The original now hangs in the Curtis Institute of Music. *Copyright © The Alfred and Elizabeth Bendiner Foundation.*

Everything comes in cycles . . . Season's Greetings, The Billy Wolfs

Billy and Irene Wolf with their six children. These annual holiday cards were among fifty that the family sent out beginning in 1936. Twenty-five of them (including these) were featured in *Life* magazine. ABOVE: The eight-seater cycle in the 1951 card was borrowed from Philadelphia's Franklin Institute. BELOW: The Swiss painted bed in the 1952 card was part of Billy and Irene's antique collection that they eventually donated to the Philadelphia Museum of Art.

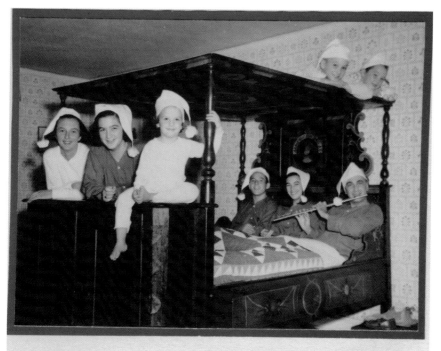

SEASON'S GREETINGS . . . THE BILLY WOLFS

ABOVE LEFT: Boris Goldovsky (standing left), with his uncle Pierre Luboshutz and aunt Genia Nemenoff prior to their 1956 three-piano tour. ABOVE RIGHT: Dmitri Goldovsky (Yuri's son). Lea's oldest grandchild was born in Moscow just prior to his father's fateful trip to Mount Misses Tau in the Caucasus during the summer of 1931. Like his father, Dmitri loved the mountains. BELOW: Lea standing in front of Mary-Lea Cottage in Rockport, Maine, sometime in the 1950s. It was this photograph that caused her sister Anna to say regretfully: "Compare Lea's mansion . . . and my *tsores* [Yiddish for 'troubles']."

MARYLEA COTTAGE   B300

ABOVE: Lea and Irene on stage at Lea's seventieth birthday Gala (February 23, 1955), the last time Lea played in public. BELOW LEFT: Pierre Luboshutz (left) with one of his oldest Russian friends, violinist Jascha Brodsky, both of whom performed at Lea's seventieth birthday Gala. BELOW RIGHT: Lea standing outside the Curtis Institute of Music after receiving her honorary doctorate from the school where she had taught for three decades (1960).

ABOVE: Anna Luboshutz with Mstislav Rostropovich at Gala event honoring her distinguished career (Moscow, January 22, 1969). BELOW: Andrew Wolf at the harbor in Camden, Maine, in the 1970s.

ABOVE: The historic Rockport (Maine) Opera House where Andrew and Thomas Wolf produced hundreds of concerts for Bay Chamber Concerts over more than half a century carrying on the summer tradition begun by Lea and other Curtis Institute of Music musicians in the 1930s. BELOW: Andrew Wolf with President Ronald Reagan, First Lady Nancy Reagan, Chinese premiere Zhao Ziyang, and violinist Isaac Stern. Andy and Stern had just played the Franck sonata at the White House, January 10, 1984.

To Andrew Wolf
With best wishes, Nancy Reagan   Ronald Reagan

ABOVE: Andrew Wolf's grave at the beautiful Seaview Cemetery in Rockport, Maine.
BELOW: Commemorative plaque honoring Lea at Mary-Lea Park next to the Opera House in Rockport, Maine.

MARY-LEA PARK
THIS PARK IS DEDICATED TO THE MEMORY OF
LEA LUBOSHUTZ
1885 — 1965
RENOWNED VIOLINIST, TEACHER AND BELOVED
MEMBER OF THIS COMMUNITY

But there is no evidence that Lea and Hofmann played concerts in London before 1926, and that was long after Boris claimed Lea was there assisting Hofmann and Betty with their domestic problems (which would have been in 1923 and 1924). There is some correspondence between Lea and the young woman in 1926 when mother and child were still in London. Lea certainly befriended Betty, but this was after two children had been born (one died in childbirth). In one of the letters, it is Lea who is seeking help with where to stay in London, a city it seems she had not visited before.[64] Boris's version simply didn't hold up.

So I was still curious about why Hofmann and Lea engaged in a musical collaboration. If Hofmann was so enthusiastic about performing the violin and piano repertoire, why didn't he choose one of the more famous Russians in America—players like Efrem Zimbalist, who joined the Curtis faculty two years after Lea, Jascha Heifetz, or Mischa Elman? The idea that it was the violin-piano repertoire itself that enticed him seemed far-fetched. Hofmann was notoriously lazy about learning new pieces—he never played Rachmaninoff's Piano Concerto no. 3, which was dedicated to him, because he didn't want to bother to learn it.

Nor was money the incentive. In fact, the fees Lea and Hofmann commanded would have been a *dis*incentive for Hofmann, whose avariciousness was legendary. In his correspondence with Lea, he complained that the total they were receiving was about half what he could earn as a soloist. As a result, he insisted on taking 80 percent of their earnings and charging her 80 percent of general expenses. Hofmann even made Lea pay for the travel expenses of his piano tuner, Maurice Gatsch.[65] None of this bothered Lea. Such was the prestige of appearing with Josef Hofmann that she would have been happy to play for even less. But while it clearly bothered Hofmann that he was making so little when he played with Lea, he continued to do so for many years.

I was in my mid-fifties before I summoned the courage to ask my mother what she really thought about the relationship. In 2001 we were driving from her summer home in Maine to the Tanglewood Music Center in western Massachusetts, where the Boston Symphony Orchestra is in residence in the summers, and where my Uncle Boris had spent many years heading the opera department. The occasion was a memorial service that had been organized in Uncle Boris's honor, following his death earlier that year. My mother was in an expansive mood, recalling Hofmann and how much Boris hated him.

"And what about you?" I asked.

"Oh, I loved him," she said. "He was my Uncle Josef. He was so good to me even though others were afraid of him and his black moods. He played at my wedding in 1933, you know, and gave me the piano as a wedding present."

This was a story I'd heard many times. Afterward, Hofmann had said he would never play at a wedding again, as it was the first time people had talked while he played, they had walked out before he finished, and they had failed to clap. And to top it off, he said, smiling, he had not even received a fee. The piano, signed by Hofmann, was still in my mother's home in 2001. Today it is in mine.

"So tell me really," I said. "Is it true what they said about your mother and Hofmann—that they were lovers?"

I expected the usual denial, but instead there was a pause. "To tell the truth, I never really knew." My hands tensed around the steering wheel as I waited for her to go on. "I have always wondered myself. He was so much a part of our lives when I came to the United States in the late twenties and in the years that followed. When I was a girl of about twelve, my mother and I used to spend weekends with him in Atlantic City. He had an apartment there. I do not think his wife knew about our visits. She certainly was never there. It was just the three of us. We always had wonderful times. He and I used to stroll on the boardwalk. These visits were not because they needed to rehearse. Mother never took her fiddle. I had my own room, of course. When I grew up, I always wondered whether I had been there to make it all seem legitimate and normal."

And with that she changed the subject.

The Decision

❦

When and how did Lea finally decide that it was time to unite the family permanently in America? Paris had been the first stable home for the family since the time of the Russian Revolution of 1917. There was a large Russian community there that could provide companionship for Gitel. Pierre was well established and could help out when needed. For a long time, Lea was reluctant to relocate again. True, she spent a lot of time in the United States since that was where she could earn a good deal of money—but it did not necessarily feel like home.

From our vantage point in the 21st century, it seems as if the United States would have been the obvious next (and perhaps, final) step in her odyssey. But the decision must have represented an enormous psychological leap, especially with a son still in the Soviet Union. Lea could not anticipate if and when the window of opportunity for Yuri to leave might come. If such a chance arose, moving farther away from her oldest child might make it more difficult to persuade him to leave. Yet, at some point, with everything weighing in the balance, Lea decided that it was best to end her long journey and settle in America.

By the end of 1927, she was clearly committed to making America the center of her professional life. In a letter to conductor Serge Koussevitzky dated October 13, 1927,[66] she asked him to engage her as a soloist with his Boston Symphony Orchestra and described her recent activities: two concerts with the Cincinnati Symphony Orchestra, four with the Philadelphia Orchestra, two solo recitals each in Philadelphia, Washington, and Baltimore, sixteen concerts with Hofmann, and ten more recitals with other pianists. Moreover, she was teaching ten students at the Curtis Institute of Music, and a new concert season in the United States was due to begin on October 28 with an equally demanding U.S. schedule. Europe could not come close to providing such opportunities.

In his reply, Koussevitzky told Lea that she should count on adding the Boston Symphony to her itinerary for the following season (she ended up performing the Prokofiev violin concerto that she had premiered in New York, appearing in Boston on December 14 and 15, 1928).[*] In a subsequent letter,[67] Lea thanked Koussevitzky for promising to engage her, adding that in one of her first concerts with Hofmann in fall 1927 in Philadelphia, the sponsors had been forced to move to the four-thousand-seat Stanley Theatre, such was the demand for tickets. There is no way Lea could keep up this pace with Paris as her base.

---

[*] The program on this occasion, in addition to the Prokofiev, included two premieres, one by Martinů and the other by Copland. All this 20th-century repertoire was too much for the conservative *Boston Globe* critic who in his December 15th review was dismissive of the music but did praise Lea's playing.

Lea accepted the faculty positon at Curtis sometime in early 1927 and nearly everything about the school made it clear that it was the place for her. Hofmann, the director, said emphatically that she would only have top students—"There are no vacancies at the Curtis Institute except for those of real genius."[68] Mrs. Bok, the school's founder and underwriter, assured Lea of her full support.

So Lea's decision to move permanently to the United States had to have come at about the time she decided to accept the Curtis position. But when exactly? Could the usual signpost—the César Franck violin sonata—be a guide? Sol Hurok had promised Lea and Hofmann a concert in Carnegie Hall. Though each had played there before, this was to be their first joint appearance, and the first in an extended tour together. The concert took place on January 30, 1927. On the program, a copy of which is reproduced in this book, the Franck was the grand finale of the performance.

The response to the concert, and especially to the performance of the Franck, was tremendous. The *New York Times*' chief critic, Olin Downes, stated unequivocally that the Franck was the "summit of the afternoon," noting the performers' "complete understanding—not merely agreement upon this or that tempo or nuance, but understanding which only musicianship and sheer hours spent with unanimity of purpose can achieve."[69] So successful was the performance of the Franck that Lea and Hofmann decided to repeat it a year later in their New York recital at Town Hall on January 17, 1928. Once again, the review was ecstatic: "The perfect unity of spirit and lofty devotion to the inner significance of the music, as opposed to mere technical display, [was] a revelation of ensemble playing in its highest perfection."[70] Incredibly, Lea and Hofmann returned to Carnegie Hall the following month, on February 27, to replace an artist who was ill, and again on April 1. Such was the demand for any musical event involving Josef Hofmann! Overexposure was simply not an issue.

For Lea, the January 1927 Carnegie Hall concert and the response to it was nothing short of a triumph. I believe that it was in the postconcert glow that Lea made her decision—or at least a tentative decision—to give America a try as a new home. After this concert, played with one of the world's greatest pianists, and especially after performing the Franck in America's most prestigious concert hall, one of the most important in the world, Lea must have decided it was the right time to commit to a new country. It might take a while to test the waters before being sure and bringing the family, but she was now ready to do so.

Once teaching began, Lea continued to concertize; Hofmann had made it clear that he wanted his faculty to be prominent on the concert stage. The first year at Curtis went well, and Mrs. Bok delivered on her promise to provide funds for additional summer instruction for students and teachers. Lea desperately wanted to see her family, so she requested a posting at her beloved St.-Jean-de-Luz in France during the summer of 1928. Four students went with her. After months of separation, she was reunited with her daughter and mother. Hofmann, ever curious about what Lea was up to, visited for an extended period—this time with his new wife.

Hofmann had given Lea a specific assignment. He wanted the Curtis school to have a first-class string quartet—an ensemble consisting of two violins, a viola, and a cello—with Lea playing the first violin. One had been formed earlier, but the two violinists were leaving the school. Hofmann wanted Lea to replace the first violinist, Carl Flesch, the very man who had objected to her appointment and who was now gone. But playing quartets was new territory for Lea—she had never played in such an ensemble before and the repertoire was unfamiliar to her. Mrs. Bok was willing to pay the travel and room and board for another faculty member to practice with Lea, and so Edwin Bachmann, who was to replace Emanuel Zetlin as second violin, came to France to join her. As the violist and cellist of the group were elsewhere, Lea summoned Boris from Budapest to play their parts on the piano. According to Boris, it was a delightful summer—full of wonderful music making and recreation. The only temporary setback was a bus trip to a bullfight in Spain that ended with a road accident. Lea was injured, though not seriously.

Playing in a string quartet is very different from playing as a soloist or even in a piano trio like the one she shared with her siblings. As it turned out, Lea's brief foray as a quartet player proved as unsatisfactory as that of her predecessors. In the first Curtis Quartet, which had disbanded the year before, the two violinists, Flesch and Zetlin, had been joined by Louis Bailly on viola and the English cellist Felix Salmond. The group did not get along well, nor did their solo training equip them for the requirements of an ensemble. Each had a unique quality of sound and there was no compromise to form a nice blend. In his history of the Curtis Institute of Music, Henri Temianka recalled:

There was a standing joke: Flesch, with Zetlin and Bailly and Salmond, had a rehearsal during which they were arguing—there was much more arguing than playing—and then they would cross the street to the drugstore, and order nickel Cokes, and they would shout in unison, "Separate checks, please!" And that was the only thing they did in unison.[71]

In Lea's case, she had a specific problem—her somewhat undependable sense of rhythm, as Boris recalled years later in his book. This extraordinary fact for someone playing concerts in major venues around the globe is not as surprising as it seems. Musical interpretation in those days allowed great flexibility in extending or compressing a musical line for effect. Rubato—the expressive and rhythmic freedom achieved by slowing down or speeding up—could be carried to such extremes that the rhythm of the line was completely changed. While the practice did not begin with the pianist and composer Frédéric Chopin, his departures from rhythmic regularity in the first half of the 19th century were legendary and influenced generations that followed. Indeed, the composer Hector Berlioz considered Chopin's rubatos so extreme that he claimed, "Chopin simply could not play in strict rhythm."*

While today's playing standards do not allow for such freedom of interpretation, skilled piano accompanists and orchestra conductors in the 1920s fully expected to follow Lea no matter what she did, since she was the soloist. Even in the Luboshutz Trio, Lea could get away with such freedom. Pierre, like Boris, always followed her, and Anna, who knew her sister's playing as well as anyone, was able to fit into the ensemble perfectly, always deferring to Lea's leadership. But in a string quartet, such playing leads to disaster. For one thing, there is no conductor to keep people together; nor a piano to act as a kind of rhythmic anchor. For another, there are now four people playing independent lines of music, often with complex musical material in very different configurations, and the players have to adhere to a common pulse, or

---

* In chapter 56 of his *Mémoires*, Berlioz says: « Chopin supportait mal le frein de la mesure; il a poussé beaucoup trop loin, selon moi, l'indépendance rythmique. [. . .] Chopin ne *pouvait* pas jouer régulièrement. » (« Chopin disliked the constraint of rhythmic regularity. In my view he went much too far in his rhythmic independence. [. . .] Chopin was simply *unable* to play in strict rhythm. »)

agree in advance to vary it in the same way. Lea assumed that everyone would follow her—after all, she was the first violinist. But her colleagues had their own parts to play that often required her to bend to their will. The cellist Orlando Cole, who played in the longtime Curtis String Quartet that followed Lea's ill-fated one, recalled:

> When Flesch left, Luboshutz came into the school and she was the first violin. And Eddie Bachmann became second violin. Salmond and Bailly remained, but Luboshutz had never played in a quartet before, and they played a concert that I remember very well—they finished the program with the Schumann A Major quartet, which is rhythmically rather involved, and Lubo got out front in the last page, in the coda. And she stopped. And Bailly stopped. And Eddie Bachmann stopped. And Salmond was playing right through till the end! Well, that was the end of *that* quartet."[72]

Aside from the unhappy string quartet experience, the Curtis Institute of Music was an institution around which Lea could build her future, and she decided she was ready to move the family. On July 29, while still in St.-Jean-de-Luz, she instructed Irina to write a letter to Mrs. Bok. She wanted her daughter to make a good advance impression demonstrating perfect manners, elegant English, and lovely penmanship. All of this was accomplished, no doubt, with the assistance of the tutor Miss B, who also helped Lea with her letters to Mrs. Bok. Lea wrote, "I am taking my daughter to America with me & Hope you will like her." Indeed, once Mrs. Bok met eleven-year-old Irina, she found her quite charming and congratulated Lea on her daughter's manners and deportment.

Lea and Irina departed on the SS *Majestic* in September 1928, the same ship on which she and Hofmann had performed together for the first time three years earlier. Irina remembered the trip fondly as she reported in her oral history three-quarters of a century later: "There were other kids aboard and I had a wonderful time playing deck tennis and running all over the ship. Mother was invited to dine at the Captain's Table and play a concert and it was all great fun on the five-day trip. When we arrived [in New York on September 22, 1928], there were press photographers . . ." It seemed ages before they cleared customs. Lea traveled with an enormous amount of luggage, concert dresses, shoes, hats, jewelry—steamer trunks full, all of which were opened and checked. Finally, a Hurok representative took them to Lea's suite at the Great Northern. On the way, Irina was amazed at seeing large groups of African Americans—a completely new experience for her.

Lea was eager to get to Philadelphia to prepare for her second year of teaching at the Curtis Institute. But before leaving New York, she shopped for appropriate clothes for Irina, and they visited the Sidney Princes, who had been so generous to Lea and had supported Boris during his years in Budapest. The Princes asked Irina whether she would like to go for an ice cream soda and whether she brought all of her dolls and toys with her from Europe. Irina did not know how to answer. She had never had an ice cream soda nor dolls nor toys. Gitel, who had been largely responsible for her care, believed that toys were an unnecessary extravagance and ice cream was a completely foreign concept. So Irina was taken on a shopping trip, which resulted in a delicious soda and the purchase of several toys. It was all quite overwhelming.

But it was Lea's colleague, Eddie Bachman, whose toy shopping for Irina produced the prize. On their adventure, Irina saw an orange teddy bear with glass eyes that she clearly coveted and that Bachmann purchased for her. This, of all the presents she received, was the one she most treasured. Though it became increasingly mangy over many decades, it remained with Irina through years of children, grandchildren, and great-grandchildren. Near the end of her life, when a rambunctious dog chewed a hole in one of the bear's paws, she carefully repaired it with red thread. She died well into her nineties with the bear still in her possession.

During Irina's first year in America, Tessie Prince recommended a boarding school, Highland Manor in Tarrytown, New York, very near the Princes' country estate in Mamaroneck. Lea went to visit, meeting with the head-mistress who was somewhat surprised that Lea had not the slightest interest in the academic program. Rather, Lea made clear that Irina was to have her own room (most girls shared) and that she was to bathe every day, rather than once every other day as was the case with the other girls. As Lea would be touring a great deal, Tessie Prince promised to serve as her surrogate mother. The Princes' chauffeur would regularly arrive on Fridays and holidays to ferry Irina either to the Prince apartment on Park Avenue in New York City or to the Mamaroneck estate. Irina loved visiting them in the country where she was able to ride horses from the Prince stable, play tennis, and even learn golf on the Princes' nine-hole golf course.

Lea was on tour in December 1928 so Irina was again with the Princes for the holidays, where she had her first experience of an American Christmas. She was dazzled by the huge tree with lights and ornaments. Under the tree were many gifts, including, for Irina, a copy of James Fenimore Cooper's *The Last of the Mohicans* illustrated by N. C. Wyeth. This too she kept all of her life. The whole experience was so thrilling that when Irina herself married and began to have children, she insisted to her Jewish husband that he provide a large Christmas tree with ornaments and lots of presents beneath it. Topped by a glittering angel, the tree was an object of some curiosity when the family rabbi unexpectedly came to visit.

This was America. This was the family's new home.

A New Home and Another "Gentleman Friend"

Lea had scant time to attend to the details of her daughter's schooling or general upbringing. She had joined a department of violin superstars at the Curtis Institute of Music, alongside Efrem Zimbalist and the greatest living violin pedagogue, Leopold Auer, now an old man of eighty-three, who had replaced the discredited Flesch as head of the violin department. Indelibly etched in Lea's mind was the day they had first met when Lea was a child and he had invited her to come study with him in St. Petersburg. Amazing to think, they now were colleagues in America.

Was Auer as superb a teacher as his reputation suggested? Possibly, though his teaching technique has been criticized for not attending sufficiently to his pupils' technical deficiencies. Auer's approach "worked best for those students capable of solving their own technical problems." According to one knowledgeable string player with a long history at Curtis, "the less talented were sometimes manacled for the rest of their playing days by technical shortcomings that hadn't been instinctively eliminated or analyzed at lessons."[73] But it hardly mattered. Auer had produced three of the greatest living violinists, men who had become American millionaires: Zimbalist, Heifetz, and Elman. For any young violin student, no other information was required.

Teaching in such company greatly enhanced Lea's reputation, and when the academic year ended, she knew she had made the right decision. Musical considerations were only part of her calculation. There was also the financial angle. She was being paid a princely sum for little work. Hofmann had arranged a salary for her of $9,600 for two days of teaching per week (five hours each day) for only thirty-two weeks with $30 an hour extra if she taught more often or during the summer. This was almost $150,000 in today's dollars, more than the cost of a nice house at that time. It was more money by far than Lea had ever earned and it did not preclude her from earning far more from concertizing. The time had now come, Lea told Gitel, to give up the Paris apartment and come to America. Pierre, who still lived there, could fend for himself. On May 28, 1929, Lea and Irina headed from Philadelphia to New York to greet the SS *Majestic*, arriving with Gitel on board.

The date is important. It was near the end of the "roaring twenties," a time of great exuberance and optimism in the United States. In this spirit, Lea's caution seems to have given way. During the heady months that preceded the onset of the Great Depression, the three generations of Luboshutz women were walking on air. Their American reunion began with a happy summer in Carmel, California, where Lea took her students. She found "a gentleman friend" who, according to my mother, she met while playing a concert in San Francisco. Long after my mother died, when I learned more about this so-called "gentleman friend," I realized that Lea, for the first time since Onissim's death, may have been exploring a serious and permanent relationship and perhaps even marriage.

The gentleman in question was one Lionel David Prince, and I have often wondered whether he was a relative of Lea's New York patron Sidney Prince. Two years younger than Lea, he was an orthopedic surgeon who had been born in California and had attended medical school at the University of California, San Francisco.[74] Was it a coincidence that Prince was a distinguished physician? Lea's sister Anna had married just such a man, and ensured a comfortable life for herself. Was it time for Lea to take a page out of her younger sister's playbook?

Although Prince was not a musician, he loved music. He was Jewish, he was comfortably well off, he was unmarried . . . and his life was untouched by scandal. Lea was no longer young—in the summer of 1929, she was forty-four years old—and rumors of sexual liaisons continued to trouble her. If she was going to now reinvent herself as a "respectable woman," it did not make sense to wait.

Once I knew the parameters of the relationship, I began my search for details. In time, through a fortuitous accident, they surfaced. My sister Catherine was packing her belongings to move to a new apartment after her husband's death in 2015. She called me, rather excited, having unearthed a box of family papers. "I have found some letters and telegrams from someone named Lionel in California," she told me. "Could this be important? Do you want them?" Did I ever!

From the letters and telegrams, it is clear that Lionel was very charming. He obviously enjoyed Lea's company, and there are many references to the intimacy of their relationship. But Lionel was not the marrying kind. He preferred his gentlemen's club—the Argonaut (founded by fellow San Francisco Jew Levi Strauss)—and his work. When he died years later, he was still unmarried. It appears that after the summer of 1929, Lea wrote him regularly and visited on occasion. But he answered only sporadically and always apologetically, wondering whether she was angry with him for being such a poor correspondent and friend. His letters are warm, friendly, and occasionally suggest something more in their future. On December 19, 1931, he sent Lea a gift and wrote: "In this gift there is a suggestion of intimacy and the thought that when you are wearing it your mind will dwell uninterrupted on memories of the past and plans for the future." A well-executed cartoon of a monkey (Lea's favorite animal) stares out from the bottom of the letter and "sends love." Lionel's correspondence appears to have maintained just enough distance to ensure that Lea would remain available but not become permanently attached. He also corresponded with Irina and was well acquainted with Boris—yet none of them ever mentioned him by name to my generation. Apparently, this particular part of Lea's story did not fit the happy narrative we were spoon-fed as children.

At some point Lea must have decided enough was enough. If the timing of the letters from Lionel is any guide, the relationship ended in 1932, when Lionel complained that he had lost much of his money in the stock market crash. It really didn't matter, he wrote, because he always had his work. Interestingly, Lea tore all the letters in half—but then decided to keep them. Though she had no need of a husband who was neither very wealthy nor totally committed to her, the memory of Lionel was something she could not easily give up.

Irina remembered the summer of 1929 in California as a high point of her childhood—she would reminisce about the nearby stable and daily horseback rides on the beach in the afternoons. Incredibly, Lea and her pupils sometimes went along on horseback (an image hard for me to imagine), though Lea was also busy learning to drive. Then there were the wonderful accomodations. Lea wrote excitedly to Mrs. Bok on June 18 that as of July 1, she would be moving into Sister Aimee Semple McPherson's cottage, which she described as "the best one in Carmel." She could not believe her luck, she said. It seemed amazing that this house of the Los Angeles–based evangelist and media superstar would even be available. "Of course you know who she is and how thrilling it is to have her place . . . It is but a few steps from the ocean so we can walk out in our bathing suits from the house."

Once they moved in, however, Lea soon found out why no one else had wanted to rent the house. Local people wanted to see McPherson, and crowds gathered regularly outside the cottage to try and catch a glimpse of the famous woman. The fact that Lea and Aimee's hair was the same color appeared to have fostered a rumor that McPherson was in residence. Soon people were climbing the high walls, looking into the courtyard. Life became so intolerable that Lea gave up the house and moved to the recently opened and fashionable Cypress Inn.

By August 8, Lea wrote again to Mrs. Bok. Her patron and friend Sidney Prince had died suddenly in New York and she mourned the man who had, for more than two decades, done so much for her and her family in America. She recalled to Mrs. Bok his assistance to Boris that made study in Budapest possible. But "aside from my great loss, we are more than happy here," she wrote. "The country seems more and more beautiful and the sun brighter." She talked of the success of her driving lessons and her hope that she might buy a Ford when she returned to Philadelphia so she could take Irene and Gitel on Sunday excursions.* In the fall, one of the earliest issues of the Curtis school magazine featured a photo of Lea's summer class in Carmel with an amusing quote that epitomizes the chauvinistic attitude toward women artists that prevailed at this time: "We cannot resist mentioning that in addition to providing her usual stimulating and high example of what an artist should be, Madame Luboshutz surprised and impressed her pupils by her virtuosity in an entirely different field—that of housekeeping."[75]

When the fall term started, Lea was quite busy, but with her mother now living with them in Philadelphia, she could place Irina in a local day school. Lea accepted recommendations of friends and enrolled Irina in a so-called "progressive" private institution—the Oak Lane Country Day School. It was based on the philosophy of John Dewey and proudly claimed that it stressed "creativity" and the arts.[76] To Lea, that sounded just fine. Irina was not destined for a "career" and might as well have some fun. And fun is indeed what Irina had, based on her reports years later. She was an exotic, fluent in four languages. As if that wasn't enough to get Irina special treatment, Lea offered to play a recital for the children, a major event that took place on March 14, 1930, and was so successful that it was repeated annually.[77] According to Irina's recollections, "I spent most of my time teaching the other kids French, making maps of the places I had lived, and not learning a thing."

Irina's school career had one near-disaster and it was of her own making. Lea had made Irina responsible for the family's personal finances: keeping records, balancing a checkbook, and writing checks. Irina became so expert in mimicking Lea's flowing signature that she also wrote notes to school explaining her absences when they occurred. As she got older, Irina figured out a way to take more and more days off and enjoy exploring the city. She wrote (under Lea's name) that she was having to visit the dentist. These notes became so frequent that the school became concerned (or suspicious) and asked Irina for the name of the dentist. Frantic, Irina (who had perfect teeth

---

* Gitel often asked to go "kahtahtsah." This Russian word (кататься), which is not precisely translatable, means to go for a ride without any particular destination in mind. In our family, it was common to say "Babushka (grandmother) wants to go kahtahtsah (for a ride)," whether the grandmother in question was Gitel or, after her death, Lea, or Irina (as each came into grandmotherhood).

and never had cavities) rushed to the dentist's office and confessed. The elderly gentlemen found the whole thing quite amusing. He made Irina promise to stop the practice and when the school eventually did call, he explained that owing to the Russian Revolution and poor dental hygiene, Irina needed extra care.

Meanwhile, Lea kept up her work on her family reunification project. Different strategies would be required for Boris and Yuri. The latter would take considerable convincing, as he was enjoying success under the Soviet system, which coddled and rewarded talented scientists, mathematicians, and physicians. With his Uncle Shereshevsky's sponsorship, Yuri had joined an elite circle of young mathematicians who were well supported by the fledgling state.

As for Boris, Lea was optimistic that after four years of Dohnanyi's tutelage, he was now ready to launch a solo career. There was no better place to do this, Lea believed, than America. Boris arrived in the United States on June 16, 1930, on the SS *Europa*, a new and impressive steamship that made the crossing in only four days. Once in Philadelphia, he immediately began practicing many hours a day so that he would be ready to play for Hofmann for the second time. Hopefully, this audition would be different, and Hofmann would appreciate the pianistic progress Boris had made.

Early in the fall, Boris and Lea traveled to Atlantic City where Hofmann kept the apartment Lea knew so well. Boris played through much of his repertoire, but all for naught. He had now studied with two men that Hofmann loathed: Schnabel and Dohnanyi. Although Boris might be an adequate accompanist for his mother and other artists, Hofmann said, he would never be a solo pianist. That was that. The great man had spoken. It was decided that Boris should enter the Curtis Institute as a conducting student. The decision was crushingly disappointing to Boris, but it turned out to be one of the most important and positive ones in Boris's life leading to a new career. As his mother often said, "Everything is ultimately for the best."

Now it was Pierre's turn to join the family in America and he moved from Paris to New York in 1931 with a new wife, the pianist Genia Nemenoff who had been his pupil at the Paris Conservatory. The family unit was almost complete. In Philadelphia, Lea rented side-by-side apartments near the Curtis Institute—one for Gitel and Irene (as Irina was now called by everyone except Gitel), the other for Lea and Boris. Other mothers might have kept both children close, but Lea's apartment was as much for the family business of music making as for domestic arrangements, and Boris's development had to be more carefully watched. Besides, over time, Gitel had done more mothering of Irene than Lea had, and Irene had become, in effect, her responsibility.

So Lea's journey finally ended. The United States would be her home for the rest of her life. Only one great hurdle remained: to get her oldest son out of the Soviet Union.

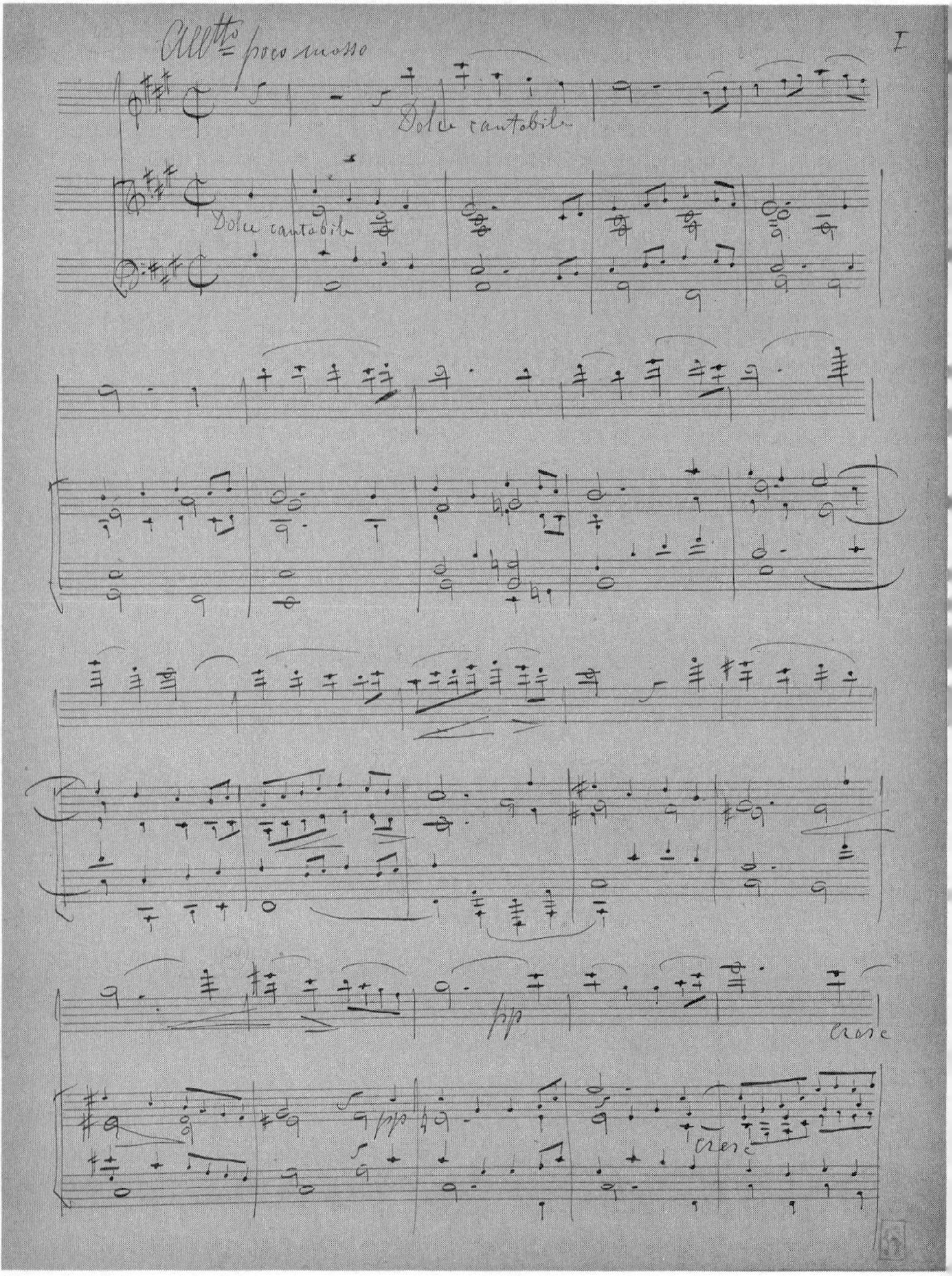
I
Alltto poco mosso
Dolce cantabile
Dolce cantabile
pp
pp
cresc
cresc

IV

TRAGEDIES

AND

TRIUMPHS

Allegretto poco mosso

(1930 to 1965)

෧ඐඬඥ

Swann heard the lovely dialogue between the piano and violin at the opening of the last movement . . . First the solitary piano, lamenting, like a bird abandoned by his companion; then the violin, listening and replying, as from a neighboring tree. It was as though they were at the beginning of the universe, as though there were only those two remaining in the world, or rather in a world closed to all the rest and constructed by a creator such that there would forever be only those two—the world of this sonata.
—Marcel Proust, *Du Côté de Chez Swann* (1913)[1]

Eugène Ysaÿe died in 1931. But the career of this violinist, to whom César Franck had dedicated his sonata for violin and piano, had been effectively over for some time. Illness had overtaken him, and his last years were increasingly difficult. Like so many European musicians, he found success in America, but by the time he died, the sonata he had premiered and championed was more famous than he. It was not only musicians who praised its greatness and beauty. The celebrated French writer Marcel Proust paid tribute to it in one of his great novels.

People who had never heard of Eugène Ysaÿe debated which performer's interpretation of the sonata was best. Violinists discussed arcane matters, such as whether a fingered slide at the beginning of the third movement should be repeated in a similar section at the end, or how expressive to make a particular pizzicato (plucked string). These questions were more important than they might appear. The sonata was now so well-known that anyone could have an opinion on any detail, and the advent of radio and recordings made it possible to scrutinize individual performances and compare one artist's interpretation to another's.

As for César Franck, though his fame had endured and even grown in the years since his death in 1890, many people who knew his name knew little else about him. Few gave much thought to the travails of this man who had finally, after the toil of many years, been inspired to complete the great sonata in 1886. It was his triumph—universally considered among the handful of greatest works ever written for violin and piano. There are many masterpieces in music, but this was his miracle.

The final movement of the Franck sonata uses the device of a canon—a musical form in which one instrument repeats a melody exactly as the other instrument has played it just a few moments earlier. The melody of the canon is based upon the single great thematic idea that recurs in all prior movements, transformed in each to reflect a different musical character. In this movement, it is rendered as a joyful song, expressed first by the piano and then imitated by the violin. It is extraordinarily beautiful—almost heartbreaking in its naive simplicity, much like the anguish of observing a child who, in a state of innocence, encounters the world. The movement's modest beginning builds steadily until, in its final moments, with the violin atop its highest string, it summons the piano to join. Negotiating an elaborate labyrinth of notes, in a passage that has been the bane of pianists for generations, the piano meets the violin in a celestial space. No one can escape a feeling of elation when the two play their final triumphant notes together.

On Being American

⌘

If anything felt triumphant to Lea in 1931, it was that she had finally settled in America with her family. Her talent, hard work, and sheer grit had paid off. In time, she was confident that her eldest son, Yuri, would also join her.

Lea and her family, like so many other Jewish musicians who came to the United States in the 1920s and 1930s, were foreigners in a new land. This foreignness was reflected in more than simply their countries of origin. For many, English was a third, fourth, or fifth language, and they spoke it with varying degrees of accuracy and comfort. They were unfamiliar with many things American, including the cavalier attitude many natives seemed to have toward living in a free society and spending money.

Their new country offered a level of security and freedom they had never before known. The lands from which they had come were beset by revolutions, wars, pogroms, and official discrimination against Jews. The United States seemed free of these conditions. Still, Lea and a whole generation of European Jewish musicians were cautious about their religion. They suspected that no country could be truly free of anti-Semitism. The easiest solution was either to play down one's religion or to pretend you weren't Jewish at all. Some, like Serge Koussevitzky and Efrem Zimbalist, who taught alongside Lea at the Curtis Institute of Music and would eventually become its director, converted and became Christians. Others, like Lea, Pierre, and Boris, did not reject their Jewishness overtly—they simply did not practice any religion at all. The only time I heard my grandmother talk about being Jewish was when ham or pork was served—meats she did not like. She would politely decline, saying that she kept kosher. This wasn't true since she enthusiastically ate lobster, clams, and shrimp, which she loved and were clearly not kosher.

European musicians rejected their broader heritage in other ways, too. Names were Anglicized. Children were discouraged from speaking anything except English in public. They were Americans, after all, and needed to succeed in the new country. Many grandchildren were discouraged from learning their grandparents' native language and certainly were not encouraged to learn Yiddish. The past, especially the nasty bits, was mostly buried. When it was acknowledged, it was as a carefully constructed mythology or amusing stories stripped of harsh realities. Lea, Boris, and Irene regularly told stories like that of Queen Elisabeth's dress or Irene's "audition" with Isadora Duncan to enthusiastic audiences of family and friends, but it was decades before I uncovered the complex circumstances surrounding these well-loved anecdotes.

When it came to passing on musical traditions, a familiar pattern was repeated across many families, including ours. New arrivals made sure their offspring learned to play instruments—a family tradition so habitual it was impossible to give up. But we also got a clear message that this was not the way young people were to make their living. In America, we could do better. Thus, we were not to consider a music school or even a music concentration in a university setting. We were to major in something that would lead to a nonmusical career, such as medicine or law. It was only my brother Andy's determination and his dropping out of Columbia University after a year that convinced my parents to allow him to audition for and ultimately attend the Curtis Institute of Music.

For European immigrants like Lea and her generation, who had worked to forge musical careers in America, the effort to be accepted extended to the music they chose to play. They had been steeped in a European classical tradition. Now they needed to find ways to make their music accessible to the general public in a country where, for the most part, such music was unfamiliar. A delicate balance had to be maintained. On the one hand, these musicians were exotic stars from abroad, and part of their mystique was their foreignness, including their charmingly unique way of speaking English. My uncle Boris's Russian accent became a hallmark, familiar to millions when he started broadcasting intermission features on Saturday afternoons from the Metropolitan Opera House in New York. People felt the outsize personalities and music of these foreigners represented high European culture, something many Americans were desperate to claim for themselves.

On the other hand, when the musicians chose what to play for audiences, programs composed exclusively of heavy classical repertoire—the kind of programs they had been accustomed to playing in Europe—did not necessarily go over well, especially in places outside of those few American cities with reasonably robust traditions of classical music. As trains carried my relatives and other European musicians on long tours across America away from the cultural hubs into small cities and towns from one war memorial auditorium to another, they needed to adapt.

And adapt they did. To be successful in these smaller places meant adjusting the music one played to suit a different kind of audience from ones to which they were accustomed. Lea was a master at this. The first half of her programs in these places often began with standard classical repertory, but sometimes with large sections of the music cut to make the pieces shorter. In some cases, if a particular movement of a sonata or concerto did not seem as if it would be appealing to the audience, Lea and others like her simply substituted a more tuneful or lively one from another sonata or concerto by the same composer. According to the cellist Orlando Cole, the legendary violinist Jascha Heifetz was not above making these compromises. Though today considered a paragon of classical musical artistry, he too would sometimes make these substitutions even when he played in New York City. He would play something listed in the program as a Mozart violin sonata, but each movement would in fact be from different sonatas that Mozart had written.[2] After intermission, there would be a series of lighter pieces ending with popular encores that were even shorter and easier to listen to.

Many of the performers, including violinists such as Zimbalist, Heifetz, and Kreisler, would also make adaptions of popular tunes from operas or even American folk songs and not only perform them in the second half of their programs, but publish them for amateurs to learn and enjoy. When my relatives did so, they lovingly referred to these pieces in Yiddish as *shmatas* (old rags—as in "that clothing he is wearing is nothing but *shmatas*").

But there was more to these programs than classical masterpieces and more popular and familiar fare. It was common practice to champion new music. As a well-known soloist, Lea would receive offers from composers eager to write music for her. This is always a tricky proposition since one never knows what the resulting composition will sound like. Most frequently, she would wait and try out pieces that had been sent to her before agreeing to perform them. There were many reasons why she might choose to include a piece in a concert program. She often liked the compositions and felt they had a future if she championed them. She was committed to introducing new music and felt it was the responsibility of prominent artists to do so (something much less common today to the detriment of the classical music field). But sometimes Lea was guided by more practical concerns: A concert engagement might depend on her debuting a new work, and getting booked and rebooked by important concert promoters was essential to her success. Lea drilled this lesson into all of the family musicians who toured in America, including my brother Andy and me when we were old enough to enter the field.

Rockport

Lea and the family spent the summer of 1930 in the town of Rockport, Maine. A tiny fishing village about halfway up the Maine coast, Rockport had been transformed by Mary Louise Curtis Bok into a Curtis Institute summer music colony. Mrs. Bok had complied with Josef Hofmann's stipulation when he became director of Curtis that funds be provided for year-round instruction, by encouraging teachers to go wherever they wanted and take students with them during the summer. She would reimburse the costs. But after a few years, it became clear that this was impractical, expensive, and did not allow opportunities for creative synergy. She decided to choose a location where they could all be together.

Mrs. Bok's father, Cyrus Curtis, who had been born in Portland, Maine, had a magnificent summer estate in Rockport. At one time, Rockport had been relatively prosperous, famous for shipbuilding, barrel making, exporting ice and lime, and harvesting seafood. But in late 1929, Rockport, like so many other towns in Maine and in the United States, was suffering. Local people whom Mary Curtis had known as children were suddenly out-of-work adults.

Enter Mary's grand plan. Long before President Franklin Delano Roosevelt put in place his New Deal program to provide work for the unemployed, Mrs. Bok created her own, with the central premise of creating a summer colony for her Curtis musicians. Mrs. Bok purchased a number of properties, many on the eastern shore of Rockport Harbor, and had them renovated into dwellings that could be occupied by faculty members, students, and their families during the summers. She purchased and repurposed a boat barn for a concert hall. For all these projects, she employed almost exclusively local workers, though for some tasks she brought in outside specialists, such as the renowned Olmsted firm for landscape design. Once the renovations and rebuilding were complete, she continued to employ local labor for ongoing maintenance, housekeeping, and cooking. In some cases, she even provided housing for the help.* In this way, Mrs. Bok kept much of the population of the local area employed throughout the Depression years.

By December 18, 1930, her largesse made national news. The *New York Herald Tribune* in a front-page story wrote that, "Through the philanthropy of Mrs. Louise Bok, widow of Edward Bok, the noted publisher, the unemployed . . . will be provided with work this winter . . . As those needing work are estimated to number eighty, this arrangement is to solve the unemployment problem in that locality . . . The population of Camden is about 3,000 and that of Rockport 2,000."

No one has ever calculated what Mrs. Bok's work program and town redevelopment project ended up costing her. But I have totaled the activities I know she funded (probably only a fraction of the whole), and by my estimate, in today's dollars, the cost was between $25 and $35 million—this in the early years of the Great Depression. No wonder my mother, years later, recalled the activity with a kind of dreamlike incredulity.

Lea was given a house to live in which she promptly named Mary-Lea Cottage in honor of her friendship with Mary Curtis Bok, and a separate studio in which to teach. When she told Mrs. Bok that, for the first time, she was learning to teach sitting down because her bow hit the ceiling of her studio when she stood, Mrs. Bok said nothing. But the next summer when Lea came to Maine and saw the building, it was capped with a new, higher roof.

Lea's teaching approach was definitely old school. One practiced basic scales, arpeggios, and familiar études that developed finger and bow technique every day and one studied the classic solo violin literature. Everyone was considered "soloist" material, so there was no time or inclination to study the violin parts of orchestra repertoire. There was a certain irony in this since

---

* Annie Spear, the head housekeeper, was provided with her own house sandwiched between the local golf course and the property acquired by my uncle Pierre. It was within walking distance of the houses she and her staff were responsible for cleaning. As of 2019, a Wolf cousin occupied that house.

many of the students did end up in orchestras—many in the first chair as concertmasters. The great chamber music literature—string quartets and quintets, piano trios (with violin), and other mixed ensemble music—was also not part of the program. Playing that music was something one could do for fun in one's spare time but it should not distract from core study.

Lea had what she called her "7 to 11 club"—any student of hers had to be up and breakfasted by seven A.M. in order to practice the requisite four hours. Lessons were held after lunch and then the students were free to swim and play. Evenings were often devoted to informal concerts. Lea's philosophy of teaching was simple and mirrored that of Josef Hofmann: Good outcomes were not the result of genius teachers. Rather, they came about when brilliant students were willing to work hard with experienced performer/teachers as their guides. Curtis had provided her with such students, and she was grateful. In an interview for the *Philadelphia Record*, reporter George M. Lang tried to replicate Lea's distinctive accent while describing her philosophy:

> "A titcher," she says, "can not mek a genius. Only Gott can do dat. A titcher can titch goot or bad and dat is very important. But de poopil must have tolent and be villing to prectice wit patience, wit hard vurk, wit schvet. Dere is no odder way."[3]

Lea believed strongly that the instructional program should include performance opportunities for her young charges. It is one thing to play for a teacher, quite another to play in front of an audience, especially one as critical as one's fellow students. Once a week, the living room of her summer cottage was transformed into a mini–concert hall. In addition, Lea wanted her pupils to hear faculty members play so they could discuss these performances with their teachers at lessons the following week. Hofmann concurred with Lea's approach; though he had no interest in performing himself, he came to many of Lea's evening musicales, including the final concert of the 1930 season, in which she played Tchaikovsky's Violin Concerto in D Major with Boris playing the orchestral parts on the piano. Whatever Hofmann may have thought of Boris's playing, he was politely complimentary.

There was one other aspect of Lea's teaching style that stood out. She believed that students could learn from one another. She instituted something called "class concerts" so students could get some performance experience in semiformal settings and she used these as teaching and learning situations. Unlike Carl Flesch's group lessons where students observed but only Flesch spoke, Lea's events included informal concert programs by students followed by talk sessions in which they discussed what they had heard and, in some cases, made constructive suggestions to one another. In her class yearbook from 1929–1930 now in the Curtis archive, she writes about what she had encountered when she started teaching at Curtis: "The attitude of my pupils toward each other was the usual one, strangers who criticized each other severely, as only young people can do. No consideration, no real friendship, no deep understanding existed between them, and each was convinced he was better than the other. There was no harmony between my students, and it was a hard struggle to overcome their attitude toward each other."

But now, she claimed, the situation had changed. And to prove it, Lea had each student write something in the class yearbook to demonstrate what he or she had learned not only about violin playing but about being part of a musical family and community at Curtis—what Lea described in all capital letters as "MUSICAL PARADISE ON EARTH." In her own words, "My class is now a wonderful group of friends, all working hard, playing for each other, never passing a jealous remark, always ready to help one another." One can read these words a bit cynically, as I did when I first encountered them, wondering whether Lea had been terribly naive. There is generally no one more competitive, critical, or cruel than a student at a leading musical conservatory. But over the years, in talking to some of Lea's students, I came to realize that much of what she said about their attitude was probably true. According to one of them, Robert Gomberg, who became a member of the Philadelphia Orchestra:

> The innovation of class concerts by Madame Lea Luboshutz seems to me one of the greatest accomplishments ever made by a modern music teacher . . . It is of great advantage to the student . . . who is trying to become accustomed to the presence of an audience. The auditors, though few in number, nevertheless played an important part in detecting mistakes in passages, intonation, tempi and degree of self control.[4]

Judging from the results of her teaching and the tremendous success her students enjoyed after graduation, her system worked. She loved her students as if they were her children and, like her children, she made them behave as if they were a family, helping one another to thrive.

Lea also loved Rockport and Mary-Lea Cottage. Irene thrived there and took to the water immediately. It is rather extraordinary to me that Lea allowed her daughter such great freedom on the open ocean. Whereas today, a thirteen-year-old visitor to the area would never be permitted on the water alone without a life jacket and would be required to stay within view of adults at all times, Irene soon mastered the art of rowing long distances unsupervised. Without donning a life jacket, she took a boat every day in good weather approximately a mile out to the Rockport Lighthouse, where the lighthouse keeper and his wife had a snack waiting for her and enjoyed hearing stories about the strange people who had invaded their little town.

By Lea's second year in Rockport (1931), the summer music colony was in full swing. Today, most of the names of the visitors would mean little to a non-musician, but at the time the Curtis faculty members who came to Maine represented musical royalty. Josef Hofmann had a beautiful house with a garage where he and his Polish assistant Karl Mickley could work on his inventions. (By the end of his life, Hofmann had over seventy patents, including the invention of pneumatic shock absorbers.) He was quite unhappy in his home life and spent many evenings playing poker at Mary-Lea Cottage.

Conductors Eugene Ormandy and Fritz Reiner came and went. The cellist Gregor Piatigorsky and harpist Carlos Salzedo brought students. There were even composers in residence including two students who would become world famous in later years—Samuel Barber and Gian Carlo Menotti. The colony became such a draw that others, not associated with Curtis, came just to be part of it. Among those who joined the poker group at Mary-Lea Cottage were the pianists Josef and Rosina Lhevinne. Both, like Lea, had been Gold Medal winners in Moscow and both had important careers in America. They were not associated with the Curtis Institute but rather with its chief competitor, New York's Juilliard School. Yet it didn't matter. They chose to spend the summer with their fellow Russians in Rockport, and even were willing to appear with them in local concerts.[5] While the poker group varied, one member was always present—Gitel, who insisted they play for money (a tenth of a cent per point) and then proceeded to cheat if she did not like the cards she was dealt, according to Irene's memories. In her halting, Yiddish-tinged English, Gitel called the game "a finef card studke mit da dvoike ist vild"—her version of "a five-card stud with deuces wild."

There was one final tradition that Lea established the first year of the Rockport summer colony, which was repeated faithfully every year thereafter. Lea felt she needed to give a public performance in some large hall to benefit a community organization. In 1930, she performed in a local opera house that had been built forty years earlier, with proceeds from the concert going to the Rockport Public Library. In subsequent years, the hospital, the YMCA, an organization sponsoring school music programs, and even the local boat club saw Lea's concert revenues filling their coffers. Helping the locals was important, especially in the Depression years. But Lea also knew that showing her appreciation to the community in this very public way would ensure that the strange band of interlopers who came every summer would continue to be welcomed.

After several such events, Lea became an extremely popular fixture in town. People treated her like royalty and attempted to address her as "Madame Luboshutz." For many, this was a difficult mouthful (no one dared call her by her first name), so at her suggestion she became simply Madame Lubo. Soon friends, colleagues, and family (including us grandchildren and, in fact, most of her professional colleagues) shortened it to Lubo, and this became the name that stuck for the rest of her life.

Yuri

After Pierre's departure from Moscow in 1925, Lea's oldest son, eighteen-year-old Yuri, had become closer to his aunt Anna and her husband, the physician-scientist, Nikolai Shereshevsky, his only near relatives left in the country. Yuri and his uncle had much in common. Both were men of mathematical and scientific interests and talents. And, given Shereshevsky's status as a respected "bourgeois specialist," his connections were extremely helpful to Yuri. Yuri wanted a career in mathematics, and Shereshevsky's unique assistance was a great boon.

With his immediate family now established in the great land of opportunity, the United States, why didn't Yuri cast his lot with theirs? Yuri, like many young people—not only in the Soviet Union but outside of it—was idealistic about his country's future after the 1917 Revolution. He and they believed that communist ideology would ultimately triumph throughout the world and that the Soviet Union was at the forefront of progress. And while Lea's career eventually became secure, that outcome was by no means clear during her early years in the United States. She had been reluctant to bring the family over until she knew things would be stable and once she did, the worldwide Depression did not augur well for her financial security. These were the very years that Yuri was establishing his career in the Soviet Union. Finally, it is important to remember that the Soviets were treating Yuri extremely well. Mathematicians were highly valued in Soviet Russia, and Yuri was a rising star in the field. In this case, the sins of the father were conveniently forgotten by the authorities.

During the 1920s, the Soviets developed new theories about how to nurture creativity. One held that leaders in a field should spend their free time together, mixing informally, discussing their work and inspiring one another. This theory was put into practice by building rural "villages" where leading specialists from a certain field were allocated adjoining plots of land and funds to build homes for use in summer and on weekends. The most famous was the writers' community Peredelkino, where Boris Pasternak and Isaac Babel lived, but villages were built for almost every profession valued by the Soviets.

Nikolai Shereshevsky was granted a dacha in a science village located in a beautiful forested area less than an hour's train ride from Moscow (though the affluent Shereshevskys could afford to be driven there by taxi). The winterized dacha was warm and welcoming, and was often visited by the family not only in summer, but during snowy months. It was still in the Shereshevsky family almost a century later. In 2014, I visited Anna and Nikolai's grandson Vladimir, who was living there permanently, enjoying retirement in the beautiful surroundings.

In Moscow, the Shereshevskys were members of the House of Scientists, an exclusive club for the Soviet Union's most distinguished scientists. The club was housed in a former mansion in the Prechistenka district, just southwest of the Kremlin and close to many scientific institutes and academies. It was an oasis of comfort, with its own garden, concert hall, restaurant, cafeteria, cinema (showing many films not permitted to the general public), conference hall, and meeting rooms. The Shereshevskys' physician-scientist granddaughter Nina, still a member when I visited in 2014, told me that she, her friends, and their children basically grew up there—when they were not away for the summer. Despite the privations of life in Moscow, the scientists' club had ample food, including fresh-baked *pirozhky* (meat pies). For the children, there were chess clubs, dance classes, tennis, and a theater group.

Besides its wonderful Moscow facilities, programs, and food, the House of Scientists maintained "tourist camps" for its members. These were in beautiful, isolated places throughout the country, like the coast of the Black Sea, a river bank in Lithuania, and the mountains of the Caucasus. Members of the House of Scientists and their families could go to these places for up to twenty-four days each year for free. Conditions in these retreats were spartan—tents rather than houses and cold-water showers. But there was always one building with electricity housing a kitchen, a dining room, and good fresh food made by a resident chef. Despite the living conditions, the scientists and their families adored these camps. For generations, the Shereshevskys continued to enjoy membership in the House of Scientists. My cousin Sveta recalled the club and the vacations as idyllic parts of her girlhood. The many forms of special treatment that the family received were not lost on Yuri. He too must have dreamed that with hard work, he could be a member of the privileged scientific elite.

Family lore says that Yuri was at least as brilliant as his father, Onissim—perhaps more so. He entered Moscow University on September 29, 1923, when he was sixteen, without being required to take an entrance exam. His career there was so successful that upon graduation, he received an appointment at Bauman Moscow State Technical University—one of the leading technical schools in the Soviet Union. The usual apprenticeship in the provinces was considered unnecessary, and he rapidly advanced to the position of associate professor. A letter to Lea, written on March 5, 1931, describes this important appointment and his impression that things like salaries for people like him are better than in America.

> Dear Mother!
>
> I just returned from Leningrad and received your letter . . . I am doing well. I am taking my vacation on July 20th and going to Caucasus. I did not have a very good winter this year: I was quite distressed at work for over half a year, since they wanted to send me to the provinces. You can understand how much it affected my mood and my work. Everything is okay now.
>
> I am now an Associate Professor at the Bauman Technical University and have a good salary—even too good. Teaching positions here are paid very well and in general, I think it is even better here than in America.[6]

In his early twenties, Yuri published a mathematical paper on the theory of functions of a real variable and its relation to integral equations—a copy of which he sent to his mother in America (she, of course, did not understand a word of it but was still very proud). At the time, this was an important subfield within mathematics and Yuri's star was rising. As he became well established professionally, Lea's pleas for him to join her fell on deaf ears. Whatever Yuri's personal desires, securing an exit visa would have been difficult, given his profession. And a further complication made any desire to leave the Soviet Union less likely: Yuri had met a fellow mathematics student at the university, Natalya Vatslavovna Levy, and married her.

Once Lea learned of the marriage, she assumed that Yuri would want to rejoin the family, especially now that he had a wife. But Boris was convinced that this was not the case. At a concert in Europe, Boris, for the first time, had worn a brand-new dinner jacket, black tie, dress shirt with studs, and patent leather shoes. A Soviet trade-mission official happened to be in attendance and, upon return to Moscow, reported to Yuri that Boris's playing was mediocre and his dress bourgeois. Yuri wrote a scathing letter. Instead of working hard on his piano playing, he claimed, Boris had wasted his time in fashionable tailor shops, succumbing to bourgeois culture and decadent capitalism.

After this, Boris had no illusions about where Yuri's political sympathies lay. But Lea was unwilling to give up. During the spring of 1931, she became quite ill. Once the school year was over, she decided to go to Europe for a rest cure and perhaps to reunite with Yuri there, at least temporarily, so they could talk things over. Josef and Betty Hofmann had convinced her to join them in Bad Kissingen, a famous spa town in Bavaria, as they were departing on May 30 for Cherbourg and would eventually end up there. Lea decided to make the transatlantic crossing with them and the conductor Albert Coates on the USS *Bremen*. The photographer Richard Fleischhut (best known today for his iconic photograph of the exploding airship Hindenburg) was also aboard and took a photograph of the four of them on June 3. It is some indication of Hofmann's fame that the photograph made its way into the collection of the German Historical Museum, where it remains to this day.

After arriving in Cherbourg on June 4, Lea traveled first to Berlin where she wrote the following letter to Yuri:

HOTEL SAVOY, BERLIN
19 June [1931]
Dear Yuri,

I got an unexpected vacation and went to Europe to take care of my health. I am writing from Berlin, where I am staying for two days. I am leaving for Kissingen tomorrow morning for 3 weeks. My address over there is: Villa Bauer Kissingen. Please write to me there, since I have not received news from you for a long time . . .

I did not send you money, since unfortunately I did not have any spare at that time: the year was not very successful. I lost almost all my money because of the [world-wide financial] crisis. I hope that things will get better and I will then send money again on the first available occasion. I had to borrow money for the trip to Europe, since I did not want to sell stocks which lost value dramatically.

You probably know what is now happening in America. Thank God I am healthy and able to work.

I would very much like to see you. . . . please write to Kissingen.

Though she did not see Yuri, Lea appeared to have a wonderful time with Josef and Betty Hofmann in Bad Kissingen, and by the time she left, she was fully recovered.[7] Their trip back to Cherbourg in the company of Albert Coates was resplendent with celebration and champagne. As she wrote (in Russian) on the back of a photograph of the four of them now in the family collection, "Dear Ones, In a few hours we will reach Cherbourg. That means that our trip is almost at an end. It was an endless delight. The master [Josef Hofmann] was in an absolutely expansive mood. We drank champagne twice a day—at breakfast and at lunch. In a word—I am happy." She left for New York on the USS *Bremen* with a large group of friends—not only the Hofmanns and Coateses but the pianists Leopold Godowsky and Leonard Liebling; the Chicago Symphony Orchestra's conductor, Frederick Stock;[*] William Paley, the founder of CBS; Berthold Neuer, the artists manager for the Knabe Piano Company, and others. She arrived in New York on August 1. Despite her concerns—the world financial crisis, her problems with her son, and her recent illness—all seemed reasonably well for her.

However, after she arrived home, Lea received disconcerting news. Natalya had been pregnant in early 1931 and the baby had been due just at the time Lea was in Germany. This alone gave Yuri a good reason not to join his mother, but he had not mentioned the child in his letters. And there was at least one other reason Yuri had decided not to come to Berlin. He was an avid and skilled mountaineer and was scheduled to use his vacation time to climb Mount Misses Tau in the Caucasus. These climbs were dangerous—the mountain was 4,427 meters or almost 15,000 feet high, and much of it was covered in snow. Yuri's plan was to go to this area, which rises at the border of Europe and Asia between the Black and Caspian seas, with some Russian and Swiss colleagues. But he managed to persuade his companions to delay the trip until he could see his new child. Nature cooperated. Natalya and Yuri's son, whom they named Dmitri, was born on July 15, 1931.

<hr />

[*]   Lea had soloed with Stock and the Chicago Symphony and the two had become friends. She had appeared as early as May 20, 1927, with him at the Ann Arbor Festival playing the Bruch concerto and short pieces by Mozart, Gluck, and Brahms.

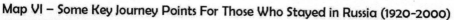

Map VI – Some Key Journey Points For Those Who Stayed in Russia (1920-2000)

Two days after visiting his wife and son in the hospital, Yuri left for the mountains. Along the way, he sent a series of postcards to his wife.

Postcard 1—written on the way to the mountains from Yuri to his wife

13/VIII
Dear T . . .
    We are traveling well. Navigating the train by compass. Will write again from Nevilomvskoy.
    Update: Milya has stomach ache, but everything else is fine. Weather is the same as in your area.
    Regards to Boris Markovich. Ylik is very popular in his beautiful coat.
    Yra,[8] *Ira, Milya*

Postcard 2

Dearest,
    I wrote only one postcard, but dropped it by accident into a box for airmail (to the right of the post window). If they don't give it to you, ask if you can buy it back.
    All . . .
    Yra

Postcard 3 from Yuri to his wife

18/VIII
    Approaching Elbrus. So far everything going as scheduled. Sending with a postman, but he only travels once a week, so don't worry about not receiving news.
    Kisses,
    Yra

When Yuri arrived at the mountain, he and his comrades set out on their climb during the final week of July 1931. That was the last anyone would hear from Yuri.

Official Notice (Izvestia #227), August 18, 1931

Центральный Совет Общества Пролетарского Туризма и Экскурсий с прискорбием извещает о гибели 30 VII при восхождении на вершину г. Миссес-Тау (на Кавказе) активных работников туристского движения альпинистов
тт. Ю. С. ГОЛЬДОВСКОГО и С. С. ЛЕВИНА (Москва)
и членов Швейцарской коммун. партия
тт. Макса МЕГЛИНА и Иосифа ХЕГГЛИНА (Базель).

The Central Committee of the Society for Proletariat Tourism and Excursions with great sadness announces the death on July 30 during an ascent on the peak of Mt. Misses Tau (Caucasus, Russia) of active participants in the tourist movement, alpinists Yu.O. Goldovsky and S.S. Levin (Moscow), as well as members of Swiss Communist Party Max Merlin and Joseph Khegglin (Basel).

Obituary of Y. O. Goldovsky and S. S. Levin

Ю. О. ГОЛЬДОВСКИЙ и С. С. ЛЕВИН

30 июля 1931 года при восхождении на гору Миссес-Т... (на Кавказе) трагически-погиб доценты Московского ме... имени Баумана Ю. О. Гольд... института возрасте 24 лет) и С. С. Левин (в возрасте 25 лет). Опытные альпинисты, они оказались жертвой несчастного случая, — их снесла снежная лавина.

Покойные товарищи принадлежали к лучшей части молодых научных работников. Талантливые математики, они дали серьезные научные исследования в области теории функций действительного переменного и интегральных уравнений. С научной работой они счастливо сочетали первоклассную педагогическую деятельность, стяжавшую им всеобщую любовь и уважение студенчества МММИ и университета. Ведя интенсивную общественную работу по организации учебно-производственной жизни института, Гольдовский и Левин являлись прекрасными образцами молодых советских ученых.

Творческая энергия, преданность делу строительства пролетарской высшей школы ушедших товарищей должны послужить примером для всех молодых научных работников.

Проф. А. Гельфонд, проф. Д. Меньшов, Д. Панов, Е. Поршнева, П. Рашевский, П. Риз, Б. Солоноуц, проф. В. Степанов, Г. Фридлендер, проф. А. Хинчин, Б. Юнович, А. Юшкевич.

On July 30, 1931, during an ascent on the mountain Misses Tau (Caucasus, Russia), Yu.O. Goldovsky (24 years old) and S. S. Levin (25 years old), both faculty members of Bauman Moscow State Technical University, tragically perished. Experienced mountain climbers, they became victims of a disastrous accident—they were swept away by an avalanche.

They represented the best part of the young scientific community. Talented mathematicians, they led groundbreaking scientific research in the area of theory of functions of a real variable and integral equations. They successfully complemented their research work with first class teaching, which earned them broad recognition and love of the student community and the University. Their active engagement in academic and administrative aspects of university life made them outstanding examples of the young Soviet scientists . . .

A month passed before Lea received the news of her son's death. Boris had gone to the tiny post office in Rockport, Maine. Among the envelopes in the day's mail was one from the Soviet Union with Natalya Goldovsky's name and return address on it. Yuri's wife had never written to Lea before, and Boris had a sense that this must portend bad news.

Letter to Lea from Natalya Goldovsky

Dear Lea Saulovna,

You and I share a terrible tragedy. Yuri is no longer with us. He fell to his death on July 30th while climbing the mountain Misses Tau in the Caucasus. I found out just two days ago when the news finally reached me.

I saw him for the last time on June 21 very briefly in the hospital because I had just returned from the delivery room one hour before his departure for the Caucasus. That way Yurochka[9] was able to see his son. His name is Dima (Dmitri) and I hope that he will look like Yuri when he grows up. Please send me your current address: when I get a good portrait, I'll

send it to you. My address is still the same, Natalya Vaslavovna
Levi.

    Your Talia

According to Irene's account, Lea sat bolt upright on the living room couch
for hours after hearing the terrible news, completely silent. It was as if she was
catatonic. She refused food. In desperation, Irene contacted Lionel Prince in
California and asked him to get in touch with Lea, which he did (a telegram
and a letter were found among Lea's things when she died). But it was Josef
Hofmann, the most important man in her life after her own flesh and blood,
who finally coaxed her to speak. When he came to see her, for the first time
since learning of Yuri's death, she got up. Quiet, composed, and determined,
she told Boris she wanted to send a telegram to her daughter-in-law in Moscow.
Yuri was dead. But there was a grandchild. Jews believe in immortality of the
seed. There was still hope to reunite the whole family.

A Matrimonial Candidate

Even while my grandmother mourned a lost son, life in America had to go on.
It was Irene who forced Lea and the family to refocus some of their attention
on the future. Gitel had always said, "Never look back, always look ahead."
Lea had learned the lesson well. And it was a young man named Billy Wolf
who would make that possible.

If there was anything twenty-four-year-old Billy Wolf knew in 1932, it was
that he was tired of Philadelphia Jewish girls. Their families were part of his
parents' tight social circle. They attended Rodeph Shalom Synagogue, the temple
where both Billy's grandfather and recently deceased father, Albert, had served
as president, and where Albert had laid the cornerstone of the new sanctuary.
The girls belonged to Philmont, the country club established by department store

magnate Ellis Gimbel in 1906 to accommodate Philadelphia Jews shunned by other clubs. They had gone to the same dancing school as Billy and engaged in threadbare gossip about the same group of acquaintances. Except for an unhappy, undistinguished year at the University of Virginia, Billy (whose real name was Walter) had spent his entire life with these girls in Philadelphia.

Many of his dates thought him a good catch. Billy was captain of his high school football team and spent many a Saturday astride his horse, fox hunting in the country. Each of his parents represented a wealthy and long-established Philadelphia German Jewish family. On his father's side, the family owned several businesses, including, at various times, the Philadelphia Phillies baseball team and a movie studio. But most importantly, Billy's father and uncles owned the eponymous Wolf Brothers Company, which manufactured all kinds of paper and packaging products. Billy himself worked for Wolf Brothers in various capacities but his favorite was in design. On his mother Minnie's side, many family members were bankers. In 1915, Minnie's brother, Howard Loeb, took over the presidency of the Tradesmen's National Bank in Philadelphia from his father, August Loeb, to become one of the youngest bank presidents in the city's history.[10] When Howard and Minnie's mother, Mathilde Adler Loeb, died at twenty-seven, her husband and parents built a grand hospital in her memory.[11] Billy often passed the building when he went into the city from his parents' suburban home.

As a third-generation American, Billy Wolf boasted a notable patrimony, in addition to his family's wealth. One of his relatives, Simon Wolf, had helped the Union with financing arrangements during the Civil War. Indeed, Simon Wolf, who named his son for President Ulysses S. Grant, had close relationships with every U.S. president from Lincoln to Wilson. Another relative, Morris Wolf, started one of the largest Jewish law firms in America and one of the largest law firms of any kind in Philadelphia. A third, Abraham Simon Wolf Rosenbach, was active as a dealer in antiquarian books and manuscripts, and built some of the great collections in America for the likes of Huntington, Folger, and Widener, all of which would ultimately be housed in great eponymous institutions. As Nathaniel Burt wrote in his 1963 book, *The Perennial Philadelphians*, "A single [Jewish] family, the Wolfs, dominate the Philadelphia scene in the present century . . . there is a Wolf for every occasion: sporty Wolfs, scholarly Wolfs, artistic Wolfs, social Wolfs, legal and financial Wolfs . . ."[12]

Only Billy's friend, Julius "Dooley" Rosenwald II, grandson of the scion of the Sears Roebuck fortune, was a better catch for the local Jewish girls. Not that Billy cared. Frankly, life at the moment (1932, when much of the world was suffering from the effects of the Great Depression) was dull. Billy poured his heart out to his older cousin, Emma Loeb, and told her his dream was to meet a foreign girl.

Cousin Emma, Mrs. Arthur Loeb, was one of the few Jewish members of the Ladies Committee of the Philadelphia Orchestra. There were plenty of Jews connected with the orchestra, but most sat on stage and played violins or cellos. Of these, many did not even speak English and none were suitable for the social circles in which members of the Ladies Committee traveled. The orchestra's board of directors and its volunteers were dependably white Anglo-Saxon Protestants. Though Cousin Emma was not, they deemed her acceptable. She was what they regarded as a "safe" Jew—someone who knew how to behave at a luncheon and who could hardly be thought of as Jewish, save her unfortunate name. Indeed, it was to Emma that the committee entrusted a particularly delicate assignment—the after-concert entertainment of a fellow Jewess, one of the orchestra's soloists, Lea Luboshutz. Lea was known to have family and friends who were recently arrived Russian Jews, and none of the other ladies on the committee were enthusiastic about welcoming fresh-off-the-boat Jewish immigrants into their homes.

The concert was scheduled to take place on Friday afternoon, November 25, 1932, with repeat performances the following Saturday and Monday. Leopold Stokowski, the Philadelphia Orchestra's conductor, had approached Mrs. Bok, who was an important patron of his orchestra. He explained that his organization was feeling the financial squeeze from the Great Depression. Could she help find soloists to perform with the orchestra? While big name soloists were a draw, the orchestra, given its precarious finances, couldn't afford to hire them. The Curtis faculty was replete with stars. Might Mrs. Bok prevail on some of her faculty to appear as soloists without fee?

Stokowski knew that if he made these requests to the artists directly, he would receive many refusals. But no one at Curtis dared turn down Mrs. Bok. In short order, it was Lea's turn. She was to appear with her great friend, the cellist Felix Salmond (another Curtis faculty member), in the Brahms Double Concerto in A Minor for violin, cello, and orchestra. By the time the concert came around and Emma Loeb had extended her invitation to a postconcert party, Lea was quite distracted. Stokowski, without consulting either her or Salmond, had arranged to have the concert broadcast, something that made Lea nervous. Unlike her brother, Pierre, who welcomed broadcasts and recordings as a way to become better known, Lea's anxiety always increased, as did her fear of memory slips or other mistakes. In the concert hall, her very presence mesmerized audiences, whether or not she played all the notes. With a broadcast or recording, only the sound of the music mattered. When Stokowski remembered that he had not informed the soloists of the broadcast, he dropped a note to Mrs. Bok on October 28, asking if she would be good enough to secure the soloists' approval. After first conferring with Hofmann, it fell to Mrs. Bok to inform Lea. Again Stokowski had been shrewd—Lea had to agree.

A few days before the concert, Emma informed her young cousin Billy Wolf that now was his chance to meet a foreign girl. Lea Luboshutz, one of two guests of honor at the concert's afterparty, had a very attractive daughter who planned to attend. What Emma did not know—or chose not to tell Billy—was that the young girl spoke perfect English and had gone to a local private progressive school long enough that she was hardly recognizable as "foreign." She also did not know that Lea and Gitel had long been on the lookout for a nice, rich Jewish boy who might serve as a suitable matrimonial candidate for Irina (as she was still called at home).

The first meeting between Billy and Irene was touched with great comedy, and was replayed many times as one of the family's classic stories. Irene was told to "act foreign," so she went back to using her Russian name, Irina, and put on her best thick Russian accent. Initially showing only lackluster interest in Billy, she pawned him off on Boris, saying, "I vant you should mit my brahzzer." Billy was not to be put off. Irene was exactly what he had been looking for. But assaulting the citadel defended by Lea and Gitel in order to see her again would be no easy feat. When the idea of a husband for Irene became a realistic possibility, her mother and grandmother suddenly got cold feet and became protective. The girl was, after all, only fifteen.

The next day, Billy, ensconced in a full-length raccoon coat, arrived at the Luboshutz apartment in his Pierce Arrow motorcar. He was refused admittance. Phone calls were also rebuffed. Gitel, as Irene's minder, had always been concerned that Irene's good looks would get her into trouble. When Irene insisted on sleeping outside on the porch during hot summer nights when the family went to Maine,

Gitel tried to talk her out of it. She feared, Irene said, that "boys would come and get me while I was asleep." When Irene refused to go inside, Gitel "got a chair and wrapped herself in a blanket and spent the night on the porch guarding me."

At first, to Gitel, Billy was no different from those other boys. But then he appealed to a family friend, Helen Lieberman, a music lover and part of the same Jewish social circle as the Wolfs. She knew Lea, and her phone call on behalf of Billy Wolf was decisive. The boy came from an extremely well-respected Jewish family, he was "suitable"—meaning rich and well-connected—and she hoped they would relent and allow him to see Irene. The boy was thus admitted to the citadel and five months after Irene's sixteenth birthday, on May 16, 1933, the girl who had been Irina Goldovsky became Mrs. Walter Loeb Wolf.

Irene looked magnificent at the wedding. Lea, who always focused on her own wardrobe for major events, had invested a fortune in a magnificent dress—a form-fitting bias cut satin gown with a silk tulle veil falling from a head band into a long flowing train. Added to this costume was a veritable armload of white lilies and gladioli. Lea had also convinced the man who many considered the world's greatest living pianist, Josef Hofmann, to play the music. Guests were astonished to see Hofmann sitting in a corner of the synagogue at a Steinway piano that he had purchased for the occasion and later gave to the bride and groom.

In many ways, Irene's wedding represented the culmination of Lea's dream. Yes, she had lost Onissim and Yuri. Her father was also dead. But the matriarchical line of Gitel and Lea had triumphed and would now continue with Irene into the next generation and beyond. And as Irene produced child after child—six in all—Lea would grow increasingly content. With Billy Wolf's financial help and with Irene's fecundity, the family prospered and grew. Boris, too, married in 1933. His wife was a fellow Curtis student, the opera singer, Margaret Codd, and Lea was pleased when they added two more grandchildren to the growing clan.

In quieter moments, Lea had to acknowledge that her aspirations had not been fully realized. She had strived unsuccessfully for years to bring Yuri to the United States and she would continue for another decade trying to entice his widow and son to join her in America. But in time she realized that this was not to be. By the end of the 1930s, the link to the Russian branch of the family was broken. Despite the successful conclusion of her journey and the fulfillment of so many of her dreams, Lea would not communicate with any of her Russian relatives for the rest of her life.

Ending a Career

❧

It is never easy to know when to end a career as a concert artist. Inevitably, one's technical powers begin to slip ever so slightly and then more rapidly. A concert artist is like a professional athlete. Frequent ailments and injury are common for a violinist, especially those associated with the neck and shoulder. On the other hand, these problems are often more than compensated for by the greater maturity and depth of one's playing. While an athlete's level of performance is easy to track objectively, this is not so for musicians. Lea did not want to be like some who had remained on the concert stage too long. She had seen the humiliation of one of these performers who she adored—Josef Hofmann—who continued to play long after his powers had been diminished by drink and other ailments. It was a sad ending for a man who had been on top of the world. She would retire sooner rather than later.

From the time of her daughter's marriage in 1933 until her retirement fifteen years later, concertizing and teaching continued to be the primary focus of her life. Her reputation was firmly established[*] and there were no longer the economic pressures there had once been. Had she not been earning money herself, she could rely on a wealthy son-in-law who was more than willing to support her. Her Carnegie Hall recitals continued (with various pianists, including both Boris and Pierre). There were also tours to Europe, though these diminished in number as Lea aged. Maintaining a presence on the concert stage for a musician over the course of a lifetime is exhausting work and arguably was more strenuous in Lea's day before the age of jet travel. It takes increasing amounts of discipline and hard work. Fortunately, for the time being, Lea was accustomed to both.

Though the economic pressure had been lifted and there was no need to realize extra cash, she felt she should probably sell one of her three great Italian instruments. She recalled what it had meant to her as a student and later in the

---

[*]   By this time she had appeared with major orchestras in Boston, New York, Philadelphia, Chicago, San Francisco, and many other cities and her concerts with Josef Hofmann had catapulted her to the top rank of performers.

early years of her career to have the magnificent Amati violin to play. Now she not only owned that instrument, but also her Stradivarius and the third violin with its uncertain Italian provenance that she had played the fateful night in Carnegie Hall when Aaron Naumburg had set in motion the purchase of the Nightingale. Lea explained the situation to Mrs. Bok, wondering whether the Curtis Institute of Music might wish to take the Bergonzi (or whatever it turned out to be) and turn it over to one of her students. Mrs. Bok agreed, purchasing the violin in 1936 and making it available to Lea's prize student at the time, thirteen-year-old Rafael Druian.

As her career was winding down, Lea still felt she had to pursue her concertizing to some extent. If she was going to teach talented pupils, she herself had to maintain high standards in her playing and provide a model of performance to her students—a tough and critical crowd to be sure. She continued to practice four hours each day and she resisted the temptation of some of her older colleagues to drop some of the more difficult pieces from her repertoire. One thing that made staying in shape easier was that she no longer had to care for children or an aging parent. Irene's and Boris's marriages in 1933 had taken them out of the house. This was followed by Gitel's death seven years later. Condolence letters came in from many colleagues and friends including Mrs. Bok and Josef Hofmann, the latter now living in California.

"Despite all the misfortune," Hofmann wrote, "I am happy that I got the opportunity of knowing the lovely 'Babuschka' when she was still amongst us. Time always will also heal your wounds. However, you need to be brave until this happens. Nothing on earth is forever, and sooner or later others will mourn us . . . Happy is he who forgets what cannot be changed anymore!"[13] But much as she missed Gitel, Lea welcomed living alone and being able to work uninterrupted. The Franck sonata remained a staple of her repertoire and a good bellwether of her capacities. When she could no longer play that well, she knew she should no longer be appearing in public. But as some of her students used to say behind her back (when she insisted that they work as hard as she did), she was "maintaining her chops."

The success of her students became increasingly important to Lea as she considered her musical legacy. In the end, her teaching record was impressive. While she never produced a leading soloist, such products were rare. On the other hand, of the roughly 150 students she taught at the Curtis Institute of Music, several won jobs in major orchestras throughout the United States, including six in the Philadelphia Orchestra alone.[14] Given that the majority of that orchestra's thirty violin positions were still held by foreign-born and foreign-trained players during her teaching career, this was an astonishing number.

Two of Lea's students became concertmasters—Rafael Druian (with orchestras in Dallas, Minnesota, Cleveland, and New York) and Henry Siegl with the Seattle Symphony. Another, Isidor Lateiner, made such a sensation as Lea's student that he was invited to solo with the Philadelphia Orchestra while still a Curtis student. Lea also had success with female students including one, Ethel Stark, who became famous as the co-founder and longtime conductor of an orchestra made up entirely of women that was invited to perform in Carnegie Hall.* Lea's track record as a teacher was so impressive that the Curtis Institute chose to bestow on her an honorary doctorate in 1960, thirteen years after she retired. By that time she was quite deaf and, though she claimed to have heard nothing during the long commencement ceremony, she looked incredibly regal in her doctoral robes. Her deportment—learned as a child at her father's knee—had not failed her.

Lea played what turned out to be her final concerts with the Philadelphia Orchestra on November 2 and 3, 1945, and the program continued her tradition of breaking new ground. It had been almost exactly five years since she had appeared with the orchestra in performances of the Beethoven Triple Concerto on November 15 and 16, 1940. Those concerts had been considered trailblazing because the three soloists (Lea, the pianist Edith Evans Braun, and the orchestra's associate principal cellist, Elsa Hilger) were all female. At the 1945 concerts, she introduced a modern concerto by her fellow countryman Nikolai Lopatnikoff. (She had premiered this piece at the Curtis Institute on May 4, 1943, while the music was still in manuscript.) It was noted by the press that even as she approached the end of her career, she was still introducing new music to the concert stage (something that many older classical musicians do not do today as it easier to stick with the familiar repertoire). Lea had been doing this since the time of her first concert tours and was not about to stop. Indeed, when she had first started playing the Franck sonata all those years ago, it was considered "new" music.

As Edwin Schloss wrote in the *Evening Bulletin*:

---

* The name of the ensemble was the Montreal Women's Symphony Orchestra and both Lea and Boris were among the performers engaged as soloists.

In choosing to introduce the Lopatnikoff concerto here, Mme. Luboshutz showed a certain amount of courage and integrity as well as good taste. A violinist of her fine gifts could have ridden to an easy triumph on one of the well-tried war-horses—the concertos of Mendelssohn, Tchaikovsky, or even Beethoven or Brahms. Instead Madame elected to enter the ranks of torch bearers and it must be said her performance shed a gratifying light.[15]

According to Schloss she played the piece "brilliantly" and was "repeatedly recalled by the audience." Other reviews were equally laudatory. One by Elizabeth Emerson Stine said "the composer [Lopatnikoff] could not have chosen [some]one more superbly endowed with the technique and style which his work demands."[16] A third by Linton Martin spoke about her "commanding authority and an impressive display of technical skill . . . that surpassed the intrinsic qualities of the concerto itself."[17] I mention these reviews because after Lea's death, when I was touring as a flutist with my Uncle Boris's opera company, he spoke often about Lea and suggested that at the end of her career there may have been some slippage in her technique. Apparently, the critics did not agree. It appeared she had decided to leave the concert stage while she was still at the top of her game.

Even though the Lopatnikoff concerto was soon forgotten, something else Lea did that day with the Philadelphia Orchestra was remembered for years—perhaps her final act as a longtime pioneering female performer who was now reinventing her public persona once again as the ever-youthful, happy grandmother. As Schloss described it, Lea "added a new touch to Academy protocol . . . Madame (seven times a grandmother, but miraculously youthful in appearance) kissed conductor Ormandy chastely on the cheek. The lucky maestro grinned, while the Friday afternoon ladies tittered and redoubled their applause." Linton Martin in the *Inquirer* did not believe Lea's behavior was so demure: ". . . she rewarded Maestro Ormandy with even more, for she marked her recall to the stage by planting what appeared to be substantially more than a merely perfunctory peck on the cheek following her impeccable performance, while her grandchildren admiringly watched from the conductor's box."[18] It is well to remember that female instrumental soloists with orchestras were quite rare in those days and the protocol of a female kissing a male conductor on stage at the conclusion of a performance—something that is commonplace today—had not been established. Once again, Lea, about to enter her seventh decade, was leading the way.

Lea ended her teaching career at the conclusion of the 1947 academic year. She gave herself one more challenge: playing a faculty recital on April 18, 1947, in front of one of the toughest audiences in the world—her students and fellow faculty members at the Curtis Institute of Music. She had been doing so annually, often appearing with Boris (as she did on May 1, 1944, and April 30, 1945) and often playing very difficult repertoire. At the 1945 concert, for example, she had performed Beethoven's challenging Kreutzer sonata. It was one of the pieces that had meant a great deal to her during her life-time and she must have recalled how she had played it with Onissim four decades earlier when they first met and later with two of her lovers, Leonid Kreutzer and Josef Hofmann. At the 1947 concert, she also chose music that was special to her—two pieces written by her beloved mentor, Eugène Ysaÿe. The Belgian violinist who had come to America in 1918 to serve as music director and conductor of the Cincinnati Symphony for four years and then returned to his native Brussels, had died in 1931. Lea was determined that his name and his music would not be forgotten.

During this period and after her retirement, Lea enjoyed being a popular local celebrity—she was someone the press loved to cover and she enoyed her final transformation into what people called "a grande dame." She was an attractive older woman with an exotic history who had succeeded in a man's field, and she had done so while retaining her delightful sense of humor and genuine zest for life. Her picture was often in the newspaper and her name was mentioned frequently in Ruth Seltzer's "must-read" society column in the local paper. As her grandson who saw her regularly and had to put up with her not infrequent moodiness and her exacting musical instruction, I often wondered what it was about Lea's personality that attracted so many people. Her story was compelling, of course, and she told it selectively and to great effect. But it was far more than that. When I watched her in a crowd, she was outgoing, friendly, likeable . . . and genuinely interested in other people. Her thick accent, and emphatic, rather iffy English, gave charm to whatever she said.

One columnist who caught it well was George M. Lang of the *Philadelphia Record*, describing a visit to her apartment for an interview (the attempt at replicating her accent is quoted directly from the article):

"Kum raight in," she said, "and tell me how glad you are to see me lookink so younk and charmink."

The reporter looked blank.

"You see," explained Madame, "I am a perfec hostess. I even gif my guests pretty spitches they shall say to me. Maybe you forget, so I help you should say somethink nize. Some pipple is so beshful."[19]

Time for the Next Generation

In 1936, Irene had produced the first of Lea's eight American grandchildren—a daughter that she and Billy named Alexandra. Several more came in rapid succession until Billy and Irene had three daughters and three sons, the last coming around the time of Lea's retirement. Boris and his wife also had produced two grandchildren for Lea—Michael and Marina—but Lea spent less time with them since they lived in Boston. Irene's family, on the other hand, lived conveniently close to Lea in Philadelphia and during the summer they all decamped to Rockport as Billy and Irene had purchased Mary-Lea Cottage when the Curtis Institute decided to close down its summer colony in 1945.

Lea was thrilled that Irene had produced so many children and believed she should oversee their musical development. Remembering her early training and knowing that a musician must begin studying early in life if he or she is to amount to anything, Lea insisted that she start teaching these youngsters as soon as they could walk and talk. Having them at hand provided the perfect opportunity for an intensive introduction to music. Lea was soon disappointed, however, to discover that American standards of childrearing were very different from what she had experienced in Russia or even what she had put her own children through. American parents—and Irene was now one of them—had lax standards and they were unwilling to browbeat their young children into practicing many hours a day. For the first three of Irene's children

(Alexandra, Nicholas, and Catherine), Lea was willing to demur. Only one chose the violin and Lea's tutelage showed little success. So with the next two children who came of appropriate age just after her retirement, she put her foot down and insisted that they would be hers to nurture in her own way. Those two children, for better or worse, were my brother Andy and me.

How we suffered. Because we were available to her on a daily basis in the summer months, instead of giving us lessons once a week and asking us to practice in between, Lea gave us lessons every day, including a practice session—supervised by her. I have mostly negative memories of my grandmother's regime. She stressed deportment, hand position, and most importantly, correct intonation (playing in tune). My clearest memory, something I cannot get out of my head to this day, was Lea's unique way of telling us a note was sharp or flat. With her thick Russian accent, she practically shrieked the word "false" at a high decibel range—pronouncing it with two syllables: "fahhhhhhhlll-seh." When she got tired of this, we received a rap with a ruler on the misbehaving finger that had been placed either too high or too low on the string.

I do have two happy recollections from that time. The first was learning how to read music—a skill I was good at and enjoyed. The second was the "concert" I gave under Lea's supervision on August 8, 1951, playing "Happy Birthday" for my father in front of the whole family. Lea, as she told us often, had played her first concert at age six. Well, I had bested her. I had played my first concert (true only for the family and only involving one tune) at five years of age.

My brother Andy and I complained incessantly about having to study violin with our grandmother, and our mother was caught between our obvious misery and Lea's imperious demand that she supervise our musical educations. Leaving things to Irene had failed to produce the desired result with the three older children. Each had taken up an instrument and then quit, though my oldest brother Nick had stuck with the violin longer than the others. He was the first of us to play a recital out of the home—in this case with his lower school compatriots—when he was ten years old. But Lea had dismissed that even though her first concert about which she bragged in her memoir was also at her school. It was now down to Andy and me and even for us she held out little hope. Around this time, she was quoted as telling a journalist, "Today my only pupils are two of my eight grandchildren. Fortunately, they are not very talented violinists. I do not worry about them being famous."[20]

But whatever she said publicly, she did harbor hopes. Despite Irene's entreaties, Lea told Irene that there would be no quitting for Andy and me. At last, a compromise was reached. We could decide whether we wanted to stay with our grandmother as violin students or switch to another instrument. Either way, she would continue to supervise our musical educations. Andy and I were delighted. "Supervision" (whatever that meant) was very different from "lessons" and daily practice sessions. The only question was which instruments to choose?

Our respective decisions turned out to be hugely consequential for our subsequent educations and professional lives. Andy chose piano. Walking out of one trap (my grandmother's tutelage), he had walked into another. There were already three professional pianists in the family (Boris, Pierre, and Pierre's wife, Genia), and his further development would now be scrutinized, critiqued, and argued about not by one family member but by four, including Lea. When it turned out that Andy was quite gifted and progressed rapidly, it made matters even worse. Now a member of the younger generation had shown real potential. From a very young age, Andy felt the pressure. His choice also had ramifications for him in terms of his relationship with Lea. Because piano was the instrument that so often accompanied the violin in the major repertoire, my grandmother continued to teach Andy—not piano technique, but actual works for violin and piano. On many summer evenings, she would take the Nightingale Strad out of the case and they would play together. She insisted that he learn most of the important sonatas for violin and piano—including the Franck. This was a gift that more than anything else shaped Andy's later career.

Meanwhile my choice of instrument was the flute. It was an instrument my musically uninitiated father had taken up when he married my mother in order to participate in the family enterprise. It soon transpired that he had no talent and he gave it up. But he had purchased a beautiful instrument and it was sitting in a closet. I decided that was what I would play. No professional musician in the family knew the first thing about wind instruments. I was left blessedly alone—or relatively so, since there was still overall supervision and monitoring of my progress, reminders to practice, and eventually concerts to prepare, which did involve Lea's close coaching.

But there were other serious consequences of my decision. I had chosen an instrument where the solo and chamber music repertoire is sparse and the career opportunities comparatively few. A violinist who wants to make a career as a performer can aspire to be a soloist, an orchestra player, a member of a string quartet, or a member of another kind of chamber ensemble. In each case, there is a vast literature of music by the greatest composers. Similarly, with the piano, as Andy soon discovered, there were many career tracks to explore and several lifetimes of great music to learn. But for a flutist, outside of flute parts in orchestra pieces, there is only a very small repertoire by the major composers. This means, effectively, that there is only one viable career track—playing in an orchestra. And while there are often more than thirty violins in a symphony orchestra, there are only four flutes. The possibilities for a performing career for a flutist in classical music are few, and in the United States, there were and are so many of us. Not only are flutists trained by teachers steeped in classical music, but tens of thousands of others receive early instruction (much of it excellent) in high school bands, then become classical players in adulthood. It is hardly a sensible choice for anyone wanting to make a living as a performing musician. But I knew none of this at the time. All I knew was that I had a shiny new instrument, a teacher with an Italian name and no connections to my family, and a chance never to touch a violin again in my life.

As part of our tutelage, Lea insisted that we attend concerts with her, just as she had done with her Curtis students. There was no better way for us to learn what repertoire should sound like than hearing it live in a concert hall. Most Saturdays during the school year she would take us to Philadelphia Orchestra concerts. Inevitably, she would drag us backstage where she would push us to the front of the line to get into the conductor or soloist's dressing room. Once inside, she would congratulate the individual, often half clothed, and introduce her two musical grandsons. While I dreaded this way of ending the evening with Lea carrying on in either Russian, French, German, or, occasionally, English, the concerts she took us to were another solid plank in our musical educations. In time, she encouraged us to take printed scores with us—to be honest, there was a bit of showing off as it made us seem much more professional—and Lea was again pleased.

Lea had something else on her agenda as well—introducing us to the César Franck sonata. Here, my brother was the main focus. Andy played the piano part night after night, with Lea playing the violin on the Nightingale (I was the dutiful page turner). Lea's tutelage was completely unsentimental. These were working sessions, not times to reminisce. Not once did she say, "You know, I studied this with the man for whom it was written." We knew nothing about her time with Ysaÿe, about the importance of the piece to our family, about the concerts with Josef Hofmann, or about her having played the piece with our grandfather the first time they met. It was all nuts and bolts.

But Andy instinctively knew the piece was special. In time, he made it a central part of his repertoire, and, like Boris and Pierre, he played the sonata with various violinists in the great concert halls of the world. Though Lea did not live long enough to know it, like her he would one day play the César Franck sonata in one of the most important concerts of his career, at New York's Carnegie Hall.

Catastrophe

"They should have known."

Growing up, I remember parents of some of my Jewish friends talking about Jews in Germany during the World War II, and about the Holocaust. They would say things like, "The Jews in Germany should have been better prepared. There were signs all around them of anti-Semitism—for decades, for generations. It didn't matter that these Jews thought of themselves as loyal Germans. It didn't matter that some of them were heroes in the First World War or held positions of power in government or business or medicine or the arts. They should have known they were not safe. Jews are never safe. We are not safe."

This always struck me as slightly nutty, or at least very paranoid. When were Jews in America not safe? When were there pogroms here? Sure, occasional outbreaks of anti-Semitism occurred in America, just like the outbreaks of violence against Catholics or Mormons during our history. But compared to other groups—especially like Blacks and Native Americans—Jews had fared well since the time of the Founding Fathers. We hadn't had a Jewish president, but we'd had just about everything else, including some pretty fabulous baseball players. What better evidence was there?

But in 2014, when I first read about my great Uncle Nikolai Shereshevsky's arrest on February 2, 1953, I thought immediately of those conversations half a century earlier. Of course, the Russian experience was very different from what led up to the anti-Semitism of Nazi Germany. On the one hand, Russia and Eastern Europe had had terrible histories of pogroms, Germany largely did not. On the other, in Russia, a sense of security and optimism was felt by many non-practicing Jews with the dawn of the Soviet Union. A break from a religious ideology on the part of the government led many Jewish writers, intellectuals, and professional people like doctors to believe that anti-Semitism was at an end.

This was certainly true for Shereshevsky and Anna. Since the 1917 Revolution, they had been loyal, respected, and hard-working citizens of the Soviet Union. Should Shereshevsky have known that the poisonous anti-Semitism that pervaded Russian history was just below the surface and eventually would catch up with him? Maybe. But he was a decorated citizen (as was his wife), a wealthy and successful physician-scientist with a fancy apartment, a valuable antiques collection, and a summer dacha. Shereshevsky didn't even identify as a Jew. Furthermore, in the 1930s, he had proven himself a loyal citizen, serving as an expert witness against other Jews during Stalin's "purges" in the 1930s. It is likely that he could not have imagined being arrested and accused of being a Jewish nationalist, an enemy of Soviet power, an American spy, and a murderer.

In fact, anti-Semitism had been muted during the early years of Stalinism and World War II, and Jews took comfort in the fact that Stalin's entourage included a handful of Jews—his right-hand man, Lazar Kaganovich, Foreign Minister Maxim Litvinov, and the head of the secret police, Genrikh Yagoda. But in 1943, a new purge was launched, targeting "rootless cosmopolitans." At first, Soviet citizens were puzzled by this term, but it soon became clear that this was just the latest label for anyone suspected—in Stalin's increasingly paranoid mind—of being insufficiently loyal. Dozens of writers, filmmakers, literary critics, and scientists were accused, imprisoned, or executed. And in 1948, the term acquired a new meaning—Jewish.

Official anti-Semitism was once more being unleashed on the Jews of Russia. In 1948, the Jewish Anti-Fascist Committee, a state-backed organization that had rallied support for the Soviet Union during World War II, was shut down. Its leader was murdered and its members were arrested. Jewish theaters, museums, and schools were also closed, and Jews were purged from the army. Local authorities across the Soviet Union, who had learned to read the political signals emanating from the Kremlin, began their own purges, firing Jews from their jobs and expelling them from party organizations. It seems that Nikolai Shereshevsky couldn't contain himself: somewhere, to someone, he expressed a "negative opinion" about the campaign against the Jews.

In Stalinist Russia, even a casual remark made in private could spell doom. Shereshevsky found himself implicated in the so-called Doctors' Plot, one of many incomprehensible episodes that occurred under Stalin. It seems to have been instigated by a particularly thuggish anti-Semitic secret police investigator named Mikhail Ryumin, who persuaded Stalin that a group of doctors had committed "medical murder," intentionally killing two Soviet leaders in their care. The result, inevitably, was a new round of purges. On January 13, 1953, *Pravda* reported that dozens of doctors were plotting to kill the leaders of the Soviet Union at the behest of the United States, Great Britain, the Jewish Joint Distribution Committee, and "Zionists." Thirty-seven doctors, including Shereshevsky, were arrested and interrogated. When they were slow to "confess," Stalin issued orders to intensify the "interrogations"—a clear euphemism for torture. After Stalin's death, his successor, Nikita Khrushchev, revealed that Stalin had planned a sweeping anti-Jewish campaign that would have culminated in the deportation of all Soviet Jews to concentration camps.[21]

Decades later, my cousins, Shereshevsky's grandchildren, recalled the terror of being herded into a single room in Nikolai and Anna's apartment while the secret police searched for "evidence." A similar search took place at their dacha. Every nook and cranny was examined, including spaces behind walls, under floors, and in chimneys. Shereshevsky's experiences as a prisoner of the Soviet secret police we can only imagine. It seems he never spoke about them to anyone.

After his arrest, Shereshevsky immediately recognized the danger he was in and became proactive. His only hope of exoneration was intervention by a high official. But whom? One man whose influence was virtually absolute was Lavrentiy Pavlovich Beria, head of the secret police apparatus, who had become deputy premier after World War II. Shereshevsky wrote him a letter on March 24, 1953:[22]

> To L. P. Beria, The Investigations Department of the Ministry of Internal Affairs
>
> From the Scientist Professor N. A. Shereshevskii, b. 1885
>
> I was arrested on February 2, 1953, and informed that I have been accused of being a Jewish nationalist, an enemy of Soviet power, an American spy, and a murderer.
>
> I absolutely reject all these charges. I must admit that, over the past 1–5 years, several people have told me about unjust treatment of the Jews—treatment connected with their work, or their inability to get work, and so on.
>
> The rumors were persistent and I tried to find an explanation for them. It seemed to me that the government perhaps had grounds for mistrusting some Jews—maybe in connection with their wish to emigrate to the State of Israel (if they expressed this wish). But there is no basis for mistrusting all Jews. In connection with this, I permitted myself in conversations with certain comrades to express my negative opinion of such measures. It is possible that I spoke tactlessly . . .

After begging forgiveness for possible transgressions in speaking about mistreatment of Jews, Shereshevsky writes extensively of his many services to the state. He cites more than one hundred journal articles he's written, the positions he has held, and the people he has trained, giving credit always to the Soviet state. "All of my achievements," he writes, "are thanks to Soviet power and have been dedicated to Soviet power."

Shereshevsky refutes the charge of spying by systematically reviewing every foreign contact he has ever had and documenting that his meetings, correspondence, and conversations have all been witnessed by others. Then comes his denial of the most egregious charge—that he is a murderer.

> With feelings of great distress, I must also reject the accusation of being any kind of murderer. Many ill people have passed through

my care during my 42-year medical career. Tens and perhaps even hundreds of thousands can thank me for curing them and alleviating their suffering. Many owe me their lives. I have performed my duties as a doctor honorably and I have never put anyone in danger.

Finally, after begging forgiveness once again for any inadvertent transgressions, he ends the letter movingly:

I am now 68 years old and my days are probably numbered. I will devote all of my remaining strength to my work and to redeeming my guilt.
I ask Your Honor to forgive me.
N. Shereshevskii

The copy of the letter is stamped "Senior Investigator for Major Crimes of the Ministry of Internal Affairs, Major Smirnov."

Though the letter was artfully written, it did not save Shereshevsky's life. It was Stalin's death on March 5, 1953, that did. Stalin's successors, Beria and Khrushchev, immediately denounced the Doctors' Plot as a fabrication, blaming Stalin and the secret policeman Mikhail Ryumin, who was arrested and shot. The accused doctors, including Shereshevsky, were released by the end of March. My great-uncle was reappointed to his job as head of the Department of Endocrinology in the Central Institute, and he again became a member of several prestigious scientific journals' editorial boards. It was as if the Doctors' Plot had never occurred.

Ultimately, I believe that the Doctors' Plot episode had the profoundest impact on Anna, not Shereshevsky. Their great-granddaughter, my cousin Sveta, told me that at the end of her life, Anna expressed just one regret—that she had not emigrated like her siblings had. This is confirmed by an incident recounted in a book published well after Anna's death in 2004 by Y. V. Geroniumus. Apparently, the choreographer, N. S. Nadezhdina, of the Berezka Folk Dance Ensemble, toured America in the 1960s, met Lea, and carried back to Anna a photograph of her sister in front of Mary-Lea Cottage in Maine. Though after the Revolution, Anna and her husband's fate had initially been far more pleasant than Lea and Onissim's, now the tide had turned. As Anna told a neighbor, she wished she had gone, but she had waited too long. Of their two lives, she said: "Compare Lea's mansion . . . and my *tsores* [Yiddish for 'troubles.']"[23]

Anna and her husband had devoted their lives to the Soviet state. Yet, in spite of the many official honors and benefits bestowed upon them, time had proven that anyone was expendable. In later life, there were many tributes and much homage paid to Shereshevsky and, after his death, to Anna including words of their devotion to the state. But by that time, Anna reserved that devotion for her family and her husband's memory.

Fortunately, Lea remained ignorant of these events. So did the rest of the family until more than fifty years after they occurred. But there was another family event—even more catastrophic—that Lea and my parents did know about, although it had been kept from my generation. It involved Genia, Pierre's wife, and her parents. Genia's family had for generations been beset by anti-Semitism. Successful in business, they had been forced to move repeatedly. On her mother's side, the Jacobs had been furriers in St. Petersburg. Her mother, Marie, was born there in 1876, one of seven children. But anti-Semitism forced them to leave and settle in Leipzig, Germany, a European capital of the fur trade, and this is where Genia's mother grew up. She became an accomplished amateur pianist and it was her love of music that attracted her, at the age of twenty-three, to a visiting Moscow shopkeeper named Aaron Nemenoff, Genia's father. Marie's suitor had an elegant beard and a beautiful voice, which was enough for her. Aaron was happy to join the family's business and was given a plum assignment—setting up a shop in Paris—a place that was considered quite safe for Jews. It was there that a son Salomon (called Mounia) was born in 1899 and a daughter, Pierre's wife, Genia, six years later.

Genia grew up in Paris, happily ignorant of anti-Semitism. To her father and mother's delight, she too became an accomplished pianist with professional aspirations. Her marriage to her conservatory piano teacher, Pierre Luboshutz, and the couple's successful life in the United States was reason enough for them to celebrate the family's good fortune. In 1938, Genia's parents accepted an invitation to join the Luboshutz family during the summer in Rockport, where Pierre had recently purchased a beautiful property only minutes on foot from Lea's cottage. Aaron and Marie were amazed to see how well Pierre and Genia were situated. Photographs show two robust and handsome older people basking in their daughter and son-in-law's success. Genia, increasingly concerned about events in Europe, suggested her parents extend their visit. But her brother back in Paris was having health problems, so her parents returned home as planned—just weeks before Kristallnacht, a coordinated anti-Semitic event in Nazi Germany that destroyed synagogues, businesses, and other Jewish buildings. Genia's parents told her not to worry, explaining that Paris was safe.

In time, of course, Paris was not safe. It fell to the Germans in June 1940. With France occupied, Genia went into high gear, using her connections to arrange for her parents to join her in America, traveling via Portugal. To her consternation, they resisted again. Her brother was still not well and they did not feel endangered. There was nothing Genia could do or say to change their minds. And then came catastrophe. In 1943, her parents were rounded up, sent first to Drancy, then to Auschwitz, part of a transport of a thousand French Jews, mostly the elderly. Of the thousand individuals on the transport, 881 were gassed immediately upon arrival. Only six were alive to see liberation in 1945. Genia's parents were not among those lucky few. As fate would have it, their son outlived them by many years.

I knew nothing of this in the years I was growing up. My great-aunt Genia was kind and generous to me, but she often seemed nervous, depressed, even sometimes paranoid. Much of this was masked by Uncle Pierre's happy-go-lucky demeanor and his wonderful sense of humor. But after Pierre's death, Genia's anxieties and feelings of persecution only seemed to worsen. During her lifetime, I never knew that this could have easily been explained. The woman had been tormented by guilt and grief. Many years after her death in 1989, some of her possessions passed to me. Among them was a photograph of Genia as a baby with her family. On the back, Genia had written in French: "My parents, my brother Mounia and me, the quite ugly little sister. 1980." And then below:

PS: when did I scribble all these things that surprise me so much? I don't recall having expressed these thoughts that keep coming back, and snatch my heart?! To lose such a family in such a terrible tragedy. I often wonder how to keep living!!!

Puzzled, I reached out to a French relative of Genia's who told me the entire tragic story. As I tried to take in the events that had caused Genia such grief, I opened one of her books, entitled *The Ten Commandments: Ten Short Novels of Hitler's War Against the Moral Code.* She had had a habit of signing her name and indicating the year she acquired a volume so this one contained her signature and the year 1943. And then below this, was another note in French that read:

1943 The fatal year! Misfortunes, pain, inexplicable or indescribable? Of suffering that will carry them to the grave!

Introducing a Third Generation to the Concert World

As Andy and I became more serious about music in the 1950s amd 1960s, Lea took increasing interest and control. Andy soon outgrew his local piano teacher and went on to study privately with a Curtis Institute faculty member, Eleanor Sokoloff, who was one of Irene's best friends and the world's then-leading pedagogue of very young piano students (even on her hundredth birthday in 2014, she was still turning out prize-winning students). Now, according to Lea, it was time to appear in public and Lea would serve as our mentor, guide, and champion. At age fifteen, Andy played his first concerto, with a local orchestra conducted by one of Boris's former fellow Fritz Reiner students from the Curtis Institute. It was a heady experience. The following summer, we played our first public joint recital in Maine. It was attended by Lea and many of the older generation of musical relatives, so for us (and for them) it was a big deal. Only four years had passed since our grandmother told the press she had no talented grandchildren. Now she was singing a different tune. There seemed to be some hope.

In December 1959, Andy got his driver's license, and we arranged a concert tour of girls' camps in Maine for the following summer. A relative of my father's, herself a camp director, shamelessly served as our promoter. Connections and help from relatives on both sides of the family continued to propel us along. On May 3, 1962, Andy and I performed together with orchestra as soloists in the Bach Brandenburg Concerto no. 5. This time our champion was the father-in-law of our recently married sister Alexandra Wolf Fogel, who served as the president of this orchestra's board. We were clearly enjoying the benefits of belonging to families with lots of musical and community ties. We had grown up as wealthy Wolfs. We were never denied anything when it came to our musical development, and the family was linked to the community in so many ways. Doors opened that were closed to others. My father and mother cheered us on as if we had achieved every milestone because of our talent and hard work and we believed them. It was only much later that I heard someone remark snidely, "It's easy to score runs when you start on third base."

Others found a certain charm to our musical and familial legacy. At fifteen, I won an audition to solo with the Philadelphia Orchestra. An article appeared in the local Maine paper that portrayed this as a victory for Lea as much as me: "Tom is the youngest grandson of Mme. Lea Luboshutz, renowned violinist, who first came to the Camden (Maine) area some years before the war as a teacher at the Curtis Summer School of Music. We can so well imagine the delight that 'Lubo' is now taking in her grandson's singular success that we can also believe that she is now ready to forgive him for not being a violinist."[24]

My Philadelphia Orchestra debut concert took place on March 12, 1962, with Andy's following on January 20, 1969. The previous spring, he had begun appearing as a soloist fairly regularly with the Boston Pops under Arthur Fiedler. I did not understand the envy of other young musicians—I assumed our good fortune was our due.

The summer after I appeared with the Philadelphia Orchestra, Lea prepared Andy for his first performance of the César Franck sonata. It was to take place in the Parish House Hall of the local Episcopal Church where we younger musicians gave our concerts. A very small venue in a tiny Maine village may not have seemed an auspicious place for a "debut"—not until one reviewed a list of the names of those slated to be in the audience. All of the family musicians would be there—Lea, Boris, Pierre, Genia—plus Mary Curtis Bok and her husband since 1943, Efrem Zimbalist. Vladimir Sokoloff, Zimbalist's pianist with whom he had played the Franck sonata on many occasions, was also coming, along with his wife, Andy's teacher, Eleanor Sokoloff, and a dozen or so other musicians whose names were known throughout the world.

The concert took place on August 20, 1962. Andy was shrewd enough to choose Zimbalist's star student of the moment, Shmuel Ashkenasi. Lea and others considered him the greatest talent then at Curtis (earlier that year, he had been a prize winner at the Tchaikovsky Competition in Moscow, the most competitive gathering of young violinists in the world), and on one occasion Lea had allowed him to play her Stradivarius. Aside from briefly loaning the instrument to violinist Isaac Stern at a party Lea gave for the visiting Soviet superstar David Oistrakh so both great artists could perform together, Shmuel was the only violinist that Lea ever allowed to touch her beloved Nightingale, so far as I knew.

Despite the fact that I turned pages for Andy the night of his César Franck debut, I have no recollection at all of the performance—only the party afterward. Playing the Franck was a rite of passage in our family, and Andy had achieved this milestone in front of a tough audience. The celebration was vibrant.

Andy's first appearance at Carnegie Hall was also a major family event. Each December twenty-fourth for the previous eight years, the violinist Alexander Schneider had conducted a special Christmas Eve concert in the Hall with friends and colleagues. In 1963, he needed someone to play one of the piano parts in a concerto for four keyboards and orchestra, arranged by Bach from music written by Vivaldi. Through one or another of our connections, Andy got the call, and Lea made sure as many relatives attended as possible. Though Andy's role was modest, it was another rite of passage for our generation of the family.

Andy's role was similarly unspectacular when, a dozen years later, he appeared again at Carnegie Hall. He had been asked to fill in in a minor role with the Boston Symphony Orchestra in November of 1975. The personnel manager of the orchestra—a good friend of the family—had called Andy and asked, "Want to make some easy money? We are doing the Saint-Saëns Organ Symphony here in Boston and later at Carnegie Hall and I need someone to play the second piano part which is easy. You would not play until the fourth movement and then only for a few bars when everyone is making so much noise that no one would hear you if you made a mistake." Andy laughed (he knew it was not quite so simple) but he happily agreed to play—the money was excellent.

However, at the concert, something occurred that Andy would never live down. The conductor, Seiji Ozawa, in taking his bows, always shook hands with the concertmaster and often with all the principal string players sitting in the inner circle closest to the podium. But because of the arrangement of the pianos, Andy was positioned in that same inner circle. So Ozawa asked him to stand and shook his hand along with the others. The orchestra players could hardly contain their laughter. "Wow, Andy," one said. "I have played in this orchestra for twenty years and the maestro has never shaken my hand onstage. You play a few bars of music and the maestro shakes your hand and gives you a solo bow. How did you do it?"

As Andy and I played more concerts, we received invaluable instruction from our Uncle Boris. In many ways, Boris was one of the most knowledgeable and sophisticated musicians we would ever know. But he was committed to making music understandable and enjoyable to people from all backgrounds. And because he was a delightful raconteur, at concerts he would often eschew formality and tell stories about the composers, the music, the era in which music was written, even about himself, the family, and his previous performances. While other musicians disdained this "dumbing down" of the concert experience, Boris drummed into us how important it was to give the audience a little help.

For our educational program for young people, Boris taught Andy how to play a shortened version of Chopin's Black Key étude as an encore, rolling a grapefruit up and down the black keys with the right hand while the left one played Chopin's written bass notes. To explain how a fugue worked, he had Andy set words to the fugue in C-sharp Major from Book I of Bach's *Well-Tempered Clavier*: "Oh mother must I go to bed, I would rather watch TV instead." By singing these words each time the fugue subject appeared in a different register, our young listeners could understand the complexity of writing and imitation in different voices. Andy and I spent a good part of our teenage years performing such concerts as a way to make extra money, and we became popular attractions, at least within our circle of acquaintances and contacts.

Our great-uncle Pierre, however, was not amused by these devices. On attending one of our programs, he quipped, "My nephews are like Klezmers," to Lea and Irene. He was referring to Jewish musicians who played popular tunes at ceremonies like weddings and bar mitzvahs. While klezmer music has achieved a level of respectability today and is often played by outstanding musicians, in Pierre's day, these were often third-rate performers who churned out unremarkable dance music. Initially Pierre intended the comment as derogatory, but over the years it became his affectionate moniker for the two of us, introducing us to his musician colleagues as "my nephews, the Klezmers."

Like her brother, Lea was unenthusiastic about Boris's populist approach to performing, so when she came to our performances, we tended to tone things down. But she had more important things to do, like making sure we practiced, long and well. This meant scales, arpeggios, études, and serious repertoire. Lea's "7-11 Club," started in her Curtis teaching years, meant practice started at seven A.M. and lasted for four hours. In those days, Lea had presided by example—she also spent those hours practicing. But by the time Andy and I were studying with her, she had retired, so at first we did not have her daily example hanging over us. As long as we put in our hours, we did not have to start at seven in the morning.

Then something occurred for which we were not prepared, which put a crimp in our summer fun and late nights. In the early 1960s, after years of self-imposed exile from countries that recognized the Franco regime in Spain, the legendary cellist Pablo Casals began to give concerts again in the United States. On April 19, 1963, he appeared with the Philadelphia Orchestra for the first time in forty-eight years. It was a major musical event. Lea was determined to go and see the man who had stayed at her Moscow apartment during one of his earliest tours of Russia.

Rushing backstage after the performance, she entered Casals's dressing room, walked up to him, and asked, "Do you remember Lea Luboshutz in Moscow? You stayed in her apartment."

"Of course I remember. And she had that wonderful sister who was a cellist and sat listening to me practice. Yes, of course, where is Lea?"

"I am she."

They embraced. Despite crowds of people waiting to greet Casals, he wanted to talk. "Tell me, Lea," he asked. "Are you still performing?"

"Of course not," she answered. "I have been retired for almost twenty years."

"But you are still practicing, of course."

"Oh no," Lea said. "I spend my time with my grandchildren, whom I hope will be musicians."

"Lea," said Casals, "that is terrible. You must practice. I am older than you and—" he paused, looking at his beautiful young wife, who was half a century younger, "I practice and make love every day. Promise me, promise me you will at least practice."

Lea agreed, and much to my and Andy's chagrin, the next summer Lea began her practice sessions at seven A.M. Each morning, she had already completed two hours' worth of practice when Andy and I straggled into the breakfast room. Our grandmother had no patience for youngsters who aspired to become professional musicians but "wasted" what she considered their most productive hours.

As our high school years were coming to an end, a gulf began to appear between what our parents wanted and what Lea saw as the inevitable next step in our musical development. Especially in Andy's case, she believed he must go to a musical conservatory. And not just any conservatory. He should attend the Curtis Institute of Music and become a student of the great pianist, Rudolf Serkin. Our parents were adamant. We were to go to a college or a university and we were to major in something other than music. A conservatory offered only one career track. A university offered many. And my parents were not alone. Many in Irene's generation had experienced what it was like to grow up in the household of a professional musician and they wanted something different for their children. No matter how musically talented, these children were to pursue a more stable and lucrative career. For the moment, Lea had lost the battle but our parents' victory was short-lived.

Going to college and moving out of a musical hothouse was a relief to me but in Andy's case, he was dispirited. He wanted to be a pianist and going to a college or university would be, in his mind, a total waste of time. He dutifully spent a year at Columbia University in New York but the following summer, he told my parents he was dropping out. He wanted to spend full time on his music. My parents realized there was no alternative and relented . . . but now there was a problem. Auditions for the next year's class of the top conservatories had long passed. It looked like Andy would lose a whole year. But Lea came to the rescue. She simply called Rudolf Serkin in Vermont at his Marlboro Music Festival and explained the problem. How she talked him into it I will never know, but the next day Andy drove to Vermont, played briefly for Serkin, and was admitted to the most competitive conservatory in the world—the Curtis Institute of Music—as Serkin's student, largely at Lea's urging.

By Reason of Strength

From the moment various members of her family had arrived in America around 1930 until her death a half century later, Lea was focused on making sure all of them had successful careers. That had always been her role and it would not stop so long as she could take her next breath. Initially, the focus was on her brother, Pierre, and her son Boris. Pierre's success came first. Since his years as a piano student in Moscow, he had always made his way, shunning the big career and working in supporting roles for the superstars. From 1926 on, he had made annual trips to America to play for people like the double bass virtuoso, Koussevitzky, and violinists Zimbalist and Kochanski,* appearing at least once in Carnegie Hall each time. He also appeared there with Lea. But fate had other plans for Pierre, and in his own genre he became very famous himself. When he and his pianist wife, Genia, settled in New York for good in the early 1930s, they formed a duo-piano team (Luboshutz & Nemenoff) that became the most important ensemble of its kind in the world, the only such recognized duo-piano team to appear with superstar conductor Arturo Toscanini.[25] They toured the world, introduced a number of new works for two pianos,[26] and made many recordings and so were far better known than Lea by the time she retired. Initially, she helped them get concerts but after a while, there was no need.

Pierre and Genia's reputation became so well established that Boris wondered whether they might include him on a couple of tours—playing concertos for three pianos and orchestra by Mozart and Bach. Pierre was especially happy because in a couple of numbers, when the program featured a concerto with a single piano, Boris was the soloist and Pierre got to conduct the orchestral accompaniment (after getting conducting lessons from Boris). Though he

---

* Pierre and Kochanski had been close friends as far back as their years in Odessa, and continued through Pierre's subsequent concerts with Paul in Russia, Western Europe, and the United States. Kochanski died of cancer at the age of forty-three in New York in 1934. Pierre was an honorary pall bearer at his funeral along with such luminaries as Arturo Toscanini, Jascha Heifetz, Vladimir Horowitz, Fritz Kreisler, Serge Koussevitzky, Leopold Stokowski, and Efrem Zimbalist.

claimed to the press that he had conducted in Russia having learned the craft of conducting from Koussevitzky, the family knew that this was stretching the truth and this was more accurately his first time ever doing so in a concert that mattered. Soon he was able to brag about the fact that he was the only family member who had received a rave review from the *New York Times* that praised both his piano playing and his conducting in the *same* concert. Clearly, Lea had nothing to worry about when it came to Pierre's career.

With respect to her sister, Anna, though she did not know the details, reports came to her from Soviet musicians who began to tour in the United States toward the end of her life that Anna had become one of the most famous cellists in the Soviet Union. Whether or not that gave her pleasure we never knew, because no one discussed Anna or the Russian relatives. It was a forbidden subject.

But it was Lea's son Boris whose development was most problematic for her. His conducting studies at the Curtis Institute of Music began, amazingly, with none other than Emil Mlynarski, Lea's old teacher from Odessa, but eventually ended up with Fritz Reiner who introduced Boris to opera. Indeed, Boris eventually established a major career as an opera producer, conductor, impresario, educator, and commentator—by the time of Lea's death in 1965, he too was far more famous than she. He never gave up piano playing entirely—I went to hear him play two Mozart piano concertos with orchestra when he was well into his seventies.[27] But his career as a pianist receded as other opportunities beckoned. Not only did he eventually establish and lead his own opera company, he was a popular commentator for the Metropolitan Opera's radio broadcasts and in the course of his distinguished career as a pedagogue, he ended up heading the opera departments of four top-flight organizations—at the Cleveland Institute of Music, the New England Conservatory of Music, the Tanglewood Music Center, and ultimately, at Lea's and his beloved school, the Curtis Institute of Music. His students went on to major careers, and many, like the opera producer Sarah Caldwell; soprano Phyllis Curtin; baritones Sherrill Milnes and Justino Diaz; and tenor George Shirley (the first African American to sing a major role at the Metropolitan Opera), went out of their way to praise his special gifts as a teacher. Boris also published many books, mostly on opera, though there was an autobiography in which Lea was portrayed fondly.

But Lea could not help herself from second-guessing both Boris's career choices and, more fundamentally, his life choices. She adored her son and believed he was a genius. Yet somehow, no matter how much he accomplished professionally, it never seemed to be enough for her. It was perhaps inevitable that no woman would be good enough for Boris in Lea's eyes and she was openly critical of his wife, claiming, quite unfairly I believe, that his marriage to Margaret had hampered his career. As a result, over time, Lea and Boris grew apart, though publicly they maintained a cordial and loving relationship. Part of the balancing act of preserving the connection while keeping Lea well separated from Margaret involved the two of them giving recitals together, which had a somewhat healing effect.

For one of his Boston programs in 1943, for example, Boris invited Lea to be a guest violinist in a lecture-recital devoted to the subject of women in music. He used a combination of flattery and the promise of a large audience to mend their somewhat frayed relationship. The mother-son event indeed stirred up interest, leading to a full house of appreciative music lovers, most of whom were subscribers to the Boston Symphony Orchestra, which was sponsoring the event. It also brought out members of the press. Boris decided to end the event with a brief question-and-answer period to give people the full flavor of his mother's personality. At these moments, Lea could turn on the charm. Almost immediately, she was asked what she thought of the pop singer Frank Sinatra, who was recording multiple hit songs and appearing in popular movies. Lea, who had never heard of Sinatra and whose English had not improved much since she first arrived in the United States, beamed. Her answer—"I think it is perfectly lovely"—surprised everyone. Boris was astonished . . . until he realized Lea's confusion. Frank Sinatra was not the Franck sonata but his mother did not know the difference.

As reported in the *Boston Evening American* the next day, "S' THE TRUTH, SO HELP US: Lea Luboshutz, noted violinist and mother of Boris Goldovsky was posed a question at a "Symphony luncheon" conducted by her son at the Copley Plaza [ballroom]. "How do you like Frank Sinatra?" Madame Luboshutz was asked . . . "I think it is perfectly lovely," was the simple reply . . . This stumped the questioner (who had heard the Voice [Sinatra] called everything except the neuter). The explanation came eventually. Goldovsky's mother understood that she had been asked her opinion of Franck's (violin) sonata . . . (She was busy—when last seen—trying to figure out who the deuce this Frank Sinatra is.)"[28]

Eventually, Lea gave up trying to influence Boris, especially as she had another concern to occupy her. It was Irene. During the 1950s, her daughter suffered a debilitating nervous breakdown. Few anticipated the crisis since Irene, much like her mother and grandmother, had always appeared to be a mentally tough matriarch. But deep down, Irene's psychological state was fragile. There had been so many terrifying moments in her childhood—being abandoned in the train station by her grandmother on the way from Odessa to Moscow when Gitel needed to escape the Red Guard with the hidden family jewels; standing alone beside her father as a three-year-old as he died; leaving Moscow with a stranger who she was told she must call Father. She had coped with all of this for years but then came one final precipitating event that led to her collapse.

As Irene recounted to a granddaughter late in her life, it was her uncle Pierre, in a moment of anger, who delivered the coup de grâce. He told her Lea was not the paragon of virtue that everyone pretended. "Your mother was never even married to your father. In fact, at the time you were born, your father was frequently living with his real wife." Irene had always been able to cling to an illusion of her parents' idyllic marriage and a brief but golden early childhood with them. Now this tiny remnant of happiness was shattered and for once she did not know where to turn for explanations. She would not speak further to Pierre who might be lying—besides she told him in anger that of course she knew that fact about her parents and it didn't bother her. She did not feel strong enough to confront her mother—the one person who had always been her bedrock of support. Nor did she trust other family members who she believed might be in league against her. She began to wonder if other happy childhood memories were a sham. Her world fell apart.

In later years, it became clear to me that there was another dynamic at work that went well beyond the story of Lea and Onissim's true relationship. There had always been a dynamic of secrecy about the past that was unnerving—something that we in the next generation would encounter again and again. As my mother described it years later in her oral history, "The past was not discussed, except in little snatches here and there. My mother simply never referred to my father . . . I never had a sense of a real person. Nor did she talk about her sister Anna, whose husband had delivered her three children . . . The message was, keep your chin up and always look ahead."[29] For Irene, keeping her chin up was no longer possible.

Billy Wolf was told enough by my mother's remarkable psychoanalyst, Eli Marcovitz, to realize that for a period of time Irene needed to be separated from her mother. Marcovitz, who was a serious amateur violinist who played string quartets every Sunday on his own Stradivarius violin and deeply admired Lea, knew that Irene's mother was a large part of her problem, and Lea's presence would complicate and delay Irene's recovery. Billy must keep them apart. Marcovitz also told Billy that Irene could only stay at home (which is what she had requested) if her time with the children could be significantly curtailed. Irene was mentally exhausted and her condition was exacerbated by her need to mother six demanding children. Others would need to take primary responsibility for their care. It was a Herculean task for Billy, especially as Lea was pressuring him constantly and he had little experience with day-to-day childrearing. Lea's wrath grew to the boiling point as she blamed Billy for Irene's condition and was furious when he would not consider the idea of Irene coming to live with her until the situation improved. We children were confused and hurt as well. But Billy rose to the occasion and in time Irene emerged a much stronger woman, one who seemed to have inherited Lea and Gitel's determination never to look back with regret but always to march ahead with optimism about the future.

With Irene apparently back to full strength, by the time Lea turned seventy, the grande dame had become quite content with her life, her family, and her place in music. It seemed that everyone loved her and musicians made special efforts to see her when they played in Philadelphia. When the Soviet violoin virtuoso David Oistrakh made his much-anticipated debut in Philadelphia once he was finally allowed to do so by the Soviet authorities, Lea gave the after-concert party for him. Among the violinists who came were her old colleague Efrem Zimbalist and the superstar American performer Isaac Stern. Never one to miss an historic opportunity, Lea took her Nightingale Strad out of the case and handed it to Isaac Stern. Beckoning to Oistrakh and the pianist Vladimir Sokoloff, she set up two music stands and got out music to the Bach concerto for two violins and accompaniment and told the three to play. To my knowledge, the guests that night were treated to the only joint performance of two of the greatest violinists of the 20th century.

On the occasion of Lea's actual seventieth birthday, Irene arranged a large event that was part tribute concert to honor her mother and part benefit for one of Lea's favorite charities. Eugene Ormandy, the Philadelphia Orchestra's conductor, spoke about how he had known Lubo, as everyone now called her, for about twenty-five years. "When I first met her she was at the peak of her career and had given recitals and solo performances with orchestras in Europe and the United States including the Philadelphia Orchestra." He went on to describe concerts they had played together and mentioned the number of her pupils now playing in his orchestra. "They are a living tribute to her as artist and teacher. Her musical contributions as a concert violinist, and as a teacher in the Curtis Institute of Music endear her to all lovers of music everywhere."[30]

The evening would not have been complete without appearances by Pierre and Genia and, of course, Boris, who served as master of ceremonies. But the pinnacle of the evening was when Lea got out her beloved Nightingale and played a short work with Boris accompanying at the piano. There was no way at this point that she could have attempted the Franck sonata. Whatever piece she played was sufficiently unmemorable that it completely slips my mind. But it didn't matter. It was Lea herself, her violin raised high, her back as straight and unbent as it had been in her prime, who brought down the house. My most special memory was of her beckoning Irene to join her on stage as the family took their bows.

As fate would have it, sister Anna was also honored at a similar event in Moscow on January 22, 1969, some time after her eightieth birthday. The host for the gala evening was the leading Soviet cellist of the time, Mstislav Rostropovich, who would later defect to the United States, become music director of the National Symphony, and, in an ironic twist of fate, join the faculty of the Curtis Institute of Music. Anna's career, in its own way, had been as successful as Lea's. From the time of the Revolution she had been a veritable workhorse, touring constantly throughout the Soviet Union and performing not only in great concert halls but in factories, aboard naval ships of the Northern Fleet at Severmorsk, and even, on one occasion, deep underground in a coal mine in the Donats Basin region for the workers. When back in Moscow, she performed almost daily on radio, not only playing compositions for cello but also transcribing and performing works from Lea's violin repertoire, including the Franck sonata. Anna was the first Soviet cellist to be awarded the title "Honored Artist of the Russian Soviet Federative Socialist Republic." With it came special status, a lifetime stipend, and the right to be buried in the cemetery at the Novodevichy Monastery, the most honored burial place in Moscow after the Kremlin Wall.

As it turned out, Anna's final resting place was only steps from the grave of the man who had done so much for her career and for Lea's—Fyodor Chaliapin. Others in the cemetery include the writers Gogol and Chekhov, the theater director Stanislavsky, and the composers Prokofiev and Shostakovich. Before Anna's death, the Moscow Music Society and the Moscow Philharmonic both honored her. But unlike Lea, Anna was never able to establish an international career as she was not allowed to perform outside of the Soviet Union. Nevertheless, she had realized her early promise as a Gold Medal winner of the Moscow Conservatory and her celebratory night was filled with music and speeches that must have touched her deeply. Imagine if each sister had been able to celebrate with the other at these special events. How sad that neither would ever know the honors bestowed on the other.

Lea died on March 18, 1965, just after her eightieth birthday. She had been diagnosed with an inoperable brain tumor and went immediately into the hospital. It was decided that there would be no major interventions and Lea was to be made as comfortable as possible. Part of making her comfortable was not telling Lea the truth about her condition. For the first four weeks, she was cheerful and anticipating a full recovery. The doctor allowed her her afternoon scotch and her room was a veritable greenhouse full of flowers and visitors. But over time she simply slept more and more and eventually lost consciousness. It was a death entirely without pain.

Boris came and went and in his usual crisp, matter-of-fact, practical way and spoke with Irene about final arrangements. To me, he seemed emotionally detached and unaffected by the event. But to my surprise, it was Pierre who seemed devastated. I had never seen Pierre cry before but his visit to the hospital completely shattered his usual jolly personality. This was the sister whom he worshipped—the one who had made so much possible for him. And this was now the end.

My mother had been clear-eyed and calm about what had to happen upon her mother's death. She decided that Lea's memorial service should be in a synagogue, even though Lea had not set foot in one for more than half a century. But Lea's grandfather had been a rabbi and her father had been a devout Jew. So Billy Wolf prevailed upon the officers of the Wolf family synagogue in Philadelphia, Rodeph Shalom, to allow Lea's memorial service to be held there, with the head rabbi officiating. The rabbi had never met Lea and he mispronounced her name badly. But he had learned enough about her that for his eulogy, he chose the biblical text and the well-known passage from Psalm 90: "The days of our years are threescore years and ten; unless by reason of strength they should be fourscore years."

Lea had lived the full fourscore years "by reason of strength." But it was music that had made that life rich, and reverberated down through generations and across the world.

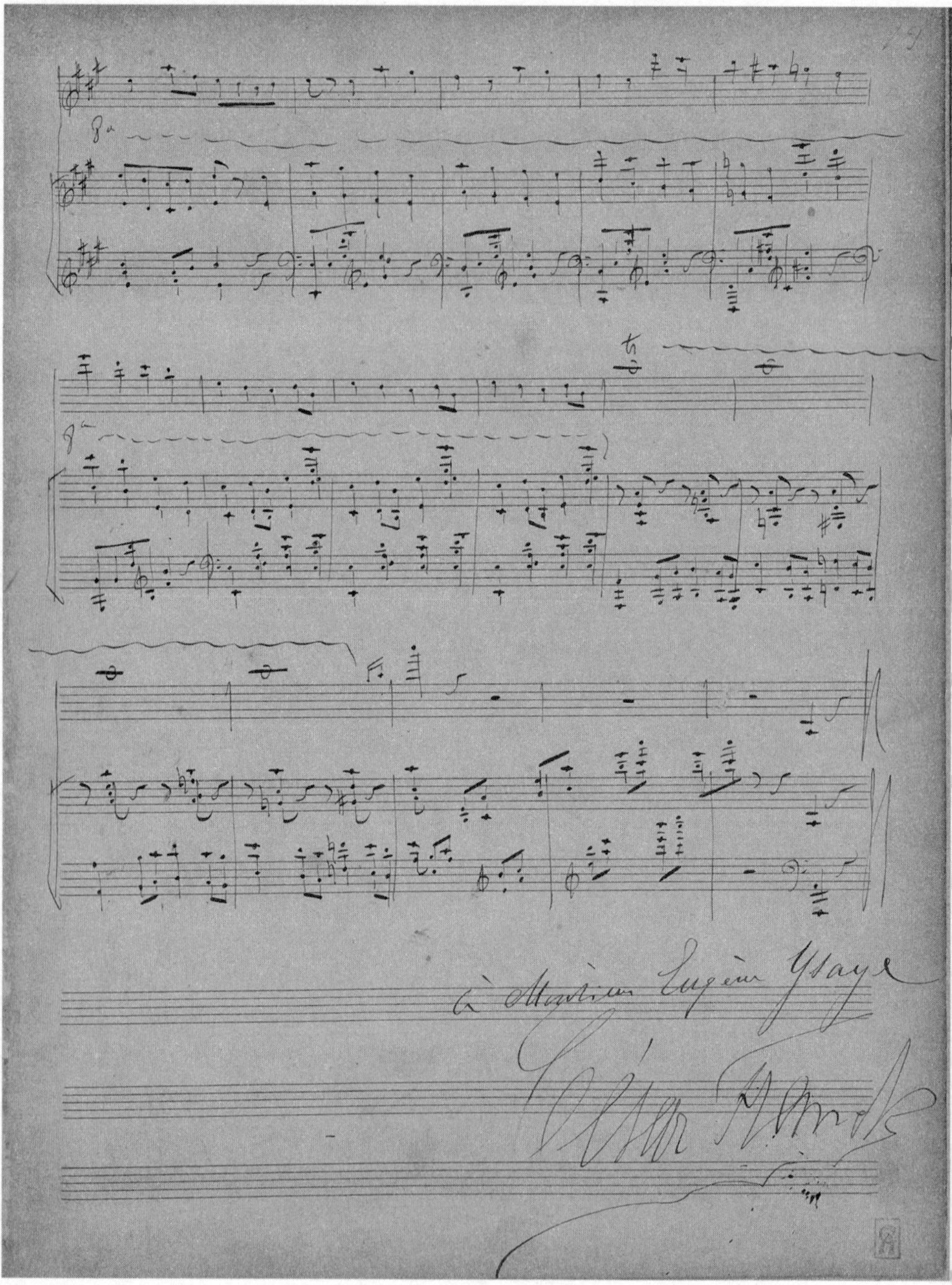
à Monsieur Eugène Ysaye

THE END OF THE SONATA

(1965 to 2018)

❧

Just as with every human life, every great piece of music must end. In examining the manuscript of César Franck's violin sonata, one finds his signature not on the first page but on the last. It is as if he is saying, "This is the end of the music—it is all I can offer." In addition to the signature, that last page bears his dedication to Eugène Ysaÿe. It was like a singular message from the composer: "To you I entrust this work. Go forth and give it continued life."

But by 1965, Ysaÿe was dead and his pupil Lea Luboshutz, who had also championed the sonata and played it throughout the world, was dead. Soon Lea's sister, who had transcribed the work for cello and played it throughout Soviet Russia, would die as would her brother, Pierre, and her son Boris, both of whom had played the sonata with her and kept it alive. Would this be the end of the family's treasured musical legacy?

Lea had struggled mightily to be sure that the sonata would live within the bosom of her family, that it would continue to provide inspiration, jubilation, solace, and triumph. She had taught the sonata to a grandchild and during her lifetime he had performed it and she had been satisfied. Though she would not live to see it, the day would come when he too would triumph with the great sonata.

Boris to the Rescue

⟨❦⟩

After Lea's death, both Andy and I were adrift. His years at the Curtis Institute of Music had not been happy ones and his confidence had become ever more fragile. His teacher, Rudolf Serkin, had been highly critical of Andy's playing and Andy suspected that Serkin would never have accepted him as a student without Lea's intervention. In retrospect, Andy's experience was not unlike Lea's with Joseph Joachim when the great violinist had decided not to take her on as a student. Trained in a distinctly Russian tradition which stressed the beauty of sound above all else, her playing (and Andy's), was not compatible with the more Germanic approach of these two musical giants. But even if someone had explained this to Andy at the time, it would have done little to console him. He was miserable and his confidence was further eroded by the fact that without Lea's door-opening abilities, his concertizing opportunities diminished.

In my own case, by the time Lea died, I was convinced that I would not pursue a career as a flutist. I had had the best of teachers thanks to Lea and the family—William Kincaid (principal flute of the Philadelphia Orchestra) and the legendary Frenchman Marcel Moyse—but neither was particulatly impressed with my playing and in Moyse's case, he could be downright cruel about it. I struggled to figure out what else to do. I toyed with the idea of medical school after spending many hours in hospitals with Lea but it was clear I was even more unsuited for that as a career choice. The one good thing about our respective situations was that Andy and I could complain to one another . . . and we did so on a daily basis.

Meanwhile, on a happier note, both of us had married and in 1970, our wives each produced a daughter within a few weeks of one another. We were thrilled that even though these babies were not the first children of our generation of the family, no one had yet selected the names of Lea and Anna. Perhaps by appropriating these names (Lea for my daughter, Anna for Andy's), the girls would bring us some of the good karma of the older generation.

One of the few musical bright spots for us was a summer chamber music series that we had organized as teenagers in Rockport in 1960 and called Bay

Chamber Concerts. Though the Curtis Institute had officially closed down its summer music colony in Maine, many of its teachers contined to come there during the summer months and bring students. Curtis often paid the costs for lessons and housing. With so many talented youngsters around, Andy and I got the idea that we would start a concert series. The main problem was money and the obvious patron was Mary Curtis Bok Zimbalist. She continued to spend the summer on the magnificent Curtis family estate in Rockport.

The young students who were around all loved the idea of playing concerts and getting Mrs. Zimbalist to pay for them. But no one was brave enough to actually meet with her and ask for the money. So I, the youngest at age fifteen, volunteered. Lea had set up the meeting and my father had driven me over and left me at the end of the long driveway (I didn't want anyone to notice that I was too young to drive). When I was somehow successful at securing a nice contribution (undoubtedly thanks to being Lea's grandson), I was anointed as the next Sol Hurok and appointed manager by acclamation. It was a lucky break for me. It was clear that no one would have wanted a flutist as part of the artistic corps of serious chamber music players, especially one whose talents did not measure up to the high standard set by Curtis whiz kids. But if they wanted me to do all the administrative and fund-raising tasks, they would have to let me play.

After Lea's death, Rockport continued to have very special associations for us and we liked to spend as much time there as possible. Soon after she died, a new park was created in Lea's memory next to the opera house where we played our concerts and was named Mary-Lea Park. It seemed as though everyone in town had known and loved Lea and this affection rubbed off on us. Nevertheless, as enjoyable as these weeks of music making were, Bay Chamber Concerts did not constitute a career nor did it begin to bring in adequate income to support our families. Andy's second daughter, Heather, and our son, Alexis, now made it all the more necessary for us to figure out what to do. So, in the absence of Lea, it was now Boris who stepped up and came to our rescue. Boris convinced his personal agent, Herbert Barrett, to put Andy on the agency's artist roster and secure some solo concert dates for him—both solo recitals and performances with orchestras. For me, Boris offered the dual job of company manager and principal flutist in his touring opera company which, because two salaries were involved, turned out to be quite lucrative. For now at least, our careers were unstalled.

Andy dutifully traveled and played concerts—mostly in medium-sized towns with small venues and audiences, and with mediocre orchestras—but he was soon unhappy again. Was this the life that he had to look forward to? He had grown up among musicians who performed with major orchestras in the great halls of the world. In Maine, he played chamber music each summer with colleagues who represented the cream of the next generation of superstars. After concerts, there was always a crowded backstage, wonderful shop talk, and lavish parties. Now he was on the road by himself, eating lousy food, staying in cheap hotels, playing for often unenthusiastic audiences who never came backstage to congratulate him or invite him to a party, in venues that had poor acoustics and bad pianos. He was lonely and miserable.

Andy's Initial Triumph

❧

Once again, Andy appealed to Boris. Was there anything else Boris could do for him? Indeed, there was. Leonard Rose was a well-known cellist on the major touring circuit and an old friend of the family. Today he is mainly remembered as being the teacher of Yo-Yo Ma, though at that time he was a leading soloist. Many years before, Lea had been his champion when as a young boy he had first auditioned and was denied admission to the Curtis Institute of Music. She had said the denial was a mistake and insisted that he be admitted the next year. Once there, he and Boris had spent good times as fellow students, especially during their summers in Rockport at the Curtis music colony. In addition, Rose recalled that some years later it was Boris, then working at the Cleveland Orchestra as assistant to the music director, who had called him, inviting Rose to join the Cleveland Orchestra as principal cellist. Subsequently, the two had played several recitals together.[1]

One day Rose mentioned to Boris that he had lost his longtime pianist. Boris suggested he consider using Andy, and after a few sessions together,

Rose took my brother on. The two started touring internationally. Through Rose, Andy was recommended to the violinist Isaac Stern. Stern's pianist had also moved on and Andy's name came up. Soon after, Andy found himself summoned to Boston's Symphony Hall where Stern was in a rehearsal with the Boston Symphony.

Andy assumed there would be some sort of audition, and so he had practiced much of the violin and piano literature that he had learned with Lea. But Stern simply said, "We will start the tour in Boston next year. Here is the repertoire and the itinerary. I assume you can do it. I will be in touch about rehearsals."

"Where will we play in Boston?" asked Andy, somewhat naively.

"Why, here in Symphony Hall, of course. Where else would we play?"

Thus, suddenly Andy was thrust into the musical big leagues. For the next several years, he played in most of the great music halls around the world—on every continent (except Antarctica)—traveling with a man who was like a benevolent uncle to him. Stern paid Andy well, introduced him to other stars of the music world, and greatly enhanced Andy's prestige. Many musicians who had ignored Andy for years began to call, and now it was Andy who turned them down because he was too busy.

One longtime friend and colleague with whom Andy had played frequently used to wonder which great musician might be calling Andy next. The friend had an uncanny ability to mimic voices and accents, and would call periodically, pretending to be this or that famous performer. On one occasion, the two had been talking about attending a Boston Celtics basketball game. The phone rang shortly thereafter, and someone with a thick Russian accent identified himself as Nathan Milstein—one of the greatest living violinists. Assuming that Milstein would not be cold calling, Andy guessed it was one of his friend's hoaxes. The caller asked Andy whether he might be free for a few concerts and named the dates. Andy played along for a while, and finally said, "So, did you get the Celtics tickets or not?"

"Sel-teecks. Vas iss Sel-teecks?"

This was no hoax. It was Nathan Milstein himself. Sadly, as it happened, Andy was not free for the dates Milstein offered. Whether it was coincidence or Andy's odd behavior on the telephone, Milstein never asked again.

Like my parents, I was thrilled that things were going well for Andy. I still played the flute off and on but due to my management training under Boris,

I was now comfortably ensconced as the executive director of the New England Foundation for the Arts in Boston and soon to start a management consulting firm to serve the cultural sector. A friend once asked me, "Aren't you ever jealous of your brother?" The answer was yes, off and on. When it came to sports, he'd been faster and more coordinated, and was always picked first to be on a team. He was more attractive to the opposite sex, which riled me even more. But when it came to music, none of our sibling rivalry was present. In retrospect, I think it had to do with the fact that we came from a family of musicians where there is rarely any illusion about talent. We all know that some have more than others. That's just how things are; the only way to do anything about it is to buckle down and work. Andy had far more native talent than I and given his penchant for practice, I knew I could never equal him there either. Thus, I had no cause to feel bad about the situation. And it wasn't as if Andy's life as a performer was a piece of cake. He once said, "You reach up and think you have perfection in your hands, and then you open your hand and it has disappeared."

That said, Andy was happy at last. Life on the road with a great musician like Isaac Stern was very satisfying and he was playing with other wonderful musicians like Leonard Rose when he was free, and running the summer festival in Rockport, which he adored. He did learn to be careful not to imitate Stern's opulent lifestyle on the road. Andy was earning good fees, but they were roughly five percent of Stern's earnings which were astronomical, befitting a superstar. On one occasion, as they planned their first concert together at London's Royal Festival Hall on December 11, 1981, Stern told Andy they would be staying at Claridges, the luxury hotel, and that Andy should save up his laundry and dry cleaning, because it was done so well there. On arrival, after several weeks on the road, Andy turned over virtually everything he was traveling with. Sure enough, it arrived back beautifully packaged, with fresh pressed flowers between the layers. He was delighted—until he received his bill. It made quite a dent in his London concert fee.

Back in the United States, the two musicians played more and more of the most important venues, ultimately preparing for their first Carnegie Hall concert together. When the night finally came on January 12, 1983, Andy was strangely calm. I was the one who was nervous! An ad in the *New York Times* had SOLD OUT written across it.[2] This was serious business.

"Are you going to play the Franck sonata?" I asked jokingly.

"Mr. Stern says that someday we will play it there, but for now, it isn't on the program."

Sitting in a box with my parents, I realized how important this concert was, especially for my mother. The family legacy would continue. Andy might not be playing the Franck sonata, but he was assuming the family mantle. It was a huge responsibility, but he seemed up to it. When the works on the printed program ended, it was time for encores. Stern announced the second encore:

"We have had a special request. We will be playing the finale from César Franck's violin sonata."

And with that they played my favorite movement in the entire violin and piano repertory.

Going backstage afterward, I could not wait to ask Andy: "Who requested the Franck?" He grinned, and said, "I did."

Andy had had a special triumph. He had played the family piece in Carnegie Hall, and many of us had been there to witness it. If only Lea could have celebrated with us.

My brother continued to tour with Isaac Stern, traveling first class, staying in fancy hotels, and playing in sold-out houses all over the world. Soon, there was talk of recordings, and Stern made it clear that the Franck sonata was high on the list. Andy called me regularly from the road, almost daily when he was in the United States. He called from the January 10, 1984, concert at the White House, followed by a banquet with the Reagans, the Chinese premier, and various Hollywood stars, many of whom were probably attending their first classical music concert;* from Miami Beach, and the over-the-top banquet following their benefit concert for the State of Israel, where Stern was an honored citizen.

After a concert in Paris, he called, especially excited. After telling me how well it had gone, he said, "You know, as I came off that stage at the end of the concert, I said to myself, 'If I never live another day, I have had the ultimate experience. It is what I have lived for. I don't need more.'"

"Jesus, man," I exclaimed. "Don't say that. Take it back. I'm superstitious. You're going to live and make music for another hundred years."

---

* The concert, which included the first two movements of the Franck sonata, was captured in an edited video of the evening released by the Ronald Reagan Presidential Library. As of 2019, the video could be found on the Internet (https://www.youtube.com /watch?v=kdYPn63wSb0).

Whether Andy heard me or not, I will never know. The transcontinental telephone line had gone dead.

The Sonata's Finale

Everything about the moment when I learned of Andy's physical collapse is still vivid in my memory. It was a beautiful spring afternoon in 1984. I had returned from giving a workshop to a group of arts administrators, and was looking forward to a walk followed by perhaps the first outdoor dinner of the year. But when I entered the hall, I saw Dennie coming toward me with a serious expression. "Andy is in the hospital," she said. "He's had a seizure. They don't know exactly what it is, but they are going to do some tests."

As I look back on the moment, I imagine myself recoiling, as if from a bullet to the gut. A few moments after Dennie spoke, I remembered Andy's words from Paris, and in my heart I sensed the inevitable. It was a few weeks before tests were complete, an initial surgery performed, a diagnosis delivered. But what I believed the day I first learned of his illness turned out to be true. Andy was going to die—and soon.

The diagnosis was a brain tumor, the same kind that had killed our grandmother, Lea—a glioblastoma. With her, it had taken eight weeks. But she had been eighty. Andy was exactly half that age and otherwise healthy. The doctor's prediction was six to eighteen months of life, with progressive loss of brain function. By the time the news was delivered, I thought I was prepared. After all, I had known from the start, hadn't I? But in the back of my mind, I had been bargaining with whatever higher powers exist for this all to be a bad dream, for everything to turn out okay. When the surgeon, a friend of Andy's and a student at his music school, delivered the news, it was he who was in tears. I was stunned.

My initial reaction was again unexpected—not grief, but fear. Andy and I had been so close for so long. We were two peas in a pod; sometimes, we seemed like a single person divided into two bodies, neither complete without the other. He was the gifted musician. That lifted the family onus and allowed me to be just a decent musician. I was the *macher*, a favorite Yiddish word in the family—the organizer, the person who could make things happen. When I played with Andy, I felt confident; I played better than my talent merited. He was always there, showing me the way musically. I could never fall too far.

And just as he supported me, I was his closet administrative support and financial amanuensis. He had successfully run Bay Chamber Concerts and more recently had taken over the directorship of a local music school, but he always asked for advice and help. It was the perfect partnership—better for the fact that it was mostly invisible to the outside world. We spoke almost every day. Even when we didn't, we were still in some kind of communication. Now it would be over—indeed, with the surgery and the prognosis, it was over already.

But I had little time to worry or weep. The second day I came to the hospital, as Andy was recovering from the operation, a cousin, Ann Wolf, approached. Ann was a few years older than me, and had recently lost her young husband, Howie, my first cousin, to cancer.

"Look, I know you must be devastated," she said. "But you need to get over it quickly, at least for now. Somebody in the family has got to step up and handle things in an unemotional way. There are doctors to consult, medical decisions, living arrangements. Linda [Andy's wife] cannot do that all by herself, and she needs some objective person she can turn to . . . Her life is going to be a living hell. You need to be there. There will be plenty of time to grieve, but it is not now."

"But she hasn't asked me for help," I said.

"Believe me, if you're there for her, she'll take it."

Ann's matter-of-fact tone was a wake-up call. Linda did lean on me for help and, much to the consternation of those closest to me, I became emotionally detached, talking to doctors, helping Linda make decisions, dealing with family and friends. In the past, I had run organizations. I had moved an opera company from city to city for Boris, getting shows on stage night after night. That was all about logistics and organization. This would be similar.

First Linda and I met with a team of doctors. I brought a notebook and wrote furiously as they spoke; Ann had said it was important to get the facts down accurately and unemotionally. Because there was no known cure for Andy's condition, the doctors recommended an experimental protocol at the

National Institutes of Health in Washington, DC. They felt that, in Andy's case, it was worth seeing if chemotherapy used in conjunction with radiation could cross the blood-brain barrier.

Then there was Isaac Stern. The concerts for the spring were over, and nothing was scheduled until the fall. But Stern needed to be given the unvarnished truth immediately. Amazingly, he took it as a challenge. Andy was going to get treatment and he was going to get better, he insisted. He just needed motivation. As far as Stern was concerned, the fall tour was on, with Andy as his pianist. And there was a new piece in the repertoire that Andy needed to learn—the A Major Fauré sonata. Stern had a piano moved into Andy's room at a residence hotel in Bethesda. Andy was in treatment only during certain hours. During the rest of the day, he should practice. Stern visited during the summer, and they rehearsed. With this generous act, one of the greatest living violinists had given Andy and all of us a great gift—the gift of confidence and hope.

Andy was disappointed to miss a special concert he had organized in Rockport for the ninety-fourth birthday of Efrem Zimbalist. Zimbalist had played such an outsized role in our lives and in the life of the summer music colony. He had agreed to come with his famous actor son, Efrem Zimbalist Jr., and his actress granddaughter, Stephanie, to hear a group of distinguished musicians from the Curtis Institute play an entire program of works written by him. Since Efrem Junior and Stephanie were both at the height of their fame at the time—he starring in the popular television series *77 Sunset Strip* and *The FBI*, she in *Remington Steele*—the event was covered by several media outlets. The *Boston Globe* even carried photos of the Zimbalists in a front page article on August 25, 1984. To Andy's frustration, he could not be released to come up for just one night and attend the concert he had so meticulously organized.

By the end of the summer of 1984, Andy seemed remarkably better. His doctors gave a cautious green light for the fall tour to Europe. The only stipulation was that I go, too, and monitor the situation. By sharing a room with Andy and being on stage as a page-turner at concerts, I could be close to him at all times. It was a remarkable moment. No one knew whether the experimental treatment had worked, but given Andy's condition, it seemed to have improved matters. Then, a week before the tour, Andy had another seizure and was back in the hospital. We called Stern and told him he should find another pianist for the tour.

The weeks that followed held many disappointments. One of the biggest is that, upon Stern's return to the United States, he did not immediately go into a studio with Andy to record the César Franck sonata. Stern was still hopeful that Andy would recover, and he felt that Andy's focus should be on treatment. I was less optimistic, and knew that this recording would be a legacy with profound meaning for Andy—his parting gift to the family. But it was not to be. The tumor was growing. Andy continued to practice, his powers slipping.

At the point where Andy could no longer read or remember names and words, another violinist stepped forward to encourage him. Joseph Silverstein, former concertmaster of the Boston Symphony and a well-known conductor, had been Andy's close friend for many years. The two played an annual Boston concert—a benefit program for Andy's music school. A 1985 event had been on the books for many months, scheduled for January 20. Like Stern, Joey (as everyone called him) did not accept the fact that Andy was not getting better. He said they should go ahead and select a program for the concert. It was hardly a surprise when Andy said he wanted to end the program with the César Franck sonata. His reasons, I'm sure, were many, but at the time he said he knew that sonata better than any other. He wanted to be sure he was programming something that his fingers knew.

By the time January 20 arrived, Andy's condition had worsened. His face was puffed up from medications and he wore a cap to hide the incisions from his surgery. His speech was poor. There were many people he did not recognize, and some who did not recognize him. But when I entered his house and heard him practicing, I was amazed. He sounded wonderful. The brain is a complex and remarkable machine; even when one part is damaged, other parts operate perfectly. Andy had spent a lifetime playing the piano, and his brain did not let him down. He and Joey rehearsed as I turned the pages of the music. I was not sure why Andy wanted me there—unable to read the notes, he was playing by memory. But he said having the music in front of him gave him more confidence.

On January 20, 1985, with a feeling of dread, I drove my parents to the concert hall. They had come from Philadelphia to be with their son at this difficult moment. Sitting on stage with Andy in the page-turner's chair, I felt paralyzed with apprehension. Andy was playing the opening music, a Mozart sonata, quite beautifully—but I knew it was by rote. So long as the deep recesses of his brain reminded his fingers of what to do, it seemed as if everything would go well. But an experienced musician has a panoply of alternative strategies for when things go awry. Andy retained none of these. What would happen if, for example, someone rushed ahead or dragged, and they got off by a beat or two? If someone forgot to take one of the repeats? What would Andy do to get back on track?

But as the first movement of the Mozart sonata gave way to the second and the third, I told myself to stop obsessing. If Andy could do this herculean task so well, who was I to sit there, turning pages and worrying? The final chords of the Mozart sounded, and I breathed a sigh of relief.

Joey had agreed to play the C major unaccompanied Bach sonata to complete the first half of the program. This would take some of the strain off Andy and allow him to rest before the César Franck sonata. Andy sat quietly backstage, not speaking. Was he nervous? Did the question even mean anything in his current condition? I did not know. I simply sat and began to worry again. Playing a Mozart sonata was one thing. But the Franck. *Oh my God . . .*

Andy had a new confidence as he prepared to walk out on stage for the second half of the program, for which I give a lot of credit to Joey Silverstein. Joey had seen so much in his career. He had played this sonata so often with so many people, young and old. He was calm and positive, not in any way indicating that this was a difficult moment. It was just like a thousand other times. No muss, no fuss. There was a concert to play.

"Okay," he said. "All ready? Let's go."

All I could think about during the first movement were the many difficult passages in the second. And when the second began, and Andy made his way through one and then another, I ticked them off in my mind, always preparing for the next. I was astonished when the second movement ended so quickly. I was dripping with sweat, but Andy just sat quietly and waited for Joey to indicate that he was ready to begin the third. Again, I worried—not about the third movement, which was fairly easy, but about the finale. Unfortunately—and I had thought about this for weeks—one of the most difficult passages in the whole sonata comes at the very end of the piece. When played perfectly, it is triumphant. When botched, it ruins everything that came before.

I sat, turning pages, waiting as the two paused before beginning the fourth movement finale. Then it began—one of the most beautiful melodies ever written—and I was crying. No matter what happened, Andy had gotten this far. I thought of Lea and Pierre and Boris and even of my grandfather Onissim, who had played this sonata the night he met Lea for the first time. They were all rooting for Andy. I know they were. He would do it.

And he did. Andy played the final passage of the Franck sonata that night as he had so often—all the notes were there. As he and Joey played the concluding chord, deafening cheers filled the hall. A miracle had taken place. Everyone who knew Andy and what he had been through over these many months understood.

For the family, it meant something else, too. A hundred years after César Franck had delivered his sonata to the world, my brother had given the family's final performance of the work. And it had been magnificent. This, even more than Carnegie Hall, even more than the White House, had been Andy's true triumph. As a reviewer wrote in the *Boston Globe*, "Wolf's playing came about as close to perfection as a mortal can hope to attain."[3]

After the concert, in the car with Dennie and my parents, little was said. Each of us realized that, barring some miracle, it was now a matter of waiting. Andy's health slowly deteriorated. There was nothing more for him to work toward. Talk of a spring tour with Stern had slowly petered out. Amazingly, though, the last person to give up hope was Stern himself. I learned years later that he called Joseph Silverstein the day after the Boston concert to ask whether he thought Andy might be up to the spring tour. Joey was unwilling to give what was essentially a musical death sentence.

"Let me send you the recording of the concert," he said, realizing that Stern, who knew Andy's playing as well as anyone, would discern the difference between his old confident partner and the pianist who had played on January 20. For most of us, it had been a remarkable performance. But Stern must have instantly heard the difference. He quietly brought on a new pianist.

Andy clung to life for almost a year. His forty-second birthday came and went on December 3, 1985. By that time, he was unconscious. On his last day, December 22, several of us gathered around his bedside. His breaths came less and less frequently. Then they stopped.

Andy's funeral service took place on December 27, 1985, at the Rockport Opera House—a building that he had helped to rescue from demolition a decade before, where he had played and produced so many concerts. Despite the time of year and the weather, many people came from faraway places.

After the service, as snow began to fall and the sky grew dark, a smaller crowd gathered around the gravesite at the Seaview Cemetery to recite the Mourners' Kaddish (the traditional Jewish prayer for the dead) as Andy's body was lowered into the ground.

Many colleagues and friends, who could not come to Maine in the middle of the holiday season, wished to pay their respects. One of these was Isaac Stern. So a second memorial was arranged at a Boston synagogue on January 6, 1986. Isaac Stern spoke about the "long and terrifying ordeal" and then of Andy as "a very rare spirit who came to me as a gift." Andy, he said, was someone "who gave me that sense of innocent joy in discovering how marvelous life and music can be." Then he took out his violin: "We musicians don't speak sometimes as well as we play." And with that he began to play unaccompanied Bach. He had decided against a selection with piano. Andy had been his pianist, and that needed to be honored. When he finished, there was a long silence. There was little left to say.

Lea's Legacy

For many years after Andy's death, I could not listen to the César Franck sonata. Every once in a while, I heard a snippet on the radio and had to turn it off. The pain was agonizing, the problem far more than simple grief for my brother. The sonata was part of a now-ended family history, and that was too painful to bear. There would be no more Carnegie Hall performances of the sonata—or any other piece—by our family. I was the only professional musician family member left, and I was a journeyman player whose work was mostly as an administrator and consultant. I did not count.

My feeling of loss was compounded when Boris's career ended soon after Andy's death. At seventy-six, my uncle was tired. He had been performing nonstop since his days as a little boy in a sailor suit. In 1984, Boris and I toured together for the last time. It had been a good run. From 1971 forward, he had taught me the classical music business. He had coached me through the writing of my first book, on touring opera, which we coauthored, giving me the confidence to write many more books on my own. He kept me from becoming a "paper pusher" as he called boring administrative posts that I had briefly held, and was largely responsible for my overall career success. Now he was calling it quits. In a *New York Times* interview with Edward Rothstein, he explained why: "Opera is entering a new era. In the last three or four years, it became available on television and on film, with glamorous settings and singers. Touring companies offer very modest productions. In the past we were very important. But I have a feeling that I have served my purpose. Opera is now becoming available to everybody."[4]

The next day, a second article marked the official end of Boris's touring company, with a photo of Boris conducting in the orchestra pit.[5] For the first time in many years, Boris seemed glum. He told me that he and Margaret had made arrangements with a burial society to simply remove their remains when they died, and he made me promise not to hold a funeral or memorial service. "No one really cares or remembers us anymore except a few family members," he told me. "And they'll probably be relieved they won't have to do anything or spend any money." I felt awkward, but reluctantly promised to abide by his wishes. In the end, it was a promise I could not keep.

The way Boris was looking back on his life troubled me. He had been director of opera at three leading conservatories (Cleveland Institute, New England Conservatory, and later in life at his alma mater, the Curtis Institute of Music). His pioneering and important work at the Boston Symphony's Tanglewood Music Center was widely acknowledged and he was perhaps America's best-known opera commentator, beloved by millions for his erudite and entertaining broadcasts for the Metropolitan Opera. His books and "Companion to Opera" records had fascinated many who loved the art form. And perhaps most importantly, his opera company had provided training to generations of American singers, many of whom became international stars and introduced the art form in live performances to millions.

I asked Boris whether he might consider my arranging for the continuation of the company he had so lovingly built. He looked at me in surprise and laughed. "Why on earth would I want that?"

I pointed out that many performing companies continued beyond the lives of their founders. "My boy," he said affectionately, in the same tone of voice he used when I was a child of five, "I formed the Goldovsky Opera to allow me to do what I believed in—teach young people how to do opera properly. I and the company are one and the same. I am finished and so is the company. Instead of asking silly questions, you need to help me close it down." So over the next few years, that is just what I did. By 1990, there was no trace of what had once been Goldovsky Opera.

One organization I felt needed to continue was Bay Chamber Concerts. Andy and I had founded it together in 1960. After my initial stint as artistic director, my brother had run it for more than twenty years, preserving the legacy of Mary Curtis Bok and her Curtis Institute of Music summer school in Rockport, Maine. Andy had hired superb musicians, helped save a great concert hall (the Rockport Opera House), and put on countless sold-out concerts. I agreed to become artistic director again, for myself, for Andy, and for my mother, Irene. I knew that she too was feeling the sense of loss—not only from Andy's death, which hit her hard, but from the gradual loss of a family tradition. The concerts at least kept some of that tradition alive. We added a new element—a national chamber music prize in Andy's memory—and we made sure there was an annual concert where the winner would perform in Andy's honor.

And so things remained for many years. In the end, it was my mother who decided she was not satisfied. Like her mother before her, she was ready to look ahead to the next chapter. Irene had become more active with the Russian Jewish émigré community, going to poetry readings and even translating some works into English.[6] Now she began to wonder whether it was worth searching for her Russian relatives—if any still existed. Boris, bitter about how the family had been treated after the Russian Revolution, had stated unequivocally that he would never return to the country of his birth. But Irene had no such qualms.

Irene's decision to go to Russia was triggered by news from her eldest grandchild, Alexa Fogel, who had just returned from the Sundance Film Festival in Utah. Alexa had noticed a listing of a Russian film directed by a woman from Moscow named Marina Goldovsky. Could that be a relative? Irene had always wondered about her brother Yuri's son, Dmitri, who had been born just days before Yuri's death in the mountains. Could this Marina Goldovsky be Dmitri's daughter? How wonderful it would be if the line had continued.

And then there was my aunt Anna's family. Irene could not remember her mother's sister (she had been four when she left Russia), and she had many questions about the rumors through Soviet musical touring artists that Anna, like Lea, had had a successful musical career. Had Anna had children? Irene was in her early seventies. If she was going to make what would inevitably be a strenuous trip to the Soviet Union, the time was now. A second granddaughter, Marya Fogel, a fluent Russian speaker, was willing to accompany her. This provided a young traveling companion who could get around on her own if necessary. Irene proposed that the two begin by searching out Marina Goldovsky, the film director. If she wasn't a relative, it didn't matter. Irene still wanted to visit the land of her birth.

The trip to Moscow took place in 1990. At first, the news was disappointing. When they tracked down Marina Goldovsky, it turned out she was not related. Once located, she pointed out a simple mistake by the Americans: in English, her surname was spelled the same as Irene's; but in Russian, it was a different name with a slightly different spelling.* Irene was so disappointed that it never occurred to her to mention her other relatives—the Luboshutz family (in Russian, Luboshitz). Why should a stranger know anything about Anna's family? It was a fateful mistake.

As it happened, Marina Goldovsky knew a great deal about Anna Luboshutz—something I only found out a quarter-century later. At the very time of Irene's visit to Moscow, the filmmaker was talking to Anna's daughter, Nadezhda—Irene's first cousin—about a film project in which she wanted Nadezhda to play a prominent part. The film, released in 1993 under the name *Dom S Rytsaryami* ("The House with the Knights"),[7] profiled people who had lived in the famous apartment house on the Arbat where Nadezhda had grown up. Nadezhda agreed to narrate a portion of the film, in which she would be introduced as, "the daughter of a well-known doctor Nikolai Shereshevsky and a brilliant cellist Anna Luboshits." In the film, she talked about her family, recalling episodes in their lives, reliving the wonderful events and the terrible ones, and showing photos of her family, including Anna and Nikolai's wedding

---

* Marina's last name in English is often given as Goldovskaya rather than Goldovsky. However, the difference in the ending is simply because she is female. In Russian, Irene's last name would have been Goldovskaya because she too is female. The only difference in the root name is a silent letter in the middle of the word.

photograph. This was the very apartment where a pregnant Lea had gone to deliver Irene. Now, many years later, Irene had been so very close to learning about her relatives and meeting her cousin Nadezhda. It was not to be.

Marina did make one suggestion that turned out to be fruitful. There might be another path for locating Dmitri Goldovsky. Had they checked a Moscow telephone directory? Astounded that such a thing existed in Soviet Russia, Irene and Marya did, and found a telephone listing for a Dmitri. They called, and a woman named Tanya answered. "We think we may be relatives. Is Dmitri there?"

The phone went silent. Then in a halting voice, Tanya said to Irene, "You are too late. My husband—your nephew, Dmitri Goldovsky—is dead." Dmitri had recently passed away after battling cancer. He had been just fifty-seven years old. Irene was devastated.

"But please come to the flat," Tanya continued. "Let us meet. And you must meet Dmitri's daughter, Marina, and her son, Ilya."

So there was a Marina Goldovsky in Moscow who was a relative! How extraordinary that Irene's brother, Boris, and her nephew, Dmitri, had both named their daughters Marina Goldovsky, and that a third, unrelated Marina Goldovsky had given Irene the idea of coming to Moscow in the first place. Irene and Marya took a taxi to a flat on the outskirts of Moscow. They were greeted by Tanya, who, with tears in her eyes, told Irene about her brother Yuri's son.

By 1980, Dmitri's wife Natalya had died of cancer. Their daughter Marina had matriculated at Moscow State University in biology, and Dima (as family and friends called him) felt very much alone. Relatives invited him on a canoe trip down a river near the ancient city of Pskov, and he decided to go. The attraction was twofold. In addition to his love of canoeing, he had an opportunity to pay homage to the greatest of all Russian poets, Alexander Pushkin, whose villa and final resting place by the walls of the Svyatogorsk Monastery are located near the so-called Pushkin Mountains by Pskov. There, Dima met a woman with whom he fell in love and spent the rest of his life. Tatyana Goussev was also a lover of Pushkin. With her, Dima gained another child, a stepson, Misha Goussev, who would become part of Irene's life some years later when he emigrated to the United States.

In the course of their conversation, Irene asked about Anna's family. Did Tanya know anything about them? Dmitri had mentioned them, Tanya said, but they had never met. Perhaps she could find out more and let Irene know. Irene and Marya were euphoric to realize that Yuri had living descendants. A few hours later, they returned to central Moscow in the same cab in which they had come. But by the time they left Russia, they had not located any of Anna's descendants.

Two years later, Irene's granddaughter, Marya, returned to Russia to explore job possibilities, and in 1993 she found a job in the Moscow bureau of the *Wall Street Journal*. At this point, Tanya reached out to tell Marya that she had located Anna and Nikolai's daughter, Nadezhda, and granddaughter Nina. The Americans (Marya, with her sister Alexa and a cousin, Heather Wolf) made contact with Anna's family and were invited to the family apartment. There, among the many pieces of antique furniture, was the very bed in which their grandmother and my mother, Irene, had been born.

The three young American women were surprised when Nadezhda told them that she knew all about the American family: They had received information from Soviet touring artists who visited America. She told them emphatically that she knew that Lea had married Josef Hofmann, that she owned two Stradivarius violins, and that Irene had had seven children. There was no talking Nadezhda out of these convictions, even though not one of them was true. Rather, they put in a call to Irene in Philadelphia. Irene and Nadezhda spoke at length. The only daughters of the two Luboshutz sisters finally had a chance to talk about their mothers, and to discuss their lives and their families. Although Irene invited Nadezhda to America, her Russian cousin died soon after. But in 1995, Anna's granddaughter Nina and her great-granddaughter Sveta came to visit. Their trip included travel to Lea's summer house in Maine. At last, the family was united.

My father, Billy, and Uncle Boris, born in the same year (1908), also died within a year of one another—Boris on February 15, 2001, and my father on January 6, 2002. Billy's memorial service was at the family's synagogue in Philadelphia, where his father had laid the cornerstone, and where my brothers and I had had our bar mitzvah services at age thirteen. We sat in pews engraved in silver with the names of various Wolf ancestors and looked up at the stained-glass windows honoring other Wolfs. I thought of all the High Holidays there with Dad, the many Shabbat services at home over which he presided, and the Seders with the extended Wolf family. I thought of my great-great-grandfather, Sergei Katzman, the rabbi in Odessa and my great-grandfather, Saul Luboshutz, who had been such a good Jew. I also thought of my grandfather Onissim, who wrote a book about the Jews of Moscow and supported Jewish causes all his life. I was glad to be in a temple marking this important family event.

Boris had asked that there be no memorial service for him, and I was in his house when a representative from a burial society arrived in an unmarked car to remove his body, per his instructions. But his prediction that no one would remember him or be interested in his passing was proven wrong just days after his death. A long, laudatory obituary appeared in the *New York Times*. Soon after, officials at the Boston Symphony Orchestra contacted me. They wanted to produce a memorial event at Tanglewood. With Boris's widow, Margaret's, permission, we planned a small event to be held at Serge Koussevitzky's personal estate at Tanglewood, with its magnificent view of the mountains and lake. But so many people wanted to come that the event was moved to the much larger Ozawa Concert Hall. And that was not all. The New England Conservatory contacted me to ask if they might mount a memorial event on the hundredth anniversary of Boris's birth. Boris had been a distinguished member of the faculty, and the school wanted to honor him. A symposium and dinner made a lovely final reunion for many whose illustrious careers had begun under Boris's tutelage.

Like her husband, Irene died at age ninety-three, on May 8, 2010, happy in the knowledge that her greatest wish—to have a large and happy family—had been fulfilled. That family had now become a clan and in her final days, Irene could count fifty-three living children, grandchildren, great-grandchildren and spouses. Though she had lost a son, a grandson, and a great-grandson, she concentrated on the bright side. She had lived long enough to see one of her grandchildren, Ira Wolf Tuton, depart on a three-continent tour as the bass player in a successful experimental rock band called Yeasayer. She had even been to one of his concerts when he was getting started as a rock musician. It didn't bother her in the slightest that Ira's music was not what she had grown up with. It was music made by her own flesh and blood. Sadly, she did not live long enough to see one of her great-grandchildren, Sasha Blair Wolf, perform at Carnegie Hall in 2016 and 2017, a little more than a century after Lea's first appearance there. Andy was not the end of the chain after all.

Late in her life, Irene added written and oral recollections to those of her mother and brother and made sure that the boxes of material she had collected about the family were carefully preserved. I agreed to take charge of what she gave us, and received additional material from Uncle Boris. But I did nothing with it for a number of years until, with my mother's death and my own advancing age, I realized I had to start. With each photo and letter, I saw how Lea had shaped the lives of three generations. Come the inevitable school assignment to collect a family narrative, nearly every grandchild and great grandchild was now retelling some version of her stories: gold medal violinist, refugee from the Revolution, performer to royalty, tale spinner, or survivor.

While the historical record increasingly came into focus, I realized that part of my task was coming to my own assessment of Lea as a musician. For years Boris had dismissed her as merely a "good" player who made it onto the stages of great concert halls as a novelty—a fiery and attractive woman who played well enough to please a crowd. Up against that appraisal I only had memories of her playing at home with Andy, deep into retirement and long after her deafness dulled her intonation.

But going through the boxes, impressions began to shift. What a career she had had! How admired she had been! And then I found a letter from Leopold Godowsky—among the most highly regarded musicians, pianists, and composers of Lea's generation. Many people assumed he was related because his last name was so close to the family name of Goldovsky. But he was Polish, not Russian, and he didn't meet Lea until both had come to the United States. In the two-page letter, written after one of Lea's Carnegie Hall recitals, he wrote:

> Your recital was to me a source of constant, unalloyed delight. What pleased me particularly is your honesty of purpose, your nobility of style, your avoidance of any virtuoso flippancy and self-exploitation, your devotion to the works you interpret, your love for the art more than the medium you selected for your expression: the violin, which you handle with complete mastery; and last—your absence of bombast and exaggeration.[8]

It was the only fan letter my grandmother had saved, and I think I know why. Here was a man who Lea respected above most others for his life of great musicianship and artistry. He had had no need to write his letter; yet he had been moved by what he heard. Perhaps I could admire my grandmother not only as the woman who had forged a successful career in the male-dominated, cutthroat world of solo violin playing in the first half of the 20th century but also someone who had been a rare and special musician.

What I desperately wanted was to hear for myself—though Lea had made that nearly impossible. She had stubbornly rejected opportunities to record after her early experiments with the still primitive technology while she was still in Russia. She believed every performance should be a new experience and an adventure for both the player and the listener and, further, that the concert hall was itself a live instrument. Hearing the same thing time after time on a recording was deadening. Rumors circulated that there existed pirated recordings of some of her early broadcasts including an amazing one of Max Bruch's Scottish Fantasy. But, search as I might, I never located any of them.

At last, I located a recording that she had made in Russia, in St. Petersburg, in the early 1900s, playing two very short pieces by Russian composers—Anton Arensky and César Cui. Brief though these musical selections were, I could now listen and form my own opinion. Lea was indeed very special. Great musicians had chosen her over and over again to perform with them, composers wrote music for her (and as in the case of Prokofiev, had given her important premieres of their works), audiences and critics loved her, and she had trained a generation of successful students. Even if her style of playing belonged to a bygone era, I could also now hear her unique musical voice.

In handing me the tea-glass holder—the *podstakannik*—that bore my great uncles' portraits, my mother had said, "Tell the story." When I finally started, I began by knitting together all the family legends I had heard growing up. And I continued the task by opening box after box, reading diaries, newspaper articles, and books. As I did so, the old legends began to dissolve, revealing a much more complex, much more human history. And it led me to wonder: More than the physical object of the tea glass holder, valuable as it may have been, was this task of telling the story the real gift my mother had given me?

Part of the answer came in the form of another anecdote about Lea that my mother had told me. Some years after she retired from the Curtis Institute of Music, Lea read about the terrible shortage of great Italian string instruments in the Soviet Union. An entire generation of remarkable young Russian violinists had access only to inferior instruments because following the Russian Revolution, so many musicians had emigrated to the West, taking their great instruments with them. Later, as these violins, violas, and cellos came up for sale, few Soviet players had the money or the legal ability to bring those instruments to their homeland.

Lea now thought about the other instrument she owned—the beautiful 16th-century Italian violin made in Cremona by a member of the Amati family. It had been a gift to her in Moscow as a conservatory student from the Polyakov family and had changed her life. Could it do so again for another rare violin talent? For her there was only one answer. Despite the high level of mid-20th-century Cold War tension between the United States and the Soviet Union, and despite what Lea and her family had experienced at the hands of the Soviets, she sent the violin back to Moscow at her own expense, asking that it be presented to a gifted young player at the same conservatory she had attended. People in the United States thought her mad, politically naive, financially and musically irresponsible. Lea's answer was simple: The violin lost all its value unless it was played. Money didn't matter. And then the drama played out again after her death, when Boris fulfilled Lea's wish that the Nightingale go to one of her gifted students rather than being sold to the highest bidder.

That student was none other than Rafael Druian who, as a thirteen-year-old at the Curtis Institute of Music, had been given one of Lea's fine Italian instruments to play. But as much as he may have loved that violin, he had heard Lea's Nightingale week after week at his lessons and he had fallen in love with it. Boris knew of Druian's keen interest in the Stradivarius and got in touch with him after Lea's death. Through a complicated financial transaction that involved the Cleveland Orchestra where Druian was concertmaster at the time, Boris made it possible for him eventually to acquire the instrument. He would play it in Cleveland and subsequently in his final concertmaster position with the New York Philharmonic. It was a special thrill to Boris and the rest of the family to hear the instrument one last time in a recording of Mozart sonatas that Druian would make with the distinguished conductor-pianist, George Szell.

Half a century later, the Nightingale has been sold for a third time since Lea owned it for undisclosed millions of dollars to an anonymous buyer whose identity has been protected by a nondisclosure agreement. The violin has been transformed from Lea's superb concert instrument into an investment—a commodity that may well spend the rest of its days safe—and silent—in a bank vault. The Nightingale may never again sing the great sonata of César Franck nor inspire moments of awe followed by wild applause . . . though I suppose one can always hope.[9]

Riding on a bus on one of Boris's opera company tours through a nondescript landscape, I asked him whether he regretted his disposition of the Nightingale. "You could have become really rich," I joked.

He replied, "Being very rich is overrated, my boy. It is neither good to be too rich nor too poor. The best thing to be is just right, like me. I have a comfortable house, food on the table, a good piano, a great library, a wonderful family . . . and like you, I am doing precisely what I enjoy most. You and I are very lucky."

Lea and her children and others in the family had experienced enough of poverty to believe that there was nothing noble about being poor. On the other hand, Lea had seen possessions lost, taken, sold, and abandoned and in the long term it seemed to cause her few moments of deep regret. Mostly, *things* were not that important to her. Instead, she sought, fought for, and kept family and music uppermost in her life. And even when her own performance career ended, she inspired all of us to champion a fierce commitment to ensuring that people with talent and passion could continue to make music at the highest level.

More than the *podstakannik*, this was the heirloom.

ENDNOTES

Prelude (1853 to 1885)

1   There are two versions of my grandmother's unpublished memoir plus random chapters that are not part of either memoir. The first version is untitled and was written in 1936 and dedicated to Mary Louise Curtis Bok. The second version is titled *LUBO: Four Generations of Music* and is undated, though she was working on it in the late 1950s and early 1960s. There are times where the differences in the versions are significant to the story, and in those cases I refer to the earlier and later versions specifically. All quotes in this book of my grandmother are from one or another version of the memoir unless otherwise noted. Where the version is important, it is noted in the text.

2   In Russian, in addition to the first or given name and the last or family name, there is a middle name—the patronymic that identifies the name of one's father. For males, the patronymic carries the suffix "–ovich," as in Onissim Borisovich (or Onissim, son of Boris). For females, the suffix is "–ovna" as in Lea Saulovna (Lea, daughter of Saul).

3   This and other facts about Boris and his two wives come from Rashel Khin-Goldovsky's diaries in Moscow, (hereafter Khin Diaries, F. 128, op. 1, ed. khr. 6), January 19, 1896. Please note that for simplicity and consistency across family names, I have used the name Goldovsky both for males and females (including Rashel). In Russian, the female name has a slightly different ending (Goldovskaya).

4   For a master list of references for each diary date, see the bibliography.

5   Khin Diaries, June 6, 1902, and September 16, 1902.

6   Ibid., May 13, 1914.

1. The Music Begins—Allegretto ben moderato (1885 to 1903)

1   All of Lea's quotes are from her unpublished memoir described in Prelude note 1.

2   The story of Onissim's summer in Bryansk is related in some detail in Solov'ev.

3   Gippius, 47.

4   Solov'ev, 11.

5   "O studente Gol'dovskom" (О Студенте Гольдовском).

6   Errera, 18.

7   Birthdates are from Anna and Pierre's Moscow Conservatory files and are given in the Old Style calendar. Anna's birthday according to the New Style was July 25 and Pierre's was July 1.

8   Sometimes one sees the Russian version of this Czech name rendered into English as Ivan Voitsekhovich Grzhimali.

9   "Rodilsya vydayushchiisya sudebnyi deyatel' Anatolii F'edorovich Koni" (Родился выдающийся судебный деятель Анатолий Фёдорович Кони). The quotation has been slightly adapted to smooth that translation.

10   All quotes of Onissim Goldovsky in this section are from Gol'dovskii (1907). The previously unpublished translations, done for this book, are by Andrea Rutherford.

11   The source for the location of this event is Irene Wolf, 8.

12   Balin.

13   Balin, 88.

14   Ibid., 110.

15   See Berdnikov.

16   Gol'dovskii (1906).

17   The complete title rendered into English is: *HELP! To Jews Affected by Crop Failure. A Literary Collection* (St. Petersburg: Isidore Goldberg Printing House, 1901).

18   A search of the Internet did turn up a portrait that was said to be that of Onissim that looked very much in the style of Pasternak. However, the painter was not identified and the sitter has only a passing resemblance to the photographs that remain of Onissim.

19   Khin Diaries, September 24, 1901.

20   Obshchestvo liubitelei rossiiskoi slovesnosti (Общество любителей российской словесности).

21   Pipes, 18.

22   Ibid., 19.

23   Balin, 113.

2. The Tempest—Allegro (1903 to 1921)

1   Balin, 111.

2   See Irene Wolf, 8.

3   Lea's portrait was shown at an exhibition of the Wanderers in 1908 and a small black-and-white reproduction was published in the catalog for that exhibition. It can also be seen in an encyclopedia of the work of this society of artists entitled *Tovarishchestvo peredvizhnykh khudozhestvennyx vystavok, 1917–1923, Entsiklopediya* (Товарищество Передвижных Художественных Выставок.1871–1923 Энциклопедия), published in St. Petersburg in 2003. The reproduction is on page 335.

4   The exhibition of Shemyakin's paintings took place at The Museum of Russian Impressionism in Moscow (October 12, 2017–January 17, 2018). The catalog includes a reproduction of Anna's portrait.

5   Saleski, 218.

6   The address comes from a notarized statement (February 14, 1911) in Pierre Luboshutz's Conservatory file signed by his father and giving his address. The statement exempts Pierre from military service as he was an only son.

7   Goldovsky and Cate.

8   See "Kak izmenilsya ideal zhenskoi krasoty za 100 let" (Как изменился идеал женской красоты за 100 лет), *Woman's Day*, Moscow, March 8, 2016. Available at: http://www.wday.ru/stil-zhizny/vibor-redakcii/kak-izmenyalsya-ideal-jenskoy-krasotyi-za-100-let.

9   Nela Rubinstein interviewed by Gregor Benko. Recording property of the International Piano Archives, University of Maryland.

10   Dates of the entries from Khin's diary about Lea in Paris include November 22 and December 5, 1905.

11   A transliteration of the Russian form of the name.

12   *HELP! To Jews Affected by Crop Failure. A Literary Collection* (St. Petersburg: Isidore Goldberg Printing House, 1901).

13   Today known as Kirovohrad.

14   March 22 according to the New Style calendar.

15   There is more than one version of this classic story. Another version is told in Malan, 237. However, the essentials of the story and Zimbalist's comments are the same in all versions.

16   June 7 according to the New Style calendar.

17   December 6 according to the New Style calendar.

18   Letters in the Russian State Archive of Literature and Art (RGALI) indicate that Lea kept Rumanov abreast of her concerts and met with him when she was in St. Petersburg.

19   From biographical information in a concert program from the Stanley Music Club (Philadelphia) 1927–1928 season. The date of the concert was October 30, 1927.

20   *Novoe Russkoe Slovo* (August 6, 1987).

21   A Russian periodical, *Rampa i zhizn'* (Рампа и жизнь), contains advertisements for these concerts. See the bibliography.

22   *Rampa i zhizn'* (1913).

23   Gol'dovskii (1906), 561–67.

24   Wolf and Whiteman.

25   Khin Diaries, February 27, 1915.

26   Goldovsky and Cate, 8.

27   Ibid.

28   Ibid., 24.

29   Ibid.

30   See Zavadskaya. I am grateful to my cousin Sveta Kuzin (Anna's great-granddaughter) for telling me about this article, which was in her family's collection, and then translating it for me.

31   See earlier note regarding advertisements for these concerts in the Russian periodical *Rampa i zhizn'* over several issues in 1913, for example nos. 41–52.

32 Gol'dovskii (1905), 72–101. Reprinted in *Nezavisimyi Psikhiatricheskyi Zhurnal*, nos. 3 and 4 (1995).

33 Gol'dovskii (1907), 313–21.

34 Gol'dovskii (1906).

35 Goldovsky and Cate, 9.

36 Khin Diaries, September 13, 1908. In the same entry, Rashel referred to Esther Chernetskaya's figure as "кувалда"—a sledgehammer.

37 One such opportunity was a tour in early 1931. The two men played their New York Carnegie Hall recital on January 24.

38 I am grateful to Professor Peter Bloom of Smith College for providing information about the Doguereaus. Some of it was retrieved from Ancestry.com on December 3, 2018. Other information was supplied by Olav Skagen, genealogist for the Skagen family in the United States (Yvonne Doguereau's married name was Skagen).

39 An advertisement for one of their joint concerts can be found in *Rampa i zhizn'*, no. 46 (November 14, 1910).

40 *Rampa i zhizn'*. This periodical includes a detailed description of the event.

41 The biographical sketch was prepared by Boris Goldovsky (Pierre's nephew) in 1971 and can be found in the Boris Goldovsky Archive at the New England Conservatory of Music.

42 Balin.

43 A. Koni's Letters to N. I. Ivanovskaya, 1899–1919, The Russian State Archive of Literature and Art (RGALI), F. 128, op. 1, ed. khr. 141.

44 Khin, Unpublished play.

45 Graham, 20.

46 Goldovsky and Cate, 25.

47 Goldovsky and Cate, 26–7.

48 Geroniumus.

49 Letter from Pierre Luboshutz to Natalya Konstantinovna and Sergei Aleksandrovich Koussevitzky (1922), Koussevitzky Collection, Library of Congress (translated by Svetlana Kuzin).

50 This information comes from Yuri Goldovsky's Moscow University file.

51 Figes, 534–35.

52 Ibid., 727.

53 Ibid., 605, 777.

54 This information is from Yuri Goldovsky's Moscow University file.

55 V. V. Rozanov's Letters, The Russian State Archive of Literature and Art (RGALI), F. 419, op. 1, ed. khr. 268.

56 The dates of the concerts were September 3, 9, and 14, and November 16 and 23. See Kotlyarov and Garmash, 170–73.

57 Charles King, 171.

58 Rahv, x–xi.

59 Khin Diaries, June 16, 1908.

60　Letter from Émile Zola to Onissim dated September 14, 1910, Goldovsky Collection, The Russian State Archive of Literature and Art (RGALI).

3. The Longest Journey—Recitativo-Fantasia: Ben moderato (1921 to 1930)

1　Goldovsky and Cate, 40.

2　Saleski, 218.

3　Irene Wolf, 11.

4　Goldovsky and Cate, 44.

5　Letter from Pierre Luboshutz to Serge Koussevitzky, Koussevitzky Collection, Library of Congress (translated by Svetlana Kuzin). This letter is undated but written from Moscow. Someone has written the date 1922 on the letter.

6　Goldovsky and Cate, 58.

7　Review of January 23, 1925, Aeolian Hall Concert of Lea Luboshutz, *The Sun* (London), January 24, 1925.

8　Saleski, 218.

9　*Le Petit Parisien*, December 1, 1924.

10　By 1930, for example, she had appeared for six successive years with the Cincinnati Symphony Orchestra, as reported in *Overtones* (1930), 86.

11　A January 10, 1927, article in the *Philadelphia Ledger* about Hofmann and Lea stated that the meeting on the *Majestic* occurred in April 1925—an obvious error, since the program from the concert is in my possession. But otherwise the gist of the story in the newspaper is correct.

12　In her memoir, Lea refers to her using a phonetic rendering of her actual Russian name—Preobrazhenskaya.

13　Sachs, 354.

14　Schneider, 80.

15　Letter from S. S. Prokofiev to Serge Koussevitzky, January 2, 1925, The Russian State Archive of Literature and Art (RGALI), F. 1, op. 929, ed. khr. 5, p. 8. References to the letter can also be found in Victor Yuzefovich's essay on the correspondence between S. Prokofiev and S. Koussevitzky 1910–1953, published in several issues of an Internet magazine, *Sem' iskusstvo* (Семь искусств). The article was published over the course of eight issues from N3(16) March 2011 to N10(23) October 2011.

16　See the January 26, 1935, *New York Times* review of a Carnegie Hall performance of the concerto, which took place on January 25, 1935.

17　The *New York Times* review of the concert appeared a day later, on November 22, 1925. Among other things, it noted Lea's personal charm and animation.

18　Goldovsky and Cate, 77.

19　Ibid., 78.

20　Ibid.

21　Ibid., 79.

22　Ibid., 74.

23 Letter to Betty Short, June 3, 1926, International Piano Archives, University of Maryland.

24 Goldovsky and Cate, 84.

25 Ibid., 84.

26 Ibid., 129–30.

27 This statement accompanied the authentification certificate from W. E. Hill & Sons and was reproduced in *The World of Strings* newsletter, published by William Moennig & Son in autumn 1983 when the violin went on sale once again.

28 Letter from Josef Hofmann to Mary Louise Curtis Bok dated February 21, 1928, Archive of the Curtis Institute of Music.

29 Letter from Josef Hofmann to Mary Louise Curtis Bok, February 21, 1928, Archive of the Curtis Institute of Music: "A friend of hers, Mr. Neuenberg [sic], has advanced the necessary money and she will repay it by and by."

30 See http://www.naumburg.org/about.php

31 A transcript of the eulogy is in the collection of the Fogg Museum, Harvard University.

32 The exact sum was told to me by a Naumburg descendent, Enid Weisz Stone. She had a copy of the will in her possession.

33 This exact quote was used in Hofmann's publicity. I saw it quoted in an advertisement in a Town Hall Luboshutz & Nemenoff program from November 25, 1938, and in a Hofmann recital program at the Eastman Theatre on January 19, 1939. Checking the original language from the *New York Times* (November 28, 1937), Hofmann's publicity people may have exercised some editing. The quote reads: ". . . he may be designated as one of the two or three living pianists who are able to forge a beauty which links the art of the present with that of the mighty past."

34 In a biographical entry in one of Lea and Hofmann's concert programs the next year (October 30, 1927, at the Stanley Theatre in Philadelphia), it mentions that Lea was the first nonfaculty member to give a concert at Curtis.

35 A printed program of the concert, together with a letter that makes reference to it (dated January 24, 1927, from Curtis violin student Ella Geer to her fiancé) can be found in the Archive of the Curtis Institute of Music.

36 Letter from Lea Luboshutz to Mary Louise Curtis Bok, January 28, 1927. This and other letters between Lea and Mrs. Bok can be found in the Archive of the Curtis Institute of Music.

37 Flesch, 355–56.

38 As cited in *New York Times*, February 28, 1926.

39 Letter from Carl Flesch to Lea Luboshutz, January 31, 1929. Luboshutz-Goldovsky-Wolf family archive.

40 Luboshutz, Lea, "European Audience of Today," *Overtones*, May 1936, 27–9.

41 Malan, 94.

42 Cole, 13 in original typescript.

43 Malan, 56.

44 Luboshutz, Lea [with students and others].

45 Quoted in Benko and McNeill.

46 Flesch, 335.

47 Interview with Eleanor Sokoloff, May 13, 2015.

48 The concert was reviewed in the London *Sunday Times*, June 27, 1926. A subsequent notice in the *London Musical Times* from August 1, 1926, looks back on a concert they played together and gives the same program but no date. I have assumed this must be the same concert, which was probably their first together.

49 *Chicago Daily Tribune* announcement of her concert with the Atwater Kent Orchestra on April 15, 1928.

50 The number of concerts is mentioned in a letter from Lea Luboshutz to Serge Koussevitzky, October 13, 1927, Koussevitzky Collection, Library of Congress.

51 Letter (in German) from Josef Hofmann to Lea Luboshutz, July 22, 1927, Collection of the International Piano Archives, University of Maryland.

52 Moore, Edward, "Hofmann Pays One of His Rare Visits: With Lea Luboshutz Tops Sunday Music List," *Chicago Daily Tribune*, November 28, 1927.

53 Temianka (1973), 230.

54 Letter to Lea Luboshutz from her representative Calvin Franklin, February 6, 1927, International Piano Archives, University of Maryland.

55 Review of Lea Luboshutz and Josef Hofmann, London *Observer*, October 10, 1926.

56 Review of Lea Luboshutz and Josef Hofmann, London *Daily Chronicle*, October 11, 1926.

57 O'Neill.

58 I am grateful to Gregor Benko, an authority on Josef Hofmann, for information regarding other violinist partners of Josef Hofmann. Personal email, February 3, 2016.

59 Olin Downes in *New York Times*, January 31, 1927.

60 Email from Gregor Benko to Thomas Wolf, March 6, 2016.

61 Letter from Josef Hofmann to Lea Luboshutz, January 23, 1928, International Piano Archives, University of Maryland.

62 Telegram from Lea Luboshutz to Josef Hofmann, March 25, 1935, International Piano Archives, University of Maryland.

63 Letter from Josef Hoffmann to Sidney Silber, October 15, 1927, International Piano Archives, University of Maryland.

64 Letter from Lea Luboshutz to Betty Short, June 10, 1926, International Piano Archives, University of Maryland.

65 Letter from Josef Hofmann to Lea Luboshutz, February 6, 1928, International Piano Archives, University of Maryland.

66 Letter from Lea Luboshutz to Serge Koussevitzky, October 13, 1927, Koussevitzky Collection, Library of Congress (translated by Svetlana Kuzin).

67 Letter from Lea Luboshutz to Serge Koussevitzky, November 4, 1927, Koussevitzky Collection, Library of Congress (translated by Svetlana Kuzin).

68 Letter from Hofmann to Henri Temianka quoted in Temianka (1973), 14.

69 *New York Times*, January 31, 1927.

70 *New York Times*, January 17, 1928. The concert took place the night before.

71 Temianka (1992).

72 Cole, 12 in original typescript.

73 Malan, 13.

74 The details of Lionel Prince's life come from his obituary in *Oakland Tribune*, March 7, 1942, 14.

75 *Overtones*, October 15, 1929.

76 Among the school's most famous graduates was the linguist, philosopher, and social critic Noam Chomsky.

77 *Overtones*, March 1930, 157.

4. Tragedies and Triumphs—Allegretto poco mosso (1930 to 1965)

1 Proust, vol. 1, 346. In this novel, Proust uses the device of a fictional sonata—the so-called Vinteuil Sonata for violin and piano—and refers to "la petite phrase" (a small phrase) that brings back many memories. On one occasion, Proust stated that the specific model for the sonata was Camille Saint-Saens's Violin Sonata no. 1 in D Minor, Op. 75 (1885). However, in the same paragraph (the dedication of *Du Côté de chez Swann* to his friend Jacques de Lacretelle), he admitted that he was not an admirer of Saint-Saëns and that for those pages in the novel he also was thinking of the A Major violin and piano sonata of César Franck, a composer whom Proust adored. As to the passage above, it specifically refers to the canonic opening of the final movement of the Franck violin sonata.

2 Cole, 43 in original typescript.

3 Lang.

4 Lea Luboshutz [with students and others].

5 See, for example, the concert announcement in the Camden (Maine) Herald, August 30, 1935.

6 All letters among Lea, Yuri, and Yuri's wife are in a family collection and were translated by Yuri's stepgrandson, Misha Goussev.

7 A photo of them together in Bad Kissingen can be found in the Archive of the Curtis Institute.

8 Yuri (as abbreviated in the postcards).

9 Affectionate nickname for Yuri.

10 Baltzell, 216.

11 Called the Mathilde Adler Loeb Dispensary, it was located near Olney and Old York Roads and was dedicated in 1878. A photograph of the building can be found in Hotchkin, 58.

12 Burt, 568.

13 The Hofmann letter is dated August 1, 1940.

14 Lang.

15 *Philadelphia Evening Bulletin*, November 3, 1945, 12.

16 Ibid., B5.

17 *Philadelphia Inquirer*, November 3, 1945, 9.

18 Ibid.

19 Lang.

20 O'Neill.

21 According to historians Jonathan Brent and Vladimir Naumov, four large camps were built in 1953 in southern and western Russia, with rumors that they were for Jews.

22 *Pis'mo N. A. Shereshevskogo L. P. Beriya* (Письмо Н.А. Шерешевского Л.П. Берия), March 24, 1953, *Almanakh Rossiya XX vek, Dyelo vrachei*, D. 15. Arkhiv Aleksandra N. Yakovleva. (Translated by Andrea Rutherford).

23 Geroniumus.

24 *Camden* (Maine) *Herald*, April 13, 1961.

25 Technically speaking, in 1935 there was another program in which Pierre was soloist with Toscanini and a second pianist (Coenraad V. Bos). They performed Brahms's Liebeslieder Waltzes. However, since Pierre and Bos did not constitute a recognized "team," it was correct to claim that Luboshutz & Nemenoff was the only duo-piano team to appear with Toscanini, as their promotional material did.

26 Pierre was constantly making new arrangements of music to enhance the limited two-piano repertoire including the works of Bach, Rameau, Gluck, Beethoven, Weber, Mendelssohn, Glinka, Johann Strauss, and Shostakovich. Other composers arranged and wrote pieces for Luboshutz & Nemenoff, including a suite from the ballet "On Stage" by Norman Dello Joio, Abram Chasins's 'Carmen' Fantasie, and a new concerto for two pianos and orchestra that Pierre commissioned from the Czech composer Bohuslav Martinů. That work's premiere by Pierre and Genia with Eugene Ormandy conducting the Philadelphia Orchestra on November 5, 1943, was considered important enough to be mentioned in the November 8, 1943, issue of *Time* magazine. Luboshutz & Nemenoff also introduced a suite for two pianos by Aram Khachaturian to American audiences in Providence, Rhode Island on October 20, 1954.

27 The concert took place at Boston's Jordan Hall on March 2, 1979, with Benjamin Zander conducting. In addition to the two concertos, Boris conducted an opening Mozart overture.

28 George Holland, "Boston After Dark," *Boston Evening American*, November 24, 1943, 19.

29 Wolf, 21–22.

30 The full statement is preserved in the Luboshutz-Goldovsky-Wolf Family Archive.

The End of the Sonata (1965–2018)

1 The information about Rose's Curtis audition comes from an interview that Irene Wolf gave to Gregor Benko in 1974. Other information comes from Honigberg.

2 *New York Times*, January 12, 1983.

3 Henry Derrick, "A Homecoming for Silverstein," *Boston Globe*, January 22, 1985, 24.

4 Edward Rothstein, "Music Notes," *New York Times*, March 18, 1984.

5 Edward Rothstein, "Opera: Goldovsky Company's Farewell," *New York Times*, March 19, 1984.

6   Kaplan, 1073.
7   Available at: http://doskado.ucoz.ru/blog/2013-02-20-9479
8   Two-page handwritten letter from Leopold Godowsky to Lea Luboshutz, Luboshutz-Goldovsky-Wolf Family Archive. The letter is not dated but it makes reference to a Carnegie Hall recital.
9   As part of the confidentiality agreements associated with the last two sales of the Nightingale, both owners refused to allow photographs of the instrument to be shared publicly. I can only imagine how upset this would have made Lea and Boris.

SOURCES AND BIBLIOGRAPHY

Few people attempting a family history could be more blessed with such rich material to work from. Members of my family were not shy about preparing personal memoirs and oral histories. In addition, because several of them were well-known in their day, a lot was written about them.

There are hundreds of books and articles in which family members are mentioned, especially in Russia and the United States but also in France, Germany, England, and elsewhere. Those who were professional musicians received much coverage. It is well to remember that reporting on classical music in Western Europe and the United States was considerably more robust during the period in which the main characters in this book were most active, making my search even more fruitful (and exhausting). Any respectable newspaper in the United States had a reviewer dedicated to classical music, and concert coverage generally appeared the day after a program was presented (often in the morning papers). Reviews and profiles of family members were commonplace not only from nationally important media markets such as Moscow, New York, Paris, Berlin, and London but also from relatively small communities where they performed. Some of this material was already in family collections; other items were available on Internet archives and even more was available in physical archives mentioned below.

When it came to primary source material, my grandmother Lea Luboshutz wrote several versions of her autobiography—none published, but all well preserved. Along with her students at the Curtis Institute of Music, she also wrote a "Class Year Book" for the 1929–1930 academic year, which provides great insights into her approach to teaching. Her son, my uncle Boris Goldovsky, wrote a published autobiography, *My Road to Opera* [with Curtis W. Cate (Boston: Houghton Mifflin, 1979)] as well as several delightful autobiographical articles including my favorite in the *Atlantic Monthly* that came out in January 1960 called "Oncle Serge" (about his years with Koussevitzky). He also wrote many technical books and articles about his work in opera. His radio lectures for the Metropolitan Opera over many years have been preserved and also contain much autobiographical material. According to Uncle Boris, *My Road to Opera* was based in part on the transcript from an oral history project sponsored by the American Jewish Committee, and he claimed that everything of importance in the Oral History Library recording was in the book. Nevertheless, I was able to track down a partial transcript and found it riveting, especially his in-depth and often unsparing and sometimes scathing analyses of various musicians of the day, which, for obvious reasons, never made it into his books. Particularly interesting was his assessment of Serge Koussevitzky, who he believed was a superb musician with a remarkable sense of orchestral sound but technically not a skilled conductor.

My mother, Irene Goldovsky Wolf, produced several reminiscences in the form of oral histories with the assistance of her granddaughter Marya Fogel Flanagan, with whom she traveled to Russia in 1990, returning there for the first time in seventy years (Nathaniel Kahn assisted with some of the interviews). There is also a recorded interview from 1974 by Gregor Benko in which she discusses Josef Hofmann. It is fortuitous that many of my mother's reminiscences describe a period when my grandmother leaves off—after the family arrived in America. I also located some written pieces that my mother submitted to a college English class in 1934. Some of these essays talk about her past in a way that shows that once she came to America, she was reconstructing her family story and eliminating many of the terrifying parts that took place in Russia and Europe. I was also pleased to have a sample of my mother's published translation work in *An Anthology of Jewish-Russian Literature*, Vol. 2 (Maxim D. Shrayer, ed., 2007, p. 1973).

With these three family authors often describing the same events, there are moments when the accounts diverge. In some cases, family archives (many of which were assembled and preserved by my father, Walter "Billy" Wolf) help resolve the problem since they contain newspaper articles and printed programs. Where it is clear which version is correct, I have gone with it. At other times, when the accounts differ, I have gone with the more likely version of events (for example, Boris's assertion that his grandparents arrived in Berlin from Moscow when they emigrated, rather than Lea's account that said they went directly to Paris—other facts seem to suggest that his version may be the more likely). In still other cases, especially where it contributes to the richness of the story, I have included different versions (for example, both Lea's and Boris's accounts of their first successful concert together in Berlin or the concert at the palace of Queen Elisabeth of Belgium where Lea and the Queen were wearing identical dresses).

There are times, too, when I have had to correct accounts that would not be possible as described. Usually these involve dates. My grandmother describes some crucial events involving Aaron and Nettie Naumburg's discussions of their gift of the Stradivarius violin as occurring in the year after Aaron's untimely death. I have no doubt that the events took place as she described them, so I backdated them to fit their actual life and death chronologies.

When I first learned that my grandfather Onissim Goldovsky had written portions of three separate books as well as additional articles, I expected little more than dry legal tomes (which is how Uncle Boris had described one of the books he had tracked down at the Library of Congress in Washington, DC). But when I finally located the books—many had been digitized and were available on the Internet and others were located by my cousin Svetlana Kuzin in Moscow—I learned that Boris's assessment was off the mark. In one book, my grandfather wrote extensively and quite personally about his post-university years and his extraordinary legal mentors. The writing sheds light on how he developed his skills and formed many of his attitudes and political views. Other books made his views of the world and his religion so stunningly clear and strong that they helped me form an impression of the man who wrote them. There were no publications by Onissim from the critical final decade of his life. But because he was active in revolutionary activities, there is much biographical information on him in several books and many articles.

Perhaps the most surprising primary source material about my grandfather and grandmother comes from Onissim Goldovsky's wife, Rashel Mironovna Khin, who kept detailed diaries between 1897 and 1917. They chronicle the daily events of her life and offer detailed observations about the many people she came in contact with. It was from this source that I learned that she and Onissim continued their marriage and close relationship even after he established a second household with my grandmother. I was also to learn of Rashel's and Onissim's encounters with such authors as Zola, Tolstoy, and Gorky and theater notables such as Stanislavsky, and of Onissim's political activities and reactions to political events. There are two versions of Rashel's diary—the longer handwritten, the shorter a typed version that she was preparing for publication. The longer version contains most of the personal information about Onissim Goldovsky, so it was a painstaking process to find the appropriate references. My cousin Svetlana (Sveta) spent months with Rashel's handwritten diary, which is housed in the Russian State Archive of Literature and Art (RGALI) in Moscow [Российский Государственный Архив Литературы и Искусства (РГАЛИ)], as are photographs and programs of my grandmother Lea and her sister, Anna. In order not to load up this book with footnotes, I have given the dates of Rashel's diary entries in the text. For those who might be interested in the cataloging of this material at RGALI that tracks with these dates, a key follows the bibliographic entry for "Khin-Goldovskaya, R. M., Diaries" (in the bibliography below).

In researching Onissim's early years, there was information about him, his parents, his brothers, and his eldest son (Yuri) as well as his high school and university records in the Central State Archive of the City of Moscow (Центральный Архив Города Москвы). Many letters that Onissim wrote, and letters written to him, are also in RGALI. All of these Moscow-based materials were tracked down by my cousin Sveta. She also found the police reports relating to his arrest in 1881 in a St. Petersburg archive. With respect to Onissim's letters specifically, some are in Russian, others in French. I had most of them translated, though in some cases either the handwriting or the archaic language made that impossible.

In looking through the writings of Onissim, Rashel, and Lea, based on the standards of late-18th- and early-19th-century Russia, my grandmother dissembled quite a bit when it came to the nature of the relationships among the three of them. For example, Lea's occasional use of the term *husband* is clearly not legally correct as she was never married. Being able to compare different versions of the same events allowed me to make some educated guesses as to what really happened, who was married to whom, and when Onissim lived with each of the women.

On the Wolf side of the family, my cousin Clarence Wolf has published two books of writings by his father, Benjamin Wolf, entitled *A Time Ago* and *En Route*. In *A Time Ago*, Clarence wrote an introduction tracing the history of the Wolf family from the time they emigrated from Germany in the mid-19th century to the time of his father's generation. This proved extremely useful, as the family is quite large and it would have been difficult for me to reconstruct what occurred. Among other books by Wolf family members, two by Edwin Wolf II include descriptions of members of the Wolf family. One of these is his now-classic biography entitled *Rosenbach* (written with John Fleming) about the famous Philadelphia bookseller Abraham Simon Wolf Rosenbach. Another is Edwin's *The History of the Jews of Philadelphia* (written with Maxwell Whiteman). I was struck by the fact that one maternal relative, Onissim Goldovsky, wrote a history of the Jews of Moscow and a paternal relative, Edwin Wolf II, wrote a similar book about the Jews of Philadelphia. Edwin also wrote a letter preserved in family archives about his trip to the little town in Germany where our ancestors lived before they emigrated.

Printed programs and newspaper reviews of concerts presented by family members, plus recordings made by them, provided a good deal of historical insights. Newspaper archives—especially that of the *New York Times*—were helpful, as were Russian periodicals collected by my Russian cousins. Family members are mentioned in so many books and articles that I will not try to catalog them here, though I have tried to provide as many sources as possible in the endnotes.

The archives of the Curtis Institute of Music include valuable material about my grandmother Lea Luboshutz (who taught there), my uncle Boris Goldovsky (who was both a student and faculty member there), and my brother Andrew Wolf (who graduated from there). It also contains valuable information (including many letters) regarding many of the others mentioned in this book including, most importantly, Josef Hofmann, Efrem Zimbalist, Leopold Stokowski, and of course the school's founder and benefactress, Mary Louise Curtis Bok Zimbalist. There was much valuable material in the Goldovsky archive at the New England Conservatory of Music, and I also drew from the archives of the Philadelphia Orchestra and the Boston Symphony Orchestra with whom various family members appeared at one time or another.

What follows is a bibliography of major sources consulted for the book.

BIBLIOGRAPHY

"A Concert by Leonid Sobinov," *Saratovskie Izvestia* [Saratov, Russia], October 11, 1924.

Ammer, Christine, *Unsung: A History of Women in American Music*. Century Edition, Portland, Ore.: Amadeus Press, 2001.

Balin, Carole B. *To Reveal Our Hearts: Jewish Women Writers in Tsarist Russia*. Cincinnati: Hebrew Union College Press, 2000.

Baltzell, E. Digby. *Philadelphia Gentlemen: The Making of a National Upper Class*. Piscataway, N.J.: Transaction Publishers, 1989.

Bebutov, David Iosifovich. *Vospominaniye* (Воспоминание) [*Memory*]. Biblioteka Istoriya (An Online Collection of Unpublished Russian-Language Historical Documents), 141–49.

Beltyukov, Sergei. *Leo Tolstoy's Family Recipe Book*. Amazon Digital Services, 2014.

Benko, Gregor and Terry McNeill. "Josef Hofmann and the First Years of the Curtis Institute of Music." Program notes for Josef Hofmann, *Casimir Hall Recital*, International Piano Archives. Recorded in 1938. 2 audio discs. University of Maryland.

Berdnikov, Lev. "Rashel' Khin-Gol'dovskaya: Kreshchenie v zhizni i v literature" (Рашель хин-гольдовская: крещение в жизни и в литературе). *Lechaim*, July 2011. Available at: http://www.lechaim.ru/ARHIV/231/berdnikov.htm

Berlioz, Hector Louis. *Mémoires de Hector Berlioz comprenant ses voyages en Italie, en Allemagne, en Russie et en Angleterre.* Paris: Chez tous les libraires, 1865.

Brent, Jonathan and Vladimir P. Naumov. *Stalin's Last Crime: The Plot Against the Jewish Doctors, 1948–1953.* New York: HarperCollins, 2003.

Briedis, Laimonas. *Vilnius: City of Strangers.* Budapest: Central European University Press, 2008, 113.

Brusilow, Anshel and Robin Underdahl. *Shoot the Conductor: Too Close to Monteux, Szell, and Ormandy.* Denton: University of North Texas Press, 2015.

Burt, Nathaniel. *The Perennial Philadelphians: The Anatomy of an American Aristocracy.* Boston: Little, Brown, 1963.

Chaikovskaya, Irina. "Zabytoye imya: Rashel' Khin-Gol'dovskaya" (Забытое имя: Рашель Хин-Гольдовская). *Chaika* 18, no. 245 (September 16, 2013). Available at: www.chayka.org

Chaliapin, I. F. *Pages from My Life.* New York: Harper Brothers, 1927.

Chicago Daily News. Interview with Artur Schnabel. June 11, 1958.

Clarfield, A. Mark. "The Soviet Doctors' Plot—50 Years On." *British Medical Journal* 325 (December 21–28, 2002): 1487–89.

Cole, Orlando. *Oral History.* Archive of the Curtis Institute of Music Archive. Philadelphia, 1992, p. 13 in original typescript.

Community Concerts' official history. http://home.comcast.net/~beckywendy/community_concerts_association_h.htm (accessed March 2014).

Dielo A. A. *Lopukhina v. Osobom Prisutstvii Pravitel'stvuiushchego senata: stenograficheskii otchet* (Дело А. А. Лопухина в особом присутствии. Правительствующего Сената: Стенографический отчет). St. Petersburg: R.I. Artsivi, 1910. Reprinted by the University of California Libraries.

Errera, Leo. *The Russian Jews: Extermination or Emancipation.* Bella Lowry (trans.). London: David Nutt, 1894.

Fateev, V. A., "A Journalist with the Soul of a Metaphysician and Mystic." *Russian Studies in Philosophy* 47, no. 3 (Winter 2008–9): 7–33.

Fauquet, Joël-Marie. *César Franck.* Paris: Fayard, 1999.

Felshtinsky, Yuri. "The Legal Foundations of the Immigration and Emigration Policy of the USSR: 1917–1927." *Soviet Studies* 34, no. 3 (July 1982): 327–48.

Figes, Orlando. *A People's Tragedy: The Russian Revolution 1891–1924.* London: Pimlico Press, 1966.

Flannery, Edward. *The Anguish of the Jews: Twenty-Three Centuries of Anti-Semitism.* Mahwah, N.J.: Paulist Press, 2004.

Flesch, Carl. *The Memoirs of Carl Flesch.* London: Macmillan, 1957.

Franck, César. *Correspondance.* Joël-Marie Fauquet (ed.). Sprimont, Belgium: Mardaga, 1991.

Frederic, Harold. *The New Exodus: A Study of Israel in Russia.* New York: G. P. Putnam's Sons, 1892. Reprinted by Bibliolife.

Gates of Repentance: New Union Prayerbook for the Days of Awe. New York: Central Conference of American Rabbis, 1978.

Geroniumus, Y. V. *V molodyie gody, avtobiograficheskie zametki* (В молодые годы, автобиографические заметки). Moscow: Moscow Center for Continuing Mathematical Education, 2004.

Gershunoff, Max and Leon Van Dyke. *It's Not All Song and Dance: A Life Behind the Scenes in the Performing Arts.* Pompton Plains, N.J.: Limelight Editions, 2005.

Getty, J. Arch, Gabor T. Rittersporn, and Viktor N. Zemkov. "Victims of the Soviet Penal System and the Pre-War Years: A First Approach on the Basis of Archival Evidence." *American Historical Review* 98, no. 4 (October 1993): 1017–49.

Gippius, Zinaida. "The Thoughtful Wanderer: On Rozanov." *Russian Studies in Philosophy* 47, no. 3 (Winter 2008–9): 34–77.

Godowsky, Dagmar. *First Person Plural: The Lives of Dagmar Godowsky by Herself.* New York: Viking, 1958.

Goldin, Milton. *The Music Merchants.* London: Macmillan, 1969.

Goldovsky, Boris. "Oncle Serge." *Atlantic Monthly*, January 1960.

Goldovsky, Boris and Curtis W. Cate. *My Road to Opera: The Recollections of Boris Goldovsky.* Boston: Houghton Mifflin, 1979.

Gol'dovskii, Onissim Borisovich, Unpublished Comments on the Draft Resolution of the All-Russian Assembly of Zemstvos, November 1904 (Проэкт Постановление II Съезда земских деятелей, 6—9 ноября 1904 г.). Russian State Archive of Literature and Art (RGALI), Moscow. F. 128, op. 1, ed. khr. 158.

———. "Psikhologia svidetel'skikh pokzanyi" (Психология свидетельских показаний). In O. B. Goldovsky, V. P. Potemkin, and I. N. Kholchein (eds.). *Problemy psykhologiya,* Moscow: I. N. Kholchev, 1905, 72–101. Reprinted in *Nezavisimyi Psikhiatricheskyi Zhurnal*, nos. 3–4 (1995).

———. "Evrei v Moskve, po neopublikovannym dokumentam" (Евреи в москве, по неопубликованным документам). In Konstantin Burmistrov (ed.). *Moskva Evreiskaya: Sbornik Statei i Materialov.* Berlin, 1906.

———. "Knyaz Urusov kak patron" (Князь урусов как патрон). *Knyaz Alexandr Ivanovich Urusov: Stat'i ego, pis'ma ego, Vospominaniya o nyem.* Moscow, 1907.

———. "Smertnaya Kazn' pred sudom Evropy" (Смертная казнь пред судом Европы). In M. N. Gernet, O. B. Gol'dovskii, and I. N. Sakharov. *Protiv Smertnoi Kazni.* 2nd ed. Moscow, 1907, 313–21.

Graham, Loren. *Lonely Ideas: Can Russia Compete?* Cambridge, Mass.: MIT Press, 2013.

Grossman, Leonid. *Dostoevsky: His Life and Work.* New York: Bobbs-Merrill, 1975.

Honigberg, Steven. *Leonard Rose: America's Golden Age and Its First Cellist.* Rev. ed. Privately printed, 2013.

Hotchkin, S. F. *The York Road, Old and New.* Philadelphia: Binder & Kelly, 1892.

Hurok, S. *Impresario* New York: Random House, 1946.

Kaplan, Igor Mikhalevich and Irene Wolf (trans.) "A Copper Penny for Good Luck." In *An Anthology of Jewish-Russian Literature.* Maxim D. Shrayer (ed.). Vol. 2. London: M. E. Sharpe, 2007.

Kassow, Samuel D. *Students, Professors and the State in Tsarist Russia*. Berkeley: University of California, 1989.

Keen, Beverley Whitney. *French Painters, Russian Collectors: Shchukin, Morozov and Modern French Art 1890–1914*. London: Hodder & Stoughton, 1983.

Khin-Goldovskaya, R. M. *Dnevniki* (Дневники). [Diaries] Russian State Archive of Literature and Art (RGALI), Moscow.

    F. 128, op. 1, ed. khr. 1: 1891–1893

    F. 128, op. 1, ed. khr. 2: 1892–1893

    F. 128, op. 1, ed. khr. 3: 1894

    F. 128, op. 1, ed. khr. 4: 1894

    F. 128, op. 1, ed. khr. 5: 1895

    F. 128, op. 1, ed. khr. 6: 1896

    F. 128, op. 1, ed. khr. 7: 1897

    F. 128, op. 1, ed. khr. 8: 1898–1900

    F. 128, op. 1, ed. khr. 9: 1900–1903

    F. 128, op. 1, ed. khr. 11: 1904

    F. 128, op. 1, ed. khr. 12: 1905

    F. 128, op. 1, ed. khr. 13: 1906

    F. 128, op. 1, ed. khr. 14: 1907

    F. 128, op. 1, ed. khr. 15: 1907–1908

    F. 128, op. 1, ed. khr. 16: 1908

    F. 128, op. 1, ed. khr. 33: incomplete pages from different years (only seven pages in the file)

    F. 128, op. 1, ed. khr. 34: 1891–1906 (later typed version)

    F. 128, op. 1, ed. khr. 35: 1914–1917 (later typed version)

Khin-Goldovskaya, R. M., Unpublished play, Russian State Archive of Literature and Art (RGALI), Moscow, F. 128, op. 1, ed. khr. 42.

Khrennikov, Tikhon. "Vdokhnovennoye masterstvo" (Вдохновенное мастерство) [Anna Luboshitz obituary]. *Sovietskaya Kul'tura*, March 21, 1974.

King, Charles. *Odessa: Genius and Death in the City of Dreams*. New York: W. W. Norton, 2011.

King, Terry. *Gregor Piatigorsky: The Life and Career of the Virtuoso Cellist*. Jefferson, N.C.: MacFarland, 2010.

"Kontsert Leonida Sobinova" (Концерт Леонида Собинова). *Saratovskie Izvestia*, October 11, 1924.

Korey, William. "The Origins and Development of Soviet Anti-Semitism: An Analysis." *Slavic Review* 31 (March 1972): 111–35.

Kotlyarov, Yuri and Victor Garmash. *Letopis zhizni i tvorchestva F. I. Shalyapina* (Летопис жизни и творчества Ф. И. Шаляпина). Vol. 2. Leningrad, Russia: Muzyka, 1989.

Kurth, Peter. *Isadora: A Sensational Life*. Boston: Little, Brown, 2001.

Kutik, Ilya and Andrew Wachtel (eds.). *From the Ends to the Beginning: A Bilingual Anthology of Russian Verse*. Tatiana Tulchinsky, Andrew Wachtel, and Gwenan Wilbur (trans.). Evanston, Ill.: Northwestern University, 2003. Accessed at: http://www.russiapoetry.net

Lang, George M. "She's Dowager Duchess of Fiddle." *Philadelphia Record*, May 9, 1945, 19.

Laue, Theodore von. *Sergei Witte and the Industrialization of Russia*. London: Macmillan, 1969.

Leonard, Carol S. *Agrarian Reform in Russia: The Road from Serfdom*. Cambridge, UK: Cambridge University Press, 2011.

Leontovitsch, Victor. *The History of Liberalism in Russia*. Parmen Leontovitsch (trans.). Pittsburgh: University of Pittsburgh Press, 2002.

Lowe, Charles. *Alexander III of Russia*. London: W. Heinemann, 1895. Bibliolife reprint.

Luboshutz, Lea. Unpublished memoir, 1936. A second version, titled *LUBO: Four Generations of Music*, is undated. There are also two other later versions.

Luboshutz, Lea [with students and others]. *Class Year Book: Violin Students of Madame Lèa Luboshutz, 1929–1930*. Archive of the Curtis Institute of Music, Philadelphia.

Malan, Roy. *Efrem Zimbalist: A Life*. Pompton Plains, N.J.: Amadeus Press, 2004.

Marcovitz, Eli. *Bemoaning the Lost Dream*. Philadelphia: Philadelphia Association for Psychoanalysis, 1982.

Mawdsley, Evan. *The Russian Civil War*. New York: Pegasus Books, 2005.

McCutchan, Ann. *Marcel Moyse: Voice of the Flute*. Portland, Ore.: Amadeus Press, 1994.

McReynolds, Louise. *Murder Most Russian: True Crime and Punishment in Late Imperial Russia*. Ithaca, N.Y.: Cornell University Press, 2013.

Milnes, Sherrill. *American Aria: From Farm Boy to Opera Star*. New York: Schirmer, 1998.

Montefiore, Simon Sebag. *The Romanovs: 1613–1918*. New York: Alfred A. Knopf, 2016.

Moorehead, Alan. *The Russian Revolution*. New York: Harper & Brothers, 1958.

Morreau, Annette. *Emanuel Feuermann*. New Haven, Conn.: Yale University Press, 2002.

"Mrs. Edw. Bok to Provide Work for Jobless in Two Maine Towns." *New York Herald Tribune*, December 18, 1930, 1.

"The Musical Luboshutz Family." In *Novoe Russkoe Slovo* (Новое Русское Слово), August 6, 1987.

Norton, Barbara T. "Russian Political Masonry and the February Revolution of 1917." *International Review of Social History* 28, no. 2 (August 1983): 240–58.

"O studente Gol'dovskom" (О Студенте Гольдовском). Russian State Historical Archive (RGIA). St. Petersburg. F. 1405, op. 88, d. 9977.

O'Neill, W. J. "Concert to Honor Mme. 'Lubo' on 70th Birthday of Violinist." *Philadelphia Daily News*, February 23, 1955.

Overtones. Curtis Institute of Music, 1929, 1930, 1936.

Piatigorsky, Gregor. *Cellist*. Garden City, N.Y.: Doubleday, 1965.

Pipes, Richard. *The Russian Revolution*. New York: Alfred A. Knopf, 1990.

"Postanovleniye II-ogo C'ezda zemskikh deyatelei, 6–9 XI 1904" (Постановление II-ого Съезда земских деятелей 6–9 XI 1904). In *Rossiiskiye liberaly: Kadety i Oktyabristi. Dokumenti, vospominaniya, publistika*. Moscow: Rosspen, 1996.

Priahin, Andrei. "From the Grand Orient of France in Russia to the Supreme Council of the Grand Orient of Russia's People." Available at: http://freemasonry.bcy.ca/texts/russia/go_russia.html

Proust, Marcel. *A la Recherche du Temps Perdu*. Paris: Gallimard, 1987.

Rachwal, Maria Noreiga, *From Kitchen to Carnegie Hall: Ethel Stark and The Montreal Women's Symphony Orchestra*. Toronto, Ont., Canada: Second Story Press, 2015.

Rahv, Philip. *A Bernard Malamud Reader.* New York: Farrar, Straus and Giroux, 1967.

Rampa i zhizn' (Рампа и жизнь), nos. 41–52 (1913) and nos. 7–10 (1914).

Rapoport, Louis. *Stalin's War Against the Jews.* New York: Free Press, 1990.

Ratcliffe, Ronald V. *Steinway.* San Francisco: Chronicle Books, 1989.

Roberts, Spencer E. *Four Faces of Rozanov: Christianity, Sex, Jews and the Russian Revolution.* New York: Philosophical Library, 1978.

Robinson, Harlow. *The Last Impresario.* New York: Viking, 1994.

"Rodilsya vydayushchiisya sudebnyi deyatel' Anatolii F'edorovich Koni" (Родился выдающийся судебный деятель Анатолий Фёдорович Кони). *Den' v istorii.* Prezidentskaya biblioteka, 2018. Available at: http://www.prlib.ru/en-us/History/Pages/Item.aspx?itemid=190

Rosenthal, Herman S. Penn. "Odessa." In *The Jewish Encyclopedia, 1906.* Available at: http://www.jewishencyclopedia.com/articles/11660-odessa

Rudd, Charles A. "A. A. Lopukhin: Police Insubordination and the Rule of Law." *Russian History* 20, nos. 1–4 (1993): 147–62.

Sachs, Harvey. *Toscanini: Musician of Conscience.* New York: Liveright Publishing, 2017.

Saleski, Gdal. *Famous Musicians of a Wandering Race.* New York: Bloch Publishing, 1927.

Schneider, Ilya Ilyich. *Isadora Duncan: The Russian Years.* David Margarshack (trans.). New York: Da Capo Press, 1981. First published in 1968 by Harcourt Brace.

Schoenbaum, David. *The Violin: A Social History of the World's Most Versatile Instrument.* New York: W. W. Norton, 2013.

Schoenburg, Nancy and Stuart Schoenburg. *Lithuanian Jewish Communities.* Northvale, N.J.: Jason Aronson, 1996.

Schonberg, Harold C. *The Great Pianists: From Mozart to the Present.* New York: Simon & Schuster, 1962.

Senkevich, Vladimir Petrovich. *Listochiki pamyati* (Листочки памяти). Available at: http://new.tsniimash.ru/main.php?id=289

Shatsillo, K. F. *Russkii liberalizm nakanunie revolutsii, 1905–1907* (Русский либерализм накануне революций, 1905-1907). Moscow: Nauka, 1985.

Shereshevskogo, N. A. and L. P. Beriya. "Letter" (Письмо). In *Almanakh Rossiya XX vek,* Dyelo vrachei, D. 15. March 24, 1953, Arkhiv Aleksandra N. Yakovleva. Available at: http://www.alexanderyakovlev.org/almanah/inside/almanah-doc/55600

Slonimsky, Nicolas. *Lexicon of Musical Invective.* New York: W. W. Norton, 1953. Page references are to the 2000 paperback edition.

Smith, Nathan. "The Role of Russian Freemasons in the February Revolution: Another Scrap of Evidence." *The Slavic Review* 27, no. 4 (December 1968): 604-608.

Solov'ev, Yurii. "Bryanskiye priklucheniya 'Russkogo Nitsche'" ("Брянские Приключения 'Русского Ницше'"). *Bryanskaya tema* 9, no. 71 (2013).

Stepanova, Anzhela. *Prisyazhnyi poverennyi kn. A.I. Urusov: Vydayushchiysya russkyi yurist i sudebnyi orator* (Присяжний Поверенний кн. А. И. Урусов: выдающийся Русский юрист и судебный оратóр). Saratov, Russia: 2012.

Stockdale, Melissa Kirschke. *Paul Miliukov and the Quest for a Liberal Russia, 1880–1918.* Ithaca, N.Y.: Cornell University Press, 1996.

Stocks, Wor. Bro. Dennis. *Russian Freemasonry.* 1988. Available at: http://www.casebook
.org/dissertations/freemasonry/russianfm.html

Storch, Leila. *Marcel Tabuteau: How Do You Expect to Play the Oboe if You Can't Peel a Mushroom?* Bloomington: Indiana University Press, 2008.

Tchaikovsky, Peter. *Eugene Onegin: Lyrical Scenes in Three Acts* (libretto). English version by Boris Goldovsky. New York: G. Schirmer, 1969.

Telepnef, Boris. *Outline of the History of Russian Freemasonry.* Whitefish, Mont.: Kessinger Publishing, 1928.

Temianka, Henri. *Facing the Music: An Irreverent Close-Up of the Real Concert World.* New York: David McKay, 1973.

———. "Oral History: Interview by Gary and Naomi Graffman." March 6, 1992, Archive of the Curtis Institute of Music, Philadelphia. Available at: https://curtisarchives. libraryhost.com/repositories/2/archival_objects/6761

Tucker, Robert C. *Stalin in Power: Revolution from Above, 1928–1941.* New York: W. W. Norton, 1992.

US Department of the Treasury, Bureau of Statistics. *The Russian Empire and the Trans-Siberian Railway.* Washington, DC: U.S. Treasury, 1899.

Walter L. Naumburg Foundation web site. Available at: http://www.naumburg.org/about.php

Weinberg, Robert. "The Pogrom of 1905 in Odessa: A Case Study." *Pogroms: Anti-Jewish Violence in Modern Russian History.* John D. Klier and Shlomo Lambroza (eds.). Cambridge, UK: Cambridge University Press, 2004, 248–89.

Welsh, Mary Sue. *One Woman in a Hundred: Edna Phillips and the Philadelphia Orchestra.* Chicago: University of Illinois Press, 2013.

Westwood, J. N. *A History of Russian Railways.* Sydney: Allen and Unwin, 1964.

Wheatcroft, Stephen. "The Scale and Nature of German and Soviet Repression and Mass Killings, 1930–45," *European and Asian Studies* 48, no. 9 (1996): 1319–53.

Wolf, Ben. *A Time Ago.* Bryn Mawr, Penn.: Privately printed, 2011.

———. *En Route.* Bryn Mawr, Penn.: Privately printed, 2012.

Wolf, Edwin II and John Fleming. *Rosenbach.* Cleveland: World Publishing, 1960.

Wolf, Edwin II and Maxwell Whiteman. *The History of the Jews of Philadelphia: From Colonial Times to the Age of Jackson.* Philadelphia: Jewish Publication Society, 1975.

Wolf, Irene (as told to Marya Fogel), Oral History, unpublished, undated.

Wortman, Richard S. *The Development of a Russian Legal Consciousness.* Chicago: University of Chicago Press, 1976.

Yandex Dictionary of Revolutionaries. Available at: http://slovari.yandex.ru

Zavadskaya, Nina Petrovna. *Predannost' Iskusstvu* (Преданность искусству) [*The Devotion to Art* (An Interview with Anna Lubushitz)]. Музыкальная жизнь *(Muzykalnaya zhizn),* Number 14, July, 1969.

FOR THOSE INTERESTED IN READINGS, RECORDINGS, AND FILMS RELATED TO THE SUBJECT MATTER AND CHARACTERS IN THE BOOK, PLEASE CHECK THE WEB SITE: www.nightingalessonata.com.

ACKNOWLEDGMENTS

Numerous people made this book possible. I am grateful to those who are mentioned here and apologize to any I may have inadvertently left out. To the extent that there are any errors in the book, they are mine alone.

My Russian cousin Svetlana "Sveta" Kuzin was my partner throughout, conducting the research in Moscow, translating material, and providing her opinions on people and events. She also provided much information on Anna Luboshutz and the extended family in Russia. In America, Andrea Rutherford was an equally important research collaborator providing translations as well as analyses of historical trends in Russia and the Soviet Union and prose suggestions.

Before my mother Irene Goldovsky Wolf's death, my niece Marya Fogel Flanagan worked with my mother to produce an oral history on which I drew. She was assisted in this effort by Nathaniel Kahn. Marya and her sister Alexa Fogel served as skilled guides on a research trip we made to Russia during the summer of 2014 hosted by cousin Sveta; her husband, Igor Kuzin; and her children, Ana and Nickolay. I am grateful as well to Sveta's mother, Nina Pugachevich Yuriev, and her uncle, Vladimir Pugachevich, for their hospitality and their insights about their grandparents Anna Luboshutz and Nikolai Shereshevsky. My late cousin Dmitri Goldovsky's daughter Marina; his half-sister, Marya Sokolovskaya; his stepson, Misha Goussev; and Dmitri's second wife, Tanya Goussev, all provided recollections about that branch of the family. In researching still another group of relatives—the Nemenoff and Jacob families—I am grateful to a French descendent, Igor Handel.

Thanks to Mary Bisbee-Beek who gave me the idea of using a piece of music as the organizing thread of the story and provided practical advice and contacts throughout the process. Once the manuscript was complete, I was thrilled that Susan Cohen of Writers House immediately saw the merits of the book and agreed to serve as my agent. She and her assistant, Nora Long, made many substantive suggestions. Jessica Case of Pegasus Books was an outstanding editor whose experience as a musician and whose knowledge of Russian language and history made her an ideal collaborator. Maria Fernandez did superb design work.

Thanks to Roy Malan for his insights about violins and violinists, along with Stefan Hersh, Philip Kass, and Michael Reynolds. I also received extensive help from Gregor Benko (including details of the life of Josef Hofmann and the pianist's relationship to Lea and other family members), Dr. Victor Yuzefovich (concerning material on Serge Koussevitzky and our family), as well as assistance from Sherrill Milnes, who shared his recollections of Boris Goldovsky. Jeff Blossom produced the very useful maps and Connie Lenzen the family tree that Kristen Weber rendered into a suitable graphic presentation. Kristen also developed the web site (www.nightengalessonata.com) that provides extra information about Lea, her family, and the book. My nieces, Irina Carriere and Heather Wolf, and their French spouses, Antoine Carriere and Krystel Poyeton, helped with translations of important French letters and passages from diaries. Jane Culbert helped edit and reorganize the manuscript countless times.

Helene van Rossum, former archivist for the Curtis Institute of Music, provided valuable material on Lea Luboshutz's, Boris Goldovsky's, and Andrew Wolf's years at that institution as well as leading me to material about the early years of Curtis. I also received help from Helene's successor Kristina Wilson. Maryalice Perrin-Mohr provided access to the archive at the New England Conservatory of Music, which contains material on Boris Goldovsky. Megan Schwenke, archivist for the Fogg Museum at Harvard, assisted in my research on the Naumburgs, and I am grateful to the Fogg staff for granting me access to the Naumburg room at the Museum. Sergei Prokofiev Jr. gave permission to access the letters between Pierre Luboshutz and his grandfather, the composer Sergei Prokofiev. Staff at the Philadelphia Orchestra (Jeremy Rohman, Katherine Blodgett, and Darrin Britting) and at the Boston Symphony Orchestra (Bridget P. Carr) located dates for specific concerts as well as photographs. Thanks to Anne Bracegirdle and Vanessa Fusco of Christie's who provided the essential information on my grandfather's *podstakannik* (tea glass holder).

I am grateful to Peter Bloom, professor of music at Smith College and an authority on 19th-century French music, for providing and translating much of the important contextual information on the family's Paris years and alerting me to the letter from Eugène Ysaÿe to César Franck concerning the latter's A Major sonata for violin and piano. Professor Bloom also translated the passage by Proust which opens Part IV of the book. My thanks to The Morgan Library & Museum for permission to use photographs of the original manuscript of the Franck sonata.

My surviving brothers and sisters—Alexandra (Sani), Nicholas (Nick), Catherine (Cathy), and Lucy—all helped with memories and suggestions. Cathy's one-woman show based on the life of our grandmother provided wonderful insights into Lea's character on which I drew. I am especially grateful to my brother Andy's widow, Linda Wolf, for her memories. Linda's husband Charles was kind enough to read the manuscript at an early stage and offer important suggestions. My children, Lea and Alexis, were helpful at many points, and Lea's research on the list of characters can help readers keep them all straight. My grandson, Asa Wolf Ferguson, spent many days helping me organize the family archive.

Others who assisted along the way include Carole B. Balin, Frances Barulich, Barbara Bentley, Laurence Berman, Rachel Chasin, Jens Deerberg-Wittram, Mike Dumont, Johan Falleyn, Joël-Marie Fauquet, Eavan Flanagan, Genevieve Gagne-Hawes, Naomi Grabel, Professor Loren Graham, Allan Green, Lina Gukasyan, Joseph Kluger, Malcolm Kottler, Alan Lurie, Julie Mancini, Patricia Manley, D'Arcy Marsh, Kelly O'Connor McNees, Katherine Sokoloff McLaughlin, Tom Morris, Dr. Alan Pestronk, Alyce Rideout, Nancy Ryan, Natalya Schetinina, Kiki Skagen, Eleanor Sokoloff, Lynn Stegner, Professor Shlomo Sternberg, the late Enid Stone, Joseph Stremlin, Livia Tenzer, Nancy Bendiner Weiss, Alice West, Kelly Harms Wimmer, and Clarence Wolf.

In the end, it is my wife, Dennie, to whom I am most especially grateful. In addition to the consistent encouragement, insights, suggestions, and extraordinary writing advice and help, she convinced me that this book would be the greatest gift I could leave for future generations of our family.

INDEX

Page references in italics indicate illustrations. BG refers to Boris Onissimovich Goldovsky; LL refers to Lea Luboshutz; OG refers to Onissim Goldovsky; PL refers to Pierre Luboshutz. Birth and death years are provided for individuals where known. Death dates are current through 2018.